D0626896

C. Eric Lincoln is Chairman of the Department of Religious and Philosophical Studies at Fisk University. He is the author of *The Black Muslims in America; My Face Is Black; The Negro Pilgrimage in America,* and *The Black Church Since Frazier.* He is General Editor of the C. Eric Lincoln Series on Black Religion, published by Anchor Press/Doubleday.

THE BLACK EXPERIENCE
IN RELIGION

THE BLACK EXPERIENCE IN RELIGION

EDITED BY
C. ERIC LINCOLN

ANCHOR BOOKS

ANCHOR PRESS/DOUBLEDAY

GARDEN CITY, NEW YORK

Library of Congress Cataloging in Publication Data

Lincoln, Charles Eric, comp.
    The Black experience in religion.

    (C. Eric Lincoln series on Black religion)
    Includes bibliographical references.
    1. Negroes–Religion. I. Title. II. Series.
BR563.N4L56   200
ISBN 0-385-01884-3
Library of Congress Catalog Card Number 73–16508

Grateful acknowledgment is made for the use of the following:

"The Genius of the Black Church," by William B. McClain. Reprinted from the November 2 and 16, 1970 issues of *Christianity and Crisis*, copyright © 1970 by Christianity and Crisis, Inc.

"They Sought a City: The Black Church and Churchmen in the Nineteenth Century," by Lawrence A. Jones. Reprinted from the *Union Theological Seminary Quarterly Review*, Spring 1971, by permission of the author and publisher.

"Caucuses and Caucasians," by Leon W. Watts. Reprinted from *Renewal*, Vol. 10, No. 7, October–December, 1970, by permission of the author.

"Black Folk in White Churches," by Gilbert H. Caldwell. Copyright 1969 Christian Century Foundation. Reprinted by permission from the February 12, 1969 issue of *The Christian Century*.

"The Case for a New Black Church Style," by Gayraud Wilmore, Jr. Published originally in *Church in Metropolis*, Fall 1968. Reprinted by permission of the author.

"Black Preaching," by Henry Mitchell. Reprinted from *Review and Expositor*, Summer 1973, by permission of author and publisher. Copyright, *Review and Expositor*, 1973.

"Martin Luther King and the Style of the Black Sermon," by Hortense Spillers. Reprinted from *The Black Scholar*, September 1971, by permission of the publisher.

Portions of *The Music of Black Americans, A History*, by Eileen Southern. Reprinted from *The Music of Black Americans, A History*, by Eileen Southern. By permission of W. W. Norton & Company, Inc. Copyright © 1971 by W. W. Norton & Company, Inc.

Portions of *Quest for a Black Theology*. Reprinted with permission from *Quest for a Black Theology*, James J. Gardiner and J. DeOtis Roberts, Sr., eds. Copyright © 1971 United Church Press.

From *A Black Theology of Liberation*, by James H. Cone. Copyright © 1971 by James H. Cone. Reprinted by permission of J. B. Lippincott Company.

"Theodicy and Methodology in Black Theology: A Critique of Washington, Cone and Cleage," by William Jones. Reprinted by permission of the *Harvard Theological Review* and the author from the *Harvard Theological Review*, 64 (1971). Copyright by the President and Fellows of Harvard College.

4.50

CONTENTS

Contents

CHAPTER V
Black Religion: Africa and the Caribbean   273

THE BLACK EXPERIENCE
IN RELIGION

CHAPTER I

BLACK RELIGION AND THE BLACK
CHURCH: MODE, MOOD AND MUSIC—
HUMANIZING THE SOCIAL ORDER

Neither scholars nor practitioners are in precise agreement over what "black religion" is, or, for that matter, whether it in fact exists. What is usually demanded as a minimum by the skeptics is evidence that "black religion" is sufficiently distinct from other forms to warrant a distinguishing terminology. The question is frequently asked: "Isn't 'black religion' simply 'white religion' in blackface?" or, "Isn't 'black religion' the same as 'white religion' except that the preaching is more colorful and protracted and the people are more 'responsive'?" What is being suggested, of course, is that black religion is a matter of external detail and not a matter of essence. It is, in the contemporary idiom, "a black patina on a white happening." Or to use a word of uncertain issue adopted by some black theologians,[1] it is white religion "blackenized."

Those who attempt to reduce black religion to nothing more than a cryptonym for the prevailing white expression of the faith run the inevitable risk of exposing how little they know about religion, or black people, or both. Whatever other derivations it may have, religion derives in part from the experiences of the people who confess it, and the white experience is not in its critical essence the black experience in America. Not yet. We need not belabor the point: suffice it to say that "Americanity," the prevailing indigenous interpretation of Christianity in America, looks to Western Europe for its ethic and for its supporting values. Behind any spectrum of values is a cultural history which is the continuing fabric of the social (including the religious) experiences of a given society. The Christian West has developed independently of any knowledge or concern for black people *as people without serious qualifications on account of color* ever since Charles Martel stopped the Moors at Tours in 732. The Protestant Ethic which provided the political and economic thrust which founded America and shaped its development was not a salient feature of African or Afro-American ideological experience. The prevailing values which illus-

---

[1] Cf. Henry Mitchell, Gayraud Wilmore, etc.

trated the practice of American religion and defined the American culture are precisely the values which created for the African diaspora a peculiar, involuntary experience which black religion attempts to view and interpret in meaningful perspective. In short, black religion is a conscious effort on the part of black people to find spiritual and ethical value in their understanding of history. Their history. This is neither parochialism nor racism. Rather it is the realization that even as God is above history He acts in history, and that somewhere in the flux, at some time the individual is confronted with the question of what God's acts mean. He must also find satisfactory answers regarding his proper response to God and how that response should be translated in terms of personal and social behavior based on his understanding of what characterizes God, i.e., what spectrum of values and what kind of behavior he supposes God to approve for Himself and for man. Out of his understanding of God, in the context of his own experience, man gropes for meaning and relevance. Assurance and reconciliation. This is religion. When the context of that groping is conditioned by the peculiar, anomalous context of the black experience in America, it is black religion.

Since the prevailing concerns of the White Church in America have had little to do with the more critical religious needs of black people it was of course inevitable that there should be black churches as a matter of mutual convenience. The real values and the primary concerns of the White Church were expressed through what took place in the local churches, and the presence of Blacks in these churches was awkward for all concerned. The traditional disparity between black and white needs and aspirations meant that there could be no meaningful black agenda wherever white Christians were gathered until that disparity was reconciled. In consequence, Blacks developed their own churches, but separate churches only relieved the physical impediments to the spiritual fulfillment of black Christians. To the degree that the white man's doctrine retained its centrality in the black man's interpretation of the faith, to that degree was the mere withdrawal from the white churches to physically distinct black churches unavailing with respect to the real needs of black Christians. The prevailing doctrine of the White Church was insidiously racist. It invited black people to believe in their own inferiority as an act of God, while suggesting that the white man was God's chosen instrument for leadership and pre-eminence in the world. It was a doctrine which invited black people to hate themselves and to hate each other, to accept subservience with gratitude and love, and to project their hopes for the most elemental human fulfillment to some other world beyond the Jordan. This was a slave-making, slave-keeping, ego-destroying doctrine which distorted the meaning of the black experience and consigned all who accepted it to an earthly life of ignominy and futility.

The answer to the perpetuation in the black churches of a doctrine obviously inimical to the interests of black Christians was a black church which would find relevance and dignity for black people in this life. The Black Church evolved, not as a formal, black "denomination," with a structured doctrine, but as an attitude, a movement. It represents the desire of Blacks to be self-conscious about the meaning of their blackness and to search for spiritual fulfillment in terms of their understanding of themselves and their experience of history. There is no single doctrine, no official dogma except the presupposition that a relevant religion begins with the people who espouse it. Black religion, then, cuts across denominational, cult, and sect lines to do for black people what other religions have not done: to assume the black man's humanity, his relevance, his responsibility, his participation, and his right to see himself as the image of God.

WILLIAM B. MCCLAIN

"What is that something that makes the Black Church unique?" First, the Christianity projected by the Black Church is a humanizing one, taking into account the social, economic, and political aspects of the world. Second, all of life is celebrated in the worship of the Black Church. Third, it has not separated the prophetic function of the church from the priestly one.

The Black Church "has sustained black people throughout the history of the black man in this nation with a gospel that has been interpreted without a dichotomy of social-religious, soul-body, priestly-prophetic categories."

The issue of the distinctiveness of the Black Church becomes more insistent as black ethnicity takes on a more prominent cast. The nature of that distinctiveness is not firmly settled even among the Black Church scholars as yet, but what black religionists *feel* it to be has received substantial articulation. McClain treats in summary fashion those elements of distinctiveness on which there is most general agreement.

William B. McClain is pastor of the Union United Methodist Church in Boston and lectures at Harvard Divinity School.

FREE STYLE AND A CLOSER RELATIONSHIP TO LIFE

Source: William B. McClain, "The Genius of the Black Church," *Christianity and Crisis*, Vol. XXX, No. 18, November 2 and 16, 1970, pp. 250–52.

Black Worship: Free-Style Affirmation

The Black Church's worship reflects an openness, a free-style and a closer relationship to life in which the sacred and secular come together to affirm God's wholeness, the unity of life and His lordship over all of life. This affirmation is not simply a temporary catharsis, but a radical contradistinction to worship in American white churches. The quietness, the apparent serenity, the orderliness of worship in the American white churches often serve to cover up the spiritual hollowness, the selfishness and narrowness that perpetuate the status quo and undergird racism. This worship is often a sentimental trip to Bibleland, where "Christ," the fairytale hero, rescues white respectability. His cross—a symbol of intervention and conflict on behalf of health, healing and wholeness—would be more appropriately replaced with a cushion while they embalm the revolutionary Jesus and His cross and turn worship into a quiet, peaceful retreat from the agonies and ecstasies of life.

Worship in the Black Church celebrates life. It celebrates the power to survive. It reflects a life-style of persons who live on the existential edge where the creative and the destructive, the wise and the foolish, the sacred and the secular, the agony and the ecstasy, the up and the down are the contrarieties of human existence in the presence of the divine. Life is affirmed with all of its complex and contradictory realities. As Lerone Bennett points out in *The Negro Mood*: "The essence of the black tradition is the extraordinary tension between the poles of pain and joy, agony and ecstasy, good and bad, Sunday and Saturday." Such a tradition encourages responses of spontaneity and improvisation, and urges the worshiper to turn himself loose into the hands of the existential here and now where joy and travail mingle together as part of the reality of God's creation.

This is the soul of worship in the black tradition, the genius of the Black Church that cannot be created or approximated, not even by the avant-garde "happenings" and programmed spontaneity of the "hip" white churches. Such worship experiences reflect liturgy and theology arising out of the happenings of a people living on the cutting edge. It calls into question the sepulchers of the American white church and the inoffensive prudential morality that issues forth from theology more rationalistic than radical, from a liturgy that is more soothing than satisfying. Worship in the Black Church tradition is a creative experience, not a book slavishly followed or a ritual rehearsed.

The Black Church maintains a clear prophetic tradition as part of a priestly function throughout its history. This tradition brings into judgment not only the institutions of society (such as political structures), but the institutional church as well. The prophetic word of the Old Testament, announcing judgment on the nation, is often heard in the Black Church and applied to contemporary America. Preaching in white churches tends to be of a much more "pastoral" nature, emphasizing individuals and their personal behavior rather than the revolutionary ethic of Jesus and the prophetic judgment on the whole community.

But the prophetic tradition kept alive in the Black Church is not confined to preaching. The thread runs throughout the whole experience of the Black Church. As Jefferson P. Rogers puts it:

Our songs and our prayers, our music and our meditations, our liturgical stance and our new theology must present the prophetic face of divine anger born of dignity and determination, undergirded by the Holy Spirit, to bring the sword in pursuit of the positive peace without which no man can experience salvation.

What is reflected in the black tradition is the coexistence of the priestly and the prophetic without the usual dichotomy.

The genius of the black tradition is to hold the tensions between the two (prophetic and priestly, affirmation and judgment) as inseparable parts of the whole message and mission of the church. Generally, the American white church decides when to be prophetic and when not. In the Black Church the prophetic is part and parcel of its priestly/prophetic existence.

The genius of the Black Church is that it has brought a people through the torture chamber of the past two centuries. It has sustained black people throughout the history of the black man in this nation with a gospel that has been interpreted without a dichotomy of social-religious, soul-body, priestly-prophetic categories. It declares that God's humanizing activity in the world is the tearing down of old systems that dehumanize and enslave and the building up of new structures and institutions to make the ordering of life more just, peaceful and human. Such structures and institutions must be responsive to the human needs of the dispossessed, the disinherited and the powerless, and accountable under God to all whom they exist to serve. The Black Church affirms the unity of life in the midst of seeming contradictions. When properly understood, it could lend the universality the church needs for renewal.

LAWRENCE A. JONES

Lawrence Jones writes about a dream widely shared by black Christian churchmen in nineteenth-century America. They dreamed of a New Jerusalem, a city in which all citizens enjoyed the full equality they heard about in the Declaration of Independence and the Constitution of the United States. Writes Professor Jones: "At different periods in the history of the last two centuries the intensity of the dream of the New Jerusalem has been in direct proportion to the prospects for achieving the beloved community . . ." In short, while the dream has persisted, there have been moments of doubt.

Jones traces the churchmen's struggle with the age-old dream through the important historical and political events of the nineteenth century —the white evangelical efforts among the black slaves; the establishment of the black mutual aid societies; the birth of the independent black churches in America; and the first national issue that confronted black religious institutions—the issue of colonization. He chronicles the anti-slavery movements and the black churchmen's efforts to educate themselves and the millions of Blacks who looked to them for leadership.

Though the black churchmen never completely realized their dream, the Black Church of the nineteenth century was effective, Jones maintains, ". . . because it was never free to separate its interior institutional life from its mission in and on behalf of the world."

Dr. Jones's essay is important because it shows how deeply committed Blackamericans have been to the *American* dream—of which the "New Jerusalem" became the only expression black people could realistically hope to share. Most of the values and experiences they hoped for were embodied in the basic Law of the Land—values and experiences all other Americans expected to realize in the present life. Since Blacks had learned that what the white man took for granted was not necessarily what Blacks could even hope for with confidence on this earth, black religion bridged the gap between hope and reality, defining the black man's citizenry to "New Jerusalem" and, in the process, reducing the competition for scarce values but making life bearable because of the certainty of future reward.

Lawrence A. Jones is Dean of the Faculty and Professor of Afro-American Church History at Union Theological Seminary, New York.

THEY SOUGHT A CITY

Source: Lawrence A. Jones, "They Sought a City: The Black Church and Churchmen in the Nineteenth Century," *Union Theological Seminary Quarterly Review.* Spring 1971, pp. 253–72.

They Sought a City

> O Yes,
> I say it plain,
> America never was America to me,
> And yet I swear this oath—
> America will be![1]

We have been believers . . .

And in the white gods of a new land we have been believers in the mercy of our masters and the beauty of our brothers, believing in the conjure of the humble and the faithful and the pure. Neither the slavers' whip nor the lynchers' rope nor the bayonet could kill our Black belief. In our hunger we beheld the welcome table and in our nakedness the glory of a long white robe. We have been believers in the New Jerusalem.[2]

It is the thesis of this paper that American Blacks, particularly the minority who joined the Christian community, pursued in the nineteenth century a dream, the twin aspects of which are poetically described in these writings of Langston Hughes and Margaret Walker. On the one hand, their primary faith was anchored in the convictions concerning sovereignty, righteousness, justice, and mercy of God. They looked forward to the New Jerusalem—the city of God. On the other hand they possessed an implicit hope, rooted in the Declaration of Independence and in the Constitution, that one day the ideals enshrined in

---

[1] Langston Hughes, "Let America Be America Again," in Langston Hughes and Arna Bontemps, ed., *The Poetry of the Negro 1746–1949* (New York: Doubleday & Company, Inc., 1949), pp. 106–8.
[2] Margaret Walker, "We Have Been Believers," ibid., pp. 180–81.

these historic documents would be actualized and that there would arise an earthly city, a beloved community, in which they would be citizens with all the rights, prerogatives, and responsibilities with which white men were invested. To be sure, at all periods in the history of Blacks in America there have been those who have despaired that the earthly aspect of the dream would ever be realized, because they have despaired of the will or even of the capacity of white Americans to make it a reality. The majority of Blacks were not exposed to, or did not accept, the vision of the New Jerusalem. But the dreams have persisted alongside each other. At different periods in the history of the last two centuries, the intensity of the dream of the New Jerusalem has been in direct proportion to the prospects for achieving the beloved community, though the struggle for the latter had never been entirely abandoned.

From the introduction of slaves into America in 1619 through the years of the Civil War, some measure of the despair of Blacks relative to achieving their dream is observable in the prominence of the heavenly aspect of the dream. There are many reasons for this despair, not the least of which were the repressiveness of the slave system and the deprived status of the black freedmen. Moreover, though the Constitution and the Declaration of Independence enunciated high-flown ideals concerning "all men," Blacks knew that they were not included in that definition. This awareness was re-enforced by custom, by law, by institutional patterns, by church order, and by judicial decisions. Before the law and in the structuring of government policy, the black man was a piece of property, though the Constitution did count him to be three-fifths of a man for purposes of determining the legislative representation of the various political units. It is an anomaly, in the constitutional sense, that property thus became one of the bases for determining the allocation of political power. Even the Church acquiesced in the judgment of the larger society in these matters. It rationalized this acquiescence by concentrating upon fitting the "souls of Blacks" for the heavenly kingdom and upon helping the slaves to adjust to their dehumanized existence on earth. If slaves had no rights which white men had an obligation to respect, the Church appeared to be saying that God had no earthly purposes with which it needed to be concerned so far as the servitude or quality of life available to Blacks was at issue. Nevertheless, it needs to be observed that whatever its misguided conclusions concerning Blacks may have been, the Church was the only established institution in the society which undertook to communicate to Blacks the ultimate beliefs and hopes which both whites and Blacks shared and by so doing tacitly acknowledged that contrary to prevailing racial ideology, Blacks were in fact children of God, human beings, and thus their brothers.

Failure of the white evangelists. The efforts of white evangelists to proselytize among the slaves met with minimal success. When the nineteenth century dawned, only four or five Blacks in every one hundred in the country were included in church statistics as Christian. By 1860 the number had risen to between twelve and sixteen. Many of these "statistical" Christians were children because the black adults appear to have been highly resistant to the Gospel. Scholars have adduced a number of reasons for the conspicuous failure of the churches in their attempts to evangelize the slaves,[3] but the central reason for the failure of the mission to the slaves lies mainly in the inability of these Blacks to reconcile the faith of the evangelizers with their conduct. They could not become adherents to a religion or worship a God whose self-acknowledged adherents acted consistently in ways that contradicted their teaching. The fifty thousand Blacks out of the one million in the country who had become Christian in 1800 did so in spite of, rather than because of, the evangelists. They were the pioneers in the faith from whom the black Christian community has grown.

However small their number in a relative sense, they were the first to grasp the dream of the "New Jerusalem." In the light of that dream, consistent with the moral imperatives that were explicit in it, and confirmed in their own humanity by its teachings, these Christian Blacks were moved to assume some measure of responsibility for the quality of life available to their fellow Blacks. The overriding and unifying concern of Blacks historically has been for freedom, and the pursuit of its prospects has been persistent, but in the last quarter of the eighteenth century those prospects were dim indeed. It is not strange, then, that though petitions were sent to state legislatures and to the Congress, the first organized activities of black Christians had the twin purposes of making available the truths of the Gospel to their benighted brethren, and to carry on ministries of benevolence and self-help. These activities were necessary because they were virtually neglected by the churches, insofar as evangelism was concerned, and because the structures of society ignored the physical needs and human rights of the disprivileged freedmen in their midst. The earliest black church was the Baptist

[3] See e.g. Winthrop Jordan, *White over Black* (Chapel Hill, N.C.: University of North Carolina Press, 1968); or Stanley Elkins, *Slavery: A Problem in American Institutional and Intellectual Life* (New York: Grosset & Dunlap, 1963).

Church at Silver Bluff, South Carolina, which was organized around 1774.[4] Still others were to follow in the 1790s, but the first self-sustaining groups organized and controlled by Blacks were the benevolent or mutual aid societies, usually found in the cities of the northeastern seaboard.[5] In most instances, these benevolent or mutual aid societies were, in fact, quasi-churches and were only prevented from being identified as such because they could not agree on a denominational affiliation, or else that did not occur as an option. Their charters emphasized the care of widows and orphans, stipends to sick members, provision for the education of orphans, and excluded persons of questionable moral character from membership.[6] For this paper, the significance of the mutual aid societies lies in the fact that they were usually organized by preachers and Christians and that their meetings very much resembled worship services.

Early mutual aid societies. Viewed from one perspective, the Blacks' churches and mutal aid societies were the means by which aggressive Blacks pursued their individual visions of their own possibilities. The first pulpits of the men who subsequently provided leadership in the churches were the mutual aid societies. Moved by a strong evangelical commitment and perceiving themselves to have been called to preach the Gospel, the societies provided an alternative to the pulpits of the religious establishment to which they were denied fully accredited access.

That this was in fact the case is illustrated in the history of the Free African Society in Philadelphia, which was organized by Richard Allen and Absalom Jones. These men formed the Free African Society only after they were frustrated in their attempt to form a religious society which they had desired to do, they report, "from a love of the people of . . . [our] complexion whom . . . [we] beheld with sorrow because of their irreligious and uncivilized state."[7] They failed in this venture because too few free Blacks shared their concern and those who did "differed in their religious sentiments."[8]

[4] Walter H. Brooks, "The Priority of the Silver Bluff Church and Its Promoters," *Journal of Negro History,* Vol. III, No. 2 (April, 1922), 172–96.
[5] August Meier and Elliott M. Rudwick, *From Plantation to Ghetto* (New York: Hill & Wang, 1966), pp. 74ff., 88–90.
[6] "Preamble and Articles of Association of the Free African Society," Benjamin T. Tanner, *Outlines of the History of the A.M.E. Church* (Baltimore, 1867), pp. 140ff.
[7] Richard Allen, *The Life, Experience and Gospel Labors of the Rt. Rev. Richard Allen* (Philadelphia, N.D.), pp. 14–15.
[8] Ibid.

As one looks at the rise of these institutions, one is struck by the variety of gifts manifested by their initial leadership. Richard Allen is a case in point. Allen was aggressive, an astute businessman, a determined organizer, and a man of unquestioned integrity and zeal. But above all, Allen and many others who led in the founding of these churches and benevolent societies were pre-eminently evangelists, deeply committed to the truth of the Gospel and zealous to communicate it to those who had not heard it. For them the "New Jerusalem" beckoned with an allure that made it desirable above all else. Nevertheless, they did not abandon their neighbors, and though their faith had an other-worldly caste, it was radically this-worldly in its day-to-day manifestation of brotherly concern.

Even though Allen was unsuccessful in establishing a church, he nevertheless continued to preach and soon had gathered some forty-two persons around him for prayer and worship. He and Jones, along with William White and Dorus Ginnings, even broached the idea of erecting a house of worship. He was opposed by both influential Blacks and by the clergy of St. George Church, who, according to Allen, "used every degrading and insulting language to us to try to prevent us from going on."[9] They were directly forbidden to continue their prayer services and meetings of exhortation, but they did not accede to these demands for the reason that ". . . we viewed the forlorn state of our colored brethren, and that they were destitute of a place to worship. They were considered a nuisance."[10] Evidently, as a result of Allen's preaching the numbers of Blacks attending the St. George Church became offensive to the whites and conditions were made so intolerable for them that they withdrew. The decision was made to affiliate with the Anglican Church because Bishop White expressed a willingness to ordain a Black to lead them. Allen refused the honor both of being ordained an Anglican priest and of joining the new congregation because he "believed that the plain and simple Gospel of the Methodist was best suited for his people."

The first black churches. Once again Allen began to gather a group around himself, which must have been disheartening, because he had helped to produce the storefront in which those who withdrew from St. George first worshiped and had committed a substantial amount of his own money in the building of the first sanctuary. Like storefront pastors of a later day, he worked in order to preach and lead a congregation.

[9] Ibid.
[10] Ibid.

Nevertheless, he persevered and in July 1794, in a service in which Bishop Asbury participated, Allen opened the new church and named it Bethel. This was technically not a schismatic movement since Bethel was an official part of the Methodist conference with ministerial oversight and services to be provided by the clergy assigned to the St. George Church from which the Blacks had withdrawn. After protracted debate over who should own the property and over the monetary considerations to be granted to the ministers, and finally after a lawsuit in the Supreme Court of Pennsylvania in which the court affirmed the right of the Bethelites to control their own pulpit and other ecclesiastical affairs, the A.M.E. Church was officially established in 1816 as a separate denomination.[11]

The experience of Allen and his group was similar to that of the congregation which ultimately formed the African Methodist Episcopal Zion Church. They separated from the John Street Methodist Society in New York because the church offered no possibility for their leaders to be ordained to the itinerant ministry. They, too, tried to maintain their ties to the Methodist Church but ultimately felt they had to withdraw. For twenty years or more, each one of these bodies sought to remain as a separate congregation within white Methodism, but in the end a formal rupture seemed the sole remaining option. The A.M.E.s were so concerned that the whites might gain control of their affairs that they wrote into their charter a provision that no person not a descendant of the African race could be a member of the church. They inserted this provision to insure control over their property, and to affirm the right of the congregation to discipline its own members and to decide its policies. They hastened to add that they did not intend

... willfully or mentally anything bordering upon schism; contrary thereto we rejoice in the prospect of mutual fellowship subsisting between our white brethren and us, and in reciprocally meeting each other in our private means of grace as visiting brethren in bands, classes and love feasts.[12]

The pre-eminent religious reasons for the founding of separate black institutions was the failure of all but a remnant of the white Christian establishment aggressively to pursue its mission on behalf of Christ among Blacks. Separate institutions were in part a response to the

[11] See Daniel A. Payne, *A History of the African Methodist Episcopal Church 1816–1866* (Nashville: Publishing House of the A.M.E. Sunday School Union, 1891).

[12] Tanner, op. cit., p. 146.

failure of white churchmen to treat their brothers with equity, respect, care, concern, and love.

As Blacks lived out the mission of the Church, it consisted of the task of freeing black men's souls from sin and their bodies from physical, political, and social bondage, and of setting the conditions of existence so that they could achieve their full humanity. But if most white churches and churchmen did not fully share this understanding of mission, black churches and churchmen had it unavoidably thrust upon them. Like their brothers outside the Church they were not free, and the single bond that bound all Blacks together, then as now, was their unfreedom. To be sure, the freedman had some prerogatives denied to the slave, but he was seriously proscribed by custom, by law, by judicial decision, and by his previous condition of servitude. Thus, not only did the churches have to deal with the internal problems common to religious institutions, they had to deal with the urgent problem of a nationally endorsed slave system, as well as with the almost universally held assumption that Blacks were inferior to whites.

The first national issue: colonization. The first national issue that confronted Blacks and their religious institutions rested upon this implicit assumption of black inferiority to whites. This was the question of colonization. It is ironic perhaps that Paul Cuffee, a black sea captain and a Quaker, had given some impetus to this idea by his successful voyage to Sierra Leone in 1815 with thirty-eight emigrants.[13] The American Society for Colonizing Free People of Color in the United States was organized in Washington, D.C., in December 1816. This organization, with its president and twelve of its seventeen vice-presidents and all twelve of its managers from the South, and all of the latter slaveholders, met with strong negative reactions from Blacks in both the North and the South. They were convinced that the purpose of the colonization effort was the removal of free Blacks, which would have the effect of discouraging further manumission and would leave the slaves more firmly in the grip of the slaveholders than ever before.

The most important meeting in public protest took place in Bethel Church in Philadelphia under the leadership of Richard Allen and James Forten. The resolutions passed by this meeting contained several important propositions delineating the objection of Blacks against the

---

[13] William J. Simons, *Men of Mark* (Cleveland, 1887), pp. 136–40. See also Benjamin Brawley, *Negro Builders and Heroes* (Chapel Hill: The University of North Carolina Press, 1937), pp. 35–40.

scheme. Many of them are reminiscent of the arguments in the current debates about civil justice and clearly articulate the vision of Blacks relative to their future in America. The preamble is instructive:

> Whereas our ancestors (not of choice) were the first successful cultivators of the winds of America, we, their descendants, feel ourselves entitled to participate in the blessings of her luxuriant soil, which their blood and sweat manured; and that any measure or system of measures, having a direct tendency to banish us from her bosom, would not only be cruel, but in direct violation of those principles which have been the boast of this republic.[14]

Furthermore, the members of the assemblage declared their abhorrence of the stigma cast upon free people of color to the effect that "they are a dangerous and useless part of the community." They insisted that they would never voluntarily separate themselves from the slave population. "They are," the resolvers declared, "our brethren by the ties of consanguinity, of suffering and of wrong; and we feel that there is more virtue in suffering privations with them than fancied advantages for a season." Then, affirming their confidence in the justice of God and the "philanthropy of the free states," they expressed their determination to leave their fate in the hand of "Him who suffers not a sparrow to fall without his special providence."

Though the possibility of attaining the beloved community in America continued to be the dream of most black Americans, there were always in their midst men who despaired of such a dream and felt that the only real solution for Blacks was to remove themselves from the presence of whites. This alternative remained alive during the nineteenth century and is alive today. Another leading churchman, Daniel Coker, one of the founders of the A.M.E. Church, espoused colonization as the solution to the situation of Blacks and was among the first eighty-eight emigrants sent out by the Colonization Society. Lott Carey, a Virginia clergyman, was among the second group of emigrants.[15] Though a man of some status in Richmond, Virginia, Carey's statement concerning his reason for emigrating might have been the reason most Blacks would have given:

[14] Resolution adopted at a Meeting in Philadelphia, January 1817. Cited in Herbert Aptheker, *A Documentary History of the Negro in the United States* (New York: The Citadel Press, 1951), I, 71–72.
[15] William A. Poe, "Lott Carey: Man of Purchased Freedom," *Church History,* 39 (1970), 39ff.

I am an African; and in this country, however meritorious my conduct and respectable my character, I cannot receive the due credit for either. I wish to go to a country where I shall be estimated by my merits and not by my complexion, and I feel bound to labor for my suffering race.[16]

Despite the enthusiasm of men like Coker and Carey, colonization did not win many converts but it re-emerged everytime black hopes were dashed by events in the nation. Thus, there was a resurgence in the fifties when the passage of the Fugitive Slave Law, the Kansas-Nebraska Act, the Dred Scott decision, the failure of John Brown's raid, and even the election of President Lincoln seemed to indicate that the realization of the dream was further than ever from realization.

(It is of interest that even Richard Allen, who was violently opposed to the American Colonization Society, should have been the principal endorser of a resolution of the Convention of People of Colour convened by him in Bethel Church in 1830, which tacitly endorsed the idea of emigration to Upper Canada.)[17]

During this period the colonizationists held three national conventions.

Among themselves they differed as to what would be the best sight. Some opted for the Caribbean area, especially for Haiti, whose ruler encouraged their aspirations. Several preferred Lower California and the Far West of the United States. But the most popular place was Africa.[18]

Some black congregations used the Colonization Society as a channel through which to support the cause of missions, but whatever usefulness the Society may have had was foreclosed for most Blacks because of the implicit racism upon which it rested.

Black Churchmen and the Anti-Slavery Movement

Despite the fact that the support which the colonization scheme garnered from the general public did not augur well for the success of their efforts, Blacks continued to pursue the elusive beloved community and

[16] Hollis R. Lynch, "Pan-Negro Nationalism in the New World, Before 1862," in August Meier and Elliott Rudwick, ed., *The Making of Black America* (New York: Atheneum, 1969), I, 48.
[17] "Address to the Free People of Color," in Herbert Aptheker, op. cit., pp. 106–7.
[18] Meier and Rudwick, op. cit., p. 121.

held on more firmly to the hope of the New Jerusalem.[19] The ever-present stumbling block was their bondage in the South and the deprivation of their human rights in the North. In this effort they established alliances with whites who, to some degree, shared their dream. Even so, the efforts in which whites and Blacks worked co-operatively are comparatively few. As might be expected, these "integrated activities" usually involved the various local, state, and national anti-slavery and abolition societies. Here Blacks discovered a remnant in the Christian community, some identified with particular churches and others outside the church, with whom they could unite in the struggle for freedom.

William Lloyd Garrison was the charismatic figure at whose invitation Blacks began to enter the anti-slavery movement in great numbers. Though there had been numerous manumission societies before Garrison sounded his militant call in 1831, Blacks were not significantly involved. Garrison's invitation to the "free colored brethren" to join him came at a crucial time in their collective history, for as one historian has observed: "In 1830 the majority of the 320,000 free Negroes were in the habit of regarding all whites as their enemies."[20] Garrison was to be the exception that challenged the stereotype. When the Garrisonian movement split in 1839, Blacks tended to align themselves along geographical lines, with those in New England, for example, remaining faithful to the old "fire-eater." From the standpoint of this paper it is significant that the eight Blacks who were founders of the American and Foreign Anti-Slavery Society in May, 1840 were all clergymen.[21]

Prior to the split, Garrison had become increasingly caustic in his criticism of white clergymen and churches. With much that he said, Blacks found themselves in ready agreement, but they had considerable misgivings concerning his suggestion that they abandon their efforts to exploit the political process in pursuit of freedom. Moreover, they had misgivings concerning some of his theological ideas, as is indicated by the following quotation from a recent study of the black abolitionists:

> On one occasion they (the Blacks) stated that Garrison's opinions were not necessarily related to the abolitionist movement, and on another they

[19] See Edwin S. Redkey, *Black Exodus* (New Haven: Yale University Press, 1969), for an overview of Black nationalist and Back-to-Africa movements during this period.

[20] Benjamin Quarles, *Black Abolitionists* (New York: Oxford University Press, 1969), p. 40; cf. Carleton Mabee, *Black Freedom* (New York: The Macmillan Co., 1970).

[21] Quarles, op. cit., p. 46.

pointed out that they were Garrison's followers so far as abolition was concerned "but on religious points, we follow Jesus."[22]

Garrison had taken the position that the Bible was not divinely inspired, and he aligned himself with the anti-Sabbatarians. This unorthodoxy struck at the bedrock upon which the faith of most Blacks rested. They believed in the Declaration of Independence and the Constitution and they believed that the political process there defined offered the best hope for eradicating slavery. Moreover, religiously, Blacks were clearly at one with the dominant religious community in affirming the divine inspiration of the Bible.

In the debate and bitterness which followed the split of the abolition movement, many criticisms which Blacks had previously muted were expressed. White workers in the old society were charged with harboring racial bias. In language familiar in our own day, a black preacher held up to ridicule a certain kind of abolitionist who hated slavery, "especially that which is one thousand or fifteen hundred miles off but who hated even more 'a man who wears a colored skin.'"[23] Blacks felt that whites in the abolition movement effectually excluded them from positions of real power, and they charged that concern for the elimination of slavery as an institution was not balanced by a reciprocal concern for the humanity of all Blacks, slave and free alike. This second-class citizenship in the abolition societies was especially galling since presumably these particular whites were their friends. Even here the ugly head of racism was reared.

A similar indictment was leveled against the American Tract Society, the American Bible Society, and the American Sunday School Union. These groups were charged with ignoring the whole issue of slavery in order not to alienate those slaveholders who offered financial support.[24] The American Board of Foreign Commissioners for Foreign Missions was the object of analogous criticism.

But if Blacks were critical of the voluntary societies, they saved their most caustic criticism for the Church and for churchmen—to whom they had looked as their natural allies. As a matter of fact, black and white Christians did share many values and concerns. Both believed that religion was a foundation stone to an ordered society and that the ordered society would to a considerable degree reflect in its laws and

---

22 Ibid., p. 42.
23 Ibid., p. 47.
24 Samuel R. Ward, *Autobiography of a Fugitive Negro* (New York: Arno Press and the New York *Times*, 1969), pp. 64ff. Ward's criticism is typical of that current in the black community at the time.

customs the commitments of the Christian community. Once again, however, the stone of stumbling in black-white relations in the churches was implicit and often explicit assumptions of black inferiority. Samuel Ringgold Ward reports that a learned divine in New Haven, Connecticut, had declared to Reverend S. E. Cornish, that "neither wealth, nor education, nor religion could fit the Negro to live upon terms of equality with the white man."[25] Or again:

> Another Congregational clergyman in Connecticut told . . . (Ward) that in his opinion, were Christ living in a house capable of holding two families, he would object to a Black family in the adjoining apartments.[26]

It is clear that opinions of this type were not restricted to New Haven, Connecticut, for Blacks early abandoned any hope that Christian churches would be the cutting edge in the effort to abolish slavery or to insure the human rights of Blacks. Nevertheless, they did not abandon their faith in God, nor in individual whites who demonstrated that they did not share the dominant racial ideologies.

It has already been indicated that the majority of Blacks were not won to the banner of Christ, or indeed were ever offered the option. Even some of those who shared the vision of the New Jerusalem couched their acceptance in certain qualifications. Nathaniel Paul, addressing a meeting celebrating the abolition of slavery in New York State in 1827, expressed confidence that slavery would be extirpated and that human rights would be accorded to black men. Without this faith, he said:

> I would disallow any allegiance or obligation I was under to my fellow creatures, or any submission that I owed to the laws of my country; I would deny the superintending power of the divine providence in the affairs of this life; I would ridicule the religion of the saviour of the world, and treat as the worst of men the ministers of an everlasting gospel; I would consider my Bible as a book of false and delusive fable and commit it to the flames; nay, I would still go farther; I would at once confess myself an atheist, and deny the existence of a holy God.[27]

[25] Ibid., p. 38.
[26] Ibid.
[27] Nathaniel Paul, "An Address Delivered on the Celebration of the Abolition of Slavery in the State of New York, July 5, 1827," in Dorothy Porter, ed., *Negro Protest Pamphlets* (New York: Arno Press and the New York *Times*, 1969), pp. 16–17.

Other black clergy and churchmen found in the Gospel a mandate for the violent seizure of freedom. Among these the most notable were David Walker and Henry Highland Garnet, the latter a Presbyterian clergyman. Garnet counselled his brethren, particularly those in slavery, to revolt as a matter of Christian obligation. He wrote:

The diabolical injustice by which your liberties are cloven down, neither God, nor angels, or just men, command you to suffer for a single moment. Therefore it is your solemn and imperative duty to use every means, both moral, intellectual, and physical that promise success.

. . . You had far better all die—*die immediately,* than live as slaves, and entail your wretchedness upon your posterity. If you would be free in this generation, here is your only hope. However much you and all of us may desire it, there is not much hope of Redemption without the shedding of blood. If you must bleed, let it all come at once—rather *die freemen, than live to be slaves.*[28]

But the promise of the dream and its possibilities for realization by other means prevailed. Some Blacks had quite folksy theological reasons for their confidence. James Redpath reported a conversation with a slave in Virginia in which a bondsman, commenting on his reaction to what he heard from the pulpit, said:

One day I heard [the preacher] say that God had given all this continent to the white man, and that it was our duty to submit.
"Do the colored people," I inquired, "believe all that sort of thing?"
"Oh no sir," he returned, "One man whispered to me as the minister said that. He be damned! God am no sich fool!"[29]

Henry McNeil Turner, later to be a bishop of the A.M.E. church, forbade his congregation to sing the popular hymn, "Wash me, and I shall be whiter than snow," for the common sense reason that "the purpose of washing is to make one clean, not white, and that white is no more a sign of purity than black, and that God is not white."[30]

Actually most black spokesmen did not join the issue at the level of critical theological reflection, but at the level of intuitive insight into

---

[28] Henry H. Garnet, *An Address to the Slaves of the United States of America* (New York: Arno Press and the New York *Times,* 1969), p. 94.

[29] *Anglo-American Magazine,* I (1859), 330. (Reprinted by Arno Press and the New York *Times,* 1968.)

[30] Bishop Henry M. Turner in Richard R. Wright, *The Bishops of the A.M.E. Church* (Nashville: A.M.E. Sunday School Union, 1963), p. 332.

the faith. Henry Ringgold Ward, a clergyman prominent in the anti-slavery movement, anticipated the observations of European theologians coming later in the century in making a distinction between religion and Christianity:

> *Religion* . . . should not be substituted for Christianity; for while a religion may be from man, and a religion from such an origin may be capable of hating, Christianity is always from God, and like him, is love . . . the oppression and the maltreatment of the hapless descendant of Africa is not merely an ugly excrescence upon American *religion* . . . no, it is a part and parcel of it, a cardinal principle, a *sine qua non*, a cherished, defended cornerstone of American faith. . . .[31]

Politics and Education

At the conclusion of the Civil War and with the subsequent passage of the 13th, 14th, and 15th amendments to the Constitution, Blacks were legally free and the dream of a beloved community in America seemed a possibility. But they soon found that freedom was more an illusion than a fact as state after state re-enacted discriminatory legislation which re-instated the system which formerly applied to the freedman. By 1896, Blacks had lost any political leverage they had gained and most of their other hopes were in shambles. Simultaneously there was a differentiation of function in the black community. As labor unions, news media, business institutions and associations, political parties and alliances came into existence, the weight the churches bore in these areas was both broadened and expressed more locally. Leadership, too, began to be diversified and secular interpretations of the dream began to dominate.

When the hope that political activity might be the means through which their dreams for America could be achieved was dashed, Blacks turned again to education, which they had long viewed as the most promising avenue to their acceptance on a parity with whites and as a means to achieving their full humanity. Like most other Americans of the period, they shared the American creed that temperance, industry, thrift, and stable family wedded to education were the keys to the kingdom.

In the period of slavery, next to a godly life, no grace was more highly prized than the ability to read and write. The benevolent societies frequently had as a part of their purpose the provision of education for the children of the community. For example, the Bethelites in Philadelphia established a First Day School in March of 1796 and six months

[31] Samuel R. Ward, op. cit., pp. 42–43.

later inaugurated a night school for adults.[32] In Newport, Rhode Island, the African Union Society, a mutual benefit society, sponsored a free school in 1808 and in 1824 established an independent black church.[33] In Boston, Prince Hall, founder of the Masonic order among Blacks, and a Methodist minister, organized a school in 1798 which was moved to the African Meeting House in 1805.[34] In city after city the black free schools were established, often by anti-slavery interests and other concerned whites, but more often than not by free Blacks. One indication of the A.M.E. Church's concern is evident in the resolution on education passed at the Nineteenth Session of the Philadelphia Annual Conference in 1834.

Resolved: That as the subject of education is one that highly interests all people, and especially the colored people of this country, it shall be the duty of every minister who has the charge of circuits or stations to use every exertion to establish schools wherever convenient, and to insist upon parents sending their children to school; and to preach occasionally a sermon on the subject of education; and it shall be the duty of all such ministers to make returns yearly of the number of schools, the amount of scholars, the branches taught, and the places in which they are located; and that every minister neglecting so to do, be subject to the censure of the Conference.[35]

Next to church buildings and related ecclesiastical activities, Blacks invested more of their resources in educational undertakings than in any other community enterprise in the nineteenth century. Some impression of the extent to which education was esteemed is conveyed by the following observation of Booker T. Washington commenting on the freedmen's drive for education:

Few people who were not right in the midst of the scene can form any exact idea of the intense desire which the people of my race showed for education. It was a whole race trying to go to school. Few were too young, and none too old, to make the attempt to learn. As fast as any kind of teachers could be secured, not only were day-schools filled, but night-schools as well. The great ambition of the older people was to try to learn to read the Bible before they died. With this end in view, men and women who were fifty or seventy-five years old, would be found in the night schools. Sunday-schools were formed soon after

[32] Benjamin T. Tanner, op. cit., p. 157.
[33] See Meier and Rudwick, op. cit., pp. 88–90, for a discussion of these affairs.
[34] Ibid.
[35] Payne, op. cit., p. 100.

freedom, but the principal book studied in the Sunday School was the spelling-book. Day-school, night-school, and Sunday-school were always crowded, and often many had to be turned away for want of room.[36]

The efforts of the black churches to provide a means for educating their members was monumental. By 1900 the Baptists were supporting some 80 schools and 18 academies and colleges. In addition, the individual associations and conventions reported the publication of some forty-four different newspapers and journals which were themselves instruments of education. The A.M.E. Church raised over $1,100,000 for educational purposes between 1884 and 1900 and supported 22 institutions providing education above the elementary level. The A.M.E. Church established its first educational institution, Union Seminary, near Columbus, Ohio, in 1844. This institution was later merged into Wilberforce University which the church had purchased from the Methodist Conference in Ohio in 1856. In 1900 the A.M.E. Zion Church was supporting, as a denomination, eight colleges and/or institutes, while the Colored Methodist Episcopal Church had established five schools during their thirty years history.[37]

These statistics of national bodies do not exhaust the extent of Blacks' commitment to education as the touchstone to the beloved community. In order to treat fully the total involvement of Blacks in the provision of educational opportunities for their children, one would have to survey all the denominations to which they belonged and to investigate their activities at the local level. Many of these activities are not available in the national statistics. Another index to the importance of education to the community is indicated by the fact that at the end of the century, the principal matters in public discussions were education and lynching, and that the nominal national leader was Booker T. Washington. In the debates that swirled around the controversial Washington, the efficacy of education was not in dispute, the style and kind of education was.

"A Dream Deferred"

Though the Black Church was effective in the nineteenth century partially because of the circumstances of history, it was effective mainly

[36] Booker T. Washington quoted in Gunnar Myrdal, *An American Dilemma* (New York: McGraw Hill Book Company, 1964), II, 883.
[37] See W. E. B. Du Bois, *The Negro Church,* Atlanta University Report No. 8, 1903 (reprinted by Arno Press and the New York *Times,* 1968) for a compilation of statistics relative to these matters.

because it never was free to separate its interior institutional life from its mission in, and on behalf of, the world. From the perspective of seventy years later, if the Black Church has had a diminishing impact it is because it has turned more and more in upon itself, and faced less and less out toward the world. The primary shortcoming of the white Christian community in the nineteenth century was that it failed to include Blacks, the mote in its eye, as a primary source of its mission.

Thus, during the nineteenth century, the black churches and churchmen vigorously pursued a dream. But in a paraphrase of Hebrews 11, they did not receive what was promised, yet the majority died in the faith that the dream was possible of achievement. What has happened to their dream is perhaps best attested by the following excerpt from the speech of Martin Luther King at the March on Washington in August 1963:

> I say to you today, my friends, even though we face the difficulties of today and tomorrow, I still have a dream. It is a dream deeply rooted in the American dream. I have a dream that one day this nation will rise up and live out the true meaning of its creed; "We hold these truths to be self-evident, that all men are created equal."

> I have a dream that one day every valley shall be exalted, every hill and mountain shall be made low, the rough places will be made plain and the crooked places will be made straight, and the glory of the Lord shall be revealed, and all flesh shall see it together.[38]

> And the dream is not yet.

[38] Martin L. King, "I Have a Dream," in John H. Franklin and Isidore Starr, ed., *The Negro in Twentieth Century America* (New York: Vintage Press, 1967), p. 146.

LEON W. WATTS

The creation of the independent black churches (A.M.E. Zion and A.M.E.) points to two things: the nature of black folk and black religion and the nature of white American Christianity. From the beginning and throughout history, black religion has reflected the struggles of black people. Watts finds that there is an "unchanging relationship between black religion in the twentieth century and black religion in the seventeenth and eighteenth centuries."

23

The Black Church represents the destiny for *all* of the black community. It encompasses the whole of the life of the black community and sustains and nurtures it.

Leon W. Watts is an ordained minister of the A.M.E. Zion Church, Publisher of *Renewal*, Associate Executive of the National Committee of Black Churchmen, and Consultant to the Department of Ministry of the National Council of Churches.

CAUCUSES AND CAUCASIANS

Source: Leon W. Watts, "Caucuses and Caucasians," *Renewal*, Vol. 10, no. 7, October–December 1970, pp. 4–6.

In the latter part of the eighteenth century, it was clear to black folks that American white Christianity was incapable of responding to legitimate black demands. The followers of James Varick and Richard Allen understood clearly that, given the choice between black people in a system of oppression and black people demanding freedom and asserting prerogatives, white people could only choose the system of oppression. To choose otherwise would have been a denial of one of the basic tenets of "whiteness" in America. White Christians could not be expected to understand the teaching "he who seeks to save his life will lose it." More importantly, Blacks could not choose to remain in a system that basically ignored and defamed them as men.

The move which created the African Methodist Episcopal Zion Church and the African Methodist Episcopal Church began to set things in perspective (1) about the nature of black folks and black religion; and (2) about the nature of white American Christianity. It was a clear indication that white American Christianity is built upon the celebration of the experiences of the oppressors, and black concerns, desires and aspirations are excluded. The role of white American churches was, and is, one of rationalizing the value systems of Americans, racism and oppression. White American Christianity undebatably has been the purveyor, sanctifier and rationalizer of the American "democratic" free enterprise system. It has sought to make holy the unholy, wholesome the unwholesome, and righteous the unrighteous.

Thus, in protest, the Black Church formalized its existence. We must clearly know and understand that the break with white American Christianity took place during the earliest days of slavery. The real question is whether or not black folks have *ever* considered themselves a part of the tradition of American Christianity.

Dr. Joseph Washington, Jr., has written: "Black Religion is unique to Negro folks, born as it was of slavery, and it ties them each to the other in times of stress by a racial bond which cuts across all other variables." Dr. Washington refers to black religion as a fifth religion. Charles Long, a black authority on African religions, raises the question this way: "Either Black folks have never been Christian in this country or we are the only Christians that country has ever had." Black religion is a unique force in American life. It cannot in any way be confused or equated with American white Protestantism, Catholicism, or Judaism. It is a separate religious force in American life, different in all aspects from the tenets of the American Religious Establishment, primarily because its basis and base of operation relates exclusively to an oppressed community. I would call black religion a fourth religious force in America. Dr. Washington calls it a fifth religious force by including secularism as the fourth dimension. It seems clear to me, however, that "secular" and "sacred" merge in black religion.

The motivations of slaves toward religion was not what their "masters" had hoped or intended. It is historically clear that black folks used the ordered language of Christianity to "turn on" a people for liberation rather than to pacify them to the condition of enslavement; to preserve a people for struggle against seemingly insurmountable odds rather than to equate their condition with the "will of God"; to free the spirit from bondage that the body might wrest liberation from the oppressors. Many historians and would-be theologians and scholars have denigrated black religion as so much "pie in the sky." Such a notion can never be reconciled with the lives of Nat Turner, Harriet Tubman, Sojourner Truth, James Varick, Denmark Vesey, Richard Allen or Frederick Douglass. Black religion motivated them and preserved them in the Struggle.

The current development of denominational caucuses is indeed a replay of the conditions which led to the formation of *all* black denominations. The same racist attitudes with regard to black demands, hopes, aspirations and desires are demonstrably present in the white American Christian Establishment today. There is no qualitative difference between the move of Varick and Allen in the eighteenth century and the move of black caucuses in predominantly white denominations today. Both caucuses and Caucasians are the same.

A few assumptions clearly illustrate the unchanging relationship between black religion in the twentieth century and black religion in the seventeenth and eighteenth centuries:

1) Black religion has always stood in contradistinction to white

25

American Christianity. It is the result of racism in the church and society. Black religion is a protest to the positions of the established American Christian tradition. It is an indictment against the religious Establishment, therefore no corollaries exist between the two.

2) The experiences of the oppressed are qualitatively different from those who are the oppressors; therefore, the basis for religious experience is different. Black religion is articulated and demonstrated by contrasting the realities of life to the assertions of American white Christianity.

3) Since theology is informed not only by revelation, scripture and tradition, but also by culture and history, theologizing in the Black Church is *necessarily* different from that of the white church. Therefore the history and culture of black people in this country must play an important role in shaping and developing a black theology. The search for our roots and the celebration of our culture is a *sine qua non* in defining the Black Church.

4) The roots of the Black Church are in protest and liberation. The explication of the Gospel of Jesus the Christ is in terms of God's liberating activities in the world vis-à-vis the oppressed community. The Black Church is a product of the oppressed community. Thus the central theme of the Black Church is black liberation.

5) As a product of an oppressed community, the Black Church has a different relationship to its community than does the white Christian Establishment. While the church in the white community is simply an institution alongside many others, the Black Church is the *major* institution in the black community. Indeed the black community and black religion are inseparable.

6) The Black Church can be and often is prophetic. American white Christianity is so inextricably bound to Americanism that white Christians can speak of God, Flag and Country as if they were synonomous terms. The propagation, perpetuation and preservation of "the American way of life" is not a goal of the Black Church. Therefore the Black Church does not confuse *nationalism* with *mission*.

7) Since the datum for black religion is the black experience, the Black Church is the only place in American society where the black experience can be celebrated with impunity. That experience bears little, if any, relationship to the experience held in common by white churchmen.

8) The Black Church is neither the victim of sixteenth century puritanism nor nineteenth century rationalism. By virtue of its history and the culture of its people, the Black Church understands that

rationality must be informed by emotional content and that there are literally no absolute values. Life is emotional as well as rational and logical; dialectical as well as normative. In the final analysis values are appropriate. The question for black religion is not normative ethics but rather, what it is a moral being?

9) Black religion is not based upon a notion of "rugged individualism" but rather its focus and drive are toward preserving the people of an oppressed community for struggle.

10) The Black Church does not experience a distinction between "sacred" and "secular" worlds. There is a merger of sacred and secular in the Black Church, since black religion and the black community are inseparable. Neither one can be defined without the other. Black ecumenicity, then, embraces the *total* black community. Black religion, in contradistinction to American white Christianity, is *inclusive* rather than *exclusive*.

Denominational caucuses are indeed representative of the ongoing protest movement in the black community. The move toward black unity and solidarity under the rubric of the Black Church, the move toward an inclusive black theology of freedom, liberation and celebration is but a renaissance of black religion in this century. It is the affirmation of the existential reality of struggle. As Frederick Douglass stated so precisely: "If there is no struggle, there is no progress. Those who profess to favor freedom and yet deprecate agitation are men who want crops without plowing up the ground."

The struggle is not a separate one for black people in white denominations over against black people in black denominations. The oppression of black people knows no caste nor class; no denomination nor faith; and the drive for liberation knows no boundaries. Indeed that is the genius of the National Committee of Black Churchmen and the genius of an inclusive black theology.

In the Black Church there lives an undaunted sense of destiny— a sense of destiny which enabled black people to survive the most inhuman form of chattel slavery the world has ever known. That destiny is liberation.

"But you are God's 'chosen generation,' his 'royal priesthood,' his 'holy nation,' his 'peculiar people'—all the old titles of God's people now belong to you. It is for you now to demonstrate the goodness of him who has called you out of darkness into his amazing light. In the past you were not 'a people' at all. Now you are the people of God. In the past you had no experience of his mercy, but now it is ultimately yours."

The Black Church does not apologize for that sense of destiny but rather *celebrates* it, shouts it from the rooftops. WE ARE INDEED "THE PEOPLE OF GOD."

The Black Church is a praising, joyful, shouting, spiritual community. Emotional! It recognizes that some realities refuse to be captured by logic and rationality. As a celebrating community it raises serious questions about *any* reality that does not have emotional content. To be emotional is part of our humanity. Spirituality is a reality of our existence.

Finally, it is evident to black religion that there are no certain assumptions. Questions about life are not raised in a vacuum. They are based upon one's experiences, his faith, his *raison d'être*. The Black Church raises questions which white people are incapable of raising because they have no basis in experience. White people, for example, cannot raise the question of the essential humanity of man. The experience of "whiteness" has been that of dehumanity. White people cannot ask the crucial questions of the relationship between Church and State for they have had no experience but that of serving the State. Certainly their violent history renders white people incapable of speaking of nonviolence. Nor can non-oppressed white people understand the message of Jesus the Christ when it speaks so clearly of liberation:

> The Spirit of the Lord is upon me, because he has anointed me to preach
>   good news to the poor.
> He has sent me to proclaim release
>   to the captives
> and recovering to sight to the
>   blind,
> to set at liberty those who are
>   oppressed,
> to proclaim the acceptable year of
>   the Lord.

GILBERT H. CALDWELL

Gilbert Caldwell sees black Christians as being called upon to be "missionaries to the gentiles," i.e., to white people. "Every encounter with our white brother could provide us with an opportunity to minister, to emancipate, to liberate him." Whether black Christians in white churches should, or will, choose to maintain these affiliations will depend upon several factors, including black recognition of the overt emotionalism characteristic of the Black Church. "The apparent serenity" of the White Church may be no more than a cover for its spiritual emptiness. Blacks need to develop a new appreciation of "soul."

Gilbert Caldwell is a Methodist minister and a Professor at the New York Theological Seminary.

BLACK FOLK IN WHITE CHURCHES

Source: Gilbert H. Caldwell, "Black Folk in White Churches," *The Christian Century,* February 12, 1969.

Today my brothers and I are raising a question: Is it or is it not possible to be black and true to the aspirations of the black community and still be a part of white Christianity? The jury is still out on that one, and it will not be coming in with the verdict for some time to come.

Some of my brothers have already decided that the answer is No. Those who follow the Honorable Elijah Muhammad say that Christianity can never speak to the needs of black people. Albert Cleage, pastor of the Shrine of the Black Madonna in Detroit, suggests that Christianity needs a "blackwashing," that the white Jesus needs to be made black because this is the way he is, the way he was and the way he must be to us. Virgil Wood of Boston's Blue Hill Soul Center seeks to effect a relationship with the Ethiopian Coptic Church. My Methodist brothers in those denominations that formed as a result of the racism of white Methodism—A.M.E., A.M.E. Zion, C.M.E.—don't seem to be ready to reaffiliate with folks who weren't ready for them in the first place.

I

Whither then the black man? All praises be to the National Committee of Black Churchmen, to the black caucus movement as it has developed in all the white denominations. Thank God for my own Black Methodists for Church Renewal. I have the feeling that if these structures had not emerged a lot of us would have received "calls" to preach in places other than the church. There is a ray of hope—not that we see our white brothers getting ready for us, but rather that through such structures as black caucuses we are beginning to see in clear terms that ours is a dual responsibility: to minister not only to the people in our black communities but also to our white brothers and sisters. For with all their sophistication and their technology and their "happenings" and their avant-gardeness, our white brothers and sisters seem to be remarkably impotent.

Ah, but you say that I am being grossly unfair to white churchmen! Why, look at you, Gil Caldwell; you are one of those "firsts"—the first black district superintendent in New England Methodist history. When I hear that "first," I cringe deep down inside; for it conveys the idea that somehow after many years, after a process of evolution, there finally emerged black men capable of providing leadership in the white institutional world. This is a lie! What is really being said is this: "At long last our institution finally reached the point where it could receive black leadership. We weren't ready before, we are not sure that we are ready now, but we are willing to give it a try!" As one who occupies one of those "first" positions I too sometimes wonder about the readiness of white Methodism.

Black men in the white church discover the presence of the same kind of white arrogance that has been a part of Western civilization's style of life. Over the years they have met this arrogance in the way the church has responded to the inner city; it is the arrogance that has asserted itself in the schools of theology (particularly in the homiletics departments), the arrogance that enables its possessors to give but not to receive. It is the arrogance to be observed in the decision-making process, the arrogance with which our regional conferences or national assemblies resort to parliamentary maneuvering to do the will of God. And the arrogance has become so overwhelming that the very suggestion of some radical change in the process is looked on as grossly heretical.

II

The future of the black man in the white church will be determined by a number of factors. I cite four:

(1) *The seriousness with which black churchmen take the black caucuses in their particular politics.* If we seriously and prayerfully engage in the deliberations of our particular caucuses they will become the source of our sustenance, our strength; they will provide the spiritual food that enables us to stand proudly amid our white Christian

brothers. The black caucus provides a base for fellowship, intellectual stimulation, strategizing, spiritual nourishment—and a kind of black ecclesiastical employment agency. It cannot afford to be just *one* of these; it must be all of these and more. We must not let ourselves get caught up in the traditional verbalizing, parliamentary shenanigans, resolutionizing, committee-creating way of doing things that our denominations have created. Instead, we must inject "soul" into the process whereby a group of committed persons make decisions.

(2) *The rapidity with which black churchmen come to grips with, and make some decision about, the overt emotionalism that is characteristic of the black church.* Many of us need to be honest enough to admit that we have rejected the emotionalism of the Black Church; we have said that it was antirational, that it simply provided a temporary catharsis for the congregation on a Sunday morning. But many of us who have served within the white church have discovered that the quietness, the apparent serenity, the orderliness of worship serve to cover up the spiritual emptiness, the selfishness and narrowness, the perpetuation of the status quo that unfortunately are part of the lifestyle of white church life.

Every black churchman, particularly those of us whose church life is nonblack, needs to develop a new appreciation for the expression of "soul" that has come out of the Black Church. Instead of rejecting and denouncing the nature of the Black Church we need to understand how God has used it to sustain a people, to help a people keep their sanity; and now in this day some of us feel God wants to use the church to empower black people and liberate white people.

(3) *The willingness of black men in white churches to recognize that, whether we can stomach it or not, in the light of our history and our experiences God is calling us to be "missionaries to the gentiles."* Years ago white people, out of a missionary motive, were moved to establish colleges in the south for black people. In the north, white Christians were moved to "serve" black people by developing settlement houses and other charitable institutions. Now it becomes clear that in this moment of history black churchmen are called to become involved in mission to today's white generation.

Our missionary style must be radically different from the one with which we have seen our white brothers and sisters operate. We black people have observed that it has been practically impossible for white people to understand the concept of empowerment, the idea of working oneself out of a job, the virtue of letting people develop their own style rather than become imitators. Whenever we come into contact with white folk, we black missionaries need to recognize our responsibility to be in mission to them.

It is evident that by and large white churchmen lack the vision, the courage, the "soul" to exist in the "new world a comin'." Interestingly, they need us now more than we need them. We know, of course, that part of our drive to re-Christianize our white brothers and sisters will have direct fallout in the black community, for we realize by now that it is white racism and the institutionalization of white racism that hampers and throttles us. Thus it is that some of my black Christian brothers who cannot see themselves in mission to "white folks" can justify their involvement because it will further empower the black community. But some of us will be involved because a close-up view of our white brothers has informed us that they are the inheritors of a congenital sickness, and that God has placed the vaccine to cure them in our hands.

Every encounter with our white brother could provide us with an opportunity to minister, to emancipate, to liberate him. What new meaning might we now find in the many meetings we have to attend and be bored by! We have been bothered by the irrelevancy and duplicity, the "order without justice," the chicanery—but now instead of simply "losing our cool" or "telling whitey off" we should be able to see a new role for ourselves in this context. We could be involved in the process of humanizing and civilizing and sensitizing and converting our white colleagues.

But, you say, there is a kind of arrogance about my presuppositions and, thus far, a display of the same kind of paternalism I have complained about. You say there are evidences of a new white man emerging. There is a thread of truth in all this. But the great challenge to black men today is that as they exert leadership they do not imitate what they have seen in white leadership—whether that be physical violence or sophisticated bureaucratic strangling. By now it must be obvious to everyone that there is a sickness in the white church; whether it is a "sickness unto death" is in a real way up to those of us who minister through it and to it.

(4) *The determination by all those who, like myself, occupy administrative and staff leadership within the white church not to take our "breakthrough" too seriously.* We cannot afford the luxury of reading the comments about our appointment, elevation or selection as printed in the daily press and in our church journals; from that source we get the impression that we are the "exceptional men," that

we were chosen because we were "different." (How often we have heard this hint!) In the minds of some, we are the overt manifestation of the church's readiness to embrace all God's children. But what every one of us knows, if we are honest with ourselves, is that there are hundreds of black brothers and sisters within the church who are as qualified as we are—or more so. We just happened to be at the right place at the right time or to attend more meetings than others did. Or perhaps—on the surface—we were not as angry or as emotional as some of our brothers and sisters were. Remembering all of this should keep us humble.

Furthermore, we should acknowledge that even though we were selected by members of the white power structure, our first allegiance is to the black community. We are where we are because the black community finally became visible to folk who had not seen it and its leadership before. We must, therefore, be careful lest we erect a barrier between ourselves and the community whence we come.

III

Some of my black brothers and sisters have been reluctant to affiliate with their respective black caucuses. They disenfranchise themselves when they say: "Now I am a part of the total church and cannot identify with any particular ethnic group. I am supposed to serve everybody." How tragic, how unfortunate that black men and women can be promoted to a level where they feel they don't have to identify with the black community, or who so mistake their responsibility that they cannot interact freely and meaningfully with the members of that community.

This kind of attitude is an "abomination before the Lord," a stab in the back of our soul brothers. And it limits our effectiveness in the white church. If there is anything our denominations do not need in their higher echelon positions at this moment it is "Negroes" who are afraid to be black, to identify with the aspirations and planning of the black community.

The next few years will be crucial for the future of the church. Even more important for some of us, the next few years will determine whether the predominantly white Christian church can receive the "new wine" black Christians have to share. If it shows that it cannot, then, we must modestly say, it has lost the chance of a lifetime. And some of us will begin to create the necessary new wineskins.

GAYRAUD WILMORE, JR.

The failure of the integration movement of the sixties and the frequent confrontations between the White Church and its black membership raises the question of whether there will be meaningful white-black Christian contact in the future. The White Church has insisted on making integration a one-way street by forcing the black Christian and the black community into the mold of the dominant white society. "The problem of the white-styled black churches today is how to recover their own self-respect by demythologizing the white cultural bag through which the faith has been transmitted to them. . ." The white Protestant denominations must stop worrying about organic union among themselves, or about closer relations with the Roman Catholic Church, and give priority to "ecumenical relations in life and work with the five great all-black denominations. . . ."

Wilmore's work with the National Committee of Negro Churches and with the Division of Race Relations of the Presbyterian Church makes him an authoritative commentator on the racial matters in the Church in America.

Gayraud Wilmore, Jr., is Martin Luther King Professor of Social Ethics at Boston University. He is the author of *Black Religion and Black Radicalism*.[1]

THE CASE FOR A NEW BLACK CHURCH STYLE

Source: Gayraud Wilmore, Jr., "The Case for a New Black Church Style," *Church in Metropolis*, Fall 1968.

It became clear that black power could not be understood or interpreted by white churches and white churchmen on the march between Memphis and Jackson in the summer of 1966. Nor was it possible to correct the distortions of what had happened, as perceptions and explanations became confused both inside the movement itself and outside. That task, as far as the churches were concerned, had to be performed by Negro churchmen who were close enough to the

[1] A volume in the C. Eric Lincoln Series on Black Religion published by Anchor Press/Doubleday.

national scene to have a panoramic view, who had been deeply enough involved with Dr. King and the Civil Rights Movement to have won their right to speak boldly, and who were black enough to challenge, without deep feelings of guilt and betrayal, the white brethren who were beginning to show signs of reconciling with the great mass of white liberal opinion and backlash *against* black power.

Something else was even more obvious by the summer of 1966. The famous slogan which the Federal Council of Churches had adopted in the late 1930s . . . "A non-segregated church in a non-segregated society" had become totally bankrupt as an expression of church action in the race field. The banner of a non-segregated society begged too many burning questions to be unfurled as a brave pronouncement of where we were and where we thought we were going. Was it not of the very nature of the church in the United States that it is, and always has been, segregated by race and class? Was there any indication that the majority of either white or black Christians wanted it differently?

Was there any reasonable expectation that churches could be de-segregated before widespread desegregation occurred in housing, public schools, and in the informal and associational structures of American society? Finally, should black Christians permit themselves to be integrated within overwhelmingly white church structures without the freedom to develop and maintain their own leadership echelons and without determinative power concerning the effect on their lives?

The Need for New Styles of Black-White Relationships

Sobered by the failure of the old civil rights movement in the North—and made wiser by the interracial confrontations which have occurred over the last several months, we approach the problem of reconciling black and white within the one church of Christ from a different direction. Black churchmen in predominantly white denominations know well that the real question is not whether these churches can become truly integrated on Sunday morning, but whether, in the next twenty-five to fifty years, these churches will have any meaningful contact with black people at all! If that question can be answered affirmatively we must inquire how that contact will contribute to the dignity and humanity of both black and white people in a time of revolutionary change.

It is not merely segregation or integration which are at stake today. It is rather the question of the viability of the Christian Church in the United States—and perhaps in Western civilization. It is the question of whether or not this church can any longer encompass within it the masses of non-white persons, who make up the majority of the peoples of the earth, without undergoing radical changes in its understanding of its purpose in the world vis-à-vis robbed, subjugated, and excluded peoples, without dismantling its organizational structures for mission and without bringing to an end its basic conformity to European theological traditions and Anglo-Saxon styles of life and structures of value. The church cannot proceed through this period of crisis as a viable and relevant institution without a radical change in its spiritual and physical relationship to black Christians—most of whom are in all black churches—and to the black community as a whole.

Historical Christian Racism

Looking back to the seventeenth and eighteenth centuries, we are amazed by the ease with which American Christians used the institution of religion to protect a double standard of human justice which suited their economic self-interest. No amount of scholarly research and eloquence by white church historians about the "deep sympathy and solicitude" the Christian slaveholder had for his slaves, or about the zeal with which the major denominations threw themselves into the task of evangelizing the slave population after the Revolution, can make us forget that the churches themselves excluded the black man from the very freedoms which they justified for white men on the basis of Christian faith.

Therein lies the core of moral corruption in the American churches today and the kernel of American racism.

The original attitude of the churches found it expedient to separate love and justice where black people were concerned and that attitude prevailed in the end. What Lincoln might have said was that the war was a test to determine whether this nation or any nation, conceived in liberty and dedicated to the proposition that all men are created equal, could extend those same ideals to black men as well as to white men and still endure. That test has not yet been determinatively made, for what was guaranteed to the freedman in the amendments to the Constitution and the early civil rights laws have never been satisfactorily delivered and the nation still endures half slave and half free. We still face the test!

Likewise, church integration has always been a one-way street. Everything black was subordinate and inferior and would have to be given up for everything white. The white church, in its accommodation to white middle-class society, attempted to make over the black man and his church in its own image and to force the black community into the mold of the white society to which the white church had always been in bondage and which it conceived to be the nearest thing on earth to the Kingdom of God in Heaven.

The Black Church Development

The black churches which split off from the white Methodist and Baptist denominations in the latter part of the eighteenth and early nineteenth century borrowed heavily from the white churches which had first evangelized them and ordained their clergy. However, these black churches were able to develop their own styles of life and their own institutions. An authentic black culture and religion were germinated. Whatever may be said of the deficiencies or excesses of their preaching and brand of churchmanship, they were the pre-eminent expression of the yearning for freedom and dignity by a people who had been introduced to a religion, but excluded from all but the most demeaning aspects of the cultural mold of that religion.

On the other hand, the black churches which remained a part of the main-line white denominations were excluded from participation in the main-line culture. They were obliged to substitute whatever they held of their own for a system of white cultural and religious values. Thus a system developed in the black church and community that could only be a poor facsimile of the "real" thing—a second-class culture for second-class Christians.

Despite the fact that the white denominations have made a lasting contribution to these churches and to their communities by establishing hundreds of churches, schools, and colleges throughout the nation (and especially in the South), it must nevertheless be conceded that, as long as these institutions remain under white control, they remain unable to interpenetrate the white cultural accretion with a distinctive black ingredient as a viable component of the American ethos. At best, they were the objects of a benevolent paternalism and either atrophied or were smothered to death in the avid embrace of the great White Father and the great White Mother. At worst, they were hostages thrown over the walls of the white churches to keep at bay the wolves of a guilty conscience and a national embarrassment. In such a situation it was inevitable that a kind of cynicism would develop on both sides, and that one day these whitenized black Christians would say, "There ain't nothing Charley can do for me but lay his money on the line and move on. That's the name of the game we've been playing with one another and if he's satisfied with it, so am I!"

Whitenized Black Churches Today

The problem of the whitenized black churches today is how to recover their own self-respect by demythologizing the white cultural bag through which the faith was transmitted to them and in which they have curled themselves up so comfortably. In so doing they may discover that the essence of the Christian faith not only transcends ultimately the ethnocentric culture of the white man, but that of the black man as well; that this Christ, in whom there is neither Jew nor Greek, bond nor free, male nor female, is also neither black nor white.

Indeed, in liberating itself from the mythology of white Christianity and standing over against the suburban captivity of the white church, the whitenized black churches may be able to illuminate a theme from the left wing of the Protestant Reformation that the American experience has increasingly made opaque. Namely, that while the church is not permitted to create its own culture alongside the secular, it does stand in a dialectical relationship to culture—more often in opposition than accommodation—its most severe critic and reformer rather than its champion and celebrant.

Black Power and Dignity

This possibility rests upon what may at first appear to be a contradictory position, but is in fact a necessary concession to the perverted reality of the black man's religious situation in America. Before the whitenized black churches can immerse themselves in ecumenical Protestantism in the United States and perform their critical and reformatory role in relationship to the total culture, these churches must immerse themselves in a black ecumenicity and in a black culture, both of which they have repudiated in the past, but for which they, nevertheless, have a peculiar responsibility.

Is this to say that the Christian faith as viewed through the black power movement is but yet another expression of an ethnocentric religion of culture? To this question we must today give a qualified affirmative answer. Qualified, because what we are seeking in the posture of black religion is temporary and transitional—a way of correcting the errors of the past and preparing the ground for the future. But we must insist that if the Christian church is to become a dynamic influence in the black community, which will continue to be beleaguered by white racism, it must become not only a religious institution but a community organization. It must develop and embrace an ideology of black power not only as a defense against the racism of the white church and white culture, but as a necessary alternative to the cynical, materialistic youth in its flight from the dehumanizing effects of a spurious white Christian culture. Is it any wonder that black Christians are resisting easy and unexamined black and white relationships?

A Word to Our White Brothers

This is a hard saying that will not be readily accepted by our white Christian brethren. But the time has come when we, who have accepted from their hands a religion devoid of an ethic relevant to our real situation and a culture in which we were never permitted to participate on equal terms, must stand back from them to reassess our relationship to our own people and to the hostile society to which the white church continues in servile accommodation and for whose sake white Christians have betrayed us—their black brothers in Jesus Christ. We must stand back and be in a strategic exodus from this unequal engagement, this degrading, debilitating embrace, until we have recovered our own sense of identity, our true relationship to the people we serve, and until the white church is ready to enter into that partnership in life and mission which is able to renew the whole church of Christ.

The National Committee of Negro Churchmen at the meeting of their Board of Directors on April 5, 1968, took action to declare the following to the white religious establishment. "We believe it would be a tragic mistake for predominately white denominations to choose to bypass this institution in an effort to relate to and invest in the urban ghettoes. The Black Church has a physical presence and a constituency already organized in these communities. It is available as a means by which the whole Christian community can deal substantively and effectively with the urban crisis, the sickness of body and spirit which we see in the metropolitan centers of America today.

We, therefore, call upon the white churches and churchmen to take with utmost seriousness the Black Church as the only, though imperfect, link with inner city life for the mission of the church and we insist that the mission structure of the national denominations must identify with and be led by the black churches if their efforts are to have either credibility or reality.

We, therefore, call upon the white churches and churchmen to reappraise their strategies and expenditures so that the rich potential of the black churches can be fulfilled with the excellent by-products of mutual respect, comradeship and ecumenical development resulting therefrom.

In the light of the above considerations and recommendations and in order to prepare black churches to better serve the communities in which they exist, the National Committee of Negro Churchmen commits itself to the development of a new and creative style of black churchmenship which will emphasize its distinctive task and opportunity. There are four interrelated dimensions for this new style of mission.

1. The renewal and enhancement of the black church in terms of its liturgical life, its theological interpretation, its understanding of its mission to itself, to the white church and to the nation.

2. The development of the Black Church, not only as a religious fellowship, but as a community organization, in the technical sense of that term, which uses its resources, influence and manpower to address the problems of estrangement, resignation and powerlessness in the political, cultural and economic life of the black community.

3. The projection of a new quality of church life which would equip and strengthen the church as custodian and interpreter of that cultural heritage which is rooted in the peculiar experience of black people in the United States and the faith that has sustained them for over two centuries on these shores.

4. The contribution of the Black Church, out of its experience of suffering and the yearning for freedom, of that quality of faith, hope and love which can activate, empower, renew and unite the whole Church of Christ."

Only under these conditions can we remain in these predominately white denominations and maintain our connection to, much less our integrity in, a revolutionary black community, where God is bringing to naught the things which are and bringing into existence the things which do not exist. Unless black churchmen and black institutions within these historic denominations redefine their role in the black community in such terms as these, there is no sense in talking at all about the task of predominantly white denominations in relation to the black community.

The evangelistic task and the renewal and unity of these two aspects, one black and the other white, of American Christianity, can be considered in the light of three possibilities.

Consultation on Church Union

First, the Consultation on Church Union (COCU) may be able, within the next ten years, to unite in one church, on a precisely calculated basis of equality, the predominantly white and the predominantly black denominations. Despite the apparent openness of the white denominations and the fact that the three largest black Methodist bodies have remained in the consultation, this seems to be an unlikely possibility for the foreseeable future. Even if the three Methodist churches were to come into the union, the Black Baptist and Pentecostal groups would be outside, and they contain such large numbers of Negroes that the interracial character of American Protestantism would be only slightly more discernible than it is today.

Indeed, one must ask if the success of COCU, even if all of the major black churches participated in the union, would affect the *de facto* segregation of the American churches in any real sense? Without limiting the power of the Holy Spirit, it is difficult to imagine that within the present century we will see a sufficient distribution of the black population throughout the nation and a sufficient diminution of color prejudice to integrate existing and new local congregations to such an extent as to have more than a small proportion of Blacks and whites worshiping together on Sunday morning. We should no longer delude ourselves if we are going to get about the real business of evangelism.

But even more important in the present climate of black awareness is the necessity of black churches dealing with their own disunity and irrelevance in the ghetto. In view of the new role that the younger clergy are discovering in relation to the black power movement, it is improbable that they will be easily persuaded to turn time and attention from the mobilization of black people for community action to prepare their people for delicate ecumenical encounters with white churches and the interminable red tape of church union.

One thing is certainly clear as one studies the COCU reports, unless the Consultation is more willing to dialogue on the thorny issues of race and face more forthrightly the psychological, theological, and structural problems of authentic church integration in an increasingly polarized and racist society, there is even less hope that black churchmen will do more than go along for the ride until the white brethren get the message that evidently has not been communicated up to now. White supremacy is dead!

The White Church Role

A second possibility emerges for the predominant white denominations in the present crisis. It is to release their most competent black urban pastors to study the total resources and characteristics of each black congregation in terms of its revolutionary function in the black community, and to recommend whatever radical reallocation of national and judicatory resources should go into these churches to cast them into a new posture and relationship to the black community. It would be highly desirable for some black ecumenical mechanism to be created in neighborhoods or sectors of the metropolitan area that would serve as a conduit, an indirect means and strategy for channeling large sums, with no strings attached, from national and regional sources to local communities. IFCO, of course, is already involved in some such intermediate operation between sources of church funds and ghetto communities. Its basic purpose and scope, however, as well as its resources, are not elaborate enough to serve the objectives envisioned in this model. What is called for is a large-scale, multimillion-dollar mission enterprise of black cluster ministries, lay apostolates, experimental ministries and ecumenical task forces in black communities, all oriented toward church community organization and militant political and economic action programs undergirded by a black theological and cultural renaissance.

The question is whether we can now design and finance this new secular mission in the black community, recruit and train both its lay and clerical leadership across denominational lines, and project it onto the vortex of the black revolution in such dramatic ways as to attract and serve not only the black poor, but also the increasingly alienated black youth, the new Afro-American student generation, and the emerging middle class.

A New Relationship

A third possibility exists in the proposals that have been put forth for the predominantly white Protestant denominations to stop worrying about organic union among themselves and *rapprochement* with Roman Catholicism and begin to enter, on an unprecedented scale, into ecumenical relations in life and work with the five great all-black denominations and about twenty-four smaller churches that comprise more than 90 per cent of all black Protestants in the United States.

This is not a suggestion that black and white denominations simply exchange fraternal greetings and enroll each other's prestigious church-men at church conventions. What is meant is that the white de-nominations begin to do joint planning for a total mission to the emerging megalopolises or regional cities with the black denomina-tions. Actually given the mission structure of many of these black churches, it may mean joint planning and strategy execution between key black congregations and key white congregations and white urban mission structures.

The inequality of financial and material wealth among these en-tities could be neutralized to some extent if the white denominations learn to accept from black hands what God has given and when black churches learn that black religion has something to give to the whole Church of Christ. White churches may give money. Black churches which are not affluent may give contributions in kind for the development and execution of various kinds of non-residential and urban fringe ministries beamed to the middle classes, joint mis-sionary education and teacher-training projects, joint liturgical study and renewal and new concepts in seminary education, recruitment, and placement. The possibilities for black-white co-operation, short of organic union, are myriad, even given the present mood, if the black churches and churchmen are given a little respect—in the pro-found sense that word has taken on in the "soul community."

It is perhaps too obvious to mention that in joint mission strategy planning and action such groups as the denominational black cau-cuses, the emerging geographical black caucuses and the National Committee of Negro Churchmen should be consulted and utilized to the fullest extent.

The three possibilities for the evangelistic advance of predominantly white churches upon territory now occupied by black congregations—whether of the white or of the historic black denominations—depend finally not upon money or real estate or equipment. Their success depends upon the determination of the white churches to attack the racism within their ranks and institutional structures with the same vigor and holy zeal with which they threw themselves into missionary activity among people of color in the South following Emancipation and in Asia and Africa in the nineteenth century.

Perhaps it will take even more effort than this in the struggle against the systemic racism and the covert racist presuppositions and myths of the white churches. But there are no real possibilities for mission in the black community, joint or otherwise, until the white church establishment begins to use church law to deal with racism among its members, to force compliance with official policy and pronouncement and to desegregate every aspect of church life—beginning with the bureaucratic structures where decision-making power lies, running through the mission agencies, educational institutions, and local churches, and continuing in decisions about questions of qualifications, recruitment, training, and creating new opportunities of meaning and worth for black leadership.

In a world that God made for all to enjoy and live in to the full, some men have taken more of their share of the power which makes the good life possible. In their dehumanization of other men they make faith in a just God impossible. The church that is engaged in the business of evangelism comes into this situation with power, speaks the word of judgment and performs the act of mercy which reveals unmistakably that the God whom it serves is the one of whom Mary said:

> "He has shown strength with his arm, he has scattered the proud in the imagination of their hearts, he has put down the mighty from their thrones, and exalted those of low degree; he has filled the hungry with good things, and the rich he has sent empty away. . . ." (Luke 1:51–53)

JOHN WESLEY WORK

The black spiritual as an art form was given international recognition through the concerts of the Fisk University Jubilee Singers who took their music to the capitals of Europe to raise funds for the struggling college a hundred years ago. Work analyzes the beauty and the value of the songs they sang. "The man, though a slave, produced the song, and the song in turn produced a better man." Blacks feel more deeply than do others, and it is the broader, deeper spirituality which has enabled black people to endure. The spirituals are songs, prayers, praises, and sermons. They have been mistakenly derided by those who cannot distinguish between the experience of slavery and the creative genius of a people *in spite* of slavery. The most effective preachers understand the spiritual and emotional needs of most Blacks and finds in the spiritual a tremendous power for arousing "feelings for the right." Even those Blacks who do not sing the spirituals openly, "sing them in their soul."

The late John W. Work was professor of Latin and History at

Fisk University and a pioneer in collecting, arranging, and presenting the black spirituals. His work at Fisk did much to legitimize the spiritual as a true art form and one indigenous to the black people of America.

WHAT THE NEGRO'S MUSIC MEANS TO HIM

Source: John Wesley Work, *Folk Songs of the American Negro,* Nashville, 1915, pp. 110–20.

"The human soul and music are alone eternal."

In the Negro's own mind his music has held, and still holds, positions of variable importance. In the darkness of bondage, it was his light; in the morn of his freedom, it was his darkness; but as the day advances, and he is being gradually lifted up into a higher life, it is becoming not only his proud heritage, but a support and powerful inspiration. The songs of the slave were his sweet consolation and his messages to Heaven, bearing sorrow, pain, joy, prayer, and adoration. Undisturbed and unafraid, he could always unburden his heart in these simple songs pregnant with faith, hope, and love. The man, though a slave, produced the song, and the song, in turn, produced a better man. The slave is perennially praised for his perfect devotion. Some attribute it to one cause, some to another. Some even go so far as to attribute it to the influence of the system of slavery, but more than any other cause, the retroactive power of his own music influenced this character of the slave. What else could he be who had such ideals ever before him? How could a man be base who looked ever to the hills? Could a man cherish the idea of rapine whose soul was ever singing these songs of love, patience and God? Neither African heathenism nor American slavery could wholly extinguish that spark of idealism, set aglow by his Creator. This idealism, expressed in terms so beautiful and strong, grew in power, and the possessor found himself irresistibly drawn and willingly striving to attain unto it. The creator of these songs had now become the creature of his own creation.

Naturally enough, when the Negro found himself free, he literally put his past behind him. It was his determination that as far as within him lay, not one single reminder of that black past should mar his future. So away went all these reminders into the "abyss of oblivion."

His music was one of these reminders and as sweet as it was to him, as much as it had helped him, it, too, must go, for it was a reminder of the awful night of bondage. It is nothing that newly emancipated slaves, sent out by schools like Fisk and Hampton, gained friends and large sums of money by singing these slave songs. That Fisk University can truthfully be said, in large part, to be a product of these plantation melodies is nothing against the fact that just after emancipation the Negro refused to sing his own music in public, especially in the schools.

When the Original Fisk Singers started out to earn money for their struggling school, they did not sing their own, but the current music of the day. It was not until they saw that they were doomed to failure that they began to use the plantation melodies, the effectiveness of which was discovered by what was apparently a mere chance. After one crushingly unsuccessful concert, the announcement was made that if any cared to remain for a while after the conclusion of the program, the company would sing a few of their own folk songs. Those who remained showed so plainly their perfect delight, that the singers themselves were astonished. People then began to talk about this new music, now knowing just what to believe about it. It was something similar to curiosity but, in fact, more than that which seized upon the people. The music made men rejoice, it made them weep, it made them ashamed, it made them better. They loved to hear it. All this was positive. The singing of these songs brought ovation after ovation. Though it was a sacrifice of a just pride to sing these songs, the sacrifice, when made, brought a new day and a new blessing. It introduced the Negro to himself! The Negro is not so different from other men in his thought as he is in his feelings. In thought, he is generic; in feeling, more specific. His feelings are broader and deeper than those of other men and they have more directive influence and power over him than other men's feelings have upon them. This spirituality is the source of his consuming enthusiasm, which has carried him over so many obstacles, to the accomplishment of the all but miraculous. The fact, however, that this feeling is so evident in all his life, work, play, and religion has led many to conclude that as he abounds in emotion he is lacking in intellect. It is almost unnecessary to state that this inference is a *non sequitur*. Like other men, the Negro is affected by his environment, only more deeply affected. He suffers more, he enjoys more. This is one reason why he seems an imitator; this is the reason why he can so easily adapt himself to his surroundings and assume cordial relations with the different phases of life. It is largely on account of this "emotional nature," which so many condemn, that he is monopolizing in different ways so much of the world's attention. Consequently, when we begin to describe the attitude of the Negro toward his own folk song, accuracy demands that we take into consideration time, place, and condition.

To our fathers who came out of bondage and who are still with us, these songs are prayers, praises, and sermons. They sang them at work; in leisure moments; they crooned them to their babes in their cradles; to their wayward children; they sang them to their sick, wracked with pain on beds of affliction; they sang them over their dead. Blessings, warnings, benedictions, and the very heartbeats of life were all expressed to our fathers by their songs. To them there is not one insignificant pause, cadence, inflexion, or expression anywhere in all these countless songs; but every note, every word, every sentiment is of tremendous import. Yes, those who lived in bondage with these songs, the offspring of their souls still love them as their comforters.

To those of the first generation, who grew up in localities illiberal and intolerant, these songs are generally objects of indifference or aversion. To them slavery is more indefensible than it was to their fathers, and present-day ill treatment adds to their indignation. Then, too, these songs always remind them of slavery and all slavery meant to their fathers; therefore, the logical sequence is that they either pass them by with "silent contempt," or they regard them with positive apathy. They take neither time nor pains to understand, or if they do this, it is only to condemn. They find all kinds of fault with them, make all kinds of odious comparisons, and "laugh them to scorn." As it is true that mankind will find fault with, criticize, and pick flaws in anything for which he may have conceived a dislike, so it is true that mankind will seek something to praise in anything for which he may have conceived a liking. There was noteworthy and interesting proof of this at Fisk University. It is clearly paradoxical that for many years it was impossible to induce the students of Fisk to sing these songs, even after that famous first company had sung this institution into new life. For years one would be as likely to hear Negro Folk Songs in St. Peter's at Rome as in Fisk University.

President Cravath had a fine helper in Professor Adam K. Spence, who led the music in chapel and who was largely responsible for the salvation of the Negro music. When Professor Spence would rise in chapel services and "start" one of these songs, requesting the students to "join in," they would "join in" with a chorus of cold silence. They knew enough to comprehend slavery dialect and bad grammar, and they would have none of either. Elijah, Messiah, and Creation were different and meant better things than the times and conditions represented by these songs. But Professor Spence would analyze and explain individual songs and show their beauty. This he did day in and day out, illustrating with his own sweet voice, and sweeter soul, the virtues expressed by the music until he finally led them to an understanding; and now, at all religious services, these songs are sung in melody abundant and divine. So important a place has this music assumed in the worship and in the life of Fisk that both teachers and students feel that something is lacking, and that there is a distinct loss, if these songs are not sung. These conditions are practically the same in a majority of the southern schools. This growing interest in his own music, the solitary connecting link between the lack of race respect and confidence and the possibility of race consciousness, is a harbinger of the New Day of Hope.

To us who have been reared in surroundings more pleasant, much of the bitterness of slavery has passed away. In the consideration and kindness of the present, the past is almost forgotten. So to this class, this folk music has a somewhat different meaning. Not consumed by fires of bitter animosity, nor fanned by winds of antipathy, we see every good point of this music. Though we could not forget that it was born in slavery, to us it is beautiful. It does not express itself in the purity of the king's English, but, oh! the crooning sweetness of the dialect! It does not employ the smoothed, well-balanced sentences of the classics, but, oh! the directness, the pithiness, the strength! Its melody does not flow in channels laid out by the great musicians, but, what is more to be praised, its melody is all its own. It is original in its beauty. In its entirety it does not touch with satisfaction the intellects of the standard composers, but it most assuredly touches the heart of all mankind. It may be our fathers' history of their enslaved past, but it is also projecting itself into a future full of bright promise, for he needs not to be called a prophet who predicts that out of our fathers' song there will be evolved a greater song, sublime and glorious.

Further, these songs are to us a storehouse of comfort. How can we ever forget those by-gone days when our mothers sang them to us as our lullabies? "This old-time religion, makes me love everybody." Think of the great blessing of being sung to sleep by such a lullaby— "Makes Me Love Everybody!" Think of the great favor of being reared in the atmosphere of "Lord, I Want to Be Like Jesus!" In times of sorrow, we have heard our mothers sing "Keep Me from Sinking Down," and often, oh! so often, "March on and You Shall Gain the

Victory," has rung with such meaning through the humble home. Can you blame us for loving these songs which have so much inspired us to be and to do?

The teachers regard this music as a desirable possession, which is worth study and understanding. They have a feeling of ownership of something original; and if teachers admire any one quality in the course of education, it is originality. They find that this music grips the hearts of the scholars and awakens interest. Teachers always welcome interest in pupils. They find in this music a refreshing departure from the routine of the classroom, giving variety to the work. Then there is around this folk song an atmosphere invigorating and inspiring. All this is of practical help to the teacher. Subjectively, the teacher is the better for an understanding of this music, for which his intelligence fits. Not only does he experience intellectual, but spiritual enjoyment as well.

The clergymen's regard is determined almost wholly by the religious power of this music. The wise preacher who really understands his people, and the preacher who helps them most, knows that he must take into consideration and give due reverence to the Negro's emotional nature, the whole world to the contrary notwithstanding. Of course, this can be overdone and it often is, but on the other hand many Negro preachers fail because they go too far the other way. They long for the reputation, "intellectual," and discountenance and discourage any manifestations of "feeling." But the arousing of a feeling for the right is a very nearly sure way of having right done. I am certain that this is psychological heresy, but experience has proved and will continue to prove that the Negro's soul obeys some such law. And the truth is, the souls of some others work the same way. Most men know the right, but it is where they have an enthusiasm for the right that they will do right. To the preacher these songs of the Negro are powers for arousing "feelings for the right." It is hardly believable that any man could remain the same and unaffected, after singing in the spirit, "Lord, I Want to Be Like Jesus," or "Were You There When They Crucified My Lord?" So it seems plain that the preacher who uses this music to add momentum to the gospel is wise.

To the musician, these songs furnish both a keen intellectual, and a deep emotional, enjoyment. He sees their idiomatic features, their characteristic originalities, their smooth exquisite melodies, their thematic values, and their possibilities. He enjoys the wonder of it, that untutored slaves could produce such music, that they could give forth such rhythm, such well-balanced periods, such lofty sentiments. He loves to take these old songs and build them into something new without destroying their individuality. He loves to select from them his themes, to be adorned in classic vestments. He loves to build harmonies congenial to their characteristics. He loves to feel that he is working with something original, separate and apart, all his own; he loves to contemplate the future life of this music, which he believes will be a glorious transformation.

Those of the second generation of freedom who have lived in the North have been more positively and deeply affected in their regard for their racial possessions and characteristics than any other class. They have come nearer experiencing civic and political freedom than their brothers in the South and have had their racial bonds greatly weakened. They simply hate the thought of slavery, despise any reference to it, and turn away from anything that reminds them of it. They naturally care nothing for the songs born in slavery. They see no beauty in them, nothing commendable, nothing worth while. They do not study them because obviously they are not fit subjects for serious thought. Among this group, Negro Folk Music finds least favor.

There are some schools attended largely by northern Negroes where the students flatly refuse to sing these songs. This is due to the fact that these students have the idea (which is often correct) that white people are looking for amusement in their singing. Some Negroes enjoy being laughed at, but they are not found in the schools. The same students assume the attitude that the rest of the world concedes to the Negroes the ability to execute well their own music, but it is beyond them to understand and execute the classics, and any attempt to do this is presumptious. To them, this is another form of circumscription which has been a hindrance and handicap. They cannot afford to recognize any limitation except those which confine the abilities of the whole human race. Some look upon this music with disfavor because they simply cannot do otherwise. They have been thoroughly overwhelmed by that powerful propaganda, which aims at impressing upon the Negro his nothingness, or at best his inferiority to other races. In their desperate effort to prove they are something, they fatuously struggle to abandon that self which the world deems inferior and to become some other self. They repudiate everything which bears the stamp of race. It is cause for sincere congratulation to ourselves that this class is growing proportionally smaller as time passes. It will finally disappear.

To those of the second generation of freedmen who live in the South, these songs are a source of encouragement. They read their story with open minds and hearts. They tell the story of our fathers' agony, the cleansing fire into which they were cast. It tells how they emerged from the fires unharmed and without the smell of smoke upon their garments, how character was brightened and faith strengthened. It tells our fathers' sublime standard of spirituality, which their children must make their very own. When they read this story and comprehend its meaning, when they catch the vision of the past, joyfully cry, "Thanks be to God for our fathers!" To be children of such forebears is a blessed inspiration; to be the heirs of such wealth of wisdom as our fathers' songs is in itself transcendant.

They are ever calling us from discouragement and fears; they lead us to face with confidence the hostile forces of life. Because we have such fathers and such inheritance, we are ashamed not to be striving ever and ever onward and upward; we are ashamed not to do our best. It nerves us to fight. Though all may not sing these songs openly, they sing them in their souls. They are a part of the very breath they breathe and of the life they live.

EILEEN SOUTHERN

Singing was a prominent feature of the camp meetings, and one most obviously affected by black participation. In fact, black-styled singing became a distinctive badge of the camp-meeting movement. The Blacks made up their songs themselves. They were not in the lyrical tradition but were a linking of isolated lines from prayers, the Scriptures, and orthodox hymns with choruses, or refrains, added as required. These black songs eventually came to be called "spirituals," and they became the official hymns of the camp meetings associated with the religious movement called the "Great Awakening."

With the development of the independent black churches, a musical component complimentary to the self-perceived image of the church was needed but was not easily come by. Southern cites the controversy over trained choirs versus spontaneous congregational singing and the controversy over the introduction of instrumental music into the churches, as important in the gradual development of the distinctive style of music in the Black Church. It is interesting to note that "concerts" and even "solos" were not readily accepted by the fledgling church and were the cause of much debate.

The preacher's attitude also figured in the development of this music. Professor Southern points to Bishop Daniel Payne of the A.M.E. Church as one who did not condone the singing of the spiritual songs in worship services. He discouraged the proliferation of the "praying and singing bands" and looked with disdain upon those who clapped their hands and stomped their feet as they sang. But in spite of Payne's protestations, the masses regarded these traditional expressions as the essence of religion, refusing in Payne's lifetime to desist from their practice.

Long before black churches were common the slaves had developed the "Invisible Church." They would steal off to secret meeting places to worship, or would meet in the cabin of the preacher, or in special cabins called "praise houses." Sometimes they sang religious folk songs with strong elements of African tradition. It was in this setting that the "shout" and the "ring dance" were most likely to take place. These shout and dance songs were sometimes called "running spirituals."

Eileen Southern is Associate Professor of Music at York College, the City University of New York.

THE RELIGIOUS OCCASION

Source: Eileen Southern, The Music of Black Americans, A History (New York: W. W. Norton & Co., Inc., 1971), pp. 93–99, 131–34, 158–63.

The Camp Meeting

The camp meeting was an American phenomenon that evolved during the "Second Awakening," a revival movement dominating the religious life of America's frontier communities during the period 1780 to 1830. Its participants were the common people, black and white, of all the Protestant denominations; its format, that of a continuous religious service spread out over several days, often an entire week. Religious services took place in a forest or woods, the members of the huge temporary congregations worshiping in large tents and living in small tents. The historic first camp meeting was held in Logan County, Kentucky, in July 1800, and drew thousands of participants. A Presbyterian minister, the Reverend James McGready, was the leading spirit in organizing the meeting, but various denominations were represented among the several preachers involved in the conduct of the services and the handling of the large crowds. Eventually the camp-meeting movement came to be dominated by Methodist ministers, who taught their own Methodist hymns to the campers in the early years. From Kentucky the idea of camp meetings traveled in all directions—northeast into West Virginia, Maryland, Delaware, Pennsylvania, and up to the northern states; east into Virginia and on into the Carolinas; south into Tennessee and down into the Deep South.

The camp meeting was an interracial institution; indeed, sometimes there were more black worshipers present than white. Foreign visitors to the States were greatly impressed by what they saw and heard at camp meetings, there being no European prototypes for the vast assemblages in forest groves. The visitors filled their diaries and travel journals with detailed descriptions of the people attending these meetings, of the sermons, of the procedures, and, above all, of the singing—especially the songs of the Blacks. Ex-slaves, too, provided descriptions of camp meetings in their writings.

At night the scene of a meeting was an awesome sight. Huge campfires burned everywhere, so that it seemed as if the "whole woods stood in flames." From three to five thousand persons or more were assembled in the huge main tent, called a *tabernacle*, to listen to the preacher-for-the-evening address them from an elevated stand. On benches below the elevation sat the other preachers. Then there were rows of seats for the people—according to some reports, one side for the Negroes and the other side for the white congregation. Other accounts state, however, that the black folk had to *stand*, not sit, in a narrow space reserved for them behind the preachers' elevation; undoubtedly, practices varied from place to place. Robert Todd, a Methodist historian who was active in the Pennsylvania-Maryland-Delaware-Virginia area, says that "a portion of the circle to the rear of the preacher's stand [was] invariably set apart for the occupancy and use of the colored people."

Occasionally black ministers preached to camp-meeting assemblies. Precedents for Blacks addressing white or interracial congregations had been set by the Methodists in their early "itinerating" practices, which sent ministers to preach in rural areas, hunting up all those who "dwelt in the wilderness." The first of the English Methodist missionaries to come to America (and, later, the first bishop of the American Methodist Church), the Reverend Francis Asbury, generally was accompanied by Black Harry Hoosier in his travels, estimated to have totaled over

270,000 miles. On some occasions Black Harry substituted for Asbury and was well received. Daniel Coker, a black minister of Baltimore and a leading figure at the organizational Conference of the A.M.E. Church in 1816, noted in his journal that he had addressed a gathering of 5,000 at a camp meeting in Maryland.

Singing in the Camp Meeting

To both participants and observers, the singing was one of the most impressive aspects of camp meetings. When the people sang their hymns and spirituals, they instantaneously formed a "superb choir." After attending a camp meeting in Georgia, the Swedish novelist Fredrika Bremer wrote:

> A magnificent choir! Most likely the sound proceeded from the black portion of the assembly, as their number was three times that of the whites, and their voices are naturally beautiful and pure.

According to a report on a camp meeting held in Pennsylvania in 1838, where there were seven thousand in attendance, the Negroes sang louder than any others, although they were greatly outnumbered:

> Their shouts and singing were so very boisterous that the singing of the white congregation was often completely drowned in the echoes and reverberations of the colored people's tumultuous strains.

The Blacks customarily continued singing in their segregated quarters long after the whites had retired to their tents for the night, and sometimes sang all night long. More than a dozen contemporary writers commented upon this unusual practice. Fredrika Bremer observed that, although the meeting she attended had lasted long past midnight, the Blacks did not go to sleep afterward:

> On the black side [of the camp] . . . the tents were still full of religious exaltation, each separate tent presenting some new phasis. . . . In one tent . . . a song of the spiritual Canaan was being sung excellently. . . . At half-past five [the next morn] . . . the hymns of the Negroes . . . were still to be heard on all sides.

Black campers made their influence felt in the camp-meeting movement in yet another way—much to the discomfiture of the church fathers. Watson observed this in his discussion of the "errors" made by Methodists of the time:

> Here ought to be considered too, a most exceptional error, which has the tolerance at least of the rulers of our camp meetings. In the *blacks'* quarter, the coloured people get together, and sing for hours together, shout scraps of disjointed affirmations, pledges, or prayers, lengthened out with long repetition *choruses*. These are all sung in the merry chorus-manner of the southern harvest field, or husking-frolic method, of the slave blacks. . . .

Such practices he condemned, pointing out that

> . . . the example has already visibly affected the religious manners of some whites. From this cause, I have known in some camp meetings, from 50 to 60 people croud into one tent, after the public devotions had closed, and there continue the whole night, singing tune after tune (though with occasional episodes of prayer), scarce one of which were in our hymn books.

Let us examine the practices of the Blacks which affected camp-meeting singing to such an extent that churchmen were moved to protest. First, the Blacks were holding songfests away from proper supervision, and this was undesirable in the eyes of the church fathers. They were singing songs of their own composing, which was even worse in the eyes of the officials. The texts of the composed songs were not lyric poems in the hallowed tradition of Watts, but a stringing together of isolated lines from prayers, the Scriptures, and orthodox hymns, the whole made longer by the addition of choruses or the injecting of refrains between verses. Finally, for their composed religious songs the Blacks used tunes that were dangerously near to being dance tunes in the style of slave jubilee melodies. None of this was acceptable to the orthodox. Nevertheless, from such practices emerged a new kind of religious song that became the distinctive badge of the camp-meeting movement.

The Camp-Meeting Spiritual

Just as the "Great Awakening" movement in the eighteenth century had stimulated a revolt among the common people against the staid psalmody of the religious establishment and had ushered in the livelier hymnody, so the "Second Awakening" of the early nineteenth century brought a reaction against the now antiquated hymns. In the noisy, folksy atmosphere of the camp meeting, songs of a different kind were demanded. There were no hymnbooks in the early years of the movement; the campers had either to sing from memory or to learn songs in the meetings. Most of the congregation was illiterate and, at any rate, it would have been difficult to read by the light of flickering campfires or torches. As a result the same kind of procedures were developed at camp meetings as had been practiced among Negroes. Song leaders added choruses and refrains to the official hymns so that the people could join in with the singing. They introduced new songs with repetitive phrases and catchy tunes. Spontaneous songs were composed on the spot, often started by some excited preacher and developed by the crowds who shouted "Hallelujah" and similar praise words or phrases between the preacher's lines. The new songs were called "spiritual songs," as distinguished from the hymns and psalms. True, the term "spiritual song" had been in use for over a century, but now it acquired a different meaning, being used to designate the camp-meeting hymn. According to modern authorities, the first collection of songs to be directly inspired by camp-meeting revivalism was published in Philadelphia in 1803, John Scott's *Hymns and Spiritual Songs for the Use of Christians, Including a Number Never Before Published*. Within the same decade appeared a number of similiar collections; among them, *The Christian Harmony or Songster's Companion* (1805), by Jeremiah Ingalls, and *A Collection of the Most Admired Hymns and Spiritual Songs with the Choruses Affixed as Usually Sung at Camp Meetings* (1809), by Joseph Totten.

The distinctive features of the camp-meeting spiritual song were the chorus, the folk-song-style melodies, and the rough and irregular couplets that referred to scriptural concepts and to everyday experiences. Frequently, as we have seen, choruses and refrains originally belonging to one song were attached to other songs. Eventually there developed a body of such "wandering verses," which became immensely popular with camp-meeting congregations. It is worthy of note that some of the verses that were to become most popular with campers appeared in print for the first time in Richard Allen's collection of 1801—for example:

> Hallelujah to the Lamb,
> Who has purchased our pardon;
> We will praise him again
> When we pass over Jordan.
> [Chorus sung with Hymns Nos. 1 and 50]

> There's glory, glory in my soul;
> Come, mourners, see salvation roll.
> [Couplet in Hymn No. 14]

> Firm united let us be,
> In the bonds of charity;
> As a band of brothers join'd,
> Loving God and all mankind.
> [Chorus of Hymns Nos. 45 and 56]

There were at least two other favorite camp-meeting verses that belonged to the Negro tradition, according to contemporary sources:

> Roll, Jordan, roll

and

> Shout, shout, we are gaining ground;
> Glory, Hallelujah.

In his book, *Methodist Error*, Watson discussed the latter along with several other verses "composed and first sung by Blacks."

Shouts in the Camp Meeting

Watson reported on a curious activity of the Negroes that took place while they were singing in their quarters after the all-camp services were ended. To him it seemed that the singers were almost dancing, and indeed they were:

> With every word so sung, they have a sinking of one or [the] other leg of the body alternately; producing an audible sound of the feet at every step, and as manifest as the steps of actual Negro dancing in Virginia, etc. If some, in the meantime, sit, they strike the sounds alternately on each thigh.

This is the earliest account of a religious dance ceremony of African origin, the "ring shout," that was to be described many, many times in nineteenth- and twentieth-century American literature. Watson apparently did not take note of the circle formation of the dancers, but he did observe the thigh slapping. As we have seen, the slaves who danced in the markets of New York City accompanied themselves with percussive sounds produced in this manner. And during the period

57

when Watson was writing, the slaves in New Orleans were drawing crowds of whites to the Place Congo on Sunday afternoons to watch a similar form of dancing. (This point will be discussed in a later chapter.)

There was another camp-meeting practice that allowed the Blacks to indulge in their traditional "shuffle step" dancing—the "farewell march around the encampment." Robert Todd reported on a typical occurrence in a northern slave state:

Usually the tide of enthusiasm on the colored side of the encampment arose and intensified as the days and nights rolled by; and reached the climatic point on the last night of the meeting. By general consent, it was understood that, as to the colored people, the rules requiring quiet after a certain hour, were, on this last night, to be suspended; and great billows of sound from the tornado of praise and singing rolled over the encampment, and was echoed back from hill and wood for miles away, until the morrow's dawning.

With the sunrise, the Blacks would begin knocking down the plank partitions that separated the white quarters from those of the Blacks. Then they would begin the "grand march round de campment,"

accompanied with leaping, shuffling, and dancing, after the order of David before the ark when his wife thought he was crazy; accompanied by a song appropriate to the exciting occasion. . . . The sound of the hammer aforesaid became the signal for a general arising all around the camp; and, in a few moments, curtains were parted; tents thrown open; and multitudes of faces peered out into the early dawning to witness the weird spectacle. Sometimes the voices of the masters and veterans among the white people would echo back, in happy response, the jubilant shout of the rejoicing slaves.

The Negro Church and Music

Several black church historians of the nineteenth century published accounts of the organization and growth of their churches, but most of these tell us little about musical practices. The A.M.E. bishop, Daniel Alexander Payne (1811–93), however, provides a wealth of information in his book, *Recollections of Seventy Years* (1888), about both religious and secular musical practices encountered in his travels about the country. It is fair to assume that what Payne wrote about the A.M.E. practices applies as well to other independent black denominations of the time. Born of free parents in Charleston, South Carolina,

Payne received his early education in that city but left at the age of twenty-three to live in the North. There he studied for the ministry at a Lutheran seminary in Pennsylvania, and after completing his studies, served as a pastor to a Presbyterian church in East Troy, New York. In 1841, however, he joined the A.M.E. Church and devoted the remainder of his life to service in that church—at various times he was a minister, historian, bishop, and college president (of the A.M.E. Wilberforce University, founded 1863). At the time he wrote his memoirs, Payne was very proud of the state of music in A.M.E. churches. He observed:

> In a musical direction what progress has been made within the last forty years! There is not a Church of ours in any of the great cities of the republic that can afford to buy an instrument which is without one; and there are but few towns or villages where our Connection exists that are without an instrument to accompany the choir.

To be sure, many bitter controversies had to be resolved before musical standards in the A.M.E. churches reached the high level boasted of by Payne in the 1870s. It will be recalled that at the first "Mother Bethel" Church in Philadelphia the elder lined-out the psalms and hymns for the congregation, just as the deacons of white Protestant sects had been compelled to do for their congregations in the eighteenth century. And just as the common people in the eighteenth century had rebelled against the introduction of new kinds of musical practices, so in the nineteenth century black Methodist old-timers fought similar battles in their independent churches. The first conflict arose when forward-looking forces in the church attempted to bring in trained choirs to join the congregation in the singing during worship services. What an uproar! Payne remembered:

> The first introduction of choral singing into the A.M.E. Church took place in Bethel, Philadelphia, Pa., between 1841 and 1842. It gave great offense to the older members, especially those who had professed personal sanctification. Said they: "You have brought the devil into the Church, and therefore we will go out." So, suiting the action to the word, many went out of Bethel, and never returned.

The split in Bethel's congregation failed, however, to solve the dispute. Although Payne had only recently become associated with the A.M.E. Church, he was drawn into the fray:

So great was the excitement and irritation produced by the introduction of the choir into Bethel Church that I, then a local preacher and schoolmaster, was requested by the leader of the choir and other prominent members in it to preach a special sermon on sacred music. This I did as best I could. In my researches I used a small monograph on music written by Mr. Wesley [founder of the white English Methodist Church], but drew my information chiefly from the word of God. The immediate effect of that discourse was to check the excitement, soothe the irritation, and set the most intelligent to reading as they had never done before.

Payne observed that similar "excitements" and "irritations" occurred when choirs were introduced into other churches of the sect, "not only in the cities but also in the large towns and villages." Conservative members withdrew from churches in many places, with the result that large congregations were supplanted by smaller ones. In Chicago the minister, the Reverend Elisha Weaver, actually was impeached by his congregation in 1857 for introducing vocal and instrumental music into the church. From the vantage point of the present time, the parallels are obvious between the development of white Protestant musical traditions in the colonial period and the growth of similar traditions in the independent black churches of the nineteenth century.

The first use of musical instruments in the church also caused conflict among black Methodists, although not to the same extent as the introduction of choral singing. The earliest performance of instrumental music in an A.M.E. church took place in Baltimore in 1848, the occasion being a concert of sacred music presented under the direction of James Fleet of Washington, D.C. In a second concert of sacred music given in the same year, William Appo directed a seven-piece string ensemble. It was not long before black congregations everywhere began to develop great pride in their choirs, their organs, and the concerts presented in their churches.

Ring Shouts and Bush Meetings. It was inevitable that Payne should come into contact with some practices that he did not condone. He disapproved, for example, of the singing of "spiritual songs" in the worship services, dismissing such songs as mere "cornfield ditties." He also protested against the custom prevailing in some churches whereby members of the congregation remained after the sermon to participate in "praying and singing bands." Payne thought the church members were acting "in a most ridiculous and heathenish way" when they formed a circle, then sang songs, clapped their hands, and stomped their feet as they moved slowly around in the circle. At camp meetings and bush meetings (meetings held in a wooded areas without the use of tents), the "bands" were even more common. When Payne remonstrated with one of the leaders about such practices, the man answered:

> The Spirit of God works upon people in different ways. At camp-meeting there must be a ring here, a ring there, a ring over yonder, or sinners will not get converted.

This traditional ritual dance was one of the most persistent of the African customs that survived in the New World. Despite the efforts of ministers such as Payne to "modify these extravagances in worship," the masses regarded the rituals as the "essence of religion" and refused to desist from their practices.

The Shout

After the regular service there frequently was held in the same room a special service, purely African in form and tradition. The most detailed account of this rite in any nineteenth-century source is given in the 1867 collection, but numerous other sources also describe it.

> The true "shout" takes place on Sundays or on "praise" nights through the week, and either in the praise-house or in some cabin in which a regular religious meeting has been held. Very likely more than half the population of the plantation is gathered together. . . . The benches are pushed back to the wall when the formal meeting is over, and old and young, men and women . . . all stand up in the middle of the floor, and when the "sperichil" [spiritual] is struck up, begin first walking and by-and-by shuffling round, one after the other, in a ring. The foot is hardly taken from the floor, and the progression is mainly due to a jerking, hitching motion, which agitates the entire shouter, and soon brings out streams of perspiration.

Generally, the gathering divided itself into two groups, shouters (that is, dancers) and singers. The latter, "composed of some of the best singers and of tired shouters stand at the side of the room to 'base' the others, singing the body of the song and clapping their hands together or on the knees." The dancers participated in the singing according to how they felt. Sometimes they danced silently; sometimes they sang only refrains of the song; sometimes they sang the entire song along with the singers. The descriptive passage concludes:

Song and dance are alike extremely energetic, and often, when the shout lasts into the middle of the night, the monotonous thud, thud of feet prevents sleep within half a mile of the praise-house.

For the participants the shout was not under any circumstances to be construed as a dance, and strictly observed rules insured that the line between "shouting" and dancing was firmly drawn. Only songs of a religious nature were sung, and the feet must never be crossed (as would happen in the dance). Among strict devotees, the feet must not even be lifted from the ground. Presumably, any song could function as a shout song or "running spiritual." In practice, however, the slaves preferred some songs to the exclusion of others, and a special body of these songs was developed among them.

In performance, a ring spiritual was repeated over and over as the shouters moved around in a circle, often for as long as four and five successive hours. The song thus took on the character of a chant, a "wild monotonous chant," and its text became the "repetition of an incoherent cry." Although the ring of shouters moved slowly at the beginning, the tempo of the music and the pace of the circling gradually quickened so that the performance eventually displayed "signs of frenzy." The religious fervor of the participants and the loud monotony of the music combined to produce a state of ecstasy in all present, and shouters often fell to the ground in a state of complete exhaustion. Their places were quickly taken by others, however, and the ring dance continued.

It can readily be seen that this religious performance belongs to the same tradition as the eighteenth-century "jubilees" and Pinkster dances, the Place Congo dancing in New Orleans, the circle dances at camp meetings, and the "Methodist praying bands" in urban areas. Here were the same ring formations, the loud chanting, the shuffling movements, the intense concentration of the participants, and the gradual build-up of the performance to a wild and frenzied state. The only missing element was the instrumental music of drums and string instruments, and to a certain extent this was compensated for by the hand clapping of the singers. Some nineteenth-century writers thought that only the Baptists had shouts. The editors of *Slave Songs* thought that the shout was "confined to South Carolina and the States south of it." From the vantage point of the present we can see, however, that the shout belonged to no one denomination nor to any one region. It simply represented the survival of an African tradition in the New World.

There were in existence more elaborate versions of the ring shout, called by some the "drama shout." A "good sister" would stand in the center of the ring. As the shouters circled around her, she would slowly lower herself, inch by inch, to her knees, and then lower yet, until her head touched the floor. Just as slowly she rose, inch by inch. Two favorite songs used to accompany this feat were "Where Is Adam?" and "Going Down to the Mire." Those persons who could demonstrate such skill, while all the time in a state of religious ecstasy, were held in high regard by the slaves. But if a person should become too intoxicated with the excitement of the performance and jump from the ground or let his feet "cross over," he was "thrown out of the church."

It will be of interest to explore briefly the nature of the relationship between the religious "ring shout" of the black Protestants and the secular ring dances of the black Catholics. The African prototype of the ritual may have had religious overtones, for in Africa the dance was an integral part of religious activity. In the European Protestant tradition, however, dancing was regarded as sinful, and slaves who were admitted into the church were compelled to "put away sinful things," such as profane songs and dancing. Obviously the ring dance was too strong a tradition to be discarded in the process of the African's acculturation to Anglo-Saxon traditions, and so the dance was sublimated into a religious ritual. On the other hand, the Catholics in the New World did not take so harsh a position on dancing, and it was unnecessary for the Blacks to give up an activity essential to their very existence. Consequently, ring dances were performed in social context. In the West Indies, where African traditions are stronger than in the United States, the ring-dance tradition is still very much alive.

CHAPTER II

BLACK PREACHERS, BLACK PREACHING
AND BLACK THEOLOGY: THE GENIUS
OF BLACK SPIRITUAL LEADERSHIP

The central figure in the Black Church is the black preacher. He has no exact counterpart in the White Church, and to attempt to see the white minister or pastor on the same plane is to risk confusion, for the black preacher includes a dimension peculiar to the black experience. That dimension is difficult to define, but it is recognized and reported by practically all observers who have given careful attention to black and white pastors in their respective roles as religious leaders. The nuances of difference are often quite pronounced. A common complaint among Blacks who become members of white churches centers around their disappointment with the way the white pastor fails to fulfill the role-expectations of his black parishioners.

In colonial America the highest status attended the clerical profession. The preachers were the best-educated men in the community, and not infrequently their functions as religious leaders gave them extensive political power as well. They set the moral standards for the community, and in the larger cities like Boston and Philadelphia the clergy represented an intellectual elite. The notion of Blacks as preachers implied certain contradictions in addition to the obvious danger of the contamination of the slaves with aspirations for freedom *this* side of Jordan. To be a preacher presupposed some kind of theological training, superior intellectual attainment, ordination, or the bestowal of "orders" by some recognized Church or communion and the ordinary freedom the profession might require. Since Blacks had little opportunity to fulfill any of these requirements, the notion of a black preacher was in most quarters considered presumptious. One famous Boston clergyman complained most bitterly about the presumptuousness of certain Blacks who had "taken it upon themselves to do the business of preaching." Another minister complained that the servants and slaves were given to the pretense of "extraordinary inspiration, and under the veil thereof

. . . run rambling about to utter enthusiastic nonsense."[1] Such were the prevailing attitudes, in spite of which a handful of black preachers such as Black Harry and Lemuel Haynes were well known and widely respected by whites. The Great Awakening ushered in the age of the informal preacher in America and did much to modify the image of the American clergy. In fact, the clerical profession in general has never recovered the status it lost when the spirit took to the brush arbors and camp meetings and took the people with it. In the informal, folk-oriented atmosphere of the Awakening, even a black preacher could exhort and be heard and appreciated. It is probable that the Great Awakening provided the first significant public exposure to black preachers, as well as the first opportunity for whites and Blacks to learn from each other. But the black preacher's style, his spirituals, and his long colorful narrative prayers had already been developed in the swamps and bayous of the Invisible Church.

By the end of the Civil War the role of the black preacher included the offices of educator, liberator, political leader, and sometimes that of physician (or healer) as well as that of advocate and spiritual leader. Unlike the white preacher, his status did not depend upon formal education or training, but upon his ability to preach the word and to represent his followers before God *and* before the hostile white world which suffered their earthly existence. Hence, the preacher's office as "advocate" had a double significance—one spiritual, the other very practical. In consequence, the role the black preacher was required to play was not always unambiguous. He had the spiritual power necessary to shake the very foundations of heaven, but his power to accomplish the earthly needs of his people was no greater than his ability to outwit the white oppressor, or, barring that, to maintain for himself and his followers a posture of pacification and obedience to the dictates of a society which demanded and expected white privilege and black submission. Accommodative leadership has its rewards, and for some black preachers the "posture" became the "fact." "Pacification" and the "Negro Church" became inseparable categories, particularly in the minds of those who were convinced that Christianity itself was an agent of white control and exploration and who saw the Negro Church as Christianity's outpost in the black community.

But the black preacher has been unduly maligned. He came from a tradition which required no education for the simple reason that the education of Blacks was *verboten* in the South, and severely cir-

[1] Lorenzo J. Greene. *The Negro in Colonial New England*, New York, 1968, p. 276.

cumscribed everywhere else. But despite the fact that he had none of the tools of sociology, economics, political science or even a systematized theology, in most instances he gave an effective leadership which advanced black survival to a marked degree at a time when mere survival itself was an accomplishment. The black preacher was pitted against a vast array of forces and powers far beyond his ken, equipped only with the confidence of his calling and the instinct for deliverance and freedom. Deliverance may come *early or late.* That is God's prerogative, and it was within this reference of "God's time" that the black preacher gauged his responsibilities and structured his leadership.

When slavery was ended, the ministry had already been established as the pre-eminent profession, and despite the established tradition of the acceptability of an uneducated clergy, the acceptable was never considered the ideal, and the first Blacks to seek to improve themselves through schooling, and then to teach others, were clergymen. The first black schools were seminaries established by the churches to produce an educated ministry.

Perhaps the peculiar genius of the black preacher derives from the fact that he has never been far from the people. He rose from among them as someone they knew and trusted—someone God had raised up in their midst. He did not have to come from far off. His credentials were most often his "gifts" as they had been observed to develop from childhood. When he made good as a preacher, the community shared in his accomplishment, and when they rewarded him for his faithfulness, it was a vicarious expression of the satisfaction the people felt with their own attainments. He was more than leader and pastor, he was the projection of the people themselves, coping with adversity, symbolizing their success, denouncing their oppressors in clever metaphor and scriptural selection, and moving them on toward that day of Jubilee which would be their liberation.

The task of the theologian is to interpret the faith in such a way as to insure its continuing relevance to the practitioner. The theological enterprise is not unlike that of the jurist whose job it is to "find" the law, and to clarify it, so that succeeding generations, who are affected by the law but who "forget" its nuances of intention, are constantly reassured of its continuing applicability. The presumption is that the law is always there, waiting only to be discovered. Similarly, the faith as a body of principles, beliefs, moral requirements and responsibilities based on the believer's understanding of the nature and behavior of

God is institutionalized in the Church, its dogma and doctrines. The theologian keeps fresh the meaning of doctrine and dogma and the relevance of the Church through his peculiar insight and knowledge about God—a formidable responsibility, but one critical to the viability of institutionalized religion.

Black religion has had the anomalous distinction of depending upon a body of theology unsympathetic to its basic presuppositions for its interpretation of the faith. Black religion begins by affirming both the righteousness of God and the relevance of black people within the context of Divine righteousness. White theology upon which black Christians depended has given little attention to the black individual or to the collective black experience in its concern with what it considered the significant aspects of the faith. The most benign presumption of white theology has been that black Christians are a kind of spiritual adumbration of white Christians, needing no special theological attention. A less sympathetic view considered Blacks *and* their religious pretensions essentially outside the circle of serious Christianity. The theological enterprise was thus addressed to white interests and to the white condition because (despite its origins) Christianity was white and Western and only incidentally concerned with whatever lay beyond the Western pale. "Inclusive Christianity" meant the "missionary enterprise" with rather stereotyped beliefs and approaches regarding those selected to be missionized.

The Black Church survived through the informal theology of itinerant preachers carrying on the traditions of the oral historians of the Old Country. Often illiterate and unschooled, they had somewhere, somehow caught a vision of the majesty of a God in whose bosom the black man could rest with equanimity and assurance. That vision sustained the Black Church until it could, in effect, raise up its own theologians to make God and His black children more relevant to each other.

The emergent school of black theologians represents the convergence and the precipitate of several historical processes. First of all, Blackamericans are but a hundred years out of the most abject form of slavery ever devised by man. In that hundred years they have gone from ground zero in the educational enterprise to that level of academic and intellectual acumen which has produced a school of philosophers and theologians. Despite the enormous handicaps laid in the way of black education for the first ninety years, Blacks have produced for themselves—and for America—an intellectual elite capable of substantially augmenting—and altering—the flow of ideas which eventually play a part in the shaping of the culture.

Secondly, Blackamericans are increasingly self-conscious about who they are precisely because they are better educated—more sophisticated than before. They always suspected that there were serious gaps in the American experience, especially concerning black participation in the unfolding of history here in the West. Now they are certain, and there is a pronounced anxiety to document the black experience and to correct the deliberate distortions and oversights of American history as presently rendered. The Black Church is a critical aspect of that history. The task of the black theologian, like that of the black social scientist, is to help America toward a less tortured version of the truth.

Finally, this is the Age of Coming of Age. Peoples and institutions everywhere which have been repressed or submerged have broken through whatever restraining forces that have inhibited being and expression, and many new forms of human activity have emerged. One such institution has been the Black Church, which for historic reasons, often in apparent contradiction with each other, has remained in the shadow of the White Church in America. All people want the kind of self-expression which offers that self-projection they see as true, or at least representative. The Black Church is in search of that identity which celebrates its most optimistic view of itself and its reason for being. Black theology is its major instrument of validation.

HENRY MITCHELL

Henry Mitchell sees black preaching (and black religion) as "the product of two streams of culture," African and Euro-American. With Woodson and Du Bois he denies a total disjunction between African and Blackamerican culture and finds in black religion in America the pronounced evidence of African antecedents. The second stream of the "confluence of two streams of culture" seems to be the preaching of George Whitefield, and other white preachers, of the "Great Awakening" in the eighteenth century. The ability to identify with the "folk," to be aware of their needs and expectations, and to use their vocabulary is critical to effective black preaching, an art few are able to master.

Dr. Mitchell is himself one of America's most celebrated preachers and is well known in Africa and America for his work on preaching and hermeneutics.

Henry Mitchell is Professor of Theology at the Rochester Divinity School, and he is the author of a book called *Black Preaching*.[1]

[1] A title in the C. Eric Lincoln Series on Black Religion published by Lippincott.

TWO STREAMS OF TRADITION

Source: Henry Mitchell, "Black Preaching," *Review and Expositor*, Summer 1973.

Black Preaching and Black Religion generally are inescapably the product of the confluence of two streams of culture, one West African and the other Euro-American. The error of E. Franklin Frazier, and many other scholars of all races, has been to assume that the former was all but wiped out, and that the latter was the basic culture and religion which took their place in America. Black scholars now have proven beyond doubt that the religion of the black masses of the United States is so clearly distinguishable from the white Protestant tradition not only because of the unique experience of oppression but, even more so, because the basic culture/religion continuum from Africa was never broken. Brilliant Black scholars of the early twentieth century like W. E. B. Du Bois and Carter G. Woodson were right after all. Whether by means of a Jungian "collective unconscious" or the "primitive" transmission system known as the "mother's milk," no folk culture, worldview, religion can be stamped out unless its bearers are massacred *in toto* or denied all forms of association, including the rearing of any of their children. It is true that slavery was hard, but not quite that hard; and African religion is still alive and doing well in the Black Church and even the black street culture of today.

The relatively similar religions of West Africa, whence came America's slaves, were much more highly developed than stereotypically pictured by missionaries and earlier historians. In fact, it was/is closely parallel at many points to the Old Testament, an idea not so new to many cultural anthropologists and students of early world religions. They needed the revelation of "God *with* us," but they were well prepared for it, as shown by their recorded response. Further, their former communal (and very humane) extended family patterns were a prefabricated kind of *koinonia* which emerged immediately as a form of the indigenous underground Black Church. As W. E. B. Du Bois said in 1903, the first Black Church was "not by any means Christian," but "gradually, after two centuries, the Church became Christian." He added, "It is this historic fact that the Negro Church of today bases itself upon the sole surviving social institution of the African Fatherland, that accounts for its extraordinary growth and vitality.[1]

[1] W. E. B. DuBois, "The Negro Church," (Atlanta: Atlanta University Press, 1903), No. 8, p. 5.

While Du Bois and Woodson used pejorative and inaccurate terms like "heathen" to describe African religions, they were quite correct in their assessment of the American Black Church while issued from it, and of the preacher and his importance, as well as his position in the religio-cultural continuum. Woodson could back up with historical evidence his contention that "The Negro ministry is still the largest factor in the life of this race."[2]

Let us now look at the components of this two-stream preaching tradition. From Africa came a culture literally full of religion and indistinguishable from it. The lofty insights into the nature of a benevolent but distant "High God" (All other heavenly beings were known to be creatures and not The Creator), and the principles of right community living were expressed in proverbs and tales, presented in highly creative ways. Yet this oral culture passed on its sacred literature or sayings in a volume and accuracy that staggers the Western imagination. The hearing might occur in ordinary conversation, in preparation for the rites of initiation for one's age set, or in the frequent festive observances and weekly rites. They might be chanted or spoken, but even the latter was done dramatically and in a highly tonal language. While the dialects differed widely, these characteristics were well-nigh universal. Thus the assumption of earlier writers like Pipes[3] that the musical quality was an addition for purposes of emotional manipulation is wholly unfounded. Intonation was an integral part of a rich group of musical languages whose speakers were purposely divided so their tongues would have to convert to their own version of English.

However, Pipes was right on target in his tracing of the confluence of the cultural streams. He gives a very plausible model of the adaptation of African oral religious expression to the purposes of Christian preaching: "The original, full-fledged, unique type of Negro preaching in America . . . existed during slavery, approximately from 1732 (the period of the great influence of Whitefield's preaching upon Negro slaves) until 1832 (. . . following Nat Turner's Insurrection) . . . some of the original characteristics and manifestations are to be found, in varying degrees, in Negro preaching today."[4]

Pipes quotes reliable descriptions of Whitefield's preaching which

[2] Carter G. Woodson, *History of the Negro Church* (Washington, D.C.: Associated Publishers, 2nd edition, 1921), p. 305.
[3] William H. Pipes, *Say Amen, Brother!* (Westport, Connecticut: Negro Universities Press, 1970).
[4] Ibid., p. 7.

indicate that it was accompanied, both in England and America, by "extreme physical manifestations"[5] very similar to the deeply imbedded patterns of African religion. This revival-launching spiritual power had some rootage, from the human perspective, in Whitefield's style, concerning which Pipes quotes Benjamin Franklin as saying that as many as 30,000 people were at one time swayed by his eloquence in an out-of-doors crowd in Philadelphia. In direct quotation he continues, "His delivery was so improved by frequent repetition that every accent, every emphasis, every modulation of his voice, was so perfectly well-turned that without being interested in the subject, one could not help being pleased with the discourse; a pleasure of much the same kind with that received from an excellent piece of music."[6] The spontaneous (no manuscript), inventive utterance and vivid description were, with their results, a way in which Blacks could finally feel at home in Christianity. It did not seem to matter that Whitefield was an advocate of slavery, along with many whose preaching had something of the same effect. It was only important that he had taken the faith from the chilly modes of the prior experiences and given it a "soul" model on which they were able thereafter to build a faith truly Christian and truly African.

The content of this preaching covered a wide spectrum of types. Miles Mark Fisher reports the African style and utter unintelligibility (to a white) of a young black preacher at an 1829 camp meeting in Indiana.[7] On the other hand, Charles Lyell, a British traveler, praised the Reverend Andrew C. Marshall, pastor of the First African Baptist Church of Savannah (strong Whitefield country) from 1812 to 1856. He considered Marshall's English to be standard, except where deviation was used for effect. The sermon, on the eagle stirring her nest, was delivered without manuscript and used "animated and picturesque language," yet it was "by no means inflated." Lyell was impressed not only by Marshall's "fine sonorous voice" and vivid imagery, but the "good practical maxims of morality . . . and the future state of rewards and punishments in which God would deal impartially with 'the poor and the rich, the black man and the white.'"[8]

That was about as far as he dared go. Black churches had been shut down for much less. No doubt Marshall, like many others, knew how

[5] Ibid., p. 60.
[6] Ibid., p. 61.
[7] Miles Mark Fisher, *Negro Slave Songs in the United States* (New York: Russell & Russell, 1968), p. 33.
[8] Fishel and Quarles, *The Negro American: A Documentary History* (Glenview, Illinois: Scott, Foresman & Co., 1967), pp. 135–36.

popular he was with whites and did all he could for his people inside the outer limits of his clout. The preaching tradition of the far-from-free black preacher in the North was usually very outspoken, however. Anti-slavery protest literature is full of addresses and sermons by Blacks. Bishop Richard Allen of the African Methodist Episcopal Church was one of a host of them, as was Presbyterian Henry Highland Garnet, one of whose addresses anticipated the contemporary black power slogan, "by any means necessary."[9] Thus, though always biblical, the black preacher's message was not always restricted solely to topics of high personal morality and hard, honest labor.

In the North, Blacks were politically insignificant until long after the Southern Rebellion; but in the South the temporary presence of federal troops enabled black preachers to sound a call from the pulpit which not only structured and stabilized the new black family and community, but gave free public education, women's rights, and universal suffrage to poor whites as well. The prophetic ministry of Martin Luther King, Jr., stood in this line of pulpit relevancy. The self-educated and "instantly" formally trained preachers of the late nineteenth century, to whom I refer as "the Black Fathers"[10] all stood in this line, building schools and businesses and publications. Dr. C. T. Walker of Augusta, and, briefly, New York City, so preached to men like John D. Rockefeller that he could be responsible for the launching of such institutions as the Harlem Y.M.C.A. And the end is not yet, for the current generation of black seminarians may well carry the tradition to new heights, by the sheer force of their numbers, advanced education, commitment to black culture, and tremendous versatility. They need only keep the level of consecration and devotion of the Black Fathers of old.

What basic assumptions underlie Black Preaching? The first assumption has to do with what preaching is. Black preaching has always assumed that preaching must be an *experience*, not merely a clever idea. It involves the totality of a person and is, consciously or not, concerned to organize feeling tones around the text.

It is understood that no such demanding enterprise can be undertaken inside human limitations, and so the understandings of spirit possession, deeply imbedded in African religion, have informed our entire history. Educated black preachers have never agreed with the tradition that eschews preparation, but all are agreed that no mere man can prepare enough to calculate, choreograph, and control the trialogue be-

[9] Carter G. Woodson, *History of the Negro Church* (Washington, D.C.: Associated Publishers, 3rd edition, 1972), p. 223.
[10] See Henry Mitchell, *Black Preaching* (New York: Lippincott, 1970).

tween the preacher, the congregation, and the very Spirit of God. Black preaching, in the best of all its traditional strands, still assumes that God Himself speaks through men who give themselves to Him in prayer and sincere preparation for the preaching event.

Another assumption is often intuitive and seldom discussed. It holds that one must "sit where they sit" (Ezek. 3:15). No amount of professional preparation must ever be allowed to put social distance between the shepherd and the sheep. In preaching, this has far-reaching implications as to language, culture, imagery, and so on.

Seminaries often hold before their students models of graduate study as opposed to ministry—men who are *obligated* to speak a language foreign to the pew. The most scholarly black preacher, if he is effective, knows and affirms the folk religion and language of his people. Unfortunate clichés and awful hymns are quietly weeded out and adequately replaced in the patient but satisfying process of what might be called acculturation. In other words, cultural and social identification with the folk does not relieve the black minister of the obligation to advance the flock spiritually, morally, and even intellectually. He simply does not call to them across a deep chasm, in words and tones that are strange to their ears. The leadership exercised in educational and political life and the deep influence on the membership are all prophetic impacts which stem from the power of inside rather than from alien communication.

How, then, does one prepare a sermon in such a tradition? The assumptions are surely not altogether unique. First, closeness to the folk makes one aware of their deepest needs, as well as their culture and vocabulary. The disclosure of need is further encouraged by the preacher's own need of the prayers, verbal response, and simple favors which employ the talent of the most obscure in the assistance of the most charismatic. The rapport thus established aids not only in subject selection but in sermon reception.

Once the subject and text are selected, the busy black pastor squeezes in as much Bible study and research as possible, as early as possible. He may be secularly employed or just extremely involved, but the object is to have time to preach from a text about which he has deep feelings and long association. Further, he must be able to major in pictures and narratives which are not only true to known scholarship but presented in living, *eye-witness* detail. A dramatic description delivered with poetic use of familiar language can convey the profoundest idea to the simplest mind and yet not offend or fail to feed the most intellectual. The black preacher works at his mental canvass as he works on his other job, or drives to the jail, or even in his sleep.

Whether he uses verbatim manuscript, outline, memory, or feels he should use one of these, the black preacher is aware of timing. The whole object is to use details, rhetorical devices, repetition and the like to teach, to create interest and suspense, and, finally, to build to the climax. One dare not start too fast or high-pitched, for when climax time comes, he will have "no-where to go." All audible art such as drama and symphony has to have a climax and so does the work of inspired art called the sermon.

Blacks and whites outside the black religious tradition have often criticized this as a cynical manipulation of deep feeling, and at times they have been correct. However, the knowledgeable black preacher knows his folk will go away with an empty feeling if he does not bring them to the level of the uninhibited celebration of the goodness of God. The sin lies not in climax per se, but in *irrelevant* climax. True climax reinforces learning with ecstasy *about the content,* in addition to giving people the strength to survive in a hostile society. That content must order not only the personal lives of black congregations, but marshall their every resource for their total liberation in our time. So great a unification and deployment of spiritual energies *has* to have such inspiration to proceed.

HORTENSE J. SPILLERS

To understand Martin Luther King and his success as a preacher, one must take into account the traditions of the southern Baptist Church. Though Dr. King received an academic training in the North where he learned the formal use of rhetoric, he also relied largely upon the emotional poetry of the traditional black sermon. "His oratory carried the emotional stuff, while his analysis carried the moral message."

The author analyzes two sermons ("The Death of Evil upon the Shore" and "Paul's Letter to the Americans") as well as the famous oration, "I Have a Dream." These three pieces belong to King's "first period." The author points out two characteristics: nominality and metaphoricality, i.e., the extensive use of nouns and adjectives on the one hand and of figures on the other. King also used repetition and amplification. He loved contrasting, and he quoted the Bible continually and made a ready use of poetry. The spirituals and the gospels are well represented in his sermons and speeches. "With King the success of his technique was more attributable to his sense of euphony and resonance than to gesture and movement."

The author concludes with the remark that "the impulse of pity, the sense of joy were endemic to King's message just as they had always been to the message of the black sermon, whose poetry was a poetry of triumph and overcoming."

Hortense Spillers is a doctoral candidate at Brandeis University. Her field is English.

MARTIN LUTHER KING AND THE STYLE OF THE BLACK SERMON

Source: Hortense J. Spillers, "Martin Luther King and the Style of the Black Sermon," *The Black Scholar*, Vol. 3, No. 1, September 1971, pp. 14–27.

A description and evaluation of the political career of Dr. Martin Luther King, Jr., will, of necessity, include an account of the southern Baptist Church in its historic influence on the life and mind of black people in this country, especially the South. Without such understanding, the moral and political lessons of the King era will be missed. To my mind, the power of his delivery, the magnificence of his pulpit style, were accountable, in large measure, for his overwhelming popularity in the South and throughout much of the nation.

The ground swell of his movement, then, was of a southern soil: highly religious and traditional in its use of a style and manner that are endemic to the black religious experience; this brings the emphasis where I want it—an exploration of King's pulpit style, poetic in texture and traditional in delivery.

The old-fashioned black preacher of the South, unlike King, rarely went to school to learn or adorn his trade. He imitated the preaching elders of his community in the selection of subject matter and content. For example, "The Eagle Stirs His Nest" is a favorite sermon of black ministers of the South. I have no clues to the age of the sermon nor where it first appeared, but I remember it from my childhood (at least twenty years ago) and would suggest that my minister heard it first from someone else. Though each minister brings to the sermon his own individuality, the material of the sermon is universal in its accessibility and appeal. The genius of sermons like "The Eagle" and "Dry Bones" lay in their technique of delivery. The minister weaves analogy and allegory into the sermon, comparing and juxtaposing contemporary problems in morality with and alongside ancient problems in morality. These build toward an emotional pitch and climax that are made possible by the minister's sense of timing and dynamics. The delivery of the message is best described by what the minister does with his voice: intonation and pitch, dynamics and rhythm, movement and timing.

These features of speech are briefly, but saliently, described by Mike Thelwell, who considers them problems in paralinguistic techniques.[1] Thelwell differentiates between two languages that the African slave adopted, after being stripped of his tribal identity and indigenous language: 1) the language that he adopted for the white overseer and slave master (Thelwell calls this the "Sambo" dialect which often appears as parody in the works of southern white humorists.) and 2) the real language (the essential, "unwigged" language) of the slave which was close to the poetry of the sermon and spiritual, "language produced by oppression, but one whose central impulse is survival and resistance."[2] Forced to adopt the language and religion of a foreign, imposed master, the slave minister found his particular historic moment under the conditions of a captured and historically-amnesiac person who would be free. The disparity between the reality and the dream molded the emotional pith of the sermon as it operated on minister and hearer.

Without the vocabulary of his white counterpart, the black minister had "to get over," so to speak, to communicate, with his power to act, to dramatize the sermon, since its ultimate effectiveness lay in his "tone of voice" rather than in his vocabulary and power of analysis. With the King James Bible as the woof of the sermon, the technique of delivery was the warp, weaving the moral lesson, spinning the emotional moment. The technique impresses me as an invariable of the black sermon, linking men as wide apart in age and temperament as the Rev. C. L. Franklin and Dr. King. That this process or technique

[1] Mike Thelwell, "Back With the Wind: Mr. Styron and the Reverend Turner," *William Styron's Nat Turner: Ten Black Writers Respond,* Boston: 1968, p. 80. The phenomenon of paralanguage was given the name by Henry Lee Smith and George L. Traeger; the problem of paralanguage is the problem of phonetic transcriptions: silence, pitch, stress, accent, terminal, and juncture. Morton W. Bloomfield and Leonard Newmark, *A Linguistic Introduction to the History of English,* New York: 1965, pp. 82–83.
[2] Ibid.

has been passed down from generation of preachers to the next, places the black sermon in the oral tradition, distinguishing it from the historical tradition where the mentifacts and ideas are enclosed in and circumscribed by the written word.

Dr. King knew the oral tradition intimately, being himself a son of a preaching father. Though he was trained in the universities and academies, his sermons were infused and enlightened by the interpretation of the gospel message as he heard it while young and growing in the southern hill-soil of Georgia. That basic and shared experience fired the response of black people by the thousands who heard him. The audience may have understood the historical-political analyses, but to be sure, the heart will long remember and take joy in the emotional achievement of the Word as King delivered it.

The most effective observer of King's style is the human ear. The recordings of his sermons, widely accessible now, will demonstrate more effectively than the pen the "how" of the process. Many of the sermons and speeches in the King Collection[3] are handwritten drafts which were later printed. This makes it possible to compare and examine the texts. King always preached a sermon; even his political speeches in their poetic detail and structure were sermons. These may be called political sermons with King James replaced by current political idealogues, interspersed and peppered with biblical allegory. The appeal, right along, was made to the emotions—one's love of inspiration, one's sense of triumph over disaster. The belief was that the inspired person, sharing a particular ethnic journey with others, will join hands with his fellows in the reaching of a common goal; for King, that goal was the full integration of black people into the American thing.

King, on his latter political career, 1965–68, was apparently turning a corner—beginning to assess the national black struggle in terms of the globe. But the early King, the King of the Montgomery Bus Boycott and the voter registration campaigns of the South, was the basic and fundamental King who believed that the idiom of non-violence would not only work as a political tact, but also as a moral purgative, cleansing the death-rot of a racist mad-land. It was from the King of these years,

[3] The King Collection of correspondence, sermons, addresses and business transactions is presently available at the Mugar Library, Boston University; grateful acknowledgment is due Dr. Gottlieb of the Library's Special Collections for permitting me access to the papers.

1954–64, that this analysis comes. I have concentrated on two of his early sermons and one of his addresses.

An explication of text is possible because King was a meticulous writer. Being an experienced preacher before he became a political leader, he knew what his audiences would like, but he did not leave the organization of his ideas to chance. The text was there as skeletal guide and outline, delineating carefully certain details of the moral and religious lesson, which to King, was one and the same. In this sense, he was part of the growing tradition of young, university-trained black preachers, who combine analysis with the manner and style of the elders. The combination is formidable, melding the traditions of the folk and the scholar. These processes, if not antagonistic to one another, are, at least, contrasting modes of expression. With the folk, the expression arises in spontaneity, springing from the emotions. Though the expression may be learned and transmitted, its impulse is emotional and its rhythms joyful, festive, and triumphant; with the scholar, the expression is cerebral, prejudged, so to speak, springing from the intellect. The intellectual statement informs and clarifies, whereas the emotional statement, which may inform and clarify as well, certainly inspires and invigorates.

A figure would simplify the distinction: the intellectual statement is like a scythe, cutting through weeds of chaos, making them a plain path, while the emotional statement is like a balm, flowing over troubled waters. It is the distinction that is made between rhetoric and poetics.[4] In the former, the speaker or writer is about the effective organization of material in a presentation of truth, appealing to the intellect. In the latter, the speaker or writer is about the presentation of ideas in an emotional and imaginative way. The emotional statement may represent the poetic mode and the rhetorical statement the intellectual mode. Both are orally rendered, both tend to persuade, in King's case, to politicize and educate in a certain way, but the difference lies in their mode of appeal and operation. Though these refer to elements in a vacuum and do not ultimately account for the chemistry and dynamics that operate between speaker and hearer, I think that they

---

[4] A short description of the origin and history of rhetoric, as a classical device of argument, is given in the Thrall and Hibbard edition: *A Handbook to Literature*, New York: 1963, p. 415. The distinction that is made between rhetoric and poetics conforms here to the old Aristotelian concept. Poetics also refer to the criticism of poetic practice: "A system or body of theory concerning the nature of poetry. The principles and rules of poetic composition . . ." Ibid., p. 361.

will be sufficient as operational terms. In King, the rhetorical style as he learned it in the academies met the poetic style of his fathers as he experienced it in the South. In his case, the poetry, basic and inviolable to his message, was that of the black sermon. His oratory carried the emotional stuff, while his analysis carried the moral message. In King, the two were complements.

A reading of the sermons reveals two important features: nominality[5] and metaphoricality. The prominent linguistic feature of the sermons is their nominality where a greater number of nouns, adjectives, and adjectival clauses abound than verbs and verb forms. Though verbal and nominal refer to written texts, I suggest that the reference works with King, since for him the text was hand-delivered first. Modification (adjectiveness) and nominality in King combine to create a picturesqueness and grandness of speech that were his hallmark. This particular feature (adjectiveness and nouness) in all its variations is at the heart of King's metaphors—the dominant poetic quality of his message.[6] The moral lesson, the political idealogues, were informed by and structured in terms of the metaphor which usually presented a picture of contrasts or opposites. The argument, then, proceeded by way of the figure which always gave rise to a mental picture or image.

This clothing of the argument in figurative dress is one of the basic differences that I perceive between poetry and prose; the poet relies on images to carry the subject, stripping his line clean and bare of certain syntactical intrusions, i.e., furthermore, consequently, therefore, however, etc. There are fewer words per idea with the poet, whereas the prose writter relies on fewer pictures and images and more words and concepts. King, while working in the conceptual and ideological, knew that the Word came alive in a figure, and he was a man of the living Word with his sights fixed clearly on this earth.

[5] This concept is borrowed from Rulon Wells, who makes an interesting description and evaluation of the verbal vs. nominal style: ed. J. V. Cunningham, *The Problem of Style*, New York, 1966, pp. 253–59.
[6] A metaphor is a figure of speech that expresses an idea or concept in terms of an image; the metaphor is an implied comparison between one or more things. One of the items in the analogy takes on the qualities of another; for example, the concept of old age may be figuratively expressed as the coming of winter, where the frost or snow or winter bespeaks the grey hair of the old man. In Thrall and Hibbard, an interesting discussion of metaphor is given by way of I. A. Richards' definition. He suggests that there is a tenor of the figure which is the idea being expressed or the subject of the comparison; the vehicle is the image by which the idea is conveyed. Thrall and Hibbard, pp. 281–82.

On May 17, 1956, King preached at the Service of Prayer and Thanksgiving in the Cathedral of St. John the Divine, New York City. The title of the sermon, "The Death of Evil Upon the Shore," gives a clue to the intent and form of the sermon. Right away, evil is given a persona, which becomes, in the context, a dramatic function. Evil represents the death of the spirit in the traditional scheme of religious thinking, but it connotes, as well, war and destruction. In King's sermon, evil specifically stands for political oppression in the name of the Egyptian Pharaohs, who were eventually put to rout by Moses and the sons of Israel. By broad analogy and principle, the American scene is here transformed into a modern-day Egypt with its appropriate Pharaohs who are holding in bondage and thrall some thirty million Blacks. King perceived a basic division of people along racial and historic lines, representing conflicting destinies and motives, one oppressing, the other resisting. The sons of Israel would advance the good—the Word of God—whereas the Pharaohs would impede the good, becoming themselves the *dramatis personae* of evil.

The modern-day Pharaohs, in their moral perfidy, would as oppressors hold back the light, while black men as the oppressed would advance the light by forcing a moral awareness upon the conscience of the Pharaohs. King's implicit message is that oppression and resistance must run parallel and contiguous until they converge with resistance cancelling out oppression. Explicitly, his statement is: History records Israel's struggle with every Egypt. In other words, oppression and resistance are invariable rhythms in the historical process. He is saying emphatically that "Every Israel" must keep on keeping on until victory is theirs. King was a persistent symbolist, seeing the struggle of his own people in terms of Israel's liberation struggle against Egypt.

The evil that will die upon the shore is pictured as the "nagging tares disrupting the orderly growth of stately wheat." In the metaphor, an image-making term is substituted for a concept, and the writer-speaker relies on the associations of the words to carry the impact. The tare is the unwanted growth, the bother, the worry, the unfaithful. In the Day of Judgment, I am told that God himself will separate the tares (the unfaithful) from the wheat (the faithful). The terms of King's metaphor, then, present a contrast, with tares representing oppression and humiliation and wheat representing order and a Christian ethic. Tares, as the disrupting, inharmonious evil, are clothed in "the garments of calamitous wars which left battlefields painted with blood, filled nations with widows and orphans, sent men home physically handicapped and psychologically wrecked." The vision is one of destruction, made vivid by the phrase: "battlefields painted with blood," as though someone had indeed, taken the energy and time to paint the earth in blood. The image betokens the extent of calamity.

King defines the struggle between good and evil in terms of religious war: "All great religions have realized that in the upward climb of goodness, there is the down pull of evil." "Upward climb" and "downward pull" sum up the contrast and carry the picture of resistance and oppression, which is a recurring motif in King's sermons. Said another way:

A mythical Satan, though the work of a conniving serpent, may gain the allegiance of man for a period, but ultimately he must give way to the magnetic, redemptive power of a humble servant on an uplifted cross. . . .

King's ear for rhythm was sure and unfailing. The cadence is strong and emphatic when he comes to: "magnetic redemptive power of a humble servant on an uplifted cross." The staccato, martial beating of "magnetic redemptive power" (all words capitalized and emphasized in their rhythmic thrust), gives way to the alternate beats of a "humble servant on an uplifted cross," where humble and uplifted are the stress words. He continues:

Evil may so shape events that Caesar will occupy a palace and Christ a cross, but one day that same Christ will rise up and split history into A.D. and B.C., so that even the life of Caesar must be dated by his name. . . .

The triumph of evil, represented in the palatial wealth of Caesar, is only temporary, for the cross of sacrifice and moral redemption, the sign of Christ, will launch a new phase of moral and imaginative awareness of men. The picture of the rising Christ, splitting history into A.D. and B.C., is an exciting and vivid picture-idea, appealing to the hearer's sense of triumph—good dramatically overcoming evil. The advent of Christ so historically significant that the dating of time started anew.

In the poetry of the black sermon, "that same Christ" and "one day" are recurrences. In their nature, they are like refrains. "This same Jesus who walked beside the sea; this same Jesus, the man of Galilee . . . this same Jesus will save your soul" are three lines from a gospel favorite that is often sung during Easter Services in the Baptist Church. The song writer takes his cue from the sermon where the preacher, in recounting the miracle and mystery of Christ, assures the hearer that

Christ is a personal, subjective savior who is concerned about the daily welfare of each individual believer. A hypothetical construction may be this:

> This same man who sits high and looks low, who rounded the world in the middle of his hands; this same man who fed five thousand and still had food left over; this same man who raised the dead, who walked the waters and calmed the sea—this same man is looking out for you and me.

By repetition and amplification, the passage builds and spins out. In many cases, the preacher's own words are echoed and verified by his audience, thus making the Word more emphatic. For example, the passage above may be interspersed thusly:

> This same man (*same* man!) who sits high and looks low, who rounded the world in the middle of his hands (the *middle* of his hands!), this same man who fed five thousand and still had food left over, (Yessuh! Had some left). This same man who raised the dead, who walked the waters and calmed the sea, (Let's hold him up, church!) this *same* man is looking out for you and me.

The phenomenon is referred to as the "Amen Corner" where the believers support and sustain the preacher by repeating certain of his own words or their own exclamations. The phenomenon was never absent when King spoke. Readers may recall King's Montgomery speech, "We're On the Move," and the unidentified man who stood at his side. (*Montgomery to Memphis* documentary.) After picking up the tenor of King's rhythm the man began to repeat the key words: "Yessuh, we're on the move!" Soon thereafter, the audience had been transformed into a vast echo chamber with King giving out the mainline, i.e., "We can't be dissuaded now . . . and no wave of racism can stop us," and the audience saying with him: "We're on the move!" This process, spontaneous in its thrust, is highly technical and consistent; the speaker, with his innate sense of timing and rhythm, knows exactly which words will be prominent and what phrases an audience will respond to because he has seen the technique work for his elders time and again.

With King, the success of the technique was more attributable to his sense of euphony[7] and resonance than to gesture and movement. King often brought together words that ended in the same sound to create a

[7] Euphony and resonance refer to pleasant sound, the pleasing combination of vowels and consonants.

kind of rhythm and cadence. In the Thanksgiving Sermon, he refers to the "humiliating oppression, the ungodly exploitation, the crushing domination" of the Egyptian Pharaohs. The combining of words that have an equal number of syllables which rhyme (same vowel and consonant sounds) creates a rhythm. This is not strictly metrical, because the speaker does not intend to make verse and meters, but the effect, the texture, is certainly rhythmical, lending itself to memory. King often referred to southern legislators as oppressive forces with their "lips dripping in interposition and nullification." This is similar in its structure to the three phrases that speak of the Pharaohs. This particular device has the effect of "setting the scene" before the hearer. The picture or image, then, is often marked by rhythm and tempo as well as contrast and opposition: "It was a frightful period in their history. It was a joyous daybreak that had come to end the long night of their captivity." The difference between night and day is the difference between oppression and liberation. In the metaphor, the concept is enlightened and clarified; identification of the problem or concept in terms of a visual image is a teaching device, for it makes the idea concrete and vivid. At the same time, the metaphor creates the poetic moment—the heightened, elevated language is most characteristic of biblical language which certainly influenced King's style.

When King's imagination set to work on an old familiar story, the story itself was enlivened to the extent of becoming life and blood, experience and option with the hearer. On November 4, 1956, King preached before his own congregation at Dexter Avenue Baptist Church in Montgomery. He updated the message of Paul to the early churches around the Roman Empire by creating "Paul's Letter to American Christians." This is a contrivance which summons the hearer's "poetic faith"—"the willing suspension of disbelief"—but the device works well, with King making explanations as he goes along: It is miraculous, he begins, that Paul should be writing 1,900 years after his last letter appeared in the New Testament; "how this is possible is something of an enigma wrapped in mystery."

The Churchillian comment used here notes the "mystery" at the same time that it dismisses it. In other words, the hearer is ready now to accept the miracle of Paul's letter to Americans. The fact that Paul, the main epistleist of the early church, is "writing" this letter says something about the emergency King felt in his own message. He goes on: "May I hasten to say that if in presenting this letter the contents sound strangely Kingian instead of Paulinian, attribute it to my lack of complete objectivity rather than Paul's lack of clarity."

King was apparently fond of ringing, resounding statement; these are earmarks of his style: "Kingian" and "Paulinian" match in tone the phrases: "my lack of complete objectivity" and "Paul's lack of clarity." Part of the hearer's joy lies in his knowing that the preacher can play with words and make beautiful, pleasing combinations of sound out of them. Paul, speaking through King, goes on to say:

> I have heard so much about you; I wish I could visit. . . . I have heard of the *fascinating* and *astounding* advances that you have made in the scientific realm. I have heard of your *dashing subways* and *flashing airplanes*. . . . Through your scientific genius, you have been able to *dwarf distance* and *place time in chains*. You have been able to *carve highways* through the stratosphere. . . . I have also heard of your *skyscraping buildings* with their *prodigious* towers sweeping skyward. . . . That is wonderful. . . . [Italics mine]

The words and passages that appear in italics are the stress words, to my mind. These were probably emphasized in the delivery and apparently selected for their pleasant sound. "Dashing subways and flashing airplanes" (all words of equal syllables, suggesting a trochaic rhythm) are onomatopoeic in their matching of the sound of the sense. "Carved highways through the stratosphere" brings the idea of civil engineering (earth-building) heavenward, preparing the hearer for "skyscraping buildings with their prodigious towers sweeping heavenward."

The imagery captures the marvel of America's technological genius which is further contrasted with her moral and spiritual failure. The nation that has been able to "dwarf distance and place time in chains," thus making the world a neighborhood, has not been able to make of that neighborhood a brotherhood:

> You have allowed the material means by which you live to outdistance the spiritual ends for which you live. You have allowed your mentality to outrun your morality . . . your civilization to out-distance your culture . . .

By building up the contrasts, King introduces one of the recurring motifs of his sermons—the passage of time and its meaning in the life of man. Though men live on earth, in a state of generation, their ultimate allegiance must go to God: "This means that although you live in the colony of time, your ultimate allegiance is to the empire of eternity. You have a dual citizenry. . . . You must never allow the transitory evanescent demands of man-made institutions to take precedence over the eternal demands of the almighty God. . . ."

In King's last sermon, delivered in Memphis, April 1968, he said that he had been to the mountaintop and viewed the Promised Land but probably would not go to the Promised Land with his followers. He felt then that his life would not be a long one, but the point, he said, was not the longevity of a man's years, but in the quality of his life. Therefore, time for him was an instrument of the eternal will, measuring and manifesting itself in the life of the ethical man. Even if denied the opportunity to live the long life, King felt satisfied at that moment that his life had been spent in the attempt to make the ethic of nonviolence a reality.

His persisting concern was with the mess that men had made of materialism and technology; the mess is betokened in the values and preferences of the society. In making the idea definite and vivid, King relied on objects close at hand:

I am afraid that many among you are more concerned about making a living than making a life. You are prone to judge the success of your profession by the index of your salary and the size of the wheel base on your automobile, rather than the quality of your service to humanity.

In the mad and violent rush for the acquisition of luxury goods, decision makers have often abused their power: "Oh, America, how often have you taken necessities from the masses to give luxuries to the classes. . . ." Though capitalism is exploitive in its practices, King did not feel that communism was an answer, and to his mind communism was the opposite of Christianity, not capitalism. In King, the communist analysis is general and incomplete: ". . . Communism is based on an ethical relativism and a metaphysical materialism that no Christian can accept." The structure of the phrases: "ethical relativism" and "a metaphysical materialism" is similar to "necessities from the masses" and "luxuries to the classes." There is a feeling of finality in the phrasing; cryptic and summarylike, these are similar to a slogan or catchword, and for that reason can be misleading.

A structure very similar to the foregoing quotations is used again and again in this sermon where King comes to question not only the abuses of capitalism and secular authority but also those of clerical authority: "A divided Protestantism and an infallible Roman Catholicism . . . a segregator and a segregated, disrupting the "I-thou" making it an "I-it."

In this instance, the key words are the modifiers, "divided" and "infallible," and the key concept that of disruption and division. In Buber's philosophy, one person's preponderance over another destroys the human relationship between the two, making it one of a master to an object or thing.

In King's estimation, segregated institutions of the South, of which the Church was the most pre-eminent example, summed up the ultimate badness of America's institutional immorality: "The underlying philosophy of Christianity is diametrically opposed to the underlying philosophy of segregation, and all the dialectics of the logician cannot make them lie down together." Just as the tares and wheat do not belong together, nor the sheep lie down with the lion, segregation and Christianity are also opposed. Dichotomies in King were not only at the heart of his metaphors, but also at the core of his reality—one was either in the camp of the ethical or among the troops of the unenlightened, and his figures ranged according to the variation on that particular theme.

King's "finest hour," perhaps, in terms of his political and oratorical achievement came in the summer of 1963 when on August 28, he delivered the now-famous "I Have a Dream" sermon in the shadows of the Lincoln Memorial. The choice of that particular sight was fraught with historic symbolism, for after one hundred years of "no win," the black man of America returned in person and spirit to the original place of the issuance of the Emancipation Proclamation to write it again in his own terms. Historians will long argue the value of "The March on Washington," which Malcolm X referred to in one of his speeches as "The Farce on Washington." To argue cause and effect in the chain of human events is the province and mandate of the historian, and King's cause, like others, will be examined in the beam eye of history. It is important that the historical judgment, however, be made in light of the cast of things at the time—where men's heads were—where they perceived they would go at that moment. Many Blacks across the country then felt that a remarkable "stride toward freedom" had been made within the decade. For them, King, on that sweltering August day, wore a crown and his sermon was that of a great coronation that many thousands had come to in order to wash their robes in the sweet springs of renewal.

An understanding of the scene is important to an understanding of the sermon itself. The black preacher has always been, historically, a beacon spirit to his people; he was the one who was most in touch with

God, assuring his listeners that even though the business of life was a cross to bear, God himself was waiting in the wings of history to secure the safe passage of those who loved Him and did His will. This simplistic and uncomplicated faith in an ultimate and final good stirred the spirit and the protest of black people long before and after the Emancipation. It was the faith that motivated and inspired the lives of agrarian Blacks of the South who had known the plow before and after the whip. When their sons fanned out through the American North and Midwest, that faith was tempered and deflected by the hard circumstances of urban reality; but even here there were the "storefronts" which in strange-name places like Harlem and the So'Side carried still, the ritual and poetry of home. "The Dream Deferred," the cruel paradox of a "Native Son," who was an alien son after all, the hoax of the "Promised Land" all stung and confused the imagination of the urban dweller, who had fled the southern backfields looking for glory.

The post-emancipation "Black Codes" of the southern legislators had locked the southern black man in an apartheid so consistently vicious that it was, perhaps, unrivaled anywhere on earth, and the Church, itself segregated, was silent in the face of the K.K.K. The North had not legislated against Blacks, but it had circumscribed them by custom and practice which made it possible for them to ride in the *front* of the bus to the program. The northern and southern experience had been different for the black man only in degree, not in kind which, North and South, was co-terminous, co-existent and co-operative. In neither place was it intended that the black man be a governor of self and kind. The Garvey Movement was little known in the South, having had brief and partial success in the North and Midwest. The Bolshevik Revolution and its early impact on that thinking of black people in America had not touched the South either and apparently affected an elite intelligentsia of the North. Here, briefly, was the black man's legacy in 1963; the feeling was: Now or Never, and the sectors of the nation each had their solution. King apparently spoke for the South and the black man's "deferred dream" of civil and human rights.

His sermon took place at a time when sense of impending triumph was at its peak, perhaps unmatched by anything in the recent past, with the probable exception of the Reconstruction Era and its promises of equality and universal manhood suffrage. The sense of racial solidarity was strong and the feeling of unity pervasive. It seemed, indeed, that the long night of captivity was surely breaking now into the joyful daybreak of liberation. King, as minister and leader, was the apotheosis, the living embodiment of that promise. His sermon was the emotional catharsis which, in a sense, washed away the tears from the tired and fevered spirit of his followers.

The language of the opening paragraph of the sermon is reminiscent of Lincolnian language; in his address at the battleground of Gettysburg, Lincoln had said: "Fourscore and seven years ago our fathers brought forth upon this continent a new nation, conceived in liberty and dedicated to the proposition that all men are created equal. . . ." By reminding the nation of its political legacy, King re-echoed Lincoln: "Fivescore years ago a great American, in whose symbolic shadow we stand, signed the Emancipation Proclamation." Briefly and straightaway King was into the heart of things—no long prelude, no long introduction. This is very close in spirit to the *in medias res* (into the heart of things) beginning of the ballad. This feeling of immediacy invests the entire sermon. "This momentous decree came as a great beacon light of hope to millions of Negro slaves who had been seared in the flames of withering injustice. It came as a joyous daybreak to end the long night of captivity. . . ." Darkness and light, daybreak and night, are seminal in King, capturing in a picturesque manner the idea of dichotomy.

Many of the motifs and images of King's earlier sermons appear in "I Have a Dream." For example, in "A Knock At Midnight," which appears in the small volume of sermons entitled *Shattered Dreams,* King talks about midnight at a time of day: a state of the individual psyche and the status of institutional morality. It was midnight all over America, and the danger zone was everywhere. The night of captivity was at its most frightful point at midnight. In *Shattered Dreams,* the sermon that gives its title to the volume, King talks of how men must behave when their dreams have been shattered and their hopes blasted, when they, like the Apostle Paul, have their vision of going to Spain and Rome in triumph transformed into the reality of a narrow jail cell. The destructibility of the dream is constant, but one must meet it with a fiery hope just as constant, which says after all: "I still have a dream."

Even after the promise of the Emancipation, the black man's dream has still been put off time and time again:

One hundred years later, the life of the Negro is still sadly crippled by the manacles of segregation and the chains of discrimination. One hundred years later, the Negro lives on a lonely island of poverty in the midst of a vast ocean of material prosperity. One hundred years later, the Negro is still languished in the corners of American society and finds himself an exile in his own land. . . .

The repetition of "one hundred years," each time amplifying the argument, heightens the feeling; the images are those of stasis, paralysis, and captivity; manacles and chains, lonely island of poverty, languishing exile all image forth the plight of the black man in America.

The marching to Washington is the same as the cashing of a check against America's justice bank. All the terms of the metaphor refer to banking and money, highlighting the disparity between the nation's wealth and the black man's poverty:

> When the architects of our republic wrote the magnificent words of the Constitution and the Declaration of Independence, they were signing a promissory note to which every American was to fall heir. This note was a promise that all men would be guaranteed their inalienable rights. . . . It is obvious today that America has defaulted on this promissory note insofar as her citizens of color are concerned. Instead of honoring this sacred obligation, America has given the Negro people a bad check, a check which has come back marked "insufficient funds." But we refuse to believe that the Bank of Justice is bankrupt. . . .

The idea of justice being a bank against which funds are drawn is a very successful and clever idea, reminiscent of other preachers' talk about "heaven's savings bank," where the earthbound Christian stores up his treasures. King's idea speaks of the quantity of the devault in materialistic terms:

> We refuse to believe that there are insufficient funds in the great vault of opportunity of this nation. So we have come to cash this check—a check that will give us upon demand the riches of freedom and the security of justice. . . .

The urgency of the demand is capitalized:

> Now is the time to make real the promises of democracy. Now is the time to rise from the dark and desolate valley of segregation to the sunlit path of racial justice. Now is the time to open the doors of opportunity to all of God's children. Now is the time to lift our nation from the quicksands of racial injustice to the solid rock of brotherhood. . . .

The saint's cry to the Lord to plant his feet on "higher ground," Owen Dodson's black mother praying that one day she with her sons will be able to strike her feet on freedom's "solid rock" are ancient themes in the Baptist Church; there are associations that may be made with King images. Implicit in the imagery is the idea of journey—long, trying and apparently endless. But in complement to that idea is one of perseverance and courage: Like the old woman who tells her story in the poem, *My Life Ain't Been No Crystal Stair,* the young person is emboldened to keep on keeping on because the way is steep for all who would walk the straight and narrow path of moral and ethical commitment. In terms of the Baptist Church, the "straight and narrow" is usually a visual reference to the Christian life of obedience, patience and humility. In King, the base of the vision is broadened, though still maintaining an overlay of religiosity.

Just as the Christian maintains his allegiance to the Kingdom of God, the black man must also maintain his allegiance to the idea of passive resistance to racial injustice: "This sweltering summer of the Negro's legitimate discontent will not pass until there is an invigorating autumn of freedom and equality. . . ." King makes an interesting switch here in the symbolic meaning of the seasons. Usually summer is a fair time. In Shakespeare, winter, not summer, is the time of discontent and fall and winter represent death. In Shakespeare's *Richard III,* Gloucester says in opening soliloquy: "Now is the winter of our discontent/Made glorious summer by this sun of York. . . ."[8] King no doubt drew his structure from the Shakespearean mold, though the valence or weight of the images is shifted. Elsewhere in King, autumn is associated with the "Alpine November of the soul." Though autumn is harvesttime, its perennial association is not usually one of invigoration and renewal, but in this context autumn presents an interesting contrast to the terrible and paralyzing heat of summer.

King continues: "The whirlwinds of revolt will continue to shake the foundations of our nation until the bright day of justice emerges. . . ." The thrust of King's message was especially significant at this time since the nation was only two summers away from the Watts Rebellion. King read the winds and America could choose to make the check good by securing the full citizenship rights of all its citizens or not. If not, then Watts would say, in effect, that there would be no justice banks for anyone. Many of King's young followers were getting tired of trying to

[8] G. B. Harrison, ed. "The Tragedy of King Richard the Third," *Shakespeare: The Complete Works,* New York: 1948, I, i, 1. 1, p. 226.

force America into the dawn of moral consciousness by singing and praying to her shrines, memorials and billy clubs. They further believed that the March would have assumed quite another character had the force of the original "steam roller" that Malcolm X speaks of been allowed to roll the banks of the placid Potomac. If there were clouds of doubt hanging over the Civil Rights Movement that day, that hour, those were they, and King implied as much: In protesting, the Negro must not allow his "thirst for freedom" have him "drink from the cup of bitterness and hatred . . . again and again we must rise to the majestic heights of meeting physical force with soul force. . . ."

King did not advocate the condemnation of the white race but the condemnation of its deeds; he felt that the distinction was real and important since many white individuals had grasped the reality that their destiny was the black man's and his freedom mightily bound to their own:

> We cannot walk alone. . . . We cannot turn back. . . . We cannot be satisfied as long as the Negro is the victim of unspeakable horrors of police brutality. We can never be satisfied as long as our bodies, heavy with the fatigue of travel, cannot gain lodging in the motels of the highways and the hotels of the cities. We cannot be satisfied as long as a Negro in Mississippi cannot vote and a Negro in New York believes that he has nothing for which to vote. We cannot be satisfied as long as the Negro's basic mobility is from a smaller ghetto to a larger one. No, no, we are not satisfied, and we will not be satisfied until *justice rolls down like water and righteousness like a mighty stream.* . . . [Italics mine]

The italicized passage comes from the prophet, Amos. It runs throughout King's philosophy and sermons, vividly depicting the pregnancy and fullness of justice and righteousness unimpeded. The figure portrays the opening of the floodgates; when applied to the concepts of justice and righteousness, the feeling is one of overwhelming power. The sentiment of the passage carries the idea of racial justice and the mandate for it both North and South. It comes to the conclusion that blacks throughout the country are reduced to a single, minimal plane because of their color, and the upshot of color prejudice manifests itself in different ways—in many places of the South, blacks have been robbed of suffrage—in the North, their voting rights turned no real political gain and capital. It is significant that King was beginning to understand the intricate involvement of color and class in the national arena. Blacks being relegated to a "lonely island of poverty" in a sea of opulence was no mere accident.

King recognized that the manhood struggle of his people, though manifesting itself differently in the different parts, demanded the energies of all the people. There was nothing especially romantic about the fight, though its language as he delivered it was intended to be a balm: "I am not unmindful that some of you have come here out of great trials and tribulations." The Scriptures speak of the great multitudes, coming up from every nation. Mahalia Jackson, great songster of gospels, sings a song familiar to the ear and spirit: "These are they from every nation on their way to the great coronation, coming up through great tribulations, on their way to the crown in glory." Behind this notion is a psalm of thanksgiving: "My soul looks back in wonder at how we made it over." King quoted from biographers, historians, and poets, but more often than not, the spirituals fired his vision.

Headlines became in King's mouth events of epic proportion: "Some of you have come fresh from narrow jail cells. Some of you have come from areas where your quest for freedom left you battered by the storms of persecution and staggered by the winds of police brutality. . . ." The language matched the importance and dignity of the subject. It was like the red-light of his message:

> You have been the veterans of creative suffering. . . . Go back to Mississippi, go back to Alabama, go back to South Carolina, go back to Georgia, go back to Louisiana, go back to the slums and ghettos of our northern cities, knowing that somehow this situation can and will be changed. . . .

A charge to keep the multitudes had, a creed and God to glorify. Here King is ardent, passionate, and burning in his desire that others see as he had seen, live as he had lived, and accept the charge of Christ to love and keep on working: "Let us not wallow in the valley of despair." Psalmist David's "valley of the shadow of death," John Bunyan's "slough of despond" are images of the Christian allegory of fall and experience. In King, the valley is also the test and trial. The captivated moved from the valley to the mountaintop, from the low places to the "rock that is higher than I." In order to lead the captivated, the leader of the captivated must move from the mountaintop (the vision) into the low and crooked places (the pit of experience). The allegory of the Christian journey, the model and vision of the suffering Christ were constants in King's terminology and concepts. He understood and interpreted the moral struggle exactly in its terms and images.

The last part of King's August sermon vividly summed up what the non-violent struggle had been about during the decade. I quote it to demonstrate its imaginative use of metaphors, its repetitive devices, and the way that it builds toward an emotional climax:

> I have a dream that one day this nation will rise up and live out the true meaning of its creed: "We hold these truths to be self-evident. . . ." I have a dream that one day on the red hills of Georgia the sons of former slaves and the sons of former slaveowners will be able to sit down together at the table of brotherhood. I have a dream that even the state of Mississippi, a desert state sweltering with the heat of injustice and oppression, will be transformed into an oasis of freedom and justice. I have a dream today that my four children will one day live in a nation where they will not be judged by the color of their skin but by the content of their character. I have a dream today . . . that one day every valley shall be exalted, every hill and mountain shall be made low, the rough places will be made plains, and the crooked places will be made straight, and the glory of the Lord shall be revealed, and all flesh shall see it together. . . .

The passage moves in contrasts, a kaleidoscope of lightness and darkness, betokening the disparity between the two by placing them side by side.

> This is the faith with which I return to the South. With this faith we will be able to hew out of the mountains of despair a stone of hope. With this faith we will be able to transform the jangling discords of our nation into a beautiful symphony of brotherhood. With this faith, we will be able to work together, to pray together, to struggle together, to go to jail together, to stand up for freedom together, knowing that we will be free one day. . . .

The thronging multitudes were with him as he went on up a little higher:

> . . . So let freedom ring from the prodigious hilltops of New Hampshire, let freedom ring. Let freedom ring from the mighty mountains of New York. Let freedom ring from the heightening Alleghenies of Pennsylvania; let freedom ring from the snow-capped Rockies of Colorado! Let free-

dom ring from the curvaceous peaks of Colorado! Let freedom ring! But not only that: Let freedom ring from Stone Mountain of Georgia. Let freedom ring from Lookout Mountain of Tennessee! Let freedom ring from every hill and molehill of Mississippi. From every mountainside, let freedom ring. . . .

And when freedom is ringing from everywhere and within the earshot of every man, the entire brotherhood of man, united under the eternal fatherhood of God can in a gesture of Thanksgiving, join hands and shout it out: "Free at last! Free at last! Thank God almighty, we are free at last!" The cycle of the imagery is brought full circle, having begun in reference to the Emancipation Proclamation and ending in what was probably the former slave's psalm of emancipation, "Free at last!"

King had moved cryptically and effectively from one phase of the sermon to the next, with the last turned into a powerful, evocative, and dramatic poem. By using a repetitive device, "let freedom ring" which unites the whole in resounding song, King heightens and sustains the passage. The audience echoed and kept pace, like in Montgomery when King asked: "How long?" the audience returned with: "Not long!" The crowd returned to him here, like the southern congregations of old, as a powerful sea wind, resounding and chanting the words of triumph and overcoming. Mrs. King observes that in those final moments of the sermon, King stopped reading from the text, being lifted and carried himself in the overflow of powerful feeling.[9] The technique requires a co-operative, concerted effort in order to be successful.

Often when audiences are slow responding to the message, the preacher will chide: "You don't have to witness!" or "I know I'm right about it!" This usually brought about the desired result. The technique was the instrument and generator of the emotional moment, and though the preacher was in charge of the technique, he was not outside or above it. His own word operated upon him as he brought the message to his followers. In that sense, he was one with his followers in a quickened response to the marvel and mystery of God through the Word.

One of the interesting typographical features of the "let freedom ring" passage is its being set out in verse form. This was perhaps a cue to King about the cadence to be adopted for those particular lines.

[9] Coretta Scott King, *My Life With Martin Luther King, Jr.*, New York: 1969, p. 239.

Prodigious, mighty, heightening, snow-capped, and curvaceous are stress words in the passage, conveying the notions of majesty and remoteness. Stone Mountain, Lookout Mountain, hill and molehill of Mississippi are symbolic of the South, and in King's view at the time the most recalcitrant, stubborn places in the nation, for they summed up the atrociously immoral condition of institutional life in the deep South. The refrain as King delivered it did not conform exactly to the written document. For example, the phrase, "let freedom ring" often framed a passage, appearing at the beginning and at the end where it sometimes began another passage simultaneously: "Let freedom ring from the mighty mountains of New York, let freedom ring . . . from the heightening Alleghenies of Pennsylvania, let freedom ring from the snow-capped Rockies of Colorado. . . ." This structuring gives the passage the feeling of continuity and unity, where one phrase is not distinct from the others except for its images and colors. In that manner, the protest of blacks was a continuum and a continuity.

It seems only natural that when freedom is ringing from all the high places of the nation, men will sing: "Free at last!" It is significant that King ended many of his sermons with quotations from gospels and spirituals; in his mouth, the sentiments came alive, perhaps more so than they'd been in some time. It was his way of summing up, for in the words of the spirituals, intellectual and peasant kinds would not only understand, but also feel together. The impulse of pity, the sense of joy, were endemic to King's message just as they had always been to the message of the black sermon, whose poetry was a poetry of triumph and overcoming.

From the most primitive times art and religion have been closely intertwined. As soon as man sought to communicate with, or proclaim his understanding of Deity, or to express his gratitude or submission to whatever he recognized as the source of his contingency, his creative genius was stirred. So he danced to express his feelings, or he carved a talisman, or composed a psalm, built a temple or cathedral, fashioned an icon, or opened his mouth and sang. In a society where most music is commercial and "romantic," and what is left for the churches often seems more insipid than inspirational, it may be difficult to remember that the first music was religiously inspired. Singing or chanting, and accompanying oneself with a rattle or drum or whistle or foot-patting or stomping, was possibly man's very first artistic expression, and in many contemporary primitive societies this form of religious art survives as a key expression of worship. Chanting and drumming, dancing and intoning are well known for their centrality in African worship and it would be astonishing if some of these expressions did not appear in some form in the Black Church. Hence, it was probably inevitable that the "spiritual," or something akin to it, would develop out of the African heritage and the black experience in America. Africans tend to be a warm and responsive people capable of a great range of emotion. Their tradition of music—vocal and instrumental—as an integral aspect of religious worship was indeed suppressed, for it would not fit the mold of traditional church demeanor in America. It was too expressive—too exuberant. But it also had a cultural tenacity which survived all efforts to destroy it.

The black spirituals are a logical and ingenious vehicle for people who are oppressed and monitored to express their religious feelings through a familiar art medium. The words and the metaphors come out of the language of the in-group and have significance only to those initiated through the peculiar experience of being black *and* Christian in America. Some black churches have been known to "rock" with feeling, a phenomenon common enough when "good preaching" and "good praying" perfectly complemented by "good singing" produced a condition of religious ecstacy—the perfect mode for which emotional religion aims.

The Black Church is a singing church—a fact well documented by the legions who have risen to fame and fortune in the world of secular music, but who began their careers in the choirs of the local black churches. Of equal importance is the fact that the transition from church choir to night club, or to stage, screen, or opera is usually accomplished with a minimum of artistic or emotional adjustment. Anyone who understands "soul" will have no occasion to marvel, for just as religion is integrated into the African's total way of life, so is there an element of religion in every form of black music. The difference beween what happens when Mahalia Jackson sings and Aretha Franklin or Billie Holiday or Bessie Smith sings may be a matter of theme and setting but hardly a matter of essence.

In many black churches there may be as many as six or seven distinct choirs or choral groups—an indication of the importance given to music in the scheme of worship. In addition, congregational singing is a prominent aspect of most black church services, and not infrequently such singing originates spontaneously, particularly if the sermon has been satisfying or effective. In earlier times, the preacher himself was expected to lead the singing, and in some churches this is still the case. It is not unusual for a successful preacher to have a "fine" singing voice as well, and occasionally in some rural or small-town churches, the minister may double as soloist. Singing, scarcely less than preaching is a central aspect of black worship, joining the preacher and his congregation in a spiritual unity which momentarily transcends the harships and injustices of this world, humanizing the social order indeed, and making it bearable.

J. DEOTIS ROBERTS

Roberts addresses himself to two questions: Why a Black Theology? and, In what respect does black theology differ from any other theology? In response to the former question, he says there is a need to reassess all experience affecting the black man's destiny; this reassessment should be done in light of the spiritual experience peculiar to black people. Black theology would differ from any other theology to the degree to which it addresses the black man's peculiar experiences of dehumanization and suffering in Christian America. In fact, according to Roberts, the problem of evil is the fundamental issue for a black theology, and the central task of black theology is the construction of an adequate theodicy.

Also vital to black theology is the question of God's providence. One of the continuing tasks of the black theologian is to find that through the faith of the black community, God is ever-present. A black theology in the expression of its idea of providence, must not be life-negating but life-affirming. The God who acts in response to the oppression of black people must be seen as all-powerful. Hence the reality of evil coupled with the existence of an all-powerful and all-loving God constitute a problem for the black theologian, for a theology of black consciousness must answer the nagging question: "What theological interpretation of evil will bring comfort and assurance to black people, enabling them to embrace the Christian style of life?"

Roberts concludes that ". . . a black theology must be a political theology in the sense that it will challenge the structures of power and seek the humanization of all institutions."

J. DeOtis Roberts is Professor of Theology and Dean of Virginia Union Theologial Seminary.

BLACK CONSCIOUSNESS IN THEOLOGICAL PERSPECTIVE

Source: James J. Gardiner, and J. D. Roberts, Sr., *Quest for a Black Theology* (Philadelphia: United Church Press, 1971) pp. 62–81.

I. Introduction: Why a Black Theology?

There has arisen most recently a crying need to interpret the spiritual dimensions of the Negro's[1] self-awareness in theological perspective. Within the past few years, the intensity of the "black experience" has deepened and widened. More specifically in the late 60s after the cry for black power had echoed throughout the land, the need for a reassessment of all experiences and relationships affecting the destiny of black men in the United States became apparent. It is not surprising that a great deal is being said about a "black theology."

Some attention should first be given to what is meant by a black theology and thus provide some guidelines for the task set before one who seeks to formulate such a statement of the Christian faith. It is to be assumed that a working definition of both "theology" and "blackness" can be found and that these meanings can be combined.

"Black consciousness" or "black awareness" describe something of the concern which presents itself to us. We are assuming that the black man in the United States has undergone a certain kind of treatment which has produced a unique type of spiritual experience both personal and collective—an experience which deserves theological analysis and interpretation. The Negro's experience is similar to Israel's experience of Egyptian bondage, to give only one example.

We will venture further to say that this experience is not only a matter of psychology but of *live* history. We have the witness of our ancestors, many of whom were slaves, and others, who together with us, have been victims of all types of discrimination (open, legal, subtle, and violent) even after the so-called emancipation. We have a "cloud of witnesses" to substantiate these claims. The souls of black men have been tried and tested in the fires of suffering. We have endured in-

---

[1] Throughout this essay "black" and "Negro" will be used interchangeably. Due to the current attractiveness of "black" as a frame of reference for Afro-Americans, this will be most frequently used. All reasons thus far given for using "black" rather than other possible designations have not been convincing. Therefore, it appears to me that "black" is a fad-type usage which was once shunned but is much used for the present.

cessant and undeserved infliction of pain due to our blackness. Thus, when we become conscious, or aware, of our blackness which accounts for this experience inflicted upon us by those who are white and who treat us thus because of the color of our skin, then we must attempt to make sense of our black experience. As Christians we must make theological sense out of our experience if we are to be both black and Christian. Our theological task is to determine what it means to be at once black and Christian in the United States.

Our blackness is a given thing. We are born black and in view of this, no choice is open to us. We have sought to escape our blackness. Some through "passing" by virtue of light skin into white society, some by seeking to belong through achievements in various fields, and some through extreme hedonism or spiritual otherworldliness. I am reminded of a Negro high-society woman who moved out of an all-black neighborhood in Chicago into an integrated neighborhood and who sent word back to her brothers and sisters: "Remember, I am thinking about you." Some have sought to escape through interracial marriage—this is especially true of athletes and entertainers who have more money and popularity than learning and insight. *The Great White Hope* is a dramatic presentation of the tragedy that often results. Even if man and wife are able to accept each other, the American society rejects them and their offspring. In a word, the black man in America confronts a "No Exit" sign in reference to his blackness.

The events of the past few years have made us painfully aware that we must face our blackness. The Ph.D's and the no-D's, the haves and the have-nots are all considered second-class citizens in a white man's world. Whether we live on the Gold Coast or in the dark ghetto, whether we are a "first" in some distinguished post or a garbage collector, to the white man the Negro is still "boss," "boy," or any number of insulting or humiliating titles. We are all united in our blackness and are therefore treated and considered as inherently inferior.

The black man in recent years has become color-conscious in the sense that he is aware that he is black and that to the white majority which controls both the wealth and power in this country, he is not equal. This means that any white man, however poor or illiterate, may assume superiority over any black man whatever his wealth, education, or position. Prejudice is a prejudgment at sight, and the black man is highly visible. Blackness is a fact of life for the Negro. It is a given, it must be accepted—it cannot be ignored, escaped, or overcome. Acceptance of blackness is the only healthy stance for the black man. In

Tillichian language, "he must have the courage to be 'black.'" One of the most wholesome and positive aspects of the black revolution is the assertion that "black is beautiful" and that we should seek "black pride." In a city in which well over half of the citizens are black, all the beauty queens are white. In spite of all evidence to the contrary, presented by the white majority, we need to be able to tell our daughters that they are black but they are also beautiful. Only in this way may we find our way to self-identity and self-acceptance.

On the one hand, blackness is ours by birth and, on the other, the Christian faith is ours by choice. What rationale may we give for a black man accepting the Christian faith? A white student recently asked me the key questions: "What," she asked, "is a black theology?" "How does a black theology differ from any other theology?" If the term theology is used in a respectable academic sense and not in a popular or journalistic sense, these questions present a serious challenge to professional theologian.

II. The Nature and Scope of a Black Theology

John Macquarrie describes theology as God-talk. Theology is theocentric. It must deal with the question of God. It also has some real concern regarding God's dealings with man. Theology includes anthropology which treats the nature and destiny of man. Paul Tillich reminds us that theology is a combination of two Greek words: "theos" (God) and "logos" (reason). Theology is reasoning about God. Theology is a study about God and about man's nature and destiny. It includes man's relation to God and to his fellowman. Christian theology treats these concerns in the context of Christian affirmations. Both philosophy and theology are concerned with ultimate questions. Whereas the philosopher may relate his presuppositions broadly to all religious experiences, a theologian must apply his faith-claims narrowly in his own theological circle, as a Christian, Muslim, or Hindu. It is our task to present a Christian theological perspective.

In a time of black-white confrontation and in a period when black men are willing to stand up to life, an escapist and sentimental Jesusology is not the answer. If the Christian faith has an answer, we must not only discover it and interpret it, but we must likewise find a way to communicate it to our brothers trapped in the dark ghetto, to the black bourgeoisie on the Gold Coast and, indeed, to the poverty-stricken and disinherited millions around the globe. All black men, in particular, share the same experience and all need a gospel of deliverance and hope. The time of need is now. Much attention has been given to the test which the Christian faith confronts in the suburbs among the "haves." The real trial of our faith is in pockets of poverty, in the dark ghettos, and among all black people in this country. We now turn to our theological task.

III. The Constructive Phase of a Black Theology

There are certain crucial problems with which the Negro Christian must deal if his faith is to be firmly established and if he is to give adequate justification for the intellectual content of his faith. The problem of God presents itself to the Negro in a unique manner. The existence, absence, and silence of God do not raise the same issues for black Christians as they do for affluent white Christians—or for "poor Whites"; for after all they are white and whiteness has priority in American life. The providence of God, the moral attributes of God, evil and God, the nearness and distance of God, are some of the important elements for forging a doctrine of God which relates to the black experience.

The black Christian generally assumes that God exists. He often asks the poignant questions: Does God care? Is God just, loving, merciful? Is God all-powerful? Why does he permit undeserved suffering? Is God near? Does he watch over all men?

The question of providence is a serious one for black theology. If faith is to be both comforting and meaningful to the black man in the United States, he must be assured that the God of the Christian creed is a benevolent and provident God. The black man must place his trust in a gracious God who superintends all his creatures. The absence of God is of academic interest, but the *presence* of God is an abiding existential concern. This is perhaps why black Christians have received so much inspiration and comfort from the Old Testament which tells how God dwells among his people and cares for them. The God of Abraham, Isaac, and Jacob is a living and present God. In the words of the psalmist, God is a "present help in trouble (Ps. 46:1)." It is rather easy to understand why black slaves and their descendants have found comfort and assurance in the Old Testament. The witness and activity of the Holy Spirit as seen in the New Testament can be of equal inspiration to the black Christian. The Holy Spirit, God dwelling within the New Israel, the church, is Life-giver, Comforter, Guide, and Strengthener. The God of Jesus who identified himself with those of low estate, must be a God who cares for and loves all men. Jesus, "a prince in beggar's garments," is born in a barn and dies on a cross. In birth, death, as in life, he casts his lot with the needy, the sinful, and the disinherited. The God of the Bible is a gracious and provident God. A black theology must develop this theme of a God who is ever-present, a God who cares, who rules, who guides and gives us "strength for the day." But this God must no longer be understood as a means of escape from life, but as one who enables us to stand up to life. The God of comfort and succor is likewise a God of power and challenge. The thrust of the doctrine of providence must not be life-negating, but life-affirming. Black theology, in asserting the presence of God, must be positive and aggressive, rather than passive, quietistic, and escapist.

Providence and creation are inseparably linked. The black man needs to know that the God of Christian faith is "the author of nature" and that, in spite of the evil and ugliness in his experience, creation is beautiful and good. The black Christian needs to have clearly presented the distinction between man's disorder and God's design. Black theology will betray the black man if it undergirds the theme: "You may have all this world and give me Jesus." Creation and all its benefits have been given to man for his enrichment and fulfillment. At this point the black theologian needs to be informed by secularity. Black people, like white people in this country, are obsessed with things as ends in themselves. Things for many black people are the *esse* (essence) of life rather than for the *bene esse* (well-being) of life. Secularism as a God-substitute (the worship of material things—or in some cases the practice of child-worship) as a quasi-religious manifestation, has overtaken all Americans —black and white. The concept of secularity emphasizes this world as a place where God is present. God as Author of nature, as Lord and Judge of creation and history, is in the here and now. Black theology must say *yes* to *this* life and the order of creation which sustains it. This affirmative doctrine of creation is a sheer necessity if black men are to have a healthy approach to the goods and services which make the present life full and abundant.

The affirmative embracement of the present life does not require a rejection of a belief in the future life. There is some real advantage in seeing the present life from the vantage point of eternity. What I am suggesting is a rejection of both "pie in the sky" and "loaves and fishes." I am suggesting a life of quality instead of a life based on quantity both here and hereafter. There is in this connection a great need to unite faith and ethics. A rejection of a valid theology often leads to the abandonment of a valid ethic. Frequently, all we have left is expediency in which one individual seeks to have his own way at the expense of his own peer group. I was not really surprised to see a sign changed in a riot-torn neighborhood from "Black Power" to "black respect" with the comment: "Stop killing your own people!" If those who advocated naked black power had a theological understanding of man, they would have been less optimistic and more realistic concerning human nature at the outset.

The moral integrity of the Divine Character has real possibilities for a black theology. Against the consciousness of unjust treatment, an unloving relationship based on racism, and the painful awareness of an unmerciful society, there is a need to believe that God is just, loving, and merciful. This is the reason, I believe, why the Old Testament prophets have had a special place in the hearts of black men. Amos' message of social justice sent from a God of justice, Isaiah's condemnation of the feast days of those whose hands are full of blood, and Micah's list of divine requirements—do justly, love mercy, and walk humbly with God—have spoken to the heart of the Negro. Then, Jesus, who came not to destroy the law and the prophets but to fulfill the promise by his life, his teachings, and his cross, demonstrates the very life of this God. Thus as scriptures are "opened up" and as we are made to see the will of God in the teachings of the prophets and the very life and example of the Son of God in the incarnation, there unfolds before us the possibility of a black theology which assures us that God in his very nature is love, justice, and mercy. The God who is love is lovingly just and his love embraces his mercy. Thus amidst all the abuses, exploitation, and injustice so abundant in our midst, we have the assurance that the benevolent, provident God in whom we trust, is loving, just, and merciful and that all evidence to the contrary, this God who is lord over life and lord of history will have the last word.

Since the theme of "power" figures so largely in black consciousness, it is important to have a close theological look at this concept. Self-determination over against determination and power over against powerlessness are at the heart of all revolutions of our time. Beginning with the Christian understanding of God, what light may we cast upon this aspect of black awareness? The black man, who lives in the dark ghetto, in a rented shack, and who works under a white boss, whose environment is regulated from city hall, whose landlord is white or Jewish and lives in the suburbs, lives an other-directed, powerless life. What does the Christian understanding of God say to this man whose life is controlled by a white landlord, a white boss, and white politicians? A few years back this man was "happy" in his plight, but now that black power has been proclaimed, he is aware and he is angry.

Even if he can find "passification" through wine, women, and song, on the one hand, and "spiritual aspirins," on the other, this is his *real* condition. What does the Christian faith have to say about God, man, and community which can make a difference to this man and his children?

Power, as such, is morally neutral. The use of power determines its moral content. Both Hitler and Gandhi used power. Hitler accepted Nietzsche's principle, "might makes right." He, therefore, asserted that the "strong do what they will" and "the weak endure what they must." Hitler used for his ends naked and brutal military force and violence. Gandhi challenged the British raj and won independence for the Indian people by another form of power. It was based upon ahimsa, or noninjury. It has as its basis reverence for life. It is rooted in Hindu scripture but is more pronounced in the Jiana and Buddhist sacred texts. Gandhi called it *satya-graha*, truth or soul force. Martin Luther King, Jr., inspired by both Gandhi and Jesus, referred to it as agape, love. This power is expressed through noncooperation and demonstrations in reference to social evils. Power, therefore, is an *instrumental virtue* when used for good ends, but it may degenerate into an *instrumental vice* when used for evil purposes. Love and goodness, on the other hand, are *intrinsic* virtues.

God is all-powerful, but his unlimited power is consistent with his character. It is indispensable to a worthy doctrine of providence to be assured that God has sufficient power to back up his love, justice, and mercy. A finite God or rather a finite-infinite God—a God limited in power, but absolute in goodness (Brightman's God)—is said to be in touch with our infirmities. He is near and related in that he has an impediment or a disability in his own nature over which his will has no control. He moves from an "eternal crucifixion to an eternal Easter," but this God is not adequate for the faith we need to confront the black experience. A God infinite in goodness, but finite in power does not satisfy an oppressed people. Black men need the assurance that God has sufficient power to sustain his love and justice. We need to know that there is no evil in the nature of God: that all evil is external to him. We need the assurance that this God is not capricious or arbitrary in the exercise of will or power, that he is benevolent and morally upright. We need to know that he never misuses or abuses his power and that his power is instrumental to his love and justice. When asked by a Muslim why I accept Jehovah rather than Allah, I could answer forthrightly that it is my understanding of God which gives me confidence in the Christian message.

Evil and God is another problem that must claim the attention of the theologian of the black experience. Any easy theoretical solution to the omnipresent fact of undeserved suffering will not suffice. The cross of Christian experience is no stranger to the life of the black Christian. Such themes as "God almighty and ills unlimited," "evil and the love of God," and "the cross in Christian experience" are not theoretical but experiential to black men. The questions: Why do the righteous suffer and the evil prosper? What is the meaning of physical pain and mental agony? These and related questions haunt the souls of black folk. What theological interpretation of evil will bring comfort and assurance to black people, enabling them to embrace the Christian style of life?

Here we are concerned primarily with moral evil as distinguished from physical pain. Any solution to the problem which attempts to explain evil away or which treats it as an illusion, will not suffice. The implication that all suffering is deserved and serves a useful purpose as a discipline, misses the mark also. I have seen the visible hate on the face of white men whose faces were reddened by my black but nameless presence. These men had come to hate a black man on sight. To the black man moral evil is real. His own black community is a "human jungle" and he is the constant victim of exploitation and abuse by white men. Moral evil is not an illusion; it is not based upon desert, but it is real and it must be faced.

Human freedom perverted by self-centeredness and selfish inhumanity resulting from sin points us in the right direction. Even so, the existence and persistence of evil in a world created, guided, and sustained by a benevolent, gracious, compassionate, and provident God said to be absolutely good and all-powerful, is difficult to overcome in theological discourse.

A realistic view of man as sinner together with an understanding of the depths of collective sin as well as personal pride and estrangement, provides some insight into this problem. A black theology must somehow maintain trust in the absolute goodness and omnipotence of God notwithstanding the fact of moral evil (both personal and social) against which we must struggle. We must confront evil and find through the resources of our faith the wherewithal to stand up to life. The character of the God in whom we put our trust, must be sufficient for our need.

The drama of Job is an excellent existential analysis of our black experience, but Job's theological solution—"a God whose ways are past finding out"—is no longer very comforting. Many theological statements, like Job's friends and mourners, have brought "false comfort" to the black man in his suffering. Is it possible for the Easter message to speak to the black experience? I believe that it is. The Christian faith is not one of escape, but of confrontation and overcoming. Jesus went *to* Jerusalem, not *around* Jerusalem, in spite of the cross that awaited him there. The cross is at once the symbol of confrontation of evil at its worst with holiness at its best, and the manifestation of "love divine, all loves excelling." The empty tomb is testimony to the *overcoming* power of love which takes us *through* and *beyond* the hold which evil and death have upon us. The grace of the cross and the power of the resurrection are the basis of our believing hope. The faith we need is that the God who is able to bring strength out of weakness will by his sanctifying grace, transform our lives in such ways that the cross in our experience may be a way that leads to victory rather than defeat.

According to our faith, it is the Son of man who suffers vicariously for human redemption. The Son of man title of Jesus refers to a heavenly or original man: man in a perfect sense and therefore man as he ought to be. This is a title of exaltation. The suffering servant title of Jesus refers to his suffering on behalf of others. It is related to Deutero-Isaiah's servant passage which states that "by his stripes we are healed." The suffering servant title refers to humiliation, undeserved suffering that is to be redemptive. Suffering is the means to redemption. Exaltation and humiliation are united in Christology. It is the Son of man who suffers redemptively for the salvation of mankind. As those who know the depths of undeserved suffering, may we somehow find a clue to its meaning in the example of Christ. To seek suffering as an end in itself is to court an empty and meaningless martyrdom. But to transform suffering into a moral and spiritual victory over evil is to live redemptively: it is to use the suffering which is ours rather than to be used by it.

IV. Conclusion: Toward a Black Theology

What is our hope as black men? Is the promise of the future greater than the sufferings and disappointments of our past? If black theology is to be messianic, even eschatological, then, in what sense? The black Christian is born on the side of oppressed humanity and must have an understanding of his faith which commits him to the quest for freedom and justice in the contemporary struggle.

There is a great need to challenge the black intellectual, the group that E. Franklin Frazier called a "new middle class" or "black bourgeoisie." They have rejected the religion of childhood which will usually be Methodist or Baptist by denomination, but they have no philosophical substitute which is adequate to construct a world view that is meaningful. They will not embrace religious cults because they are mass-dominated. The Daddy Grace, Father Divine, and Black Muslim movements are usually unacceptable because of the large lower-class Negro membership. According to Frazier, when they decide that science doesn't have all the answers, they turn to faith healing and psychic phenomena. It has become a fad in cities to make a novena though they are not Catholics. They may even leave the church altogether and trust in "chance." Chance becomes a God-substitute.[2] If members of this new black middle class turn to religion, it is likely to be compartmentalized from all other aspects of life. Not all persons in this middle class are well-educated. Some are in this group by virtue of business success, political appointments, entertainment, sports, and the like. The religion of this class, where it does exist, is often a blind, anti-intellectual fundamentalism. It is a faith which they have been driven to, usually in middle life or old age, "by the ills that flesh is heir to." To use the language of the spirituals, they have arrived at this blind faith "by the troubles of this world."

The goal of black theology must somehow reach the "haves" among the Blacks who have deceived themselves into a social bankruptcy. According to Frazier, they have aimed at "nothingness" for their lives have been emptied of "both content and significance."[3] It is a fact that Frazier's analysis is alarmingly accurate and that a theology which speaks to the black experience must have the new middle class as well as the lower class of Blacks in view. A black theology must have as its goal the sociological and spiritual unity of the black community. To be the people of God, black Christians "must enter into covenant" with one another. The beloved community must be inclusive of black men and women from all stations in life. Pride in blackness must not only remove self-hate; it must erase the hatred, distrust, and tension that exist in the black community. Recently I had dinner with ten or twelve black students who were a "black caucus" on an integrated campus. Among several important concerns of the students was a desire to bring the black domestic servant into their caucus. They had found a "unity in blackness" which their parents had ignored, even rejected. Such a discovery deserves theological interpretation and must be an integral

[2] E. Franklin Frazier, *Black Bourgeoisie* (New York: Collier, 1962), pp. 172–75.
[3] Ibid., p. 195.

part of any black theology. Our common experience in blackness must issue into a deeper understanding of our oneness in Christ. A class and color conscious black church is a luxury which no black community can afford. We are one people both in nature and grace.

One black student who had done a great deal of serious reading in religious literature, but who was not yet convinced by the claims of Christianity, asked whether or not the Christian faith is against all forms of exclusiveness and if so, is it not incompatible with black nationalism? A black theology cannot ignore this important issue. Our "getting together" as black Christians is to discover who we are. When we know our identity, have gained our self-respect, and are fully confident as a people, we will be in a position to be reconciled to others as equals and not as subordinates. If we can take our black consciousness up into our Christian faith, we will find it not only unmanly but unchristian to be reconciled on less than an equal basis. Our faith tells us that all are one in creation, sin, and redemption. As Christians we know that the practice of love is a two-way street and that the ties we have with the faithful lead us in and lead us out.

The ecumenical movement has taught us that as we seek a worldwide fellowship, we are driven to discover more clearly who we are as Baptists, Methodists, and so forth. The "black caucus" movement has created a "black ecumenism." We are seeking through these small fellowships to arrive at self-identification in order that we may know our past, our talents, our uniqueness as a people of God. In large integrated bodies we have been "mere faces in the crowd." We have been nameless, anonymous, culturally and historically disrobed, and religiously inhibited. We have not known ourselves; neither have we been free to be ourselves. The church, as the people of God, should be a fellowship in which everyone belongs—can be himself and do his own thing—"in the Lord" and under the direction of the Holy Spirit.

A black theology must combine the "inner felt" and the "outer known." We must combine our subjective experience with objective knowledge. Among the existent creative theological movements, the theology of hope may be the most satisfying in forging a constructive theological statement of the black experience. The theme of hope for an oppressed people is exhilarating and political theology which places Christian faith firmly on the side of the disinherited with equality and reconciliation as its goal, is attractive. Therefore, in sum, the end is only the beginning. A statement by Herzog in his essay "God, Evil, and Revolution," seems to say well what I would like to stress in my final words:

Revolutionary changes seem a real possibility offered us to arrive at a better use of power. On the one hand, the Christian is compelled to stand at a critical distance from man's revolution so that he will not identify the tentative and relative of revolutions with absolute goodness. On the other hand, he is constrained, in this attitude of critical distance, to the deepest involvement in revolutionary change, since only here can he find the concrete foretaste of God's coming Kingdom in which God will make all things new.[4]

[4] Frederick Herzog, "God, Evil, and Revolution," *The Journal of Religious Thought*, Vol. XXV, No. 2, 1968–69, pp. 27–28.

JAMES H. CONE

Sources are the formative factors, the data of theological construction; the norms are the criteria which determine how the data are to be used. The sources of black theology include the black experience, black history, black culture, revelation, scripture, and tradition.

The norm or hermeneutical principle "is decisive in specifying how sources are to be used and by rating their importance and by distinguishing the relevant data from the irrelevant." Black theology must therefore begin with a norm which relates the condition of the black people to that of the biblical tradition. The black condition is one of oppression in a white racist society. Consequently, black people "want to know what God has to say about the black condition . . . or what is He doing about it." But the norm for black theology must be anchored in the black community's experience of Jesus Christ, for black liberation has no meaning outside of the Christian perspective. It is not the "white Jesus" of American tradition that is meant. This white Jesus must be destroyed and replaced by a "Black Messiah." "The norm of all God-talk which seeks to be black-talk is the manifestation of Jesus as the Black Christ who provides the necessary soul for black liberation."

James Hal Cone is Professor of Theology at Union Theological Seminary in New York, and a prominent member of the emerging school of black theology.

THE SOURCES AND NORM OF BLACK THEOLOGY

Source: James H. Cone, *A Black Theology of Liberation*,* (New York: J. B. Lippincott Company, 1970), pp. 50–81.

* A title in the C. Eric Lincoln Series in Black Religion published by Lippincott.

The Function of the Sources and Norm

Though I have alluded already to some of the factors which shape the perspective of black theology, it is necessary to say a word about what are often designated as sources and norm in systematic theology. The sources are the "formative factors"[1] that determine the character of a given theology, and the norm is "the criterion to which the sources . . . must be subjected."[2]

The Sources of Black Theology

There are many factors which shape the perspective of black theology. Since black consciousness is a relatively new phenomenon, it is too early to define all of the sources which are participating in its creation. The black community as a self-determining people, proud of its blackness, has just begun, and we must wait before we can describe what its fullest manifestation will be. "We are God's children now; it does not yet appear what we shall be . . ." (I John 3:2a). Even so, at this stage, we must say a word about the present manifestation. What are the sources in black theology?

1. *Black Experience.* There can be no black theology which does not take seriously the black experience—a life of humiliation and suffering. This must be the point of departure of all God-talk which seeks to be black-talk. This means that black theology realizes that it is man who speaks of God; and when that man is black, he can only speak of God in the light of the black experience. It is not that black theology denies the importance of God's revelation in Christ; but black people want to know what Christ means when they are confronted with the brutality of white racism. The black experience prevents us from turning the gospel into theological catch phrases and makes us realize that they must be clothed in black flesh. The black experience forces us to ask, "What does revelation mean when one's being is engulfed in a system of white racism cloaking itself in pious moralities?" "What does God mean when a policeman whacks you over the head because you are black?" "What does the Church mean when white churchmen proclaim they need more time to end racism?"

The black experience should not be identified with inwardness, as implied in Schleiermacher's description of religion as the "feeling of

1 See John Macquarrie, *Principles of Christian Theology* (New York: Charles Scribner's Sons, 1966), p. 4.
2 Tillich, *Systematic Theology*, Vol. I (Chicago: The University of Chicago Press, 1951), p. 47.

absolute dependence." It is not an introspection in which man contemplates his own ego. Black people are not afforded the luxury of navel gazing. The black experience is the environment in which black people live. It is the totality of black existence in a white world where babies are tortured, women are raped, and men are shot. The black poet Don Lee puts it well: "The true black experience in most cases is very concrete . . . sleeping in subways, being bitten by rats, six people living in a kitchenette."[3]

The black experience is existence in a system of white racism. The black man knows that a ghetto is the white way of saying that black people are subhuman and fit only to live with rats. The black experience is police departments recruiting more men and buying more guns to provide "law and order," which means making the city safe for white people. It is politicians telling blacks to cool it *or else*. It is George Wallace, Hubert Humphrey, and Richard Nixon running for President and Nixon winning. The black experience is college administrators defining "quality" education in the light of white values. It is church bodies compromising and debating whether blacks are human. And because black theology is a product of that experience, it must talk about God in the light of it. The purpose of black theology is to make sense of black experience.

The black experience, however, is more than encountering white insanity. It also means black people making decisions about themselves which involve white people. Black people know that white people do not have the last word on black existence. This realization may be defined as black power, which is the power of the black community to make decisions regarding its identity. When this happens, black people become aware of their blackness; and to be aware of self is to set certain limits on other people's behavior toward oneself. The black experience means telling whitey what the limits are.

The power of the black experience cannot be overestimated. It is the power to love oneself precisely because one is black and a readiness to die if white people try to make one behave otherwise. It is the sound of James Brown singing, "I'm Black and I'm Proud," and Aretha Franklin demanding "Respect." The black experience is catching the spirit of blackness and loving it. It is hearing black preachers speak of God's love in spite of the filthy ghetto, and black congregations responding, "Amen," which means that they realize that ghetto-existence is not the result of divine decree but of white inhumanity. The black experience is the feeling one has when he strikes against the enemy of black hu-

[3] David Llorens, "Black Don Lee," *Ebony*, March 1969, p. 74.

manity by throwing a live Molotov cocktail into a white-owned building and watching it go up in flames. We know, of course, that there is more to getting rid of evil than burning buildings, but one must start somewhere.

Being black is a beautiful experience. It is the sane way of living in an insane environment. Whites do not understand it; they can only catch glimpses of it in sociological reports and historical studies. The black experience is possible only for black people. It means having natural hair cuts, wearing African dashikis and dancing to the sound of Johnny Lee Hooker or B. B. King, knowing that no matter how hard whitey tries, there can be no real duplication of black soul. Black soul is not learned; it comes from the totality of black experience, the experience of carving out an existence in a society that says you don't belong.

The black experience is a source of black theology because the latter seeks to relate biblical revelation to the situation of black people in America. This means that black theology cannot speak of God and his activity in contemporary America without identifying him with the liberation of the black community.

2. *Black History.* Black history refers to the way black people were brought to this land and the way they have been treated in this land. This is not to say that only the American white man participated in the institution of slavery. But there was something unique about American slavery, namely, the white man's attempt to define black people as nonpeople. In other countries the slaves were allowed community, and there were slave rights. Slaves were human beings, and their humanity was protected (to some degree) by certain civil laws. Black history in America means that white people used every conceivable method to destroy black humanity. As late as 1857 the highest court of this land decreed that black people "had no rights which the white man was bound to respect." The history of slavery in this country reveals the possibilities of human depravity; and the fact that this country still, in many blatant ways, perpetuates the idea of the inferiority of black people shows the capabilities of human evil. If black theology is going to speak to the condition of black people, it cannot ignore the history of white inhumanity committed against them.

But black history is more than what whites did to blacks. More importantly black history is black people saying No to every act of white brutality. Contrary to what whites say in *their* history books, black power is not new. It began when the first black man decided that he had had enough of white domination. It began when black mothers decided to kill their babies rather than have them grow up to be slaves.

Black power is Nat Turner, Denmark Vesey, and Gabriel Prosser planning a slave revolt. It is slaves poisoning masters, and Frederick Douglass delivering an abolitionist address. This is the history that black theology must take seriously before it can begin to speak about God and black people.

Like black power, black theology is not new either. It came into being when black churchmen realized that killing slave masters was doing the work of God. It began when black churchmen refused to accept the racist white church as consistent with the gospel of God. The organizing of the African Methodist Episcopal Church, The African Methodist Episcopal Zion Church, the Christian Methodist Church, the Baptist Churches and many other black churches is a visible manifestation of black theology. The participation of the black churches in the black liberation struggle from the eighteenth to the twentieth century is a tribute to the endurance of black theology.

Black Theology focuses on black history as a source for its theological interpretation of God's work in the world because divine activity is inseparable from the history of black people. There can be no comprehension of black theology without realizing that its existence comes from a community which looks back on its unique past, visualizes the reality of the future, and then makes decisions about possibilities in the present. Taking seriously the reality of God's involvement in history, black theology asks, "What are the implications of black history for the revelation of God? Is he active in black history or has he withdrawn and left black people at the disposal of white insanity?" While the answers to these questions are not easy, black theology refuses to accept a God who is not identified totally with the goals of the black community. If God is not for us and against white people, then he is a murderer, and we had better kill him. The task of black theology is to kill gods who do not belong to the black community; and by taking black history as a source, we know that this is neither an easy nor a sentimental task but an awesome responsibility.

3. *Black Culture.* The concept of black culture is closely related to black experience and black history. We could say that the black experience is what the black man feels when he tries to carve out an existence in dehumanized white society. It is black "soul," the pain and the joy of reacting to whiteness and affirming blackness. Black history is the record of the joy and the pain. It is those experiences that the black community remembers and retells because of the mythic power inherent in the symbols for the present revolution against white racism. Black culture consists of the creative forms of expression as one reflects on the history,

endures the pain, and experiences the joy. It is the black community expressing itself in music, poetry, prose and other art forms. The emergence of the concept of the Revolutionary Black Theater with writers like LeRoi Jones, Larry Neal, Ed Bullins, and others is an example of the black community expressing itself culturally. Aretha Franklin, James Brown, Charlie Parker, John Coltrane, and others are examples in music. Culture refers to the way a man lives and moves in the world; it controls his thought forms.

Black theology must take seriously the cultural expressions of the community it represents so that it will be able to speak relevantly to the black condition. Of course, black theology is aware of the danger of identifying the word of man with the Word of God, the danger Karl Barth persuasively warned against in the second decade of this century. "Form," he writes, "believes itself capable of taking the place of content. . . . Man has taken the divine in his possession; he has brought him under his management."[4] Such a warning is necessary in a situation alive with satanic creatures like Hitler, and it is always the task of the church to announce the impending judgment of God against the power of the state which seeks to destroy the weak. This is why Bonhoeffer said, "When Christ calls a man, he bids him come and die." Suffering is the badge of true discipleship. But is it appropriate to speak the same words to be oppressed? To apply Barth's words to the black-white context and interpret them as a warning against identifying God's revelation with black culture is to misunderstand Barth. His warning was appropriate for the situation in which it was given, but not for black people. Black people need to see some correlations between divine salvation and black culture. For too long Christ has been pictured as a blue-eyed honky. Black theologians are right: we need to dehonkify him and thus make him relevant to the black condition.

Paul Tillich wrote:

> I am not unaware of the danger that in this way [the method of relating theology to culture] the substance of the Christian message may be lost. Nevertheless, this danger must be risked, and once one has realized this, one must proceed in this direction. Dangers are not a reason for avoiding a serious demand.[5]

Though Tillich was not speaking of the black situation, his words are applicable to it. To be sure, as Barth pointed out, God's Word is alien

[4] Karl Barth, *The Word of God and the Word of Man*, trans. by Douglas Horton (New York: Harper and Row, Publishers, 1957), p. 68.
[5] Tillich, *Systematic Theology*, Vol. III, p. 4.

to man and thus comes to him as a "bolt from the blue," but one must be careful about which man one is speaking of. For the oppressors, the dehumanizers, the analysis is correct. However, when we speak of God's revelation to the oppressed, the analysis is incorrect. His revelation comes to us in and through the cultural situation of the oppressed. His Word is our word; his existence, our existence. This is the meaning of black culture and its relation to divine revelation.

Black culture, then, is God's way of acting in America, his participation in black liberation. Speaking of black art, Don Lee writes: "Black art will elevate and enlighten our people and lead them toward an awareness of self, *i.e.*, their blackness. It will show them mirrors. Beautiful symbols. And will aid in the destruction of anything nasty and detrimental to our advancement as a people."[6] This is black liberation, the emancipation of the minds and souls of black people from white definitions of black humanity. Black theology does not ignore this; it participates in this experience of the divine.

4. *Revelation.* Some religionists who have been influenced by the twentieth-century Protestant theologies of revelation will question my discussion of revelation as the fourth source rather than the *first.* Does this not suggest that revelation is secondary to the black experience, black history and black culture? Is not this the very danger which Karl Barth pointed to?

I should indicate that the numerical order of the discussion is not necessarily in order of importance. It is difficult to know which source is more important since all are interdependent and thus a discussion of one usually involves the others. No hard-and-fast line can be drawn between them. A perspective is an expression of the way a community perceives itself and its participation in reality, and this is a *total* experience. It is not possible to slice up that experience and rate the pieces in terms of importance. Since *being* refers to the whole of reality, talk about one aspect of being forces one to consider the totality of being. I have tried to choose a method of discussion which best describes the black community's encounter with reality.

I do not think that revelation is comprehensible from a black theological perspective without a prior understanding of the concrete manifestation of revelation in the black community as seen in the black experience, black history, and black culture. For Christian faith revelation is an event, a happening in human history. It is God making himself known to man through a historical act of human liberation. Revelation is what Yahweh *did* in the event of the Exodus; it is Yahweh tearing

[6] Llorens, op. cit., p. 73.

down old orders and establishing new ones. Throughout the entire history of Israel, to know God is to know what he is doing in human history on behalf of the oppressed of the land.

In the New Testament, the revelatory event of God takes place in the person of Christ. He is the event of God, telling us who God is by what he does on behalf of the oppressed. For Christian thinking the man Jesus must be the decisive interpretive factor in everything we say about God because he is the complete revelation of God.

This analysis of the meaning of revelation is not new in Protestant circles since the appearance of Karl Barth. The weakness of white American theology is that it seldom gets beyond the first century in its analysis of revelation. If I read the New Testament correctly, the resurrection of Christ means that he is also present today in the midst of all societies effecting his liberation of the oppressed. He is not confined to the first century, and thus our talk of him in the past is important only insofar as it leads us to an *encounter* with him *now*. As a black theologian, I want to know what God's revelation means right now as the black community participates in the struggle for liberation. The failure of white theology to speak to the black liberation struggle only reveals once again the racist character of white thought.

For black theology, revelation is not *just* a past event or a contemporary event in which it is difficult to recognize the activity of God. *Revelation is a black event*, i.e., what black people are doing about their liberation. I have spoken of the black experience, black history, and black culture as theological sources because they are God himself at work liberating his people.

I am aware of possible pantheistic distortion of my analysis. But this risk must be taken if theological statements are going to have meaning in a world that is falling apart because white people think that God has appointed them to rule over other people, especially black people. Besides, people who are unduly nervous about pantheism inevitably move toward a deistic distortion of faith; and the god of deism may as well be dead. Our risk is no greater than the risk inherent in Hebrew prophecy; and do I need to mention the risk of Christ? Christian theology, if it is going to have relevance in a revolutionary situation, must take the risk of pointing to the contemporary manifestation of God, and this necessarily involves taking sides. Should God's work in the world be identified with the oppressors or the oppressed? There can be no neutrality on this issue, neutrality is nothing but an identification of God's work with the oppressors.

Black theology takes the risk of faith and thus makes an unqualified identification of God's revelation with the liberation of black people. There can be no other medium of encountering the contemporary revelatory event of God in this society.

5. *Scripture.* Black theology is kerygmatic theology. That is, it is theology which takes seriously the importance of Scripture in theological discourse. There can be no theology of the Christian gospel which does not take into account the biblical witness. It is true that the Bible is not the revelation of God; only Christ is. But it is an indispensable witness to God's revelation and is thus a primary source for Christian thinking about God. As John Macquarrie says, "It is one important way . . . by which the community of faith keeps open its access to that primordial revelation on which the community has been founded."[7] By taking seriously the witness of Scripture, we are prevented from making the gospel into private moments of religious ecstasy or into the religious sanctification of the structures of society. The Bible can serve as a guide for checking the contemporary interpretation of God's revelation, making certain that our interpretation is consistent with the biblical witness.

It is indeed the *biblical* witness that says that God is a God of liberation, who calls to himself the oppressed and abused in the nation and assures them that his righteousness will vindicate their suffering. It is the Bible that tells us that God became man in Jesus Christ so that his kingdom would make freedom a reality for all men. This is the meaning of the resurrection of Christ. Man no longer has to be a slave to anybody but must rebel against all the principalities and powers which make his existence subhuman. It is in this light that black theology is affirmed as a twentieth-century analysis of God's work in the world.

From this, however, we should not conclude that the Bible is an infallible witness. God is neither the author of the Bible, nor are the writers his secretaries. Efforts to prove verbal inspiration of the Scripture are the result of men failing to see the real meaning of the biblical message: the liberation of man! Unfortunately, it is the very emphasis on verbal infallibility which leads us to unimportant concerns. While churches are debating whether the whale swallowed Jonah, the state is enacting laws of inhumanity against the oppressed. It matters little to the oppressed who authored Scripture; what is important is whether it can serve as a weapon against the oppressors.

It is interesting that there is a close correlation between political and religious conservatism. Whites who insist on verbal infallibility are often

[7] Macquarrie, op. cit., p. 8.

the most violent racists. If one can be sure, without the possibility of doubt, regarding his view of Scripture, then he can be equally sure in enforcing his view in the society as a whole. With God on his side there is nothing that will be spared in the name of "the laws of God and men." It becomes an easy matter to kill blacks, Indians, or anybody else who questions his right to make decisions on how the world ought to be governed. Literalism always means the removal of doubt in religion, and thus enables the believer to justify all kinds of political oppression in the name of God and country. During slavery black people were encouraged to be obedient slaves because it was the will of God. After all, Paul did say "slaves obey your masters"; and because of the "curse of Ham," blacks have been condemned to be inferior to whites. Even today the same kind of literalism is being used by white scholars to encourage black people to be nonviolent, as if nonviolence were the only possible expression of Christian love. It is surprising that it never dawns on these white religionists that oppressors are in no moral position to dictate what a Christian response is. Jesus' exhortations "turn the other cheek" and "go the second mile" are no evidence that black people should let white people beat the hell out of them. We cannot use Jesus' behavior in the first century as a literal guide for our actions in the twentieth century. To do so is to fall in the same trap that the fundamentalists are guilty of. It destroys the freedom of the Christian man, the freedom to make decisions without an ethical guide from Jesus.

Scripture then is not a guide which makes our decisions for us. On the contrary, it is a theological source because of its power to "renew for us the disclosure of the holy which was the content of the primordial revelation."[8] The God who is present today in our midst is the same God who revealed himself in Jesus Christ as witnessed in the Scriptures. By reading an account of God's activity in the world as recorded in Scripture, it is possible for a community in the twentieth century to experience the contemporary work of God in the world. The meaning of Scripture is not to be found in the words of Scripture as such but only in its power to point beyond itself to the reality of God's revelation; and in America, that means black liberation. Herein lies the key to the meaning of biblical inspiration. The Bible is inspired because through reading it a community can encounter the resurrected Christ and thus be placed in a state of freedom whereby it will be willing to risk all for earthly freedom.

[8] Ibid.

6. *Tradition.* Tradition refers to the theological reflection of the church upon the nature of Christianity from the time of the early church to the present day. It is impossible for any student of Christianity to ignore tradition because the New Testament itself is a result of it. The possibility of going back to the Bible without taking into account the tradition which gave rise to it and which defines our contemporary evaluation of it is unthinkable; for tradition controls (in part) both our negative and positive thinking about the nature of the Christian gospel.

Though tradition is essential for any theological evaluation of Christianity, black theology is not uncritical of it, particularly the history of western Christianity since the fourth century. The "conversion" of Constantine to Christianity and his subsequent enactment of it as the official religion of the Roman Empire (replacing the public state sacrifices) raises some serious questions about Christendom, especially the possibility of it remaining true to its origin and task. It could be argued that this is the beginning of the decline of Christianity so evident in contemporary American society. Is it possible for the church to be the church (*i.e.*, a church committed unreservedly to the oppressed in society) and at the same time an integral part of the societal structure? I think not. If the gospel of Christ is the gospel of and for the oppressed in the society, the church of Christ cannot be the religion of the society. But it seems that the official church which has been most responsible for the transmission of the gospel tradition has played also the role as the political enforcer of "law and order" against the oppressed by divinely sanctioning the laws of the state and thus serving as the "redemptive" center of an established order. The long bloody history of Christian anti-Semitism is a prominent case in point.

The Protestant Reformation in the sixteenth century did little to change this emphasis. Luther's identification with the oppressors in society enabled him to speak of the state as a servant of God at the same time the oppressed were being tortured by the state. It is impossible for the oppressed who are seeking liberation to think of the state as God's servant. In most cases, the state is responsible for the condition of human enslavement and is thus the enemy of all who are interested in human freedom.

Luther's concern for "law and order" in the midst of human oppression is seriously questioned by black theology. While it may be doubtful whether his doctrine of the relation between church and state prepared the way for Hitler's genocide of the Jews in Europe, it did little to prevent it. In fact, his condemnation of the Peasant Revolt sounds very much like white churchmen's condemnation of ghetto rebellions.[9]

The other Protestant reformers, especially Calvin and Wesley, did little to make Christianity a religion for the politically oppressed in the society. Though no man is responsible for everything that is done in his name, one may be suspicious of the easy affinity of Calvinism, capitalism, and slave trading.[10] John Wesley also said little about slaveholding and did even less.[11] We are told that Wesley's Methodism prevented a

[9] I am not suggesting that Luther had no place in his theology for resisting the state. As P. S. Watson pointed out, Luther believed that it was the job of the preachers of the Word to rebuke rulers publicly when they failed in their duty. "Such rebuking Luther himself knew well how to undertake. Even in the case of the Peasants' Revolt, he laid the entire blame for the rising at the door of the Princes—W.M.L., IV, 220ff.—whose sins he also frequently denounces elsewhere, and in no measured terms" (Watson, *The State as a Servant of God* [London: Society for Promoting Christian Knowledge, 1946], p. 65n.).

Black Theology can appreciate Luther's speaking out against the evils of the Princes (a trait that is typical of many theologians), but, and this is the problem with Luther, he was a "law and order" man even at the expense of the oppression of the poor. Watson reminds us of his unqualified insistence that "one must not resist the government *with force,* but only with knowledge of the truth; if it is influenced by it, well; if not, you are innocent and suffer wrong for God's sake." (Cited by Watson, op. cit., p. 71n.) Now such advice will not go over well in the black community. Indeed it sounds too much like white ministers telling black people to be nonviolent while they enslave them. It could be that we can excuse Luther (after all, he lived in the sixteenth century!), but certainly not white religionists who use him as the guide for their thinking on the black revolution in America.

[10] See Max Weber, *The Protestant Ethic and the Spirit of Capitalism,* trans. by Talcott Parsons (New York: Charles Scribner's Sons, 1958), and J. R. Washington, *The Politics of God* (Boston: Beacon Press, 1967), Chapter IV.

[11] Of course, this is not to say that Wesley was completely silent on this issue. It was hard for any sensitive man during his time to ignore the question of slavery altogether. My point is simply this: in reading his sermons and other writings, one does not get the impression that slavery was one of the burning issues on Wesley's mind. Indeed, for Wesley Christianity seems to be primarily "personal" (a deliverance from sin and death) and not too political. His preoccupation with sanctification and what that entails seems to have distorted his picture of the world at large. Perhaps the later followers distorted the real Wesley by placing an undue emphasis on the "warm heart." But at least the Wesley that has come to us seems very white and quite British, and that ain't no good for black people who know that the Englishmen are the scoundrels who perfected the slave trade.

Black Theology must counsel black people to beware of the Wesley brothers and their concern for personal salvation, the "warm heart" and all that stuff. What black people do not need are warm hearts. Our attention must be elsewhere—say, the political, social and economic freedom of black people!

revolution in England, but I am not sure whether we should praise or condemn him on that account. The behavior of the white Methodist Church in America, with its vacillation on slavery and colonization, is consistent with Wesley's less than passionate approach to the issues.

Black theology believes that the spirit of the authentic gospel is often expressed by the "heretics" rather than the "orthodox" tradition. Certainly the so-called Radical Reformers were closer to the truth of Christianity in their emphasis on Christian discipleship through an identification with the oppressed of the land than was Luther, who called on the state to put down peasants.

Regarding what is often called tradition, black theology perceives *moments* of authentic identification with the ethical implications of the gospel of Christ, but they are rare. When black theology speaks of the importance of tradition, it focuses primarily on the history of the Black Church in America and secondarily on white western Christianity. It believes that the authentic Christian gospel as expressed in the New Testament is found more in the pre-Civil War black church than in its white counterpart. The names of Richard Allen, Daniel Payne, and Highland Garnet are more important in analyzing the theological implications of black liberation than Luther, Calvin, and Wesley. This is partially true because they are black but more importantly because inherent in their interpretation of the gospel is political, economic and social liberation. These men recognized the incompatibility between Christianity and slavery. While the white church in America was rationalizing slavery through clever exegesis, the black ministers were preaching freedom and equality.

The Black Church in America was founded on the belief that God condemned slavery and that Christian freedom meant political emancipation. Highland Garnet even argued that it was both a political and Christian right that slaves should rise in revolt against their white masters by taking up arms against them.

> Brethren, it is as wrong for your lordly oppressors to keep you in slavery as it was for the man-thief to steal our ancestors from the coast of Africa. You should therefore now use the same manner of resistance as would have been just in our ancestors when the bloody footprints of the first remorseless soul-thief was placed upon the shores of our fatherland.[12]

[12] Quoted in B. E. Mays, *The Negro's God* (New York: Atheneum, 1968), p. 46.

Black theology is only concerned with the tradition of Christianity which is usable in the black liberation struggle. As it looks over the past, it asks: "How is the Christian tradition related to the oppression of black people in America?"

The Norm of Black Theology

In the previous section, we attempted to set forth the basic sources of black theology. It is appropriate now to analyze the hermeneutical principle or norm which is operative in black theology as it makes a theological determination regarding the sources. Sometimes it is possible to perceive the norm of a particular theology through an evaluation of the selection and analysis of the sources; but this is not always true, since most theologies share common sources. As we have pointed out, the difference between Barth and Tillich does not lie in their choice of sources. The crucial difference is in their use of the sources, which is traceable back to their definition of the theological norm.

The theological norm is the hermeneutical principle which is decisive in specifying how sources are to be used by rating their importance and by distinguishing the relevant data from the irrelevant. For example, most theologians would agree that the Bible is important for the theological task. But there are sixty-six books in the Bible, and how are we going to decide which books are more important than others? The answers to this question range from the fundamentalist's verbal-inspiration view to the archliberal view that the Bible is merely one of many records of man's religious experiences. In all cases, the importance and use of the Bible are determined by the theological norm which is brought to the Scripture. Theologies with a kerygmatic consciousness would like to think that the norm arises from Scripture itself, but this is not always easy to determine. What is certain is that the theologian brings to the Scripture the perspective of a community, and what is to be hoped is that that community's concern is consistent with the concern of the community that gave us the Scriptures. It is the task of theology to keep these two communities (biblical and contemporary) in constant tension in order that we may be able to speak meaningfully about God in the contemporary situation.

Black theology seeks to create a theological norm which is in harmony with the black condition and the biblical revelation. On the one hand, the norm must not be a private norm of a particular theologian but must arise from the black community itself. This means that there can be no norm for the black community which does not take seriously its reality in the world and what that means in a white racist society. Theology cannot be indifferent to the importance of blackness by making some kind of existential leap beyond blackness to an undefined universalism. It must take seriously the questions which arise from black-existence and not even try to answer white questions, questions coming from the lips of those who know oppressed existence only through abstract reflections.

If theology is to be relevant to the human condition which created it, it must relate itself to the questions which arise out of the community responsible for its reason for being. The very existence of black theology is dependent on its ability to relate itself to the human situation unique to oppressed men generally and black people particularly. If black theology fails to do this adequately, then the black community will and should destroy it. Black people have heard enough about God. What they want to know is what God has to say about the black condition. Or, more importantly, what is he doing about it? What is his relevance in the struggle against the forces of evil which seek to destroy black being? These are the questions which must shape the character of the norm of black theology.

On the other hand, black theology must not overlook the biblical revelation. This means that black theology should not devise a norm which ignores the encounter of the black community with the revelation of God. Whatever it says about liberation must be said in the light of the black community's experience of Jesus Christ. The failure of many black radicals to win the enthusiasm of the black community may be due to their inability to take seriously the religious character inherent in that community. It is not possible to speak meaningfully to the black community about liberation unless it is analyzed from a Christian perspective which centers on Jesus Christ. This accounts for the influence of Martin Luther King, Jr. As a prophet, with a charisma never before witnessed in this century, King preached black liberation in the light of Jesus Christ and thus aroused the spirit of freedom among black people. To be sure, one may argue that his method of non-violence did not meet the needs of the black community in an age of black power; but it is beyond question that it was King's influence and leadership in the black community which brought us to the period in which we now live, and for that we are in his debt. His life and message demonstrate that the "soul" of the black community is inseparable from liberation but always liberation grounded in Jesus Christ. The task of black theology is to build on the foundation laid by King by recognizing the theological character of the black community, a community whose being is inseparable from liberation through Jesus Christ.

This is an awesome task for black theology. It is so easy to sacrifice one for the other. There is a tendency, on the one hand, to deny the relevance of Jesus Christ for black liberation especially in view of white prostitution of the gospel in the interest of slavery and white supremacy. One can be convinced that Jesus Christ is the white man's savior and god and thus can have nothing to do with black self-determination. And yet, what other name is there? It is the name of Jesus which has a long history in the black community. Black people know the source from which the name comes, but they also know the reality to which that name refers. Despite its misuse in the white community (even the devil is not prohibited from adopting God's name), the black community is convinced of the reality of Christ's presence and his total identification with the suffering of black people. They never believed that slavery was his will; and therefore every time a white master came to his death, black people believed that it was the work of God inflicting his judgment in recompense for the sufferings of his people. Black theology cannot ignore this spirit in the black community if it is going to win the enthusiasm of the community it serves.

Black theology must also avoid the opposite error of speaking of Christ without reference to black liberation. The post-Civil War black church committed this error. It is so tempting to take the white Jesus who always speaks to black people in terms of white interest and power. He tells black people that love means turning the other cheek; that the only way to win your political freedom is through non-violence; he even praises Martin Luther King, Jr., for his devotion to him, though he knows that King was always enemy in spirit and that he chose King because he thought King was the least of the evils available. He tries to convince us that there is no difference between American democracy and Christian freedom, that violence is no way to respond to inhumanity. Black theology must realize that the white Jesus has no place in the black community, and it is our task to destroy him. We must replace him with the Black Messiah, as Albert Cleage would say, a messiah who sees his existence as inseparable from black liberation and the destruction of white racism.

The norm of black theology must take seriously two realities, actually two aspects of a single reality: the liberation of black people and the revelation of Jesus Christ. With these two realities before us, what then is the norm of black theology? The *norm of all God-talk which seeks to be black-talk is the manifestation of Jesus as the Black Christ who provides the necessary soul for black liberation.* This is the hermeneutical principle for black theology which guides its interpretation of the meaning of contemporary Christianity. Black theology refuses to accept any norm which does not focus on Jesus Christ, because he is the essence of the Christian gospel. But when we speak of the Christian gospel, we have merely scratched the surface by saying Jesus is at the center. It is so easy to make his name mean intellectual analysis, and we already have too much of that garbage in seminary libraries. What is needed is an application of the name to the concrete affairs of men. What does the name mean when black people are burning buildings and white people are responding with riot-police control? Whose side is Jesus on? The norm of black theology, which identifies revelation as a manifestation of the Black Christ, says that he is those very black men whom white society shoots and kills. The contemporary Christ is in the black ghetto, making decisions about white existence and black liberation.

Of course, this interpretation of theology will be strange to most white people and even some blacks will be made to wonder whether it is really true that Christ is black. But the truth of the statement is not dependent on white or black affirmation, but on reality of Christ himself who is presently breaking the power of white racism. This and this alone is the norm for black-talk about God.

JOSEPH A. JOHNSON, JR.

As liberator, Jesus is the power, love, and wisdom of God. Johnson bases his discussion on St. Paul's mystical experience with God which gave him the power to live a free, righteous life.

Johnson argues that the tragedy of the interpretations of Jesus by the white American theologians during the last three hundred years is that Jesus has been too often identified with the oppressive structures and forces of the prevailing society. Hence the quest, via black consciousness, for a "Black Messiah."

The world of white theologians is severely limited: "This severe limitation of the white theologians' inability to articulate the full meaning of the Christian faith has given rise to the development of black theology." Johnson says black theology is a "product of black Christian experience and reflection. It comes out of the past" and is redemptive for the future.

But Blacks must "detheologize" their minds in order to recover the essential humanity of Jesus, for "The white Christ of the white church establishment is the enemy of the black man." To be a Christian, says Johnson, is to join Christ "at the crossways of the world," to participate in His ministry of love and liberation.

Joseph A. Johnson, Jr., is a Bishop of the Christian Methodist Episcopal Church.

JESUS, THE LIBERATOR

Source: James J. Gardiner and J. DeOtis Roberts, *Quest for a Black Theology* (Philadelphia: United Church Press, 1971), pp. 98–111.

Jesus is the Liberator. He is the revelation of the wisdom, the power, and the love of God. This was the message which the early Christian preachers were commissioned to proclaim. This message was called the Kerygma. We preach Christ, Paul shouts. At the heart of the Kerygma lies this fundamental christological affirmation: Jesus is the Liberator! Jesus is the Emancipator!

The tragedy of the interpretations of Jesus by the white American theologians during the last three hundred years is that Jesus has been too often identified with the oppressive structures and forces of the prevailing society. His teachings have been used to justify wars, exploitation of the poor and oppressed peoples of the world. In his name the most vicious form of racism has been condoned and advocated. In a more tragic sense this Jesus of the white church establishment has been white, straight-haired, blue-eyed, Anglo-Saxon, that is, presented in the image of the oppressor. This "whiteness" has prevailed to the extent that the black, brown, or red peoples of the world, who had accepted Jesus as Lord and Saviour, were denied full Christian fellowship in his church and were not accepted as brothers for whom Jesus died.

The Limitations of White Theology

To be sure, during the past fifteen years we have entered, insofar as the black community is concerned, into one of the most exciting periods in the life of the black people of this country. For more than one hundred years black students have studied in predominantly white seminaries and have been served a theological diet, created, mixed, and dosed out by white theological technicians. The black seminarians took both the theological milk and meat and even when they had consumed these, their souls were still empty. Those of us who went through the white seminaries did not understand why then. We had passed the courses in the four major fields of studies; we knew our Barth, Brunner, and Niebuhr. We had entered deeply into a serious study of Bonhoeffer and Tillich, but we discovered that these white theologians had described the substance and had elucidated a contemporary faith for the white man. These white scholars knew nothing about the black experience, and to many of them this black experience was illegitimate and unauthentic.

The black man's religious style was considered subhuman by many of the white theological seminaries of this nation and the emotional nature of his religious experience was termed primitive. For the black seminary student to become a great preacher really meant that he had to *whitenize* himself. He had to suppress his naturalness and remake himself in the image of a Sockman, Fosdick, or Buttrick. You see, insofar as the white seminaries were concerned, there were no great black preachers, and if a black preacher was fortunate to be called great by the white community, it meant that he was merely a pale reflection of the white ideal.

The young black seminary student today has been introduced into a whole new experience—one fashioned by the late Martin Luther King, Jr., but clarified and profoundly interpreted by Frantz Fanon, Malcolm X, Stokely Carmichael, and Ron Karenga. The young black seminary student today has been tried by every conceivable ordeal that sadistic racial minds can devise; from the fire hoses to vicious dogs, from tear gas to electric animal prods. They have matched wits with the white racist of the power structure and are helping to pull down the system of segregation and discrimination. They have no objection to the combination of such words "black and power," "black and theology," "black and church," "black and Christ," "black and God." They believe Du Bois who wrote, "This assumption that, of all the hues of God, whiteness is inherently and obviously better than brownness or tan leads to curious acts." They are not shocked, nor are they discouraged if the term black power seems to offend or frighten white or black Americans. To these young blacks, black power means consciousness and solidarity. It means the amassing by black people of the economic, political, and judicial control necessary to define their own goals and share in the decisions that determine their faith. Fanon, Malcolm X, Carmichael, and Karenga forced the black seminary students to ask these questions: What do these white American and European theologians of a white-racist-dominated religious establishment know about the soul of black folks? What do Barth, Brunner, and Tillich know about the realities of the black ghettos or the fate of black sharecroppers' families whose souls are crushed by the powerful forces of a society that considers everything black as evil? Could these white theologians see the image of the crucified Jesus in the mutilated face of a rat-bitten child, or a drug addict, bleeding to death in a stinking alley?

We have learned that the interpretation of Christian theology and of Jesus expounded by white American theologians is severely limited. This is due to the simple reason that these white scholars have never been lowered into the murky depth of the black experience of reality. They never conceived the black Jesus walking the dark streets of the ghettos of the North and the sharecropper's farm in the Deep South without a job, busted, and emasculated. These white theologians could never hear the voice of Jesus speaking in the dialect of Blacks from the southern farms, or in the idiom of the Blacks of the ghetto. This severe limitation of the white theologians' inability to articulate the full meaning of the Christian faith has given rise to the development of black theology.

The Commission on Theology of the National Committee of Black Churchmen has issued a statement on black theology. In this document black theology is defined:

> For us, Black theology is the theology of black liberation. It seeks to plumb the black condition in the light of God's revelation in Jesus Christ, so that the black community can see the gospel is commensurate with the achievement of black humanity. Black theology is a theology of "blackness." It is the affirmation of black humanity that emancipates black people from white racism thus providing authentic freedom for both white and black people. It affirms the humanity of white people in that it says "No" to the encroachment of white oppression[1]

The black scholars are indebted in a measure to white theologians.

[1] "Black Theology: A Statement of the National Committee of Black Churchmen," June 13, 1969.

We have learned much from them. However, the white theologians in their interpretation of the Christian faith have ignored the black Christian experience. Many have felt that this black Christian experience was devoid of meaning and therefore could be omitted in their exposition and interpretation of the Christian faith. To be sure, this was a grievous error. The omission of the black Christian experience by white interpreters of the Christian faith meant that the message of the Christian faith thus interpreted was oriented toward the white community. Therefore this message had nothing significant to say to the black man who is now struggling for identity and dignity. The black theologians were forced to look at the black Christian experience and interpret this experience so as to ascertain what the black Christian experience has to say to the black man concerning the vital matters of the Christian faith. Black theology is a product of black Christian experience and reflection. It comes out of the past. It is strong in the present and we believe it is redemptive for the future.

The Quest for the Black Jesus

The reason for the quest for the black Jesus is deeply embedded in the black man's experience in this country. The black man's introduction to the white Jesus was a catastrophe! Vincent Harding reminds us that the Blacks encountered the American white Christ first on the slave ships that brought us to these shores. The Blacks on the slave ship heard his name sung in hymns of praise while they died chained in stinky holes beneath the decks locked in terror and disease. When the Blacks leaped from the decks of the slave ships they saw his name carved on the side of the ship. When the black women were raped in the cabin by the white racists, they must have noticed the Holy Bible on the shelves. Vincent Harding declares, "The horrors continued on American soil. So all through the nation's history many black men have rejected this Christ—indeed the miracle is that so many accepted him. In past times our disdain often had to be stifled and sullen, our angers silent and self-destructive. But now we speak out."[2]

One white perceptive theologian, Kyle Haselden, has observed:

> The white man cleaves Christian piety into two parts: the strong, virile virtues he applies exclusively to himself; the apparently weak, passive virtues he endorses especially for the Negro. "Whatsoever things are true, honest, just, pure, lovely" belong to the white man; "whatsoever things

[2] Vincent Harding, "Black Power and the American Christ," *The Black Power Revolt*, ed. Floyd B. Barbour (Boston: F. Porter Sargent, 1968), p. 86.

are of good report" belong to the Negro. The white man takes the active and positive Christian adjectives for himself: noble, manly, wise, strong, courageous; he recommends the passive and negative Christian adjectives to the Negro: patient, long-suffering, humble, self-effacing, considerate, submissive, childlike, meek.[3]

White theology has not presented us with good theological reasons why we should not speak out against this gross perversion of the Christian faith. White theology has not been able to reshape the life of the white church so as to cleanse it of its racism and to liberate it from the iron claws of the white racist establishment of this nation. White theology has presented the Blacks a religion of contentment in the state of life in which they find themselves. Such an interpretation of the Christian faith avoided questions about personal dignity, collective power, freedom, equality, and self-determination. The white church establishment presented to the black people a religion carefully tailored to fit the purposes of the white oppressors, corrupted in language, interpretation, and application by the conscious and unconscious racism of white Christians from the first plantation missionary down to Billy Graham.

The white Christ of the white church establishment is the enemy of the black man. The teachings of this white Christ are used to justify wars, exploitation, segregation, discrimination, prejudice, and racism. This white Christ is the oppressor of the black man, and the black preacher and scholar was compelled to discover a Christ in his image of blackness. He was forced to look at the teachings of Jesus in the light of his own black experience and discover what this black Jesus said about the realities of his own life. The black preacher, seminary student, and scholar had their work cut out for them. If Bultmann's task was to demythologize the New Testament, the black preacher and scholar had to detheologize his mind of the racist ideas which had crept into interpretations of Jesus and to see him in the depth of his full humanity.

We remind you, we were asked to address ourselves "in the general area of understanding and communicating the Christian faith in today's revolutionary society." The first requirement is one of admitting the inadequacies of an understanding of the Christian faith which is used to support our contemporary racist society. Black and white scholars must read again the scriptures with new eyes and minds so as to hear the words of Jesus in their disturbing clarity.

[3] Kyle Haselden, *The Racial Problem in Christian Perspective* (New York: Harper & Bros., 1959), pp. 42–43.

The subject of all preaching is Jesus Christ. As Paul says, "We proclaim Christ—yes, Christ nailed to the cross; and though this is a stumbling block to Jews and folly to Greeks, yet to those who have heard his call, Jews and Greeks alike, he is the power of God and the wisdom of God (1 Cor. 1:23–24, NEB)."[4]

A Recovery of the Humanity of Jesus

Detheologizing demands that we recover the humanity of Jesus in all its depth, length, breadth, and height. Jesus was born in a barn, wrapped in a blanket used for sick cattle, and placed in a stall. He died on a city dump outside Jerusalem.

The New Testament presents with disturbing clarity its record of the birth, ministry, and death of Jesus. There is no attempt to hide the stark realities which confronted Jesus from the barn of Bethlehem to the city dump of Jerusalem. The realism is naked and stark. Jesus was born in a barn. He died on a city dump. Even the place of the birth of Jesus is identified with the needs and the conditions of people. Where the need is the deepest, the situation most desperate, and the pain the sharpest, that is precisely where Jesus is. We repeat, even in the birth of Jesus, the Gospels of Matthew and Luke identify him with the needs, the suffering, the pain, and the anxieties of the world. You see, most of the world's babies are not born in the palaces of kings or the government houses of prime ministers, or the manses of bishops. Most of the world's babies are born in the ghettos of corrupt cities, in mud houses, in disintegrated cottages with cracked floors and stuffed walls where the muffled cries of unattended mothers mingle with the screams of newborn infants.

Bultmann writes about the offense of the incarnation of the word.[5] He contends that the revealer appears not as man in general, that is, not simply as a bearer of human nature but as a definite human being in history—Jesus of Nazareth—a Jew. The humanity of Jesus is genuine humanity. The writer of the Gospel of John has no theory about the preexistent miraculous entrance into the world or of the legend of the virgin birth. You know this legend or myth is presented to us in the Gospels of Matthew and Luke. The writer of the Gospel of Mark, the evangelist of the Fourth Gospel, and Paul teach a high Christology without reference to the virgin birth.

Permit us to make this suggestion: Suppose we would omit the phrase

---

[4] From *The New English Bible, New Testament,* op. cit.
[5] Rudolph Bultmann, *Theology of the New Testament,* Vol. II (London, SCM Press, 1955), pp. 40–41.

"of the Holy Spirit" from Matthew 1:18 where it is recorded that "Mary had been betrothed to Joseph, before they came together she was found to be with child," what would this teach us about the humanity of Jesus? The reaction of many would be instantaneous and we would be accused of teaching "a doctrine of the illegitimate birth of Jesus." These objectors would insist that the birth of Jesus was due to a special act of God in and through humanity and that since Jesus is who he is and has done what he has done, this requires that his entrance into the world through humanity must be unique. Those who advocate this position forget the teachings of Jesus in particular and the New Testament writers in general concerning all life. Jesus taught that all life comes from God and that the birth of every child embodies and expresses a unique act of God.

Who Jesus was, was determined not necessarily by the manner of his birth but rather by what he did. John Knox states that the first form of the christological question was "What has God done through Jesus?"[6] The New Testament writers go to great length in presenting and discussing the saving deed of God through Jesus.

It was the belief of most writers of the New Testament that God was at work in the life and deeds of Jesus and that what God was doing in Jesus had both soteriological and eschatological significance. The conviction shared by most New Testament writers was to the effect that the last days had finally dawned and that God was acting decisively for man's salvation, renewal, and liberation. Again John Knox notes that the supreme importance of Jesus was determined more by his role and function than by his nature and further, "the christological question, which was originally a question about the eschatological and soteriological significance of an event, has become a question about the metaphysical nature of a person."[7] What must be done, therefore, if we are to understand the meaning and significance of Jesus, the Liberator, is to go behind the metaphysical speculation concerning him and ascertain and study those events which were foundational and believed by writers of the New Testament to possess saving and liberating significance. Men knew Jesus in terms of what he had done for them. J. K. Mozley states, "There is in the New Testament no speculative Christology divorced from the gospel of the Saviour and the salvation he brings."[8] The early Christians were not seeking abstract definitions con-

[6] John Knox, *On the Meaning of Christ* (New York: Charles Scribner's Sons, 1947), p. 49.
[7] Ibid., pp. 55–56.
[8] J. K. Mozley, "Jesus in Relation to Believing Man," *Interpretation, A Journal of Bible and Theology* (January 1958), p. 11.

cerning the person of Jesus. The language of the early Christians was experiential, functional, and confessional. The foundation for the theology of Paul is the experience of what God had done for him in his own conversion, and he is basically interested in Jesus as the Redeemer, Revealer, and Liberator.

Brunner has argued that the titles given to Jesus in the New Testament are verbal in nature and character. They all describe an event, a work of God, or what God has done through Jesus in and for mankind. Further, Brunner writes: "Who and what Jesus is can only be stated at first at any rate by what God does and gives in him."[9]

Brunner insists that all christological titles must be understood not in terms of their substantive implications but in terms of their verbal functions. The term *Christos* may be interpreted as the one in whom and through whom God is to establish his sovereignty. The title *Son of God* is functional and it suggests an office and *the work* of the Liberator rather than a description of his metaphysical nature. Even the title *Immanuel* is defined in terms of its functional implications because this title means "God is with us." The title *Kyrios* describes the one who rules over the church. And finally, the title *Saviour* points to the one who is to bring the healing, salvation, and liberation for which mankind yearns.[10]

The significance of Jesus for religious living is determined by what Jesus has done for mankind and all the christological titles applied to Jesus emphasize his gift of liberation to and for men.[11]

The divinity of Jesus is a divinity of service. His humanity was stretched in service so as to include the whole world of man in its miseries, slavery, frustration, and hopelessness. The New Testament word used to express this deep concern for men is *splagchnizesthai*. This word means to be moved with compassion, and it is used to describe an emotion which moved Jesus, the Liberator, at the very depth of his being. This word also indicates the depth of Jesus' concern and identification with others. Whenever the Gospel writers used this word *splagchnizesthai* in reference to Jesus, they were attempting to describe the manner and the way in which Jesus identified himself completely with others and how he entered into the world of their misery and suf-

[9] Emil Brunner, *The Christian Doctrine of Creation and Redemption* (London: Lutterworth Press, 1952), p. 272.
[10] Ibid., p. 273.
[11] Ferdinand Hahn, *The Titles of Jesus in Christology* (New York: World Publishing Co., 1969), pp. 347–50; Oscar Cullmann, *The Christology of the New Testament* (London: SCM Press, 1959), pp. 3–6.

fering, their slavery and hopelessness, and provided the means for liberation and renewal.

The men and women of the New Testament period who witness this ministry of service, love, and liberation reach the astounding conclusion that Jesus is the Revelation of a new kind of freedom and has made available to men the liberating power of God's love. Jesus is God acting in the service of men, thereby enabling them to realize their God-given potentials as human beings and as sons of God.

The Christians of the first century saw in Jesus, the Liberator, the answer to their most distressing problems. Jesus in his ministry, identifies himself with all men. The early Christians believed that he provided the answer to their most disturbing problems and whatever they needed he was sufficient. The writers of the four Gospels interpreted Jesus in the light of what they considered to be the greatest need of mankind. For the writer of the Gospel of Matthew, Jesus is the new Rabbi; for Luke, he is the great Physician; for Mark, he is the Stranger satisfying the deepest needs of men; and for John, Jesus is the Revealer.

The people of all races, because of his service, are able to identify with him and to see in his humanity, a reflection of their own images. Today the black man looks at Jesus observes his ministry of love and liberation and considers him the Black Messiah who fights oppression and sets the captive free.

Committed to the Message and Mission of Jesus

The radicalness of the humanity of Jesus is not only expressed in his service but also in his speech. We must permit his speech to address, probe, disturb, and challenge us. Prof. Ernst Fuchs has called the rise of the gospel a speech event—an opening of a new dimension of man's awareness, a new breakthrough in language and symbolization. Professor Fuchs writes: "The early Church is itself a language phenomenon. It is precisely for this reason that it has created for itself a memorial in the new stylistic form of the Gospel. Even the Apocalypse of John, and more than ever the apostolic epistles, are creations of a new language that transforms everything with which it comes into contact."[12]

The words of Jesus have the rugged fiber of a cypress tree and the jagged edge of the crosscut saw. His language is extreme, extravagant, explosive as hand grenades which are tossed into the crowds that lis-

12 Ernst Fuchs, *Studies of the Historical Jesus* (Napierville, Ill.: Alec R. Allenson, Inc., 1960), p. 68.

tened to him. A tremendous vigor and vitality surges through his words. In Jesus' words, "A man with a log in his eye tries to pick a cinder out of his brother's eye." In the words of Jesus "a giant hand hangs a millstone around the neck of one who exploits a little child and hurls the sinner into the midst of the sea." In the words of Jesus, "a man asks for bread and is given a stone, another asks for fish and is given a snake." In the words of Jesus, "men strain at the little gnats and gulp down the camels." In the words of Jesus, "a mountain develops feet and casts itself into the sea." He attacks the religious establishment of his day—the religious leaders, the ordained ministers with such phrases as "you hypocrite," "you blind guides," "you blind Pharisees," "you brood of snakes," "you serpents," "you murderers."

Jesus spoke with authority and with power!

In the city of Nazareth where he was reared, this dark, long-haired, bearded ghetto lad of Nazareth took over the synagogue service and read his universal manifesto of liberation:

> The spirit of the Lord is upon me because he has anointed me; he has sent me to announce good news to the poor,
> to proclaim release for prisoners and recovery of sight for the blind;
> to let the broken victims go free,
> to proclaim the year of the Lord's favour (Luke 4:18–19, NEB).[13]

The reading of this liberation manifesto caused debates, rebuttals, accusations, counterrebuttals, wrath, anger, and hate. The Gospel of Luke is explicit in describing the reaction of the religious establishment to the manifesto of liberation of Jesus. "When they heard this, all in the synagogue were filled with wrath. And they rose up and put him out of the city, and led him to the brow of the hill on which their city was built, that they might throw him down headlong. But passing through the midst of them he went away (Luke 4:28–30)."

Liberation was the aim and the goal of the life of Jesus in the world. Liberation expresses the essential thrust of his ministry. The stage of his ministry was the streets. His congregation consisted of those who were written-off by the established church and the state. He ministered to those who needed him, "the nobodies of the world," the sick, the blind, the lame, and the demon-possessed. He invaded the chambers of sickness and death and hallowed these with the healing words of health and life. He invaded the minds of the demon-possessed and in those dark chambers of night he brought light, sanity, and order. Jesus ministered to men in their sorrow, sin, and degradation and offered

[13] From *The New English Bible, New Testament,* op. cit.

them hope and light and courage and strength. He offered comfort to the poor who did not fit into the structure of the world. Jesus comforted the mourner and offered hope to the humble. He had a message for the men and women who had been pushed to the limits of human existence and on these he pronounced his blessedness.

The people who received help from Jesus are throughout the Gospels on the fringe of society—men who because of fate, guilt, and prejudices were considered marked men; *sick people,* who must bear their disease as punishment for crime or for some sin committed; *demoniacs,* that is those possessed of demons; *the lepers,* the first-born of death to whom fellowship was denied; *gentiles,* women and children who did not count for anything in the community; and *the really bad people,* the prostitutes, the thieves, the murderers, the robbers. When Jesus was pressed for an explanation of the radicalness of the thrust of his ministry, his answer was simple and direct. "Those who are well have no need of a physician, but those who are sick; I have not come to call the righteous, but sinners (Luke 5:31–32)."

The greatness of Jesus is to be found precisely in the way in which he makes himself accessible to those who need him, ignoring conventional limitations and issuing that grand and glorious welcome— "Come unto me all ye that labor and are heavy laden and I will give you rest."

The Gospel of Mark records the healing of Peter's mother-in-law. Please listen to this passage. "And immediately he left the synagogue, and entered the house of Simon and Andrew, with James and John. Now Simon's mother-in-law lay sick with a fever, and immediately they told him of her (Mark 1:29–30)." Now, verse 31 tells us what Jesus did: "And he came and took her by the hand and lifted her up, and the fever left her; and she served them."

Jesus is saying to his disciples the only way to lift is to touch. You cannot lift men without touching them. Jesus is saying to the church— the people of God—the church must not be locked in its stained-glass fortress with its multicolored windows, red-cushioned seats, crimson carpets, and temperature-controlled auditorium where according to Kierkegaard, "An anemic preacher preaches anemic gospel about an anemic Christ to an anemic congregation."[14]

The church building must be a point of departure, a departure into the world, into the dirty here and now.

We are challenged to continue in our world Jesus' ministry of love

[14] Sören Kierkegaard, *Attack upon Christendom,* tr. by Walter Lowrie (Princeton: Princeton University Press, 1946), p. 30.

and liberation. We must recognize that to be a Christian is to be con-temporaneous with Jesus, the Liberator. To be sure, to be a Christian is not to hold views about Jesus but rather to become a contemporary with Jesus in his ministry of suffering and humiliation and of love and liberation. To be a Christian is to be committed to the man Jesus in spite of the world's rejection of him, in spite of Christendom's betrayal of him, and in spite of the social and intellectual stigma involved in ac-cepting and following him. To be a Christian is to stand with Jesus and participate in his ministry of love and liberation at the crossways of the world where men are crucified on the crosses of poverty, racism, war, and exploitation. To be a Christian is to try again to introduce Chris-tianity into Christendom and to set free again the powers of the love and liberating ministry of Jesus, the Liberator.

WILLIAM JONES

Black theology must first ask: Is God a white racist? And it must be founded on a viable theodicy. Because black theology starts with black suffering, and because its aim is black liberation, it cannot take for granted the universal love and goodness of God. Methodologically, *the black experience* must be "the Supreme Court"; black liberation must be the theological goal; and black theology must reappraise radically all the traditional theological concepts and oppose white-racist theology. It must proceed *de novo*. The non-racism of God is the first point the black theologian must take. How do black theologians Washington, Cone, and Cleage fare in that respect?

Joseph Washington, Jr., assigns to Blacks the role of "suffering ser-vants" and "the chosen people," with the mission of witnessing to the humanity of God and of saving America. But, biblically, one cannot talk of the suffering servant without mentioning in the same breath, even if eschatologically, the liberation, the liberation from suffering. Washington does not point to the black liberation, present or future, which would entitle him to call Blacks suffering servants, but rather seems to imply the perpetuity of black suffering. His soteriology applies more to whites than to blacks. In short, he fails to prove that God is not a white racist.

In James Cone's theology, God is The Great Liberator. Blacks being oppressed, God will liberate them. But the question of *why* Blacks are oppressed is not even raised in relation to God. According to Cone, one cannot talk of God independently of his liberating acts, but he fails to mention any involving Blacks. Nothing in Cone's theology definitively denies the racism of God.

In Cleage's system, God has liberated Blacks in history, for the Jews of the Exodus were Blacks, and so was Jesus. Moreover, God himself is black, or more precisely, "non-white." The use of the *imago dei* concept can easily lead to total anthropomorphism. Cleage understands black suffering as a punishment for sin, that of failing to resist the oppressor. But the gap between sin and punishment thus created is unacceptable and leaves the question of the non-suffering of the whites for their racism unanswered. We do not know from this whether God is a white racist, or not.

William Jones is Assistant Professor of Philosophy in the Yale Divinity School. He is the author of *Is God a White Racist? A Preamble to Black Theology.**

A QUESTION FOR BLACK THEOLOGY: IS GOD A WHITE RACIST?

Source: William Jones, "Theodicy and Methodology in Black Theology: A Critique of Washington, Cone, and Cleage," *Harvard Theological Review*, 64, 1971, pp. 541–57.

Our study criticizes the respective theodicies and methodologies of Joseph Washington, James Cone, and Albert Cleage. Our argument is reducible to the following propositions. (1) On the basis of their own presuppositions, the point of departure for black theology must be the question: Is God a white racist? (2) Accordingly, a viable theodicy, one which refutes the charge of divine racism, must be the foundation for the edifice of black theology. (3) The theodicies of the above theologians leave the issue of God's racism essentially unresolved. Consequently, the remainder of the theological system lacks adequate support.

I

The argument of Richard Rubenstein[1] provides the initial framework for our analysis. The oppression and slaughter of the Jews in

* A title in the C. Eric Lincoln Series in Black Religion published by Doubleday.
[1] *After Auschwitz* (Bobbs-Merrill Co., 1966).

World War II led him to conclude that two key elements of his theological tradition must be scraped: God as active in *and* sovereign over history, i.e., the politics of God, and the Jews as God's chosen people. Though he does not use the following language, his argument raises the question: Is God an anti-Semite? And to raise the latter question is, as Moltmann correctly suggests,[2] to revive the theodicy question.

The implications for black theology are clear. In the light of black suffering—a suffering which may exceed that of the Jews—[3] the unsavory and, some will say, blasphemous question must be put at the outset: Is God a white racist? Once raised, the methodological consequences are equally clear; a viable theodicy must be the first order of business before construction of the rest of the theological system can begin. This is not to say that a theodicy must, numerically, be the first chapter. We suggest, rather, that the theodicy question must control the theological enterprise. Christological and eschatological options, for instance, must be weighed in terms of their value to the theodicy problem. Black theology, we purport to show, must be an extended theodicy.

One should not conclude that Rubenstein's argument makes the theodicy question central for black theologicans. To be exact, the methodological position they adopt, in part, forces the issue to center stage. If black suffering is in any way crucial for the black theologian, if reflection upon black suffering is the starting point for his theology, then the theodicy question must precede all others. For each of the figures in our study, black suffering, explicitly or implicitly, is central.

Explicitly: "The point of departure for black theology," according to Cone, "is the question: How do we *dare* speak of God in a suffering world . . . in which Blacks are humiliated because they are black? This question . . . occupies the central place in our theological perspective."[4] Implicitly: if black liberation is the goal of black theology, black suffering, in the final analysis, is its starting point. To regard liberation as the *summum bonum* necessitates that its opposite, suffering as oppression, is an aspect of the *summum malum*. The pre-condi-

---

[2] "Since we experience reality as history and no longer as cosmos, the fundamental theodicy question is still with us and is more pressing than before. For us it has no longer only its old naturalistic form, as in the earthquake of Lisbon in 1755. It appears today in a political form, as in the question of Auschwitz. . . . We ask the question: *An Deus sit?* ('Whether God is?') on grounds of history and its crimes. . . ." *Religion, Revolution and the Future* (Charles Scribner's Sons, 1969), p. 205.

[3] BASIL DAVIDSON estimates that slavery, "before and after embarkation," cost Africa fifty million blacks. *Black Mother* (Atlantic-Little, Brown Co., 1961), p. 80.

[4] CONE, *A Black Theology of Liberation* (Lippincott, 1970), p. 115.

tion for black liberation as the objective for black theology is the prior affirmation of black suffering as oppressive.

Because of the nature of suffering in general *and* black suffering in particular, the question of divine racism cannot be avoided. Suffering is multievidential; it can express a relation of *favor* or *disfavor* between man and ultimate reality. Consequently, in the face of suffering, whatever its character, one must at least entertain the possibility that the relation of disfavor obtains.

The peculiar character of black suffering points to the same possibility. There is, first, its maldistribution. It is suffering confined to a specific ethnic group; it is not spread, more or less impartially, upon mankind as a whole. Black suffering, then, manifests the scandal of particularity to the degree that it is balanced by white *non*-suffering instead of white suffering. There is, second, its enormity. If we accept the statistics of Davidson, the issue is more acute for Blacks than for Jews. Finally, black suffering is not catastrophic but extends over long periods of history. One is tempted, accordingly, to interpret its causal nexus in terms of purpose and thereby person—not the operation of some indifferent natural law. Actually, the same observation could be made for each characteristic of black suffering.

We contend that the peculiar nature of black suffering raises the *question* of divine racism; we do not conclude that it *answers* the question. We do insist that black theology, precisely because of the fact of black suffering, cannot proceed as if the goodness of God for *all* mankind were a theological axiom. The black religionist must press the issue at the outset, and, most important, he must demonstrate—not assume —its falsity.

Our argument is strengthened when we show that there are determining factors besides suffering that oblige black theologians to ponder the issue of transcendent racism. We purport to show that black theology is committed to a *de novo* approach, and in the latter context divine racism is a genuine option. The implications of the concept of black consciousness for theological method establish our point.

Black religionists, today, identify black consciousness with a specific theological method. Because it recognizes the Negro's inauthentic attraction and commitment to white theology—a theology of racism and oppression—black consciousness fosters the development of a counter theology, a black theology, a theology of liberation. Black consciousness requires, in short, a theological movement not simply beyond white theology, but in conscious opposition to it.

This means in general methodological terms that the black experience must control the theological enterprise. More specifically, it means (1) that black theology must adopt a method of correlation. The starting point for theological reflection must be the issues and questions that emerge from the black experience, and the answers, i.e., the black theology, must be consistent with that experience. (2) The black experience must function as the theological singular. As the theological Supreme Court, it passes final judgment upon the functional or dysfunctional quality of each part of the theological tradition. (3) A theological concept is functional if and only if it advances the cause of black liberation. (4) As a consequence of the foregoing—and here we come to the significant point for our analysis—black theology is methodologically obliged to conduct a radical and comprehensive appraisal of classical theological concepts to determine if each possesses sufficient "soul" to be included in the emerging black theology. The appraisal must be total—not even God or Jesus Christ can *a priori* be regarded sacrosanct; they, too, must be jettisoned if they flunk the test. Because black theology suspects that the norms of the Christian tradition are racist, it must proceed, as it were, *de novo*. The entire tradition must be placed under a strict theological ban until each part demonstrates its orthodoxy, the enhancement of black liberation. And since from a *de novo* perspective, the claims, God is a racist and God is a "soul" brother, are on equal footing, can consideration of the former claim, we ask, be avoided? Indeed, our previous discussion permits us to say that black theology methodologically contradicts itself if it both adopts a *de novo* approach and emphasizes black suffering, but fails to ask the troublesome question of divine racism. Once the issue is broached, the mandatory next step for black theology is to refute the charge, i.e., formulate a viable theodicy.[5]

That a viable theodicy is crucial to the methodological consistency of black theology can be supported on other grounds, and again, in terms of the black theologians' presuppositions. Central to each is the doctrine of the politics of God; man must discover where God is at work in human history and join His effort of human liberation. But the politics of God, in the context of black theology, presupposes that

[5] It is not our intent to establish deductive requirements for a viable theodicy. We contend that the issue of divine racism emerges from the events and crimes of history. The answer, likewise, must appeal to historical data and not a mere rational or theoretical formulation unsubstantiated by the actual history of blacks. It will become clear that the presuppositions of the black theologians—the politics of God, the priority of the black experience, etc.—dictate that the actual black experience, past, present, or future, must be the arena for debate, and not abstract possibilities.

God is, in fact, for the liberation of Blacks. He is not, in other words, a racist. It is obvious, however, that a politics-of-God approach presupposes a prior demonstration that God is not a racist or else it begs the question. Is it possible to construct a black theology with the politics of God as the second story without a foundational theodicy which refutes the charge of divine racism? And what has just been argued for relative to the politics of God holds as well for another crucial category in black theology: Blacks as God's chosen people. This is particularly the case if one makes vicarious suffering, as Washington does, defining for the elect.

Finally, if black theology defines itself as a theology of liberation or revolution, the theodicy question is again controlling. For if the impulse to liberation is to obtain, the suffering implicit in the present situation of Blacks must be interpreted as oppressive. Clearly, not every theodicy provides the requisite interpretation. Indeed, certain ones, e.g., a theodicy which entails quietism, must be labeled counter-revolutionary. Our point is this: a theology of liberation must formulate not just a theodicy, but one with a specific character. Moreover, to clear the field for itself, it must spell out the deficiencies of alternative theodicies.

Our summary can be brief: the foundation the black theologian constructs for his system must be a theodicy which refutes the claim, God is a white racist. Whether Washington, Cone, and Cleage supply the indispensable rebuttal must now be determined by critically analyzing their respective answers to the theodicy question.

II

Washington's theodicy is an elaboration of the suffering servant theme. God is engaged in human history for a purpose which will not be frustrated. He fulfills his plan, totally or in part, through the vicarious suffering of an elect group. Black suffering, which must be the suffering of the entire group, is the means by which God's plan is realized.

Washington moves between two different but related soteriological roles for blacks. There is, on the one hand, a universal mission to the total human family which parallels the saving role of another chosen people, the Jews. Their task is "to witness to the one God," while the mission of Blacks "is to witness to the one humanity of the one God."[6] The realization of the universal mission of Blacks both begins with and hinges upon the successful completion of a more particular assignment:

[6] WASHINGTON, *The Politics of God* (Beacon, 1969), p. 158.

the concrete salvation of the white oppressor in America from the shackles of his own racism and white folk religion, i.e., irreligion.

Blacks should not seek to evade the suffering inherent in their roles; actually, they could not, even if they hoped for release. Since one's status as suffering servant-chosen people is rooted in God's choice, a choice consequently that cannot be nullified, one cannot choose not to be the suffering servant-chosen people. One can choose not to be obedient to the demands of one's mission—but only at the peril of rebelling against God himself. Washington is willing to affirm that, ultimately, the only hope for the success of black liberation is to follow the path he describes—through the valley and shadow of vicarious suffering. For it is this path alone which God demands and therefore nurtures.

The deficiencies of Washington's theodicy, in our view, are severe, if not fatal. Before describing them, it is necessary to isolate the structure of his argument and thus provide a framework for our criticism.

The argument appears to have the following structure: (a) If Blacks are the suffering servant-chosen people, then the charge of divine racism is refuted. (b) Blacks are the suffering servant-chosen people. (c) Therefore, the charge of divine racism is refuted. To round out the argument it is necessary to show that the category of the suffering servant-chosen people, the cornerstone of his theodicy, carries two meanings for Washington, and each constitutes a refutation of divine racism. To be chosen means that one has found favor in God's sight. Chosenness is also essentially related to one's salvation.

Clearly the validity of his argument is contingent upon his establishing (b). We question whether the label of suffering servant-chosen people is justified on the basis of Washington's evidence.

An analysis of Isaiah 53:5–12, the section Washington cites as support for his classification, is our point of departure. Our reading concludes that *two* conditions are required to index an individual or group in the category of suffering-servant. (1) There is the fact of suffering, but suffering as a necessary condition. (2) There is a radical shift in the status of the suffering individual group which we will name the *liberation event* or factor. The shift comprises something similar to the principle of "from last to first." If we call (1) the situation of humiliation, then (2) would designate exaltation or reward. The references, "I will divide him a portion with the great" and "He shall divide the spoil with the strong," supply the general sense of (2) that is intended. Even where the liberation event is interpreted eschatologically, i.e., the change in status is yet to come, it is on the basis of the eschatological event that the present suffering, for instance, is alleged to be unjustified. Two rhetorical questions summarize our point. Can we speak of Jesus as Lord if we speak only of the cross and omit the resurrection? Can we speak of Blacks as suffering servant-chosen people if the only evidence given is their suffering?

The point can be put in another way. Without the liberation event how can we differentiate between two mutually exclusive alternatives, vicarious suffering and suffering as deserved punishment? Is it not premature to classify someone as suffering servant-chosen people *prior* to the occurrence of the liberation event?[7] Is it not incumbent upon Washington, from the methodological standpoint, to designate the liberation event(s) for Blacks which justifies the label, chosen people-suffering servant?

One might argue that the eschatological option is available for black theology; the liberation event is yet to come. This option, from our vantage point, is a theological dead end, for, in the final analysis, it leaves the issue of God's racism unresolved until the eschaton. Prior to the actual eschatological event, and in the face of black suffering, God's favor and disfavor relative to blacks remain equally probable.

Moreover, it would appear that Washington further undercuts the strength of his theodicy when he acknowledges that the reason for God's choice of Blacks as suffering servant-chosen people "is no more fathomable than His choice of Israel to be His 'suffering servant.' "[8] Does not the uncertainty regarding the reason for the election make problematical Washington's stipulation of a specific purpose for the selection?

Washington's theodicy is even more questionable when we consider that it appears to entail a consequence which is clearly consistent with the concept of a racist God: the *perpetuity* of black suffering. He appears to establish an either/or situation in which both alternatives involve suffering. There is, on the one hand, the inevitable suffering associated with Blacks as suffering servant; on the other, Blacks suffer because "Negroes will always be black and objectionable to whites."[9] The former cannot be evaded because it expresses the will of ultimate

---

[7] Though the category of deserved punishment stands in essential contradiction to WASHINGTON's position, he gives it only scant attention. The following seems to be his only "refutation" of the alternative of deserved punishment. "Historically, the systematic victimization of the African and the American Negro has been accepted as the punishment of the will of God. But this very belief sparks the reality so opposite, the truth of hope; these victims bear the marks of those blessed of God to do his work of love . . . ," p. 176.

[8] WASHINGTON, op. cit., p. 173.

[9] Ibid., p. 173.

reality, the latter because Blacks are powerless in a racist society. Consequently, the Negro has the choice either "to be what he is, 'suffering servant,' the source of power, or fatalistically acquiesce in suffering. . . ."[10]

Black suffering will be terminated, according to Washington, only when their soteriological mission is complete, and this may not occur until the eschaton. In a similar vein he concludes: "The continuing chastisement of the Jews may be to the end of time."[11] If I understand Washington correctly, he is affirming that Blacks will not be liberated until their assignment is *successfully* concluded. "The Negro will receive no reward until all are healed."[12] In reading Washington, we have the nagging suspicion that black suffering is intended as much for white liberation as for black freedom. In fact, one could argue that the position is weighted in favor of white freedom since black reward is contingent upon the success of their soteriological assignment. The suspicion grows even stronger when we note that slavery, for Washington, is a necessary part of God's purpose and, moreover, less "bruising" than the present mission.[13] If this were not sufficient to make one distrust the God he represents, Washington further asserts that though God's purpose demanded the exodus of the Jews from bondage in Egypt, the will of God for the Negro does not include a similar exodus. We do not think it unfair to suggest that Blacks should at least ponder over God's purpose and motive if it involves the type of suffering Washington describes—particularly without a corresponding suffering for whites. Washington's theodicy, we submit, does not disprove the charge of divine racism, rather it has the net effect of reaffirming the charge.

III

It is to Cone's merit that he avoids a theodicy which implies the perpetuity of black suffering. Indeed, the opposite impulse informs his approach. The elect are not chosen to suffer for the other, not even indirectly; their election entails, instead, their release from suffering and bondage. Yet his theodicy, in our view, is also a failure since it does not falsify the assertion, God is a white racist.

[10] Ibid., p. 166.
[11] Ibid., p. 158.
[12] Ibid., p. 160.
[13] "Slavery was but the means for inextricably binding the Negro and the Caucasian. Without this binding the immeasurably more bruising work of releasing whites from their blasphemous bondage to whiteness and racial superiority cannot be done," op. cit., p. 157.

The logical structure of Cone's argument parallels that of Washington. Three steps can be indicated. (1) A class is posited that involves a special and favored relation to deity. For Washington, as we saw, this class was the suffering servant-chosen people; for Cone, the *oppressed*. (2) It is argued that Blacks are members of the class in question. (3) The conclusion follows: God is not a racist.

The major support for Cone's argument boils down to an exegetical demonstration that the liberation of the oppressed is the core of the biblical *Heilsgeschichte*. This, in turn, is the ground for the other pillar of his theodicy: "The *liberation* of the oppressed is a part of the innermost nature of God."[14] Making liberation the essence of God serves a dual purpose. It links Blacks to the biblical acts of liberation, and, consequently, it answers, at the same time, the question of divine racism. If "liberation is . . . the essence of divine activity,"[15] racism, by definition, is not possible. Thus, God's acts of liberation in the past, which are the clue to his character, purpose, and motive, are sufficient grounds for Blacks to rest assured that he has made their liberation his concern and is in their midst as they struggle towards freedom. Cone is willing to conclude that if God is not "identified totally" with the goals of blacks, he is a murderer, i.e., a racist, and the only appropriate response for Blacks is deicide.[16]

One other feature of Cone's theodicy deserves special attention. His approach does not explain the "why" of black suffering; nor does he seek to harmonize it with God's will or purpose. He is content to see white racism as the cause. The weight of his argument falls upon what God has done for the oppressed in the *past* and, thus by implication, what he is now doing about black oppression. Black suffering does not imply divine racism, because God is presently participating in the black struggle for freedom.

If our analysis is correct,[17] Cone's position is vulnerable at crucial points. The first crucial issue is whether the first step of his argument begs the question; the same question can also be put to Washington. To posit a class that presupposes a favored relation to God—and the term *oppressed* carries this stipulative meaning for Cone—is to exclude the alternative of God's disfavor by definition.

Of equal importance is whether Cone has substantiated the claim that the liberations of *Blacks* is essential to God's being. We wish to

---

[14] Cone, op. cit., p. 121.

[15] Ibid.

[16] Cone, op. cit., 59–60.

[17] We have not included Cone's treatment of theodicy in *Black Theology* and *Black Power* on the assumption that his later work presents his definitive position.

show that, on his own terms, the claim can be corroborated only by pointing to concrete acts of God in behalf of *black* liberation—not acts for some other group. That is, once the issue of God's racism is raised, the fact of his liberating activity for non-blacks, e.g., the Israelites, is irrelevant to the charge, God is a white racist. The exodus may refute the accusation of anti-Semitism but not racism.

Our criticism gains clarity when we consider Albert Cleage's response to the same issue. That God is liberating Blacks is established by Cleage at the outset in terms of his concepts of the blackness of God, Jesus and the Jew. The *physical* blackness of God and Jesus—not their symbolic blackness—partially confirms their status as "soul" brother and assures their active participation in the struggle for black freedom. By regarding the Jews as black, he guarantees, again at the outset, the fact of God's liberating effort in behalf of the *particular* group at issue. In summary, the scandal of particularity, which is raised by virtue of the nature of black suffering, can only be answered by reference to the particularity of God's liberating activity, e.g., an exodus for *Blacks*.

Let us consider some decisive statements from Cone himself to show that they support our interpretation. "There is no revelation of God without a condition of oppression *which develops into a situation of liberation.*"[18] What can this statement mean except that revelation presupposes the two conditions we detailed in the previous section: suffering and the liberation event? Must we not conclude that in the absence of the latter, there is no revelation, and consequently, no knowledge of God's nature? In the absence of the liberation event *for Blacks,* is it possible to speak of the liberation of Blacks as implicit in God's innermost nature?

Other statements yield the same conclusion. He rejects the suggestion that knowledge of God "as he is in himself" is possible and also the view that we can know God "independently of his liberating work."[19] When we combine these with another claim, our criticism is justified. "Black theology," he claims, "cannot accept a view of God which does not represent him as being for Blacks and thus against whites . . . We must know where God is and what he is doing in the revolution. There is no use for a God who loves whites the *same* as Blacks."[20] Does not Cone's position here push him to the conclusion that Blacks can know God as for them, as liberator, only if there are concrete acts of black liberation where the hand of God is detected? To conclude that God is on the side

[18] CONE, 91. Emphasis supplied.
[19] CONE, op. cit., 133.
[20] CONE, op. cit., 131–32.

of Blacks because he has participated in the liberation of non-blacks is to assign a character to God which, in Cone's own terms, has not been established. It is to speak of God "independently of his liberating acts." Is it not comparable to arguing that since Huey Long was on the side of the oppressed, i.e., Southern whites, he was also on the side of Blacks?

Finally, can we fail to give full weight to this point? The conditions Cone cites as the basis for saying Blacks are oppressed and thereby the beneficiary of God's liberating work—"Blacks are humiliated because they are black"—are, in fact, the same conditions one would expect if God were a racist.

We submit that Cone has not substantiated the one fact which his own position asserts must be shown if God is not a murderer, namely, that black liberation is a part of his innermost nature. If this is the case, the remainder of the system is without a sturdy foundation. Obviously, the equation between black theology and the Gospel he advocates becomes suspect. Further, the black factor of his theology would lose its support. It is on the basis of God's identification with the oppressed, i.e., Blacks, and his assumption of their condition that he is able to speak of a black Christ. But if the issue of God's relation to Blacks remains unresolved, there is no basis for speaking of a black Christ.

What options are available to Cone to authenticate the liberation event for Blacks? He can adopt Cleage's approach which makes the exodus, for instance, an act of black liberation since the Jews, in Cleage's system, are black. Another possibility is to isolate the liberation factor or progress of events through a survey of black history, but his own position makes this option unattractive. His claim, previously considered, that God must be for Blacks and against whites has this methodological consequence: he can prove that God is on the side of Blacks only if he also marshals empirical warrant for God's opposition to whites. It is embarrassing even to mention that whites have been on top for centuries. Moreover, he could not legitimately speak of a progressive improvement for Blacks if their status *relative to whites* did not measurably improve. An appeal to white racism as the cause of black suffering would simply shift the issue to another level. The central question would then be to account for white racism in the context of God's sovereignty and his alleged opposition to whites.

The option of eschatological confirmation, the liberation event(s) is yet to come, also appears to be closed by Cone's own position, though his thought may be inconsistent here. It should be clear that an eschatological verification would not fit with his argument that Blacks must know here and now whose side God is on, for, as we have already argued, the actual effect of eschatological confirmation is to leave the issue of divine racism unresolved until the eschaton.

Moreover, Cone rejects the concept of eschatological compensation for this-worldly suffering, but curiously, he introduces something strikingly similar in content and intent. He finds it necessary to postulate "the future reality of life after death"[21] for various reasons: to substantiate that God is on the side of Blacks, to insure that fear of death will not lead to defeatism and thus diminish one's total commitment to the struggle, to assure that the death of the black freedom fighter is not meaningless, etc. One wonders, however, what the real difference is between the eschatological perspective he accepts and the one he rejects. The slave eschatology promised compensation for those who suffer patiently here; while Cone's eschatology guarantees reward and meaning for those who die valiantly here. Though the difference reflects a much needed corrective for black ethics, is it an improvement on black theodicy? I raise this question because the following possibility sticks in my mind. Consider: the promise of a future reality after death motivates Blacks to make the ultimate sacrifice for their liberation, and this is the means by which a racist God beckons blacks to suicidal efforts and thus accomplishes black genocide.

IV

The core of Cleage's position seems to be a complex of categories which he does not explicitly relate to the theodicy issue. As we suggested above, the concepts of the blackness of God, Jesus, and the Jews, along with the view of the particularity of the divine action for liberation, constitute an answer to the question of divine racism. Since these categories also form the core of Cleage's total system, their description and criticism would require another article. Our admittedly incomplete analysis must, accordingly, be an outline of the argument we would present if space and time permitted.

Cleage's refutation of God's racism is reducible to two points. (1) To be on the side of Blacks requires that one be like them, i.e., physically black; thus the necessity of a black God and a black Jesus. (2) Since not everyone who is black is also a "soul" brother, there must be concrete evidence of God's activity in their behalf. Here the major evidential materials are the exodus and the revolutionary ministry of Jesus, the Black Messiah, to the black nation, Israel. The same point is

21 CONE, op. cit., 247.

affirmed when Blacks are considered as the chosen people, which means that God is working for their emancipation.

It is important, for purposes of criticism, to recognize the logical connection between (1) and (2). In the final analysis (2) is dependent upon the demonstration of (1). It is only on the basis of the blackness of God, Jesus, and the Jews that the exodus, for instance, becomes an event of black liberation. Thus, it becomes necessary to consider how he defends the particularity of God's saving activity based on an identity of pigmentation with the specific group in question.

The concept of the *imago dei* is the ground for claiming that God is black. Specifically, according to Cleage, we must describe God as some "combination" of the actual characteristics of the human family considered in terms of their numerical representation. Since an empirical analysis indicates that there are black men, red men, yellow men, and "a few, a mighty few, white men," it can be concluded that God must be some combination of red, yellow, and black, "with just a little touch of white, and (hence) we must think of God as a black God."[22] To reach the latter conclusion Cleage emphasizes the American view that one drop of black blood makes one black.

Though Cleage's argument refutes the charge of divine racism, it must be noted that he depends upon an interpretation of the *imago dei* concept which leads to very dubious consequences, and these undercut the value of his refutation. It is obvious that the "combination" interpretation of the *imago dei* can be applied to other features of the divine nature as well. If we conclude that God is a combination of the various hues represented in the human family, must we not also apply the combination interpretation to the category of weight, size, sex, intelligence, etc. The logical consequence, it appears, would be total anthropomorphism. Moreover, since Cleage utilizes the combination interpretation in an exclusive way—"Certainly thou must understand that as black people, it would be impossible for us to kneel before thee, believing thee to be a white God—"[23] would not a plurality of gods, each with a different color, be necessary to accommodate the human family of worshippers?

Special note, moreover, should be made of the fact that Cleage does not establish that God is black but only *non-white*. Accordingly, it is also appropriate to speak of a yellow messiah or a red messiah.

We turn now to Cleage's explicit treatment of black suffering, and here he utilizes the category of *deserved punishment*. This interpretive

---

[22] CLEAGE, *The Black Messiah* (Sheed and Ward, 1969), pp. 42–43.
[23] Ibid., pp. 46–47.

framework, at first glance, seems odd, for it would appear to entail quietism. If the suffering is deserved, then evasion is inappropriate. Further, if it is the result of God's disfavor, then it is futile, as Father Paneloux observers in *The Plague*, to try to escape the full brunt of the punishment. Cleage avoids the albatross of quietism by making quietism itself the sin which is being punished. Blacks are being punished because of their failure to affirm their manhood by challenging every dehumanizing act of the oppressor.

To round out this side of the theodicy other features must be described. God's nature, i.e., the morality of the universe, requires an atoning act for each sin. The atonement must be man's work, and the act of atonement must be the antithesis of the sin under question. "For every moment of cowardice, there must be a moment of courage."[24] In sum, our suffering will continue until we have made total restitution for our past sins, and it is presupposed that the sins of the father are visited upon the son.

We would question whether the category of deserved punishment can carry the weight Cleage places upon it. We find it difficult to describe the nature of the sin which requires the degree of suffering Blacks have experienced since coming to America. Is the sin to be traced to an African past? It would seem that the character of black suffering in Cleage's analysis raises the issue of the commensurability of sin and punishment. To make our point another way. We argued that the crucial issue for Washington and Cone was the identification of the liberating event for Blacks; for Cleage, it is the identification of the sin for which black suffering is the restitution.

What we are suggesting, indirectly, is that Cleage's position carries within it a hint of the perpetuity of black suffering. His argument that every sin must be matched by an antithetical act is open-ended to the extent that one can never know when full satisfaction has been made. And one wonders why God insists upon parity between sin and suffering when it is allowed that God was willing to "break the very laws of the universe"[25] for his chosen people.

Nor is it apparent that his position can accommodate white non-suffering. In the light of continued black suffering and white non-suffering, what are we to conclude about whites, particularly when we invoke the rigid principle of equal satisfaction for each sin? Has another people replaced Blacks as God's chosen? Must we conclude that God has broken the rules of the universe in their favor by nullifying

[24] CLEAGE, op. cit., p. 271.
[25] CLEAGE, op. cit., p. 242.

the necessity of punishment for their crime of white racism? In general terms, Cleage must explain how it is that Blacks are God's chosen people in light of the fact that whites were allowed to get on top and stay there. Cleage's framework would allow him to conclude that black suffering is due to black sin, therefore the issue of the status of whites is irrelevant. We admit this, but such a line of argumentation would also sever, it appears, any causal connection between white racism and black suffering.

In sum, we find Cleage's theodicy to be an unsure answer to the question of divine racism.

V

A description of our positions falls beyond the scope of this article, but we must emphasize that it does not enlist the position of divine racism. We would see black suffering in particular and suffering in general as simply a matter of powerlessness. We would also find the framework of humanistic existentialism to be a more viable framework for black theology than the scaffolding we find in Washington, Cone, and Cleage. We hope to have more to say on these themes in the near future.[26]

[26] Cf. my forthcoming work, *Is God a White Racist? A Preamble to Black Theology.*

CHAPTER III

BLACK RELIGION AND BLACK PROTEST

Some critics have argued that black religion is essentially black protest and nothing more. This argument holds that God and history have simply been made adjunctive to the politics of liberation, and that religion has somehow been degraded by making it a vehicle for the political aspirations of black people. This is, of course, the perfect complement to the ancient dogma that God loves and values man's *soul* whatever his condition of life, and that in consequence the religious enterprise ought to be directed to the perfection of the inner life, leaving to the Almighty the regulation of status and condition in this life. Black religion rejects such a doctrine and affirms instead the belief that *all* of man belongs to God, not just his soul; and that man has responsibilities to God, to himself, and to other men which require a condition of freedom for their execution. In short, the perfect worship of God cannot occur when one is in some form of bondage to another and acquiesces in that bondage. If, then, black religion is a religion of protest it takes its departure from the assumption that God wants man free; that man, in the image of God, must be free to do God's work—to respond responsibly to the requirements of the faith.

Black religion is the spiritual pearl of the black experience, an experience in which human bondage was a principal component. Since religion is in some sense an institutionalization of certain cultural experiences, that protest against the lingering vestiges of unfreedom, which recall the harsh experience of slavery, may well be expected to characterize the expression of black religion. Religious leaders who are best remembered, and who are held in highest esteem by the black community, have almost invariably been protest leaders as well. Nat Turner, Gabriel Prosser, Lott Carey, Henry Highland Garnet, Adam Clayton Powell, and Martin Luther King, Jr., are all examples of men whose spiritual leadership included important commitments to black protest.

However, to see black religion *merely* as a covert form of political protest is to oversimplify matters to the point of distortion. In the first place, there could have been no religion for Blacks had not the controlling whites been convinced that Christianity, should it be permitted the Blacks, would strengthen white control and increase the level of black acceptance for black servitude. To a very marked degree, this speculation was correct. Blacks who found Jesus in the white man's church, or who accepted spiritual care and oversight under the aegis of the white man's religion, soon found themselves inevitably more sympathetic to the white man's plans for non-whites. The white man's Christian interpretation of reality made the white man's black burden seem more onerous and more sacrificial, and it made the black man's inherent inadequacy so obviously an element of his God-ordained culpability as to soften considerably his attitude toward the whites who suffered the Blacks to live among them and learn the ways of civilization. Those Blacks who drove their masters to church of a Sundays, handsomely dressed in the cast-off clothes of the Big House, and who were suffered to sit in the church galleries and listen to the white minister intone the virtues of black obedience and submission were too closely identified with the system to protest it. They developed a vested interest, small though it was, in the maintenance of things as they were. They shared the master's status, the master's discarded wealth, and the master's understanding of God's will for man, the distinctions God seemed to be making between white men and black men notwithstanding.

Hence the religion that developed in the white man's church was not a religion of protest. The "protest" in black religion comes from that other spiritual stream which flowed from the fount of the "Invisible Church," the cultus of that indigenous religion of the black diaspora that seeped through the soil of slavery and watered the hopes and aspirations of all those who would be free.

CALVIN B. MARSHALL III

In the latter part of the eighteenth century, a number of independent black churches were established because the white churches were inclined to be racist. From the beginning, these black churches were concerned with freedom for black people. In the twentieth century, however, some became "acculturated" and forgot their mission to the black community.

Black people in this country are said to illustrate one of four basic negative conditions: First is the *Afro-Saxon Mind*, which is "the psychological urge to be white"; second, the *Syndrome of the Colonized*, which is expressed by nonconfidence which characterizes the powerless majority; third, the *Slave Mentality,* which implies acceptance of the inferior status as God-ordained. Fourth is the *Super-Militant* or the *Right-On-Brother,* who has "superficial understanding of his present condition and little or no viable strategy for his future."

There is a fifth and positive condition, though: the *transcendent condition:* "Having transcended the past, embracing and understanding the present and moving toward the future with cold dispassionate precision on an agenda of black liberation, this group understands the potential value of the black church to the liberation movement." This attitude can be symbolized by the Cross and the Fist, adopted by the National Committee of Black Churchmen. The Reverend Calvin Bromlee Marshall III is pastor of the historic Varick Memorial African Methodist Episcopal Zion Church in Brooklyn, now known as the Church of Black Liberation. Varick is the "Mother Church" of the African Methodist Episcopal Zion denomination, founded by free Blacks who withdrew from the white John Street Methodist Church over the issue of segregation. However, the National Committee of Black Churches is made up largely of Blacks in the New York area who hold stiff positions in the national and international structures of the major white denominations. The Black Economic Development Conference produced the controversial "Black Manifesto" in 1966, calling for "reparations" from the churches and synagogues of America for their complicity in three centuries of black exploitation.

Marshall is the Chairman of the Board of the Black Economic Development Conference, Inc., and a member of the Executive Committee of the National Committee of Black Churchmen. He is Professor of Pastoral Care, the Institute of Black Ministries, the Conwell School of Theology in Philadelphia, Pennsylvania.

THE BLACK CHURCH—ITS MISSION IS LIBERATION

Source: Calvin B. Marshall, "The Black Church—Its Mission Is Liberation," *The Black Scholar,* Vol. 2, No. 4, December 1970, pp. 13–19.

In this article I shall attempt to set forth the role that the Black Church must play in the revolutionary struggle for the total liberation of black people.

Let me attempt to do so by setting forth certain guidelines or a particular context from which this article will be written. One, although I am cognizant that the black liberation movement is not confined to the

North American Continent, or the Western Hemisphere—I nevertheless shall write this article from this perspective. Secondly, being well aware of the fact that the Black Church is only one of the institutions in the black community, I nevertheless shall deal exclusively with the role of the Black Church in the struggle. This is not to be misunderstood that the Black Church is the only institution capable of bringing about black liberation. Thirdly, I shall constantly make references to the historical role of the African Methodist Episcopal Zion Church. I want it clearly understood that I am in no way setting forth this denomination as the only black denomination who has a history of involvement in the struggle, but I am simply using the A.M.E. Zion Church as an example because it is the denomination to which I belong and I am more familiar with its historical role and its contemporary role in the struggle for black liberation.

In the latter part of the eighteenth century, black people on the North American continent almost simultaneously began to secede from the white church establishments in this country and during that period the two major black Methodist denominations were founded. Historical records also set forth that independent black Baptist churches were also founded during this period of time. It is quite apparent to us as we study the history of the foundation of the Black Church that this phenomena took place not because of any great doctrinal, liturgical, philosophical or dogmatic disagreement with the white church institution, but purely and simply because Blacks became aware of the fact that, in spite of the Christian pronouncements on the part of the white church establishment, the white church was inextricably locked into slavery and racism.

Take for an instance the case of the A.M.E. Zion Church. James Varick, Peter Williams and others withdrew from the John Street Methodist Church, in New York City, in 1796. The immediate issue was the refusal to commune blacks at the chancel rail along with other communicants who happened to be white. This act became the straw that broke the camel's back so to speak. Nevertheless, it was not an isolated act, but just one of the more obvious ways in which the Methodist Church said to black people that you are inferior. James Varick and his followers withdrew and founded a church in a blacksmith's shop. From this humble beginning a denomination with more than a million members has come about.

Almost simultaneously Richard Allen withdrew from the Methodist Church in Philadelphia, essentially for the same reasons, and formed the

Bethel A.M.E. Church which today is the largest black episcopally governed church in America.

From its very beginning the A.M.E. Zion Church was dubbed the freedom church, and for one hundred years it produced some of the greatest freedom fighters that the race has ever known. Among them were such stalwart figures as Fred Douglass, Harriet Tubman, Sojourner Truth, Joseph Charles Price, James W. Hood and Alexander B. Walters. There is no doubt in my mind that the Zion Church from its beginning, up through the abolitionists movement, the Civil War, and Reconstruction, clearly saw itself as a church whose mission was one of liberation. One only has to read the life stories of some of her leaders and follow the minutes of many of her annual and general conferences to realize that the undergirding motivation of this organization was the acquisition of full freedom for the black man in America. Unfortunately, as the church entered the twentieth century other things and other priorities seemed to replace the burning zeal that the church once displayed for liberation.

Her record during the past seventy years, as it has to do with the liberation struggle, cannot match what her record was prior to this century. This characteristic, however, is not unique to any one single black denomination but seems to have been the fate that befell the entire black church movement in this country. Ironically, in this century the church increasingly sought to become more and more like the white church that she had cast off. To some degree it is understandable; yet to those of us who look at the Black Church today it is not justifiable. You see, the Black Church became very self-conscious and like individual black people she as an institution began to seek her legitimacy in the white community. She started to judge herself by white standards and her values became increasingly white as she sought her authenticity in that community, forgetting that she was authentic because black people are authentic; and in seeking approval from the broader white community the fires of liberation were dimmed, and she became increasingly more conservative. Her conservatism was seen in many ways, from the changing of her music to her emphasis on dignity, quietness in worship, seminary-trained clergy and organizations upon organizations. While these things are not necessarily negative in character, her preoccupation with the quest for more sophistication was becoming her very undoing. For while she sought to be integrated in the main stream of America, she forgot about her poor, about her hungry, about her sick, and about her imprisoned.

Being accepted by the National Council of Churches meant more to her than being accepted by the people of the black ghetto. Trips to the Holy Land became more important than trips through the streets of her impoverished neighborhoods—to see, to feel, to hear, and to taste the plight of her people. She became an organization of joiners; she built her structures, organized her self-indulgent programs and then opened her doors and invited good, orderly and decent people to come. She forgot that her mission was one of salvation-liberation and she ceased to be found in the arenas where men were struggling to throw off the yoke of oppression and slavery. She no longer understood her role in terms of revolution and change. She became status quo oriented and stagnant. In so doing, she not only betrayed her founding fathers but she betrayed the Christ whose gospel she yet claimed to be preaching. While generations of black preachers lost sight of the radical and revolutionary nature of the Christian gospel. They forgot that Jesus the Christ stood in opposition to the religious, political, and social status quo of his day because he found those positions to be oppressive and dehumanizing to his people. Somehow the meaning of the death of Christ was lost and simply relegated to the symbolic observance of breaking bread and sipping wine. We were able to talk about the crucifixion of Christ without really understanding that here was a radical, a revolutionary who was put to death for treason. Christ was an anarchist pure and simple. Christ was a Malcolm X. One of the reasons it became so easy for us to forget about the real reasons and the real meaning behind the death of Christ was the fact that if we could do so we would then absolve and remove ourselves from suffering and struggle.

This past summer, I was invited by the Christian Education Department of my denomination (A.M.E. Zion Church) to deliver a sermon at its quadrennial session held at Livingstone College. Since the theme of the conference was "The Black Experience" I chose the subject: "Arm Your Minds to Meet the Demands of the Struggle for Black Liberation." This sermon was based scripturally around first Peter, the fourth chapter. The chapter starts off with these words: "For as much then as Christ has suffered for us in the flesh—arm yourselves likewise with the same mind." This entire chapter deals with an admonition to the church to take up the mantle of struggle and it clearly sets forth that the church will be judged severely if she neglects to do so. The reactions to this sermon were varied. Some of the younger clergy, a few of the older clergy, along with a fairly large amount of lay people received it favorably and accepted the call that was issued to the church to re-enter the struggle for black liberation. Eleven of the twelve Bishops present in Salisbury, North Carolina, boycotted the sermon because of my reputation as the troublemaker in Zion Church. One older clergyman who was in attendance referred to the sermon as the insane tirade of a demented mad man. Subsequent to the Salisbury experience, a four-column article appeared in the A.M.E. Zion weekly newspaper, *The Star of Zion,* blasting me and some of my colleagues, including a Bishop of the church, who were vocal in the cause for black liberation at the Salisbury Conference.

The issue facing the majority of black churchmen and black churches is, Will we or will we not involve ourselves in the struggle for black liberation? Fortunately, we have but one choice, for if the Black Church is to survive she must enter the arena of struggle. If she does not do so, her existence is indeed irrelevant and her demise will be welcomed. For no institution needs to exist in the midst of black people unless it is inextricably bound to the liberation struggle of our people. Many churchmen see this and certainly the growth and development of the National Committee of Black Churchmen is indicative of this insight. The involvement of key black churchmen in the development of the Black Economic Development Conference, Inc., their support of the programmatic demands of the Black Manifesto, lends credence to the fact that there are black churchmen who understand the role that the Black Church must play in the liberation struggle. The life generated by these churchmen gives us some assurance that there is viability within the Black Church and that it can be moved, in spite of tremendous opposition, into the very core of the struggle. For it should indeed be the very core and hub around which the struggle exists, given its historical role on the North American Continent.

One of the well-known prayers to be found in Methodist-Episcopal liturgy is the prayer known as the prayer for "all sorts and conditions of men." It beseeches God to meet man in whatever conditions that man happens to be found in. The Black Church as she is moved toward the struggle for black liberation must meet the needs of various sorts and relate to black men in various conditions. There are four conditions that I would like to set forth in which the majority of black people find themselves in the Western Hemisphere at this moment in history.

After stating the four conditions which are essentially negative, the fifth condition which is essentially positive will be obvious. The first condition I would like to deal with is the *Afro-Saxon Mind.* Many black people in America and the Caribbean are suffering from what I choose to term the Afro-Saxon Mentality. These people usually think of themselves as being middle class and in many instances tend to be more affluent than the average black, although this is not always true. An example of this is the fact that one can observe a minor civil servant or shop clerk in Barbados or Jamaica who might not be making more than twenty-five dollars a week, and yet these persons are afflicted with the Afro-Saxon Mentality. Color is still very much a factor, especially in the Caribbean, with those who are infected with this disease. In America some of the symptoms of those who are suffering from this disease is preoccupation with getting out of the black ghetto and into integrated neighborhoods, joining interracial churches, country clubs, yacht clubs, etc. In short, achieving all of the status and success symbols of the white community.

The Afro-Saxon Mentality is the psychological urge to be white, and so strong is the urge that men who have black faces and who have suffered the reality of the black condition yet seemingly can brush aside their blackness and embrace values that are white. It is fair and accurate to say that most black people in America beyond the age of twenty, at one period or another, have suffered from this malady. For it affects us in so many subtle ways. And even those of us who are liberated in our minds can remember at some point of our lives being influenced by the white man's standards of beauty and by his standards of right and wrong. Many black people of all ages, from various backgrounds, are still thinking with the white man's mind, although we have pointed out that the so-called black middle class seemed to succumb to this malady more easily than their less affluent brothers. It must also be noted that many poor Blacks are yet struggling for the day when they can become integrated, white, and acceptable.

The Afro-Saxon condition is a problem of identity and of values. Those black people who are still thinking, acting and reacting white are simply doing so because they have never achieved, or have lost, a sense of identity. One of the reasons the Black Church opted from the struggle for liberation was because it lost its sense of identity and in losing its black identity it assumed a white identity. The identity crisis also can be seen in the difficulty we encounter when we try to organize people around political, social and economic issues in the black community. Take for an example the school problem in the Oceanhill-Brownsville section of Brooklyn in 1968 where a valiant struggle was waged for community control of the schools. The reason why the black community lost this struggle was simply because the so-called big black preachers did not see it as their struggle. The frugal West Indian homeowners in the area did not see it as their struggle and most of the "good middle-class, church-going" black people did not see it as their struggle and could not identify with it. It was seen as the struggle of some loud-mouth welfare mothers, a few young radical black preachers with their white liberal Clergy sympathizers, and the struggle of the black militants.

What was misunderstood or, more correctly, what was never understood on the part of the black community in Brooklyn about the Oceanhill-Brownsville struggle is that we were struggling for power. Political power, financial power, and self-determinative power. What happened in the Oceanhill-Brownsville situation is characteristic of the kind of behavior that one can expect in a community when many of its people have black faces but white minds. For the Afro-Saxon Mentality is devisive, it alienates us from one another and it causes us to have an inflated sense of our own value while it destroys our sense of real community. The greatest challenge to the Black Church as we move it back into the struggle is the sickness of identity for most of the people to be found in most of our churches that are plagued with Afro-Saxon Minds.

The second condition that faces the Black Church as it seeks to relate to the problems of black people is the *Syndrome of the Colonized*. We must come to understand that many black people who are poor, who are living in the ghetto, and are eking out a living in the rural South, who seem to lack the incentive to improve their conditions are suffering from the Colonized Mentality. Although many of them consciously will proclaim that they are as good as and equal to any other people, long years of powerlessness in the black condition causes them subconsciously to see themselves as an inferior breed. There is a resignation to conditions as they are and a sense of nonconfidence in their ability to take into their own hands their social, educational, and political destiny. Many of us who have been mentally liberated would accuse me of sounding like a patronizing white social-scientist, however, let me cite an example that can be duplicated again and again in urban ghettos across this country.

This summer through our storefront ministries program (a center operated by Varick Memorial A.M.E. Zion Church and the Black Economic Development Conference, Inc., located some eight blocks from the church at the eastern edge of Bedford-Stuyvesant), the ministerial staff of our church tried to organize an eight-tenant-apartment building for a rent strike. After weeks of talking, pleading, and reassuring the tenants of that particular building, we were only able to get two tenants to go along with the strike. The opinion of the other six was—although the living conditions were deplorable: broken stairways, inadequate electricity, faulty plumbing, lack of heat in winter, etc.—there was very little that they could do about it and they expressed fear of getting into legal trouble and of getting dispossessed and not having anywhere to live. Here is an example of people caught in a black ghetto, a black colony that is being exploited every day by white merchants, tradesmen, landlords, and politicians and who feel completely powerless in and of themselves to reverse these conditions. Using the same example, the two tenants who did withhold their rent, indicates that with the proper kind of involvement, assistance, and assurance from the church, colonized people will begin to move no matter how minute these movements might be in the beginning.

It is this great host of people that the Black Church has most conspicuously neglected and it is among those people that we must find our credibility. For to be found in this number are the welfare families, the households that are headed by women, the alcoholic husbands, the teenage drop-outs and dope addicts, and the sons who are being slaughtered in Vietnam. This is the *powerless majority*—these are the superfluous people. They constitute the church's mission.

The third condition are those who are afflicted with the *Slave Mentality*. Unlike those who are living under the Colonized Syndrome, there are Blacks who feel that their inferior status has been indeed decreed by heaven and they are justly proud of being orderly and knowing their place. They bear more resemblance to the Afro-Saxon mentality than to the Colonized Mind. However, the marked difference between them and the Afro-Saxon is that they do not delude themselves with the notion that they have entered into the mainstream of white society. They are contented in being the good, God-fearing, patriotic colored servants. That state of servitude can be seen from the loyal colored maid, to the one small town Midwestern colored doctor who it tickled to death that his white masters recognize him and allow him to be their token nigger on the staff of the local general hospital, although it is painful for us to admit, far too many Blacks still are caught up and willingly so in the Slave Mentality.

I recall an incident going back only a few years when as a young pastor in the city of Peekskill, New York, I took exception with the treatment that was accorded a group of young black people from my church in a local restaurant by its proprietor. I subsequently wrote a letter to the local newspaper complaining about the racial abuses that were heaped upon us. The letter caused some furor in the town and a great deal of negative reactions from many of the officials of my church. I was told by one of the Trustees of the church that I was a troublemaker, that our young black people were disorderly, that the white people of Peekskill were among the best white people to be found anywhere and if we would stay in our place we would get along alright and not have any trouble from white folks. In the eight years from 1960 to 1968 that I pastored in this town and sought to give leadership to the black community, I engendered similar reactions from so-called decent, law-abiding Negroes at least two or three times a year. Unfortunately, many of those contented serfs still populate the Black Church and they are probably the group that stands in the greatest opposition to the church becoming a relevant viable tool for black liberation. However, the Black Church can no longer listen to this white Jesus crowd and in spite of them the church has to be moved forward on a black agenda. It will necessitate in some instances moving them aside, going over them, undermining them, but whatever is necessary to be done must be done to shake the Black Church loose from those who are plagued by this Slave Mentality.

The fourth condition is that of the *Super-Militant* or the *Right-On-Brother*. The Super-Militant or the Right-On-Brother is usually a graduate of one of the three categories that I have described. In most cases, however, he would more than likely be one of those who has thrown off the Colonized Mentality and now absolutely rejects everything about his past. He possesses a very superficial understanding of his present condition and little or no viable strategy for his future. His rhetoric is often what he calls revolutionary, and he is convinced that ideologies formulated in other times, in other places, by other people under other circumstances can be adopted and superimposed upon black people as they struggle for liberation. He tends to be young, between fifteen and thirty, and he tends to adopt a very distinctive kind of life style. Very often he will wear a natural or Afro hairstyle and a beard. In some instances he will adopt an African name and African dress. He talks violence, and in some isolated instances practices violence, in almost all cases without any programmed and strategic patterns for his violence. Consequently, he is more successful in bringing about additional violence on the heads of black people than he is in the perpetration of violence against the oppressor. He, in short, goes bear hunting with a switch. He very often expresses a total rejection of the Black Church and writes Christianity off as a white man's religion. When he is challenged on this score, it becomes quite apparent that he has little awareness of the history of the Christian Church and does not realize that black people were involved with the church from its inception.

In most instances the average black churchman, and churchgoer, is afraid of him and intimidated by him because although "his thing" is not all together, the average churchman, or churchgoer, is coming from a position that is equally unreal and, therefore, cannot counter the arguments, accusations and abuses hurled against them by the Right-On-Brother or the Super-Militant.

The young people that I have described with all of their faults yet probably produce the most vocal and active challenge to the Black Church and are potentially the best allies that the church can find as she moves toward the struggle for black liberation. One thing that they clearly know and understand is that something is wrong. Their powerlessness has led them to anger. Their anger has forced them to grope for their identity and for answers to the question of being. They reject what has been, and violently so. They do not possess the answers; they have not found the viable strategy, yet on the other hand they seek not to be white. They refused to be colonized. Slavery is an abomination to them and liberation is a burning quest for them. The Black Church must open its arms to the militant. The Black Church must seek to embrace the Panthers, the Five Pereneters, the Republic of New Africa, etc. For we must be mindful that these groups and individuals have moved into the vacuum that once was filled by the Black Church.

I have just described four conditions that are essentially negative conditions. In doing so I have attempted to point out how each of these conditions present a challenge to the Black Church to move forward in the struggle for black liberation. The fifth and obvious condition that now faces the Black Church is a very positive one. There is an increasing number of serious radical no-nonsense black people in America. They represent a wide age range and they come from the streets and they come from the universities. They come from various black institutions, including the church, and the thing that bands them together is their uncompromising commitment to black liberation. They exist in the *transcendent condition*. Having transcended the past, embracing and understanding the present and moving toward the future with cold dispassionate precision on an agenda of black liberation, this group understands the potential value of the Black Church to the liberation movement, but at the same time it will ruthlessly reject itself and will be led in this rejection by radical black churchmen themselves.

We call upon the Black Church to cease being a sounding brass and a tinkling symbol. We call upon the church to reinterpret itself in the light of its historical past and to seek its legitimacy and its authenticity in terms of the liberation struggle.

The Cross and the Fist

It is quite appropriate that the most viable group of churchmen in this country, the National Committee of Black Churchmen, have adopted for their symbol the Cross and the Fist. For the one is symbolic of struggle and the other is symbolic of a unity and a power that must be brought to bear if our struggle for liberation will be successful. The Black Church must understand again the meaning of the cross. We must understand that salvation and liberation only comes as we commit ourselves to struggle. We must reject many of the programs that we have been giving our money, our time, and our energies to. For it is the role of the church to struggle against the forces of injustice and to struggle against the structural inequity of this society. It is not our role simply to have programs to build large sanctuaries, to have beautiful services, and then return to business as usual. What we must be doing is struggling day by day against the social, political, and economic forces of depression within this society, to liberate our people. In clenched fist we must work to bring about the unity of black people, for in unity there is power and in power there is the ability to bring about change. The Black Churches' only Mission at the beginning of the seventh decade of the twentieth century is Black Liberation.

ALBERT B. CLEAGE, JR.

To be black in a world dominated by whites is to experience an unrelieved succession of indignities; to be disadvantaged in every area; to meet obstacles at every turn. Hence, the black man must have his own religion, for religion and its church must meet the peculiar needs of the people who espouse it. Religion is not fixed; it changes with the times and with the needs of its practitioners. In America, the church was developed to meet the needs of white people, and the black man's mistake has been a prolonged attempt to work within the framework of the white man's religion, a religion not conceived in his interests or with his needs in mind. "If religion doesn't meet the needs of the people, religion is nothing, and if it's geared to meet the needs of some other people, that doesn't help you any."

Cleage maintains that Israel was a black nation, that the Bible was written by Black Jews, and that the Old Testament is the history of Black Jews. "Jesus was a Black Messiah. He came to free a black people from the oppression of white gentiles."

Dr. Cleage has become the most articulate spokesman for Christian black nationalism since Marcus Garvey. Well-educated, urbane and soft-spoken, Cleage is not a man to be dismissed peremptorily. For twenty years his ministry was in mainline churches committed to the principle of racially integrated memberships. Today his followers are all black and can be found throughout America.

Albert Cleage, Jr., is a clergyman of the United Church of Christ and pastor of the Shrine of the Black Madonna in Detroit.

A NEW TIME RELIGION

Source: Albert B. Cleage, Jr., *The Black Messiah* (New York: Sheed and Ward, Inc., 1971), pp. 100–14.

I want to talk about the Church and what it means to be black in a white man's world. Our scripture reading is a very simple one. It says, if you have come into your neighbor's power, you have to do something to get out of it. You have to stay awake. "Give your eyes no sleep, and your eyelids no slumber. Save yourself like a gazelle from the hunter." Then, down a little farther, in the tenth verse, "A little sleep, a little slumber, a little folding of the hands to rest, and poverty will come upon you like a vagabond and want like an armed man." I just want you to think about those words as we consider the Church and its relevance to black people in today's world.

I was in a barbershop recently and everyone was arguing about religion. The interesting thing to me was that each one was arguing against some religion he had heard preached down home someplace. The one arguing the loudest came from West Virginia, and he must have had a real wind-burner in his church when he was a boy. The dangers of hell fire had scared him half to death every Sunday morning, and he still hasn't recovered. As soon as anyone admitted that he was a Christian, he would start arguing with things that preacher back in West Virginia said thirty years ago. He didn't have any idea that Christianity could be anything other than the gospel preached in his little home-town church.

The Church has come a long way in thirty years. I don't mean the whole church. I know a lot of preachers who are preaching just like they were thirty years ago in some little country church in West Virginia. But we have come a long way in what we expect of a church because we have come a long way in the kind of problems we face and the kind of questions we are trying to grapple with. "What does it mean to be black in a white man's world?" is a new problem for us. Just a little while ago we refused to recognize this. We wouldn't admit that it was a white man's world because as far as we were concerned we were all white together. Some of us were just a little "dark white." So today, when we talk about the problem of being black in a white man's world, we have changed our whole position. We no longer identify with the white man and think of ourselves as being a part of his world. Now we know that we are a separate black people. We have a separate culture and a separate history. We realize this today and we are not ashamed of it. We have come a long way, and these changes which are taking place in our thinking impose strange new demands upon the Black Church.

What does it mean to be black in a white man's world? Obviously it means that we have difficulties everywhere we turn, because black people are powerless and white people are powerful and are ruthless in the use of their power to maintain white supremacy in a white racist world. It means that in every area of life we are disadvantaged and must be able to survive and move ahead against overwhelming obstacles. The Black Church must understand our dilemma and must offer leadership in complex areas totally unknown to the down-home, fire-and-brimstone preacher.

The Black Church must offer leadership in areas in which most of us are confused if it is to survive. Few of us really understand what it means to be black in a white man's world. Many of us are just getting over the illusion that we are a part of the white man's world. Because we don't realize our powerlessness, we are confused. A black person will talk logically for five minutes and then he will say the most absurd things because he refuses to accept the obvious implications of things he knows to be true.

The most ignorant people I have talked to since the Detroit Rebellion have been black professional people. They could have been living thirty years ago. Many of them haven't changed one iota in their thinking. They can sit there in their silk suits and be just as out of touch with reality as a small-town black preacher. Obviously we cannot expect them to play any part in the struggle to make the Black Church relevant.

One group kept arguing all night that I was unfair to them because I tell people that the black middle class is not doing its part. I said, "That's right, you're not doing your part." They contended that just living and maintaining their position was a real contribution. They hadn't even begun to face the implication of being black in a white man's world. They were black on the outside but just as white as they could be on the inside. Oh, they knew in a vague kind of way that they were black. They knew there were whole areas of life which were closed to them. But they hadn't faced its implications.

The Black Church faces this kind of confusion in the black community as it seeks to face the problem of being black. These people will tear up a church, or leave it, if the preacher talks too much about racial problems or the struggle to get black power. They will admit that they don't believe in anything all black.

What does it mean to be black in a white man's world? A black mother called me last week. Her boy had gone to school dressed in an African Dashiki and the principal had called him in and told him that he couldn't wear it because it was disrupting the school. The boy said, "This is the dress of my people, I have a right to wear it if I want to." He tried to tell the principal about the black man's heritage and suggested that if the Irish can wear green ties on St. Patrick's Day, he could wear an African Dashiki. The principal expelled him. So the mother put on her African outfit and went to talk to the principal. She told him more about the history and culture of Africa than he cared to know until the principal finally said, "Let's forget the whole thing. He can wear anything he wants to wear." But the mother said, "I'm not about to forget it, now that you brought it up." And she talked to him all afternoon.

This is another response to being black in a white man's world. This boy was black. His African Dashiki and his African heritage meant something to him, and the white man is not used to any black person having something of his own that means anything to him. Now the boy is back in school, and a whole lot of other black boys and girls are wearing Dashikis because they know the man doesn't like them. The Black Church, too, must speak to the needs of black people who are proud of their African heritage.

But we are confused on so many things. The Black Teacher's Workshop, a very advanced group of black teachers, invited some black young people to present their ideas. Some of the young people thought that getting skills, learning something, was important, but some of the college-age "black nationalists" thought that all you had to do was to "come out of your black thing." One of the kids suggested, "I still think it would be better if we came out of our black thing knowing something." The younger kids were right in wanting the schools to teach them skills. They wanted Afro-American history and Swahili, but in addition, they wanted to be learning skills to equip them to fit into the twentieth century.

It is not enough to just learn how black you are. That's the problem of being black in a white man's world. You have to stop and figure out what's important at every step of the way. Both the young folks were sincere and the older folks were sincere. The problem wasn't that they were not sincere. It's difficult to be black in a white man's world and know what to do all the time. You have to figure it out, you have to think, to plan, to plot. Being black in a white man's world is not easy and the Black Church cannot survive if it tries to ignore the problem and pretend that it does not exist.

Our young people went down to the anti-war demonstration in Washington. My daughter went. She said that there was a beautiful black contingent. They insisted on going in their own buses and when they got there they had a separate place to meet, a black caucus. There were hundreds of black young people from all over the country, from as far away as Los Angeles and San Francisco. And there they faced it again, How can you be black in a white man's world? Should they march on the Pentagon with the white kids and get whipped up in an integrated protest? And they had to sit down and argue it out right there before they could do a thing. They had gone to Washington, but they were not sure exactly what they wanted to do. Finally, they decided, "This is the white man's thing. Let them go get whipped up about their thing at the Pentagon, and we'll get whipped up about our thing somewhere else."

So they paraded and had their own separate black anti-war demonstration. They tied up traffic all over Washington. They marched to Howard University and held a rally there. Black young people had their own caucus and made their own decisions. Every time I see black folks getting together, trying to figure something out, I know it's a problem. And it's not going to be something that is all cut and dried. We have to think every minute, and we have to figure every minute. And we are going to have differences, but as long as we are trying to decide it in terms of what is best for us, it's going to come out all right. The Black Church must become a part of this important decision-making that black people are doing everywhere and in every area of life.

What is the role of the Black Church in all that is happening, where nothing is just accepted at face value? Can the Black Church adjust and survive, or must it be destroyed and rebuilt from the ashes? As black people begin to re-evaluate, they more and more tend to kick out religion and the Church. They say this is a white man's thing. He has used it to keep us in subjection all these years. We'll just put it aside and forget it. That is just one of the many problems we must figure out if we are to survive as black men in this white man's world.

I would like to suggest that we approach the problem of the Black Church in a much too unsophisticated way. The role of the Church and religion is always adjusted to meet the needs of a people. Religion is not just something that goes on the same way from the beginning of time right on down. Religion and the Church constantly shift to meet the needs of a people. Religion isn't the same today as it was thirty years ago, a hundred years or two hundred years ago. It is shifting and changing all the time. One of the things that confuses us when we talk about religion is that we tend to think of it as something fixed, final and settled. The man in the barbershop was arguing about a religion that he heard preached thirty years ago, but he thinks it's the same today.

Once there was a unified Christian Church which dominated the Western world. The Church told kings what they could do, and if a king got out of line, the Pope made him crawl for miles to beg forgiveness. The Church was really running things then. That was the old Roman Catholic Church which existed before the Protestant Reformation. The Protestants broke away from the Catholic Church, and today, Protestants give a lot of reasons to explain why they broke away. The Catholics were corrupt and immoral and a whole lot of bad things were going on. But that wasn't enough to make folks break away. You know yourself that a whole lot can go on in a church and everybody will just look the other way. There had to be a logical reason why so many people found so many reasons to get out of the Catholic Church at this particular time.

I am suggesting that this split had to do with the simple fact that the Church must adjust to meet the needs of the people. The Protestants, with their Reformation, placed a new emphasis upon the rights of the individual. In the old Catholic Church, the individual didn't have much in the way of rights. The Church, the institution, the group had the power. The individual was forced to conform. People in general were getting tired of conformity and restrictions. The Protestant Reformation merely gave expression to the growing desire of people to free themselves from this monolithic church which controlled everything. The Protestant Reformation declared the freedom of the individual.

Freedom is a funny thing. Protestants declared the individual's right to worship according to the dictates of his conscience. But freedom, once announced, could not be restricted. So the Reformation declared the freedom of the individual in many other areas: his freedom to get rich, his freedom to exploit, and his freedom to take whatever he wanted. The other side of Protestantism was capitalism, with each individual having the right to do almost anything necessary to make a profit. And in the artistic and intellectual areas also, books, paintings, poems and music began to reflect the chaos of individual revolt. Obviously people wanted something new. They wanted a change. They wanted individual freedom from the restraints of an institutionalized omnipresent God.

The Church can always justify the changes it is forced to make. When the people wanted freedom from the control of a powerful church, they went back to the Apostle Paul, the evangelist of individualism. Every time Martin Luther, the leader of the Protestant Reformation, sat down to search out an escape from church power and domination, he would always go back to the Apostle Paul. Finally he found the phrase he needed, "We are saved by faith," and he said, "That's it! The Church can't save you. Each individual is saved by himself. We are saved by faith." He took this little concept of individual salvation and made a revolution out of it. Do you know why people paused to listen to this almost meaningless half-truth? Because they wanted freedom from the control of the Church and here was a man who said: "You aren't saved by the Church; you are saved by your own faith." And they said, "Lord, that is what I have been waiting to hear somebody say." And so the whole Protestant thing came into being. "We are saved by faith." Each individual decides everything for himself. The Bible is a sufficient rule of faith and conduct, as interpreted by the individual. The Church doesn't decide. You read the Bible and the Holy Spirit tells you what's right and what's wrong.

This pure individualism was so extreme that Protestant churches never really accepted it in practice, after the organization of Protestant churches. In today's world, society borders on chaos as a result of this Protestant individualism. Individualism merely means that each individual feels that he is the most important thing in the world. Your whole life is built on getting what you can for yourself as an individual and getting ahead as an individual. Your concern for your little family is merely an extension of your self-centered individualism. Today, the whole fabric of society is falling apart because there are so many individuals who have no sense of unity. There is no cement to hold society together. The Hippies reject a decadent society. Many motion pictures portray the step-by-step disillusionment of society and contribute to it. In this kind of world, the Church seeks to hold back the tide by trying to come back together. The Church Universal broke up because people wanted to be free, wanted to be individuals. Today, people are sick of being free, sick of being individuals, and so the Church is trying to find its way back together. This is the ecumenical movement. Denominations merging and making little flirting gestures toward Rome, suggesting that maybe we can all come back together and have one big church that can dominate the world again. Today, people are looking for the kind of security which a unified church might offer. The very simple fact is that people make the Church serve their needs.

In the United States the Church was developed to meet the white man's needs. He decided what it should be. He decided the form, the structure, the theology, everything. The black man's church has tried to work within the framework of the white man's decisions because we were so hell-bent on being integrated that anything he said had to be right. Only recently have we begun to understand that the whole development of the Christian Church has been something the white man was building for himself. We have been going along with the program and making only minor modifications to suit our own needs. Everywhere the Black Church tries to be like the white man's church. They go through the motions and the more education black worshipers have, the harder they try. They even try to copy the dead emptiness of the white folks' service, the little rhythmless songs with nothing to pat your foot to all through the service.

Have you ever heard a black preacher trying to sound white? He gets up and tries to whisper at you and tell you how nice everything is. That's only in churches for well-to-do black folks who don't go to church often, anyway. This is the most ridiculous black church there ever was because it doesn't have any relationship to the needs of black people at all. We don't like the music. We don't like the preaching. We don't like anything about it and the only black people who attend are black people who have a need to pretend that they really like to do things the same way white folks do them. A black church which is a copy of the white church cannot meet any of our needs. Some black folks take pride in sitting through a service and saying to themselves as they suffer, "If white folks came in here, they wouldn't know that this was not a white Church." They think that that's the highest compliment they can give themselves. Sometimes they even put a white preacher on the staff to make the illusion complete. It is as completely ridiculous as it is pathetic.

Now, the old down-home churches, Baptist, Methodist, or what have you, were in a sense a replica of white folks' religion. But there we took white folks' Christianity, twisted it around and made it fit at least a few of our needs. When you worship in a down-home black church, at least you feel good. The music is good, you can jump up and down, you can shout and feel free—free like you are home. To help you feel good and release tension is meeting at least some need. You caught hell all week. The white man was driving you, and all week you have wanted to tell him off but you couldn't because you didn't want to lose your job. You took insults because you didn't want to get whipped up and go to jail, and on Sunday you just let yourself go.

So the uneducated black preacher who can "shout" a congregation on Sunday morning is more meaningful than the most sophisticated middle-class black pastor who whispers a sermon that's unrelated to anything in the black man's experience because he is trying to sound like a white minister. If it doesn't meet the needs of a people, religion is nothing, and if it's geared to meet the needs of some other people, that doesn't help you any. There was a whole lot in the old time black church that was good. It was built wrong because we didn't know any better then. But it tried to satisfy the needs of black people. All the shouting and emotionalism that people laugh about offered an escape from oppression and we had to have some kind of escape. From somewhere we had to have some kind of escape. From somewhere we had to find the strength to get through another week.

We had sex and alcohol on Saturday night and church on Sunday morning. All week we would be waiting for Saturday night and Sunday morning. We don't have to be ashamed of that because it is the truth. If we hadn't had Saturday night and Sunday morning, we never would have made it this far. We took the white man's individualism, turned it around and made it an escape from oppression. On Sunday morning we would feel good together. We didn't have to talk about the problems of the world. In fact, we didn't want to talk about them. We just talked about up yonder and Jesus taking care of us. And we knew that one of these days God was going to shake the white man over hell-fire and take us up to heaven through the Pearly Gates. It was such a wonderful thought that God was just. We knew that if God was just, there was no place but heaven for us. We could look at the white man all week and we knew where he was going. He was headed straight for hell.

Besides, we never had money enough to get from payday to payday, and that's still true for most of us. The Black Church offered deliverance. You came to church, you were broke, you were hungry, you had no job, you were sick or whatever it was and the Church offered you deliverance. God delivered a whole lot of us a lot of times. You can't explain it, but things would happen, and we would say, "God did it." That is why the Black Church was valid. It related to the needs of black people.

Why did this down-home black church put so much emphasis on sin, little petty sins like drinking, fornicating and adultery? Because the Church knew that there was not only Sunday morning but there was also Saturday night. And a people seeking escape from oppression might very easily make Saturday night extend over the entire week. Then the Church could not have saved and delivered them on Sunday morning. The Black Church was preaching to the real everyday needs of black people. The Church had to keep black people from going too far in finding escape through sins of the flesh.

So the down-home black church was not irrelevant to the needs of black people, but it met those needs only partially and superficially because essentially it was but a slight modification of the white church; it taught black people that they had been saved by a white Jesus because of the love of a white God. It could not come to grips with the black man's powerlessness. The white man's church and religion are designed to meet *his* needs, not ours. We cannot borrow a church which meets our needs from the white man. The white man's church is inescapably an instrument for the preservation of white power. The

Black Church must be something different—separate and apart from the white church—because black people and white people have different needs.

Let me say it this way. The oppressor, the white man, needs a religion that gives him an opportunity to find escape from the guilt of his oppression. He knows that his oppression is destroying black people all week. He knows that he is responsible for a system of oppression that keeps little black children in inferior schools. He knows that everything he does is designed to reduce black men to permanent powerlessness and inferiority. He needs a religion that can give him escape from these feelings of guilt. His religion has to give him an individual escape from guilt. The white Christian finds the basis for this religion in the New Testament, in the Epistles of the Apostle Paul. He must find escape from the guilt of white racism in a faith in universal brotherhood. This faith provides "escape techniques" for the white Christian, without in any way endangering white power and domination.

A white Christian can go out into the community and do little brotherhood acts. He can fight for "open occupancy." He can do little, almost meaningless acts of face-to-face kindness which in no way touch the problem of the black man's powerlessness. That's his religion.

But our religion is something different. The black man's religion is essentially based on the Old Testament concepts of the Nation Israel, God's chosen people, and our knowledge that the problems of the black Israelites were the same as ours. When we read the Old Testament, we can identify with a black people who were guided and loved by God. Everything in the Old Testament speaks directly to our problem.

We know that Israel was a black nation and that descendants of the original Black Jews are in Israel, Africa, and the Mediterranean area today. The Bible was written by Black Jews. The Old Testament is the history of Black Jews. The first three Gospels, Matthew, Mark, and Luke, tell the story of Jesus, retaining some of the original material which establishes the simple fact that Jesus built upon the Old Testament. Jesus was a Black Messiah. He came to free a black people from the oppression of the white Gentiles. We know this now to be a fact. Our religion, our preaching, our teachings all come from the Old Testament, for we are God's chosen people. God is working with us every day, helping us find a way to freedom. Jesus tried to teach the Nation Israel how to come together as a black people, to be brothers one with another and to stand against their white oppressors.

There is no way in the world that a black man can teach the same thing in his church that the white man teaches in his church. The white man is not going to admit that Jesus was black. He is going to twist history to make it fit the pattern of white supremacy. He will continue to paint pictures of Jesus looking the way he wants him to look. He knows that all of those pictures painted during the Middle Ages are lies. He knows that the religious films which have come out of Hollywood are all white supremacy lies. Jesus was black, and he did *not* preach universal love. Remember the white Gentile woman who came to Jesus asking him to heal her daughter? "I don't have time to waste with Gentiles. I have come to the house of Israel," Jesus said.

Our whole religion, then, since we are black people, becomes different. There are many ways to say it. God is trying to help people stand up as men, and if anything in our religion makes us less than men, there is something wrong with our religion. *God says that we are created in his image. That means that we have to have some kind of power. You can't stand up as a man if you are powerless. That means that the Black Church must dedicate itself to the task of building Black Power. Don't worry because white folks are afraid of the words "Black Power." Say "Black Christian Power," if you want, because that is what it amounts to. Black God-given Power.* That is what we are talking about. God wants his chosen people to have power because if they don't have power, they are slaves. They are sick because there's no way to live without power and be well.

It is God's will, then. If God created us in his own image, he doesn't want us running around acting like lap dogs for white people. He wants us to stand up and be men, to fight for the things that belong to us, to build a heritage to hand on to our black children. This is what God wants. This is what we have to preach from the black pulpit. We can't really care what white people are preaching. They can be talking about brotherhood and love, day in and day out, but black people must learn to love one another. The white man stands separated from God by his oppression. God cannot look with favor upon the white man. If *we* can see that he acts like a beast, what must God think of him? When God looks down upon the white man, what can he say? He's oppressing everybody in sight; he's abusing people; he's robbing them of manhood. That is the white man's sin, so what can the white man do to rid himself of that sin? He must seek brotherhood and universal love. He must rid himself of this thing which he is doing. An oppressor is always in a peculiar relationship with God because he's filled with guilt.

Our relationship with God as black men also makes special demands upon us. God is disgusted with us because we have crawled too long. God did not intend for us to accept slavery and oppression for almost four hundred years. God has been ashamed of us for those four hundred years. God demands that we fight; that we throw off the shackles of bondage now; that we stand up as free men now; that we come together as black brothers now, in the cause of black freedom. We must fight, and die if need be, that black people may be free with the power to stay free. This is what God demands of black men.

So God is demanding different things of black men and white men. Don't let white people confuse you. Everytime I speak some place, they say, "You're a preacher; you shouldn't be talking about power." I tell them, "You do what God wants you to do. You get down on your knees and ask forgiveness for all of the sins you have committed against black people, but don't ask me to get down there with you, because God is asking something different of me." That's why our church here, The Shrine of the Black Madonna, is so important. We are pointing the Black Church in a new direction. We understand where we are going and why.

To the Black Revolution we bring the stabilizing influence of the religion of the Black Messiah, Jesus Christ. The Black Revolution is not going any farther than the Black Church enables it to go, by giving it a foundation, a philosophy, and a direction.

Angry, frustrated black people running up and down the street are not going to make a Black Revolution. Our Black Revolution depends for success upon a people who are welded together into a Black Nation and who can fight together because they share a common faith. That's why this church is so important. We are the wave of the future. The Black Church is in the process of being reborn, and we, here, are participants in that tremendous beginning. It is hard to be a black man in a white man's world. But if you don't have a black man's religion and if you can't be a part of a black man's church, it's almost impossible.

Heavenly Father, we thank thee for this fellowship, for the opportunity of coming together in thy house as black brothers and sisters dedicated to the accomplishment of thy will, the freeing of thy people everywhere. Give us the courage, the wisdom, the unity, and the love for each other, necessary to accomplish this task. Bless this Church and bless this house, that we may be in fact thy chosen people. Help us that we may follow in the footsteps of the Black Messiah, thy Son, our Lord and Savior, Jesus Christ. Give each of us

*the courage to do the things which must be done. Give us the
courage, if we are not yet a part of the Black Nation, to come forward,
as we open the doors of the Church, and become followers of the
Black Messiah. Give us the courage to wipe from our hearts and
minds those little twinges of Uncle Tomism that still linger there.
Help us to come forward and say: "I am not ashamed to worship a
black Jesus." Help us, God, as we open the doors of the Church that
people here and now may feel the persuasive touch of thy spirit.
These things we ask in his name. Amen.*

PRESTON N. WILLIAMS

Professor Williams offers the black theologian one of two alternatives:
loyalty to a God concerned with the oppressed, most of whom happen to
be black, or loyalty to Blacks, most of whom happen to be oppressed.
Williams opts for loyalty to God rather than to a racial group. The
Black Revolution must be based on universal principles which "will
provide adequate bases for the participation of all men"—an alternative
which "relies upon beliefs and values associated with the Christian faith
and American constitutional principles." Williams cautions Blackamericans to realize that they "are included within the American Dream
and that white Americans will seek to procure the black man's full
equality as a citizen."

However, the ultimate protection for the black man's human rights
is not in "democratic constitutionalism" but in the creative act of
God. White Americans *are* responsible for their historical malfeasance
respecting Blacks, and "liberation of the black man requires reparations
as well as promise-keeping." Yet, despite the soundness of the reparations idea, James Forman's Black Manifesto missed the point, for
"Blacks are not seeking a worn-out Marxist-Leninism to replace a
worn-out capitalism."

Preston N. Williams is a Professor in the Harvard University
Divinity School.

THE PROBLEM OF A BLACK ETHIC

Source: Preston N. Williams, "The Problem of a Black Ethic,"
The Harvard Theological Review, Vol. 65, No. 4, October 1972.

Either one is loyal to the God who works on behalf of the oppressed, most of whom happen to be black, or one is loyal to the Blacks, most of whom may be oppressed and some of whom may have a peculiar place in the plan of God for this day. My alternative is loyalty to God or whatever symbol may stand for the ultimate and eternal source of meaning and value. Rather than argue about how black should be used in ethics or what is the nature of the loyalty owed to the black community, I shall offer an alternative way of stating the revolutionary demand of Blacks. Hopefully it will motivate Blacks to continue vigorously to seek their rights but at the same time it will provide adequate bases for the participation of all persons. Our alternative relies upon beliefs and values associated with the Christian faith and American constitutional principles. Our mix is determined by reliance upon some prima-facie duties acknowledged by the generality of mankind.[1] They are interpreted in the light of the black experience in America. We set them forth here as three essentials for the liberation of Blacks and whites in America.

The first requirement is promise-keeping. Black Americans must come to know that they are included within the American dream and that white Americans will seek to procure the black man's full equality as a citizen.

One must never forget that Blacks alone of all the inhabitants of America have been classified as non-members of the Western Christian moral universe. Roger B. Taney, the Roman Catholic Chief Justice of the U. S. Supreme Court, giving what he considered to be a descriptive and historical statement about civilized whites, stated on the basis of a strict interpretation of the Constitution that whites from the beginning of the Republic did not acknowledge black Americans to be a part of the people and that "they had no rights which the white man was bound to respect."[2] Although the Civil War ended slavery, the history of Jim Crow, racial discrimination, and prejudice demonstrates that white Americans still believe themselves superior to black Americans. If the Supreme Court decision of 1954 indicated that a liberal construction of the Constitution would make black Americans candidates for the fulfillment of the American dream, then the process of implementing the decision has

[1] W. D. Ross, *The Right and the Good* (Oxford: Clarendon Press, 1930), Chapter 2.
[2] Source 19 Howard 393. Roger B. Taney: Dred Scott v. Sandford. [CONE also thinks this case to be significant. See his *Black Theology and Black Power,* 9–10.]

disclosed that the majority attitude of white America is still very close to that of Judge Taney.

No one, we presume, supposes that any change in public opinion or feeling in relation to this unfortunate race in the civilized nations of Europe or in this country, should induce the Court to give the words of the Constitution a more liberal construction in their favor than they were intended to bear when the instrument was framed and adopted.[3]

Because Taney's arguments of 1857 were nullified by the 13th, 14th, and 15th amendments to the Constitution, it is our contention that black Americans are participants in the promise of the Declaration of Independence and the Constitution. Daily, however, white Americans continue to break these promises and act as if Blacks have no rights which a white man is bound to respect. One record of these broken promises is to be found in the "Report of the National Advisory Commission on Civil Rights."[4] Black Americans thus have a claim upon white America because of its failure to keep the promises acknowledged in the act of making the black American a citizen.

Edward C. Banfield in his volume, *The Unheavenly City*, suggests that the failure of promise-keeping is the responsibility of the Blacks whose lower-class cultural style has unfitted them for middle- and upper-class-ification.[5] Not all Blacks are so indicted, but there is the clear conviction that non-racial factors are more important than racial factors in black victimization. Future-oriented Blacks succeed; present-oriented Blacks become deserved victims for which society bears no responsibility.[6] Without attempting, here, to argue the soundness of Banfield's view I would want simply to assert that my approach would claim, as does Liebow's in *Talley's Corner*, that Blacks are present-oriented because of the failure of whites to keep the promises and that when this situation is altered, lower-class Blacks, too, will leave the so-called lower class.[7] The most important matter is promise-keeping. Blacks must be seen as having as valid a claim upon the resources of America as does any future-oriented upper- or middle-class white. Exclusivism based upon any conception of white superiority

[3] Ibid.
[4] Report of the National Advisory Commission on Civil Disorders (New York: Bantam Books, 1968).
[5] E. C. BANFIELD, *The Unheavenly City* (Boston: Little, Brown & Company, 1970), 85–87.
[6] Ibid., 211–12.
[7] Ibid., 219; E. LIEBOW, *Talley's Corner* (Boston: Little, Brown & Company, 1967), 222–31.

—race or class—must be rejected.[8] The first essential for the liberation of the black man is promise-keeping, a recognition by white Americans that black Americans have a full claim upon American ideals and resources and that this claim cannot be wholly determined by the capricious white will.

Because the black American's human rights, like that of the white American, are rooted ultimately in the creative act of the divine and not democratic constitutionalism, America as a people can be held responsible for its failure to honor from the beginning the black man's promissory note. Liberation of the black man requires thus reparations as well as promise-keeping. The wrong done the black American must be amended. James Forman's "Black Manifesto" was correct in urging white America to repair the wrong done to black America. His presentation of the problem in terms of class struggle and economic-political issues was, however, too superficial and glossed over the real concerns of the Black Revolution. Blacks are not seeking a worn-out Marxist-Leninism to replace a worn-out capitalism. They have gone beyond the call for simply economic and political remedies. They desire the decent respect "to which the Laws of Nature and of Nature's God entitle them."[9] Having been treated as beast and chattel, they demand now that the whites perceive in them the person of Christ and fulfill the injunctions of the Gospel:

for I was hungry and you gave me food, I was thirsty and you gave me drink, I was a stranger and you welcomed me, I was naked and you clothed me, I was sick and you visited me, I was in prison and you came to me.[10]

The scriptural passage has several advantages over the "Black Manifesto." It suggests that the meeting of the specific material needs of Blacks is not to be wedded too closely with any economic or political program. Such programs we know too well are frequently more linked to their party ideology and goals than to persons. Marxist-Leninism, as well as non-violence and integration, is no exception. The scripture presses, however, for justice, beyond measure, to persons. It sees in the other, the black American, the face of the Christ who claims from the disciple, the white American, his all. The demand placed upon

[8] I find BANFIELD's class-ification distasteful and pejorative because he feels lower-class culture to be pathological. Ibid., 54. His view is a subtle form of racism despite his protest and apparent desire to find solutions to current problems.
[9] Declaration of Independence.
[10] R.S.V. 25:35, 36.

the black American differs from that borne by his white brother. In spite of the times the injunction of Martin Luther King, Jr., is still appropriate. ". . . in winning our freedom we will so appeal to your heart and conscience that we will win you in the process."[11]

The Christian affirmation that Blacks and whites are equally the sons of God and must act toward each other as toward the Christ serves as a ground for reparations because white Christians have seldom so acted and should desire to atone for their sins of omission and commission. Another ground for reparations is evident in the words of King which immediately precede the ones just quoted.

> . . . We will match your capacity to inflict suffering with our capacity to endure suffering. We will meet your physical force with soul force. We will not hate you, but we cannot in all good conscience obey your unjust laws. Do to us what you will and we will still love you. Bomb our homes and threaten our children; send your hooded perpetrators of violence into our communities and drag us out on some side road, beating us and leaving us half dead and we will still love you.[12]

The truth of this passage, while no longer self-evident, points to the fact that Blacks are owed reparations not simply for wrongs done in slavery but also for wrongs done today. The truth exists, however, on two levels, one of which is seldom acknowledged. There is the physical deed, and this is quite frequently seen and acknowledged. In addition, there is the spiritual deed, and this is seldom perceived or assessed by whites. Reparations are owed the black American because in race relations King and white Americans—liberal and conservative —turned the Christian ethic topsy-turvy. Blacks were urged to become either Sambo-type[13] persons or "more Christ-like Negroes."[14] In either case pathological elements remained in or were introduced into the life style of Blacks. More especially not only normality but the Christian faith and ethic were distorted. King's actual ministry was more adequate than his words. Under his leadership Blacks made "strides toward freedom" and they did learn to become somebodies. In the process they outgrew his strategy. Blacks need now to right the Christian ethic and demand that whites bear the burden of their

[11] M. L. KING, JR., *Stride Toward Freedom* (New York: Harper & Brothers, 1958), 217.
[12] Ibid., 217.
[13] S. M. ELKINS, *Slavery* (New York: Grosset & Dunlap, 1963), 130–31.
[14] S. P. FULLINWIDER, *The Mind and Mood of America.* (Homewood, Illinois), 27–28, 238–39.

sins. Moreover Blacks themselves need to learn how to further alter their social environment and thus help create the conditions for normal and Christian character development. This achievement will depend upon the transfer of power from white to Blacks, the loss of status by whites, and an alteration of the standards by which persons, actions, and things are evaluated. Reparations demand thus a willingness on the part of whites to accept the loss of status entailed in repairing the affectivity of the black American and rebuilding his self-esteem, the loss of power involved in restructuring social institutions, and the change of cultural perspective implied in opening white Americans to new patterns of interactions that implicate them in acknowledging and adopting some black styles as the most adequate expression of the human. More than large grants of money is demanded. Together with the money, there is needed a metanoia, μετώνοιω, i.e., a complete reorientation of the person and of social institutions to true standards of justice. Since it is the height of injustice to treat those who are unequal as equals, reparations are indispensable. The ground for reparations is present wrong as well as past wrong. Its focus will be the person and the human group, not passé socialist programs or capricious fantasies. Without reparations there can be no liberation of Blacks in America. Removal of black self-hatred and distrust and white racism is unthinkable without compensatory programs. As a consequence neither the huckster of revolution nor the self-righteous liberals and conservatives should be permitted to obscure this issue.

Some of the evils of the present which legitimate the ethical correctness of reparations result from white America's failure to keep promises made. The national policy of "if you're black stay back, if you're brown stick around, if you're white you're right" has meant that race or class programs in America have never been properly implemented in relationship to the black poor. Caste status has distorted every portion of their lives and "last hired, first fired" has made them even in time of affluence subject to full manipulation by others. Liberation of Blacks therefore requires increased concern for accountability and responsibility. Not only whites but also Blacks must be held accountable for their deeds. It is well that during these days there is a United States Commission on Civil Rights that monitors the government's performance in this area. It is unfortunate that the practice is not more widespread among institutions, groups, and persons active in race relations and that the practice where present is not scrupulously honest.

Black-white relations in America exist at the level of distrust. That is why negotiations of differences always come to rest upon the question of the conditions to be related to co-operation. Too frequently the question has been resolved by the adoption of a "take it or leave it" position by one party to the dispute. White fear of Blacks quite frequently leads to white acceptance of confidence games. Black powerlessness and real, urgent needs often cause Blacks to develop new styles of ingratiation. Both actions are terribly wasteful of resources and further erode the modicum of trust that exists. Moreover, they tend to develop men and programs of deceitfulness and duplicity which make racism more intractable. What is needed in order that persons might know what promises have been made, judge the nature of promise-keeping, and assess properly reparations is better means of accountability and measurement of responsibility. Distrust can be removed only when people are able to place confidence in the agent and means of racial change.

Our concern heightens the necessity for new means of reporting and evaluation but it does not do away with the need for new types or forms of evaluation. It asserts instead that Blacks and whites must strive more diligently than ever before to find culture-free, class-free, race-free instruments of evaluation. The easy declaration of some whites that a particular action or policy is objective and fair must be challenged on the basis of its consequences. The belligerent cry of some Blacks that nothing they do can be measured by any except "the community" must be challenged on the basis of the fact that their conception of "the community" arbitrarily excludes most black people. Because there is among Blacks and whites a limited quantity of moral resolve, expertise, and financial resources, all persons and groups engaged in fighting racism must be held accountable. The fragile nature of trust between Blacks and whites requires sensitivity to what is productive of mutuality and a building of new attitudes and traditions upon those successful interactions.

Promise-keeping, reparations, and responsibility, if practiced by black and white, will provide America with a means for finding, through conflict and co-operation, racial justice. I am not questioning the importance of theologizing about the human condition of black persons and the black community. That too is an endeavor essential for liberation. I am concerned that ethics permit and encourage rational debate and free choice. Black theology should enhance not erode those essentials, for black persons know best of all persons what can be the fruit of irrationality and gut emotions.

C. D. COLEMAN

In order to fulfill its ". . . divine destiny . . . of redeeming and remaking a spiritually denuded society," the Black Church must take four tasks upon itself: it must "recapture its historic relationship with the black community; it must take its place in the vanguard of the Black Revolution; it must utilize the potentials of its young people; and it must lead black youth beyond blackness to destiny."

To accomplish the tasks posed by the "new agenda" and to become more relevant to the masses of black people, the Black Church must also:

shift present priorities from fruitless conferences and conventions to direct-action programs facing the lives of the black masses; hold a summit meeting of top executives and leaders from black denominations and black caucuses in dialogue with black community-action groups;

teach black youth the ". . . values and principles related to the use of power . . ." so that they may understand the true meaning of black power and blackness as forces for renewing society and not destroying it; and

lead black youth to the realization that nobility is less determined by skin color than by acts, and that black awareness ". . . will deliver us from the madness of the American power structure . . ." and make it possible for Blackamericans to remake society.

Because the Black Church is itself in transition, its agenda often lacks depth; sometimes it lacks clarity, too, for an operational agenda for revolutionary change is often *ad hoc* by necessity. Coleman's understanding of the Black Church's "divine destiny," the "redeeming and remaking a spiritually denuded society" may not be fully realized through his agenda of "four tasks," but certainly the cause will be advanced. The possibility of the Black Church ever being all to the black community it once was is probably remote. The Church was what it was precisely *because* the black community was structural and conditional as *it* was. Effective religion must speak to the existential condition.

C. D. Coleman is General Secretary of The General Board of Education of the Christian Methodist Episcopal Church.

AGENDA FOR THE BLACK CHURCH

Source: C. D. Coleman, "Agenda for the Black Church," *Religious Education,* November–December, 1969, pp. 441–46.

The Black Church Must Recapture Its Historic Relationship with the Black Community

The first priority for the Black Church is to recapture the leadership of the black people. It must reclaim the unqualified trust and commitment traditionally associated with the Black Church and the black community. It must restore its original identity with the fortunes of black people.

Originally, the church was the very expression of black people themselves. It represented the first successful exercise of collective strength created through a sense of common expression and a common estate of being. Dating back to the Revolutionary War, the first independent efforts of black people to organize this unbreakable bond resulted in the formation of a church. Although the Black Church fully accepted American-Protestant values which are identical with white middle-class values and white cultural hegemony, it nevertheless represented a vortex of power for black people. The Black Church began as a strong answer to white exclusiveness, as a means of coping with social isolation, and out of the realization that even the teachings of Jesus Christ himself are not sufficiently persuasive in the ethics of white people to make them treat black people as equal human beings.

The organization of the Black Church was the first important step forward in preserving their ethnic culture and developing black consciousness. It gave an outlet for the frustration resulting from their social isolation and formed a basis for their social cohesion. For black people their church was their "thing," giving them the opportunity to develop identity and make their own leaders who knew firsthand their hurts and problems. As an authentic and unrestricted expression of themselves, it was the bastion for developing self-pride and finding self-fulfillment. The Black Church was all these things in one, having total empathy with the community; feeling its sensitivities, hearing its every feeble cry, and ministering, as it could, to every need.

Another gift of the Black Church to the "Black Tradition," which must be reclaimed, is the gift of hope—a toughness that allows one to stand straight and tall, and, even in losing, never give up.

Unfortunately the Black Church did not break from white cultural hegemony which is inherited along with American Protestantism. Therefore many Blacks spent the first half of the twentieth century vainly trying to become "Black Anglo-Saxons" or carbon copies of white-middle-class America. The word *black* became taboo, and gave way to the word *colored* as the respectable racial designation. At the same time, the established Black Church tended to become more and more urbane in its outlook and less and less serviceable to the black community, more and more a copy of the white-middle-class church and less and less responsive to the frustration of black people. As disdain for blackness increased, some "colored" churches selected their leadership on the basis of shade of skin color; persons of lighter skin shade occupied the more important positions.

By this time the Black Church was the "colored" church and out of touch with black people, forgetting their language and being insensitive to their needs, their struggles and their aspirations. In short, the Black Church had ceased being black. The spirituals which were born out of the souls of the masses were replaced by the "hymns of the church," which did not speak to the souls of black people. Attempts were made to correct the grammar and eliminate the dialect of spirituals. Some "colored" churches refused to sing spirituals at all. Gospel songs, a natural product of the black experience and expressions, were downgraded, and emphasis was placed on anthems, chorales and fugues. Alas, the Black Church became mulatto.

With the advent of a greater emphasis on civil rights by mid-century, the Church became one of the agencies advocating social change, especially in the realm of race relations. This time, however, it was not the undisputed leader of black people but one of the coalition. It was obvious that the Church had lost its leadership in the black community and must earn again the right to be called "leader." In order to follow the path where destiny leads, the Church must again become the expression of the soul of black people. It must give up white-middle-class church values which are more concerned with buildings and rituals than with conditions of people. The Black Church must learn that white-middle class solutions will not dissolve black community problems, especially with the black community fighting for self-determination and the white power structure determined to maintain the status quo.

Unless the Black Church moves quickly to lead the black community beyond their blackness, it will forfeit the leadership to less positive forces. At this point in the confrontation, the Black Church has the opportunity to speak to and for black people as no other agency can do, because it is a part of the very existence of black people. It is interwoven into their mentality as no other institution can ever be. It can once again become the most powerful factor in the community if it moves now. It can keep causes just and noble. It can prevent blackness from becoming an end within itself. It can keep the black community loving God and country. It has done all these things before and can do so again if it selects new priorities. It can no longer seek the respectability and comfort of suburbia. It cannot specialize in a ministry to the black elite only but must live with and minister to the masses. It must become outraged at the pains of injustice and the covert violence of a racist society. The agenda for the Black Church is not so much going to lunch with the mayor, as it is camping on the mayor's doorstep until the cause is heard; not so much giving nice prayers at civic gatherings, as it is pricking the conscience of civic gatherings. It is not so much merging with white churches as it is remaking white churches, confronting them with the burning truth, relentless love and righteous judgments of Jesus Christ, the Liberator, as he is revealed today through the perspectives of the black experience. The business of the Black Church at this moment is being present wherever wrong reaches out for justice, wherever the poor seek jobs and food, and wherever victims of prejudice cry out their hurt. It must deal positively with institutionalized racism and legalized forms of violence. The violence that occurs without a hand being lifted, or a foot being raised; the violence that is being visited upon black people every hour of every day; the refusal to train and employ; the run-down and rat-infested shacks; the overcrowded and neglected all-black schools; the "no-down-payment" stores that charge many times the original price for the cheapest product; the supermarkets that raise prices in black neighborhoods; the rats, the roaches, the stench and flies of the city dump; these covert acts against black people are no less violent than the overt counteraction of an angry mob burning, looting and pillaging, neither of which is right and both of which are intolerable.

The business of the Black Church at this moment in history is to mount and sustain an attack upon these evils. This will require shifting present priorities from fruitless conferences and conventions to direct-action programs; from petty church politics to constructive encounters with the problems plaguing black people. This is the first agenda item: the Black Church must become black again and be the champion and expression of black people.

The Black Church Must Take Its Rightful Place in the Vanguard of the Black Revolution

The imperatives of this hour demand that the Black Church speak as the authoritative and united voice of its people. This voice cannot be that of one congregation, one denomination, any one black agency, committee, or black caucus. It must be a voice resulting from a Black Church summit meeting involving top executives and key leaders from black denominations and leaders of black caucuses in dialogue with representatives from black action groups. The need for a Black Church summit is obvious. A summit meeting could enable black denominations to divest themselves of wasteful competition, petty jealousies, and encumbrancing institutional interests. It could provide a cohesive base for co-ordinating the efforts of the black revolt. This would prevent further fragmentation of the black community which must now choose among numerous black activist groups, all seeking the same goals, but by diverse, and sometimes dubious, methods. A summit meeting, if convened now, could keep the leadership out of the hand of ultraradical and ultranationalist groups whose motives are blackness for blackness' sake. Out of a summit meeting, the Black Church could assume a more relevant, supportive, and pastoral relationship with black activists who represent some of the most brilliant, resourceful and courageous young people in the nation. Such a summit should consider among other things, strategies, plans, and designs for a massive appeal to black and white Christians and all people of good will for capital resources, time and talent, to be used in a nation-wide ecumenical ministry to bring an end to white racism in all its manifestations and salvage millions of young people who languish on reservations, in ghettos, Appalachia, and migrant labor camps, trapped in educational, cultural, economical, moral and spiritual hopelessness. It should devise ways of reintegrating the thousands of progressive and dedicated young black men and women who have turned away from the Church of their fathers which nurtured them through the long, long night. The Black Church can no longer afford the luxury of silence.

The current crises in the social order, the continuing disregard for sanctity of human life and personhood, and the present ferment in the religious order make it obligatory that the Black Church initiate a summit meeting immediately or be found sleeping through a revolution which it should be leading.

The Black Church Must Utilize the Potentials of Its Young People

This generation of young black Americans are some of the best equipped youth in the world for effecting constructive social change. They have been tried by the ordeals of fire hoses, vicious dogs, tear gas, mace, clubs and every form of inhumane incarceration that sadistic minds could concoct. This gave them the endurance point that defeated brutality and endowed them with a courage unexcelled by any group who has ever fought for freedom in America. They matched wits with the worst racists of the power structure and helped to pull down the system of segregation. They matched wills with demagogues and tyrants and faced them down. They marched thousands of miles; they suffered thousands of insults; and they endured countless abuses. But, bloody and brutalized as they were, they could still sing and believe, "We Shall Overcome."

Black young people are well fitted to renew human institutions and overhaul out-worn structures and systems; they are more aware of inequities and more concerned to right social evils than any youth generation in American history. This generation is exposing the materialism and hypocrisy of our society with deadly accuracy. They have the freshness of vision, the necessary impatience, the will and desire to participate in the new birth of this nation. Black youth have come to the awareness of themselves that is significantly different from that of their elders. They are aware of the absolute necessity of power for existence in a pluralistic society. They have no objection to the combination of the words "Black" and "Power." And they could not care less if it seems to offend or frighten white Americans. To these young people "Black Power" means black consciousness and solidarity. It means the amassing by black people of the economic, political and judicial control necessary to define their own goals and share in the decisions that determine their fate. Ethnic power is a fact of life and existence in America. The potentials of the power of young black Americans is tremendous. The Black Church should see to it that this power is used constructively. It must address itself to a realistic attitude toward "Black Power." The fact is, before any ethnic group can enter the open society it must first close ranks. Black power is a way of doing this if it calls black people to unite, to recognize their heritage, and to build a sense of pride in themselves and their ancestry. The Church must speak to young people about power, "Black Power." Black power does not automatically mean black violence, black separatism, black supremacy, black racism, or anti-whiteness any more than white power automatically means white violence, white separatism, white supremacy, white racism or anti-blackness. The truth is that it can and will mean these things if the Black Church does as the white church did and fails to take a stand for the just and unbiased use of power for the good of all God's children.

Destiny demands that the gifts of blackness be used to renew society and not destroy it; to make this a free and open society, not to indulge anger or appease vanity. "Black Power" must be used for these noble ends, and it is the responsibility of the Black Church to give youth the correct interpretation of power.

The Church Must Lead Youth Beyond Blackness to Destiny

The excursion into black awareness, which is attracting so many of our young people and gaining increasing acceptability among middle-class adults, is necessary in the process of self-identity. But it holds both peril and promise. The peril lies in the danger that blackness will become a panacea and will be substituted for the essentials of survival. The prime purpose of black awareness is to give answers to the question, Who am I?; to give pride in ourselves, our history and our ancestry. It is not a substitute for nobility—only deeds can make men noble. It is not a license just to do one's own "thing" in one's own way. Neither is it a substitute for ability. In an open society, ability is the key to survival, and it will take all the intelligence, energy and shrewdness we can bring to bear to change a stubborn racist society. There is the danger that black awareness for black awareness' sake can create the illusion of superpower and the delusion that black people can go it alone. There is also the peril that blackness will be used as a gauge to measure the worth of others. The promise which black consciousness holds, however, is far greater than its perils. The promise is, if we share the recognition of the meaning of this moment in history, our blackness will become a gift that will deliver us to be brothers to all men; that will enable us to lead the way in building a new kind of freedom, a new kind of man and a new kind of world. Our blackness, if properly used, will deliver us from the madness of the American power structure and make it possible for black Americans to remake society with patience, faith and love, which the dark past has taught us. If with our gift of blackness we can achieve this, history will bless us for leading the fight for all men to have, not just freedom, but opportunity; not just legal equality, but human ability; not just equality as a right and a theory, but equality as a fact and practice.

This is the role which destiny demands of the Black Church in these crowded hours, and perhaps it is also the role against which the Black Church will be judged in the pages of history.

CHAPTER IV

BLACK CULTS AND SECTS:
ALTERNATIVES TO TRADITION

America is a country in which there is no officially established religion, and by law no attempt is made to regulate religion except, of course, in those occasional instances where public policy, or the public welfare may be involved. Partially because of such broad-gauge religious freedom and partly because of the wide spectrum of cultural interests represented in this country, the proliferation of religious denominations, sects, and cults has been unimpeded since the founding of the Republic. In consequence, the number of more-or-less distinctive organizations representing various nuances of religious beliefs and practices runs into the hundreds. Some have fewer than a dozen members; others number their memberships in the millions. Some are quite private and are scarcely known outside their own constituencies. Others tend toward the bizarre in doctrine or ritual and may receive more attention than is warranted by their numbers or influence.

Because religion in America is so "fragmented" or "sectarian," it is seen by some as "the scandal of the Church." The supporting notion of this argument is that religion is, or ought to be, unitary—*one*—and that sectarianism threatens, if indeed it does not destroy summarily, the integrity of the faith. This need not be the case, for the integrity of the faith is often reduced to a matter of human interpretation reflecting in part the needs and experiences, actual or vicarious, of the believers. In consequence, believers, or potential believers with different needs may find the faith as projected, incompatible. Those who are thus excluded by a predetermined expression of what the faith is, or who subsequently discover its understanding does not speak effectively to their conditions of existence, eschew or leave a particular organized cult of worshipers in search of another reflecting a religious view more consistent with *their* needs as they see them. Hence, the division and redivision into denominations, sects, movements, cults, etc., represents a continued search for religious relevance on the part of those who have not found it in previous experiences with existing religious organizations. Such a "questing" is probably exaggerated in the United States precisely because of (1), traditions of religious freedom—there having been no established Church to proclaim an "official doctrine," thereby implying the outlawry of non-conforming groups, and (2), because of the unevenness and the contradictions in the vast number of cultural and ethnic experiences which make up the "American experience." It will be readily understood how the black experience, differing radically from that of other ethnic and cultural groups, and under continuing pressure to define its meaning in the context of American Christendom, would very likely reflect a wide spectrum of dissidence and experimentation in its search for a religious truth relevant to black people in America. So it is that Blacks have been impelled to search for relevance over the whole spectrum of American religious interpretation, from the Society of Friends, through the mainline "white" denominations, to the various white sects, black sects, and even to Mormonism, a Church which specifically excludes them from the full benefits of belief. This then is the story of the black search for religious relevance in America.

JOSEPH R. WASHINGTON, JR.

Blacks were not "holiness prone" because of any inherent heathenism. Rather, many poor Blacks found no welcome in the independent black churches. "Some received the fragments of white religion during their spiritual hunger and alienation," although the Holiness movement was not specifically aimed at Blacks. For the Holiness people, the world's great problem is sin, and sin can only be overcome through an encounter with God which enables one thereafter to gain sanctification and lead a perfect life. The "life" (of holiness) often spawned interracial fellowships and created missionary opportunities for Blacks seeking to save their fellows from the wages of sin. The marks of holiness included an emotional experience of conversion, sanctification, striving for perfection, the guidance of the Holy Spirit, revival, and strict puritan morality.

Joseph R. Washington, Jr., is Professor of Religious Studies and Chairman of Afro-American Studies at the University of Virginia. He is the author of *Black Religion and the Politics of God*.

THE BLACK HOLINESS AND PENTECOSTAL SECTS

Source: Joseph R. Washington, *Black Sects and Cults** (New York: Anchor Press/Doubleday, 1972), pp. 60–82.

*A title in The C. Eric Lincoln Series on Black Religion published by Anchor Press/Doubleday.

It is important here to sketch quickly the historical line of this search for perfection and holiness to dispel the widely held assumption that Blacks are holiness prone because of their heathenism. Indeed, a minority of Blacks went the route of holiness and formed permanent black sects seeking perfection without concern for social reform. Those who went this way, and do today, did so because they received the fragments of white religion during their spiritual hunger and alienation. Poor Blacks were nearly brushed aside in black independent churches just as black independents had been left without dignity in white churches. There was no help for their real poverty in black churches and there was no opportunity for them to express their fears. As the Holiness movement became national, it spread sporadically to Blacks and attracted those who found no satisfaction in black churches and who without social stability were ripe for the simple, clear, religion. "You are helpless, a deprived sinner. There is nothing you can do for yourself morally, spiritually, or socially. God alone can do it. Turn to him!"

The message was the same for whites and Blacks. The only problem in the world is sin. The only way to overcome sin is through an encounter with God and its resulting special experience, thus arousing the will to perfect sanctification or a life free from sin, both of which assured one of being among the saved in the golden age to come, for which one only need wait in patient holiness. There was no other message around that met the quiet desperation of forsaken Blacks and temperamentally suggestive whites. Moreover, this movement gave Blacks an opportunity to be missionaries among fellow Blacks, bringing to them an answer to their troubles in a packaged religion they could put together with other like-minded, without the need of clergy. In some cases the Holiness movement brought poor whites and Blacks together in interracial fellowships. Emotional spasms, treeing the devil, jerks, trances, prophecies, speaking in tongues, and all the undisciplined religious expressions which are considered the black man's special province, these extravagances were first taught by whites and only later by Blacks. A new generation of whites instructed a new generation of Blacks in a narrow religious conduct which had no accompanying means of release in social reform or social criticism. It would stay longer with Blacks because they would stay longer on the bottom of poverty. In time, poor Blacks would turn in their deepest despair to the more flashy social representation and dramatic action of the cults, the left wing of the Pentecostal movement, which would both heed and take advantage of this cry for help.

Involvement in Pentecostal sects and Holiness groups by Blacks left destitute by their own and disowned by the society is not surprising, for they were following in the footsteps of whites who were working to the ultimate an old, old spiritual haunt. In fact the religion of delirium predates Christianity, while running throughout its history. Gifts of prophecy, visions, trances, dances, gifts of tongues, and shouting in ecstasy may very well be primitive traits, but it is the white primitives who gave them their history in Western culture.

While there is historical precedent for exotic spirituality, the red-hot religion of Holiness in the search for perfection took hold of the American people via the firebrand Methodism demonstrated by George Whitefield. He must be credited with introducing the method of a quick decision for Christ in the presence of a great company. Yet, the basic message which Whitefield brought proved to be more lasting. As a follower of John Wesley, he set the pace for Methodists who would pump spiritual religion into the nineteenth-century frontier America, controlling and giving it a peculiar stamp.

The impact of Methodism extended beyond the technique of revivalism to its basic teachings. John Wesley stressed the doctrine of perfection as a state which one must strive to attain. Perfection was taught as the fruit of salvation, being the gift of God through his Holy Spirit to a deprived and doomed soul, helpless in himself. Those who traveled the highways and byways preaching Methodist doctrine were instructed to save as many souls as possible in as short a span as possible "and with all your power to build them up in that holiness without which they cannot see the Lord." The way to receive perfection, or holiness, was through an instant conversion experience or justification, the knowledge of which would come in an emotional outbreak after one had thrown himself on the mercy of God and received the Holy Spirit in his heart. From that moment on one was to seek a second blessing or sanctification, working thereafter to gain perfection or freedom from sin.

With the coming of the national Holiness movement a permanent sect arose, with its membership mainly among the poor. Previously, holiness and perfection were a rural or frontier phenomenon. An urban America constantly being replenished by the rural poor guarantees the Holiness tradition. At least among Blacks, the rural South is far more the territory of the independents than it is the natural homeland of the Holiness movements. The marks of Holiness sects are set in affirmation of an emotional experience of conversion, the experience of a second blessing or sanctification, the need to strive for perfection, the guidance of the Holy Spirit in all events of life through visions or dreams, the fundamentalism of their faith, the practice of revival techniques, the expectation of the Second Coming of Christ, and a strict Puritan morality.

Sanctified or Holiness groups among Blacks differ from independents not only in their status but the seriousness with which they practice their beliefs. They speak in tongues which are believed to be a gift of the Holy Spirit, or the baptism of the Holy Spirit, and they do so without apology. They seek the pure religious life and hold up the rules by which their members are judged, without flagging zeal. Members fall by the wayside, some of them are as hypocritical as the independents, but they do so at peril of being read out of the fellowship.

Insofar as the independents can trace their beginnings directly back to early evangelical Methodists and Baptists, Holiness, Pentecostal, and Sanctified Blacks do so indirectly. Their real beginnings are rooted in the 1886 revival in the mountains of eastern Tennessee and western North Carolina, which spilled over into the national Holiness movement of 1887, dominated in time by white Baptists and Methodists who felt they had no opportunity to exercise their gifts of the spirit in the parent body. These whites left their denominations and formed Pentecostal groups which were fallouts from the Outpouring of the Latter Rain Movement at the close of the nineteenth century. Holiness or Pentecostal Blacks split off from their white associates for many of the same reasons as the independents before them. When whites continued to sing their popular hymn—the words to the chorus follow—it was time for the Blacks to leave:

> My heart was black with sin,
> Until the Savior came in.
> His precious blood, I know,
> Has made it white as snow.

In other cases, a strong black personality coming under the influence of these sects and finding no room for expression within an independent black congregation departed from it to form his own.

Elder Lucy Smith is atypical in her success, but in her history, methods, and beliefs, she illustrates well the early development of black Holiness and Pentecostal meetinghouses.

Lucy Smith was born in 1875 in Georgia. She migrated to Atlanta in 1909 and relocated a few years later in Chicago. Reared a Baptist, she found no satisfaction in either the historic Olivet Baptist Church on Chicago's South Side, or the less prestigious Ebenezer Baptist Church.

Consequently, Lucy Smith made her way to Stone Church, a white Pentecostal fellowship where

> in 1914 I received my baptism and came into the works of the Lord. I continued going to Stone Church until I received my calling, which is divine healing.

This calling was responded to by scores of migrants, who aided her move from the single-room prayer-meeting sessions that began in her home in 1916 to the establishment in the 1930s of the All Nations Pentecostal Church on a fashionable street.

Elder Lucy Smith was a "black Puritan preaching holiness," variously described as elderly, corpulent, maternal, dark-skinned,

> a simple, ignorant, untrained woman with deep human sympathies, who believed absolutely in her own power to help and heal other people. Calm and serene in that faith, she had drawn together a following from the back streets of Chicago.

Elder Smith's services were typically emotional, sparked by shouting, rolling, and "speaking in tongues." Her reputation was made on the strength of healing power:

> Come to my Church more often and witness how many hundreds of men and women I heal—all kinds of sores and pains of the body and of the mind. I heal with prayers—jus' lay my hand on the troubled place and pray, and it all goes away.

Yet, something more than this rare power accounted for her success:

> I started with giving advice to folks in my neighborhood. This made me realize how much a good talking does to many people. Very soon they started coming more and more, and so for the last seven years I've been preachin' to large numbers. I'm building a new church; it will soon be finished. You should come to see my new place. You wouldn't believe that these folks with barely enough to live on are the very people who helped build my new large church.

Her church services were enjoyed by persons to whom she brought joy as a temporary substitute for their deep pain and suffering:

> The members of my church are troubled and need something to make them happy. My preaching is not about sad things, but always

about being saved. The singing in my church has "swing" to it, because I want my people to swing out of themselves all the mis'ry and troubles that is heavy on their hearts.

White people were welcome. They had as exciting a time in Elder Lucy Smith's services as did Blacks. Some whites were healed, like the one with tuberculosis "who had got so offensive we had to hoist the window while we prayed for him." Symbolizing the bridge between her black and white religious past, Elder Smith is a model for understanding the Holiness and Pentecostal types:

My church is for all nations and my preachin' for all Christians. I distribute clothes and food to the poor and I make no distinction of color. Even poor whites come in and receive help.

Whether they are identified as Holiness or Pentecostal, the roots of these groups are identical. They differ in emphases, depending upon the particular peculiar interest of the white sect left behind, or the special concern of the leader. The following characteristics of black Holiness, or Pentecostal, sects neither differ from white patterns nor from each other except that one body will hold to one and not the other as a matter of practice rather than principle: speaking in tongues, puritan morals, foot washing, divine revelations, divine healing, visions, trances, jerks, prophecies, testimony, Scripture quotations, quickening sermons, singing, dancing, fasting, biblical literalism, fundamentalism, adventism, perfectionism, and tithing. Some sects are anti-trinitarian, baptizing in the name of the "Father only" and others in the name of "Jesus only," the latter including the Apostolic Church of Jesus Christ, 1915, Indianapolis, and the Church of Our Lord Jesus Christ of the Apostolic Faith, Incorporated, New York City, 1919. But such distinctions are not theologically or sociologically significant, based as they are on exegeses carried forward in the oral tradition or created out of vivid imaginations. If one notes the urban concentration of these sects and the fact that they are often more numerous than independents, though not in total membership, it is not difficult to see how important they are as halfway houses between independents and cults. This importance lies not simply in increasing numbers, competition with independents, or in creating cults. Even more does this influence lie in a not uncommon tendency to prove that Jesus was black. The conclusion most often drawn from such an assertion is not that because Jesus was black, Blacks are superior, rather that blackness is to be cherished. More often than not, though segregated by intention, these groups tend to engage in interracial fellowship in the spirit at a much greater rate than independents.

The beliefs and styles which these groups share in common provide little room for distinction among them. One result is the distinctive flare of an individual personality who feels the necessity of focusing upon some idea which flashed across his mind in order to compete in the jungle of tongues. The lack of distinction in belief and styles leads to the creation of striking names, a few of which are indicated here with place and date of origin: The Fire-Baptized Holiness Church of God of the Americas, 1922, South Carolina; Church of God in Christ, 1895, Tennessee; Free Church of God in Christ, 1915, Oklahoma; Free Christian Zion Church of Christ, 1906, Arkansas; Church of Christ, Holiness United States of America, 1894, Alabama; Triumph the Church and Kingdom of God in Christ, 1936, Alabama; The Sought Our Church of God in Christ and Spiritual House of Prayer, Incorporated, 1947, Georgia; Church of the Living God, Christian Workers for Fellowship, 1902, Arkansas; The Latter House of the Lord for All People and the Church on the Mountain, Apostolic Faith, 1936, Cincinnati; Church of the Living God, the Pillar and Ground of Truth, 1925, Arkansas; Apostolic Overcoming Holy Church of God, 1919, Alabama; the National David Spiritual Temple of Christ Church Union, 1932, Missouri; Christ's Sanctified Holy Church, Colored, 1903, Louisiana; the House of God, the Holy Church of the Living God, the Pillar and Grounds of the Truth, House of Prayer for All People, 1914, Washington, D.C.; and the House of the Lord, 1925, Michigan.

Not the least important fact about these permanent black sects is their existence as a result of white religious movements. As the independents resulted from the first white proddings, the pioneer evangelical outreach of present-day establishment religion, so the permanent black sects are the result of the lower class whites, who reacted against conventional culture religion. That is, black religious life is the product of a penetration by whites, not once but twice.

This is not to hold that Blacks have not been fantastically creative with white religion. The very fact that Blacks have made so much out of the little given them that whites can no longer see their own devious hand within black religion—and, therefore, categorically assert that Blacks are "given to emotional exercises," as if whites are not, or that "formal worship is rather an exception" among Blacks—the very fact of this widespread nonsense points clearly to black creativity in religion. This attitude finds common ground with black chauvinism.

Religion as spirituality or charismatic power was certainly not invented by Blacks. It certainly is not their private domain. To be sure, there is little evidence of sophisticated theological reflection on the part of black Holiness types. Their very existence, like that of comparable whites, testifies or is a testimony against a rational faith. Where theology is seriously invited among white fundamentalists, they have long since risen above poverty and the helplessness which is so conducive to Holiness. With respect to organization, black sects have done as well as whites on a comparative basis.

Sects have been generally described as lower class, small, loosely organized, local, perfectionist, ascetic, unstable, antiecclesiastical, antistate, lay-oriented, isolationist, exclusive, future-oriented, short-lived, and rigidly moral. This description would seem to support a definition of white or black sects as a movement seeking to satisfy "individual needs by religious means," in revolt against a secular and religious system. This may well accurately state the case for white lower- or middle-class sects. The emerging point of difference is crucial between white and black sects. A black sect cannot long exist in this society with the belief that religious means can satisfy individual needs. This is true of the traditional or accommodationist black independents, which wish to be viewed as a church-type but must be viewed as sect-type, first, because their tradition prevents a universalism which would include racists, thus, their very existence serves as a protest against the religious and secular system; and, second, though they are neither aggressively hostile nor passively indifferent to the systems, they cannot hold to a belief in religion as the solver of personal problems in the face of black consciousness.

On the other hand, neither can Holiness or Pentecostal black sects. These Blacks are sectarian, but they are increasingly structured, having existed for more than fifty years in some instances. Consequently, we have called them permanent, though they might well be called established sects were it not for the middle-class connotation of establishment, which would put them in league with Theosophy or Quakerism. Nevertheless, it would seem that Holiness or Pentecostal sects, permanent though they may be, are forced by their religious affirmations to hold to religion as the only solvent. But the very fact of increasing organization and settled existence in urban areas forces upon them a compromise with respect to social problems, though none with respect to basic beliefs. One cannot become a member of the Apostolic Church of God in Chicago without giving evidence of baptism by the Holy Spirit. Yet, its pastor, the Reverend Arthur M. Brazier, is a member of the Illinois Advisory Board of the U. S. Civil Rights Commission and president of The Woodlawn Organization, founded by none other than Saul Alinsky. In the foreword to his book on TWO, Brazier states:

> The church led the way in understanding and implementing the struggle of the black man for identity, dignity, and self-determination in Woodlawn. Withdrawal of the church into a purely spiritual ministry is indefensible, especially from a biblical Christian view. To do nothing is to take sides with the Establishment in maintaining the oppressive status quo against the black community. By positively affirming the rights and the gifts of the black man and by helping him take effective action, the church can underscore the preaching of the gospel of salvation in Christ by responsible living in Christ.

As if to drive out forever the stereotype, Brazier is adamant:

> Any church, whether it be Baptist, Pentecostal, Methodist, Catholic, that gives support to the immoral system of repression, by silence or by saying, "Our role is to preach the gospel and to save souls only," is denying Christ and his clear teaching and example. The church can lead the way in changing the status quo, or by silence she can join the forces of oppression.

Here is a Pentecostalist who cannot be dismissed as being a wild radicalist. He must be seen and accepted as both the product of a permanent black sect and an indication of the difference Blacks make in the religion of whites. He is a wave of the future.

There is a further basic assumption generally held by white people. It is that Blacks who are Holiness or Pentecostal believers are ignorant, mentally unbalanced, unstable, primitive, rank fools, and just plain different. It may well be that this is more true of whites than Blacks, but in any case there is no evidence to justify the prejudice that black Pentecostals are any more emotionally unstable or subject to mental illness than are church-types, white or black. In fact, it is a wonder that there are not many more psychotics resulting from the high-powered religion of black Pentecostals. The truth is, these Holiness types are under so much oppression in the midst of so much obvious affluence until what is generally assumed to produce emotional stress really produces emotional power, which really guarantees mental health in an unhealthy society. The trouble, of course, is that this power too often goes begging. We cannot stand in judgment upon permanent black sects for not being on the forefront of social reform. We can only stand in awe when they are at the edge of reconstruction, as they increasingly are. We stand in awe of their power to break religious traditions and the oppression which forces them to do so.

But the really creative power of fundamentalist Holiness and Pentecostal Blacks has been ignored or obscured. Sometimes this has occurred because students of black culture see these sects as deviants. Other wish to capture the dynamics of black cultural life for secular Blacks by distorting the past. Whether guided by the Marxist assumption that religion is the "opiate" of Blacks or the Freudian presumption that it is "the future of an illusion," students of black culture who fail to make the connection between religion and black culture, in the past and present, simply refuse to credit Blacks with what they have done for themselves. In their opposition to religion, perceived in its repressive dimensions apart from its creative ones, some black culture enthusiasts seek to make black people over into purely secular masses, severed entirely from the religious past, convinced that they are complimenting Blacks. In fact, such distortions insult the black creativity where it is not blunted. This use of black culture for whatever bias is hardly in the best interest of Blacks.

There are, of course, students of black culture who vividly see religion as the base of black people's creativity. The key to this creativity is music, blues, jazz, gospels, and the synthesis of all of these which forms "soul music." Soul music is the creation of the black masses and finds greatest expression in the fundamentalistic congregations. In the attempt to protect the creativity of Blacks, every effort is made to eliminate all common ground between white and black Holiness sects, on the mistaken assumption that if there was a connection there would be no creativeness among Blacks. So, a single connection is forged between the religion of slaves and the post-slavery black Pentecostals. By leaving out the missing link, the creative process among black masses as opposed to the black middle class is prevented from coming into full view as a reinterpretation of white demonstrativeness. Blacks made a thing of beauty out of what for white Pentecostals and Holiness sects seemed pure torture.

White Pentecostals provided the opportunity for the creativity in the black sects which distinguished them from whites and blacks in traditional religion. Blacks incorporated the secular music.

The arousements which are so much a part of the black congregations of the masses did not simply result from African continuations and white evangelical mutual penetration. However, even in the rural South, independents dominated the religion of Blacks in the immediate postslavery period. Independents took on the model of middle-class whites. It was the second wave of Holiness and Pentecostal white evangelicals that reinforced the old-time religion among Blacks left untouched by middle-class Blacks and whites. They were the imperialists who sought to capture all America for their religious fundamentalism and emotionalism. The low-culture enthusiasts in religion reached whites who reached Blacks at the end of Reconstruction, when Blacks were cut off from their moorings. To reveal this link permits us to see the bridge between secular and religious Blacks by way of the gospel music and other instrumentations which made their way into black religion through these new Blacks, free but directionless. The tremendous contribution of black Pentecostals and Holiness sects to black culture is lost because they are overlooked in the effort to establish a direct connection between contemporary blacks and African survivals.

The most obvious African survival of the slave experience was the music: religious spirituals, work songs, "shouts," "field hollers," and antiphonal singing. The most apparent African heritage in the music of Blacks was its rhythms. The spirituals originated in the souls of slaves, created out of Christianity provided by whites and the American experience. Spirituals were left behind by Blacks with the slave experience. They were brought to the attention and appreciation of whites as art songs sung by Blacks on concert stages, but spirituals never became a dynamic part of the postslavery black religious worship of independent or permanent sects. After whites reached Blacks with their evangelical religion of fire, Blacks were permitted to have their places of worship, on a few plantations, because the church was reserved for whites and some of the household Blacks. These meetinghouses of field slaves were called "praise houses." Even here, although Blacks were permitted a measure of freedom of expression, whites were generally present as overseers, and after the Nat Turner rebellion the meetinghouses were virtually shut down. Due to the nearly complete isolation of Sea Island slaves, off the coast of South Carolina, reached by white evangelicals but not black independents or radicals, "praise houses" continued there longer than anywhere else.

The benches are pushed back to the wall when the formal meeting is over, and old and young, men and women, sprucely dressed young men, grotesquely half-clad field hands, the women generally with gay handkerchiefs twisted about their heads and with short skirts, boys with tattered shirts and men's trousers, young girls bare-footed, all stand up in the middle of the floor, and when the "sperichil" is struck up, begin first walking and by and by shuffling around, one after the other, in a ring. The foot is hardly taken from the floor and the progression is mainly due to a jerking, hitching motion which agitates the entire shouter and soon brings out streams of perspiration. Sometimes they dance silently, sometimes as they shuffle they sing the chorus of the spiritual, and sometimes the song itself is also sung by the dancers. But more frequently a band, composed of some of the best singers and of tired shouters, stands at the side of the room to "base" the others, singing the body of the song and dropping their hands together or on their knees. Song and dance are alike extremely energetic and often, when the shout lasts into the middle of the night, the monotonous thud, thud, of the feet prevents sleep within half a mile of the praise house.

It is just to this isolated case that one is sent for proof of African-originated characteristics in black religion.

The fact is, one instance not withstanding, Blacks were not generally permitted by their white controllers to engage in dancing or use musical instruments (especially drums) in worship. This came only with freedom and the Pentecostals when Blacks were out from under perpetual white supervision, though not white stimulation. We need to come now to the several forces working upon Blacks which gave rise to a tradition of emotional religion and musical creativity not known before the Civil War.

The masses of black folk were at a loss following the Civil War. They drifted aimlessly, where they were cut from all previous ties or were without any stake or opportunity in the land. By and large, Blacks in churches, especially in the cities, were a cut above the masses with respect to economic possibilities, but a cut below them with respect to freedom from the dominant white religious style. Though they had their freedom, Blacks in the greatest numbers were unable to make capital out of it or turn it into an asset. Whereas the social conditions were not the same as in slavery, they were worse off with respect to the psychological impact. Whether in the rural or urban areas, Blacks combatted their sickness of body, mind, and soul with their music, their rhythm. Submerged in a secular society, free of religious restraint for the first time, Blacks used the spirituals, chants, hollers, and shouts of their condition. With the same music and rhythm that created the religious spiritual, free Blacks created the blues.

The blues differed from the spirituals in being personal and secular rather than communal and religious.

The new sound of the blues and the experiences of the cities set up the conditions for response to the Holiness and Pentecostal movement, which broke forth among whites at this time. Blacks could go to church or sing the blues, but neither of these provided any answer to the terrible depressed conditions plaguing Blacks. As we have seen earlier, and for those reasons, the Holiness movement filtered down to Blacks and gave a definite answer to their troubles and a way out to be found in a highly excitable religious experience. The Holiness movement seemed to be a sufficient answer for desperate Blacks, for it broke out like wild fire among the masses. It grasped the Reverend C. P. Jones in Selma, Alabama, and in 1894 this Baptist preacher left to found The Church of Christ, Holiness U.S.A. And it shook the Reverend C. H. Mason of Memphis, Tennessee, causing him to leave his Baptist church in 1895 and organize The Church of God in Christ in an old gym at Lexington, Mississippi. At Wrightsville, Arkansas, in 1899, the Reverend William Christian received the baptism of the Holy Spirit and formed the Church of the Living God, Christian Workers for Fellowship. There were hundreds of others.

The black experience did not permit these Pentecostals and Holiness churches by the hundreds simply to follow in the steps of whites. They did adhere to the general teachings of whites, adding individual touches here and there with regard to doctrines, rituals, and organizational structure. But, it was the combination of suffering and music which turned these sects around, providing the cohesion which has enabled them to be permanent rather than fly-by-night inspirations. Remembering the spirituals, hearing blues and jazz on the streets, and being of the streets, the Holiness and Pentecostal sects brought into their religious services everything that was denied Blacks in slavery or was denied by black independents: dancing, tambourine playing, hand clapping, and screaming, as well as the usual healing, speaking in tongues, and prophesying adapted from whites. As Blacks became more mobile they increased in number and variety the instruments used in their services, in keeping with the new ones used by the blues and jazz men. This fantastic combination of white and black forces was developed into a new creation which dominated Blacks in the South, rural and urban alike. The power of these groups gave birth to the cults. It was in such a context of Pentecostalism that Father Divine and Daddy Grace found their answers. Blacks created a whole new religious music in gospel songs which revolutionized music in the black congregations through the leadership of jackleg preachers and evangelists who went from rags to riches by means of bringing the secular world of blues and jazz into worship. Such sects have become permanent, they have made a lasting contribution because they affirmed the spirit and feelings of the black masses, so beautifully expressed in blues and jazz, and disguised this secular form in spiritual garb. It was a new creation, this gospel music. In time it would be recognized with blues and jazz as soul music. But in its beginning, it was the religion of the masses and invaded lower-middle-class Baptist and Methodist congregations only after Blacks surged forth en masse to the urban centers North and South, making demands that the senior choir move over and share with the gospel chorus.

Very few black congregations today do not engage in gospel music, if no more than by inviting a gospel quartet or chorus in on special occasions. Those black churches that see gospel music as sheer commercialism, "low culture" they might say, are generally members of communions in which the number of Blacks are small. The very nearly universal presence of gospel music, the formula of which is familiar,

> similar wails and cries linked to various tumbling strains and descending figures, statements and counter-statements, call and response, compulsive participation, arrangements combining spirituals, blues, jazz,

makes it appear that the pattern is natural to Blacks learned by every child by heart in a church, continuing an uninterrupted line from the urban ghetto to the rural South to the slave era to West Africa. But in fact, Blacks have become increasingly more African of late. The progressive and competitive drive to return to the roots of the African heritage is indicative of broken periods, of the need to relearn the forgotten past, or search for the lost, unknown past. The communication of the black experience through gospel music is the direct contribution of lower-class-black fundamentalists. They synthesized the forces playing upon them in a period when the masses were cut off from Africa, as well as mainstream Blacks and whites. Theirs was a new creation out of a new experience, not a simple reiteration of a past. Nothing substantiates more fully the radical newness of lower-class Blacks than the resistance with which their culture and religious music met for so long a period.

In time, what was the special creation of Pentecostals and Holiness black sects became contagious among all lower-class-black congregations. The back Holiness people left the Baptist and Methodist churches because they could not exercise therein their gifts of the spirit, but their spirited ways returned to dominate the scene to the extent that black Baptists and Methodists now claim this heritage as their very own, failing to credit the special gifts of Pentecostal and Holiness types.

In the past, the creative dimensions of these permanent black sects, and their potential for the future solidarity of Blacks, have been ignored due to the huge constituencies of Baptist, the heroic beginnings of Methodists, and the order and stability of both. There is another factor. The assumption that a sect is by nature a small, reactionary, short-lived group whose growth and influence correspond with a period of acute distress among Blacks and fade with the crisis. The permanency of these black sects is a testimony to distress and crisis as a way of life among Blacks. This reality and the process of realism making its way, slowly to be sure, in these religious bodies signify possibilities which are rooted in substantial qualities of the authentic black experience. They are in touch with the masses. Organization is growing among them. In their strategic position lies the key to black unity. And they may yet use it. To unite the masses and pressure the independents may be a calling they will heed. What seems to be their weakness may prove to be their strength. Unshakable religious beliefs and authoritarian structure may in a generation or two work together for good with a sensitivity to the black style and an increasing social conscience. They may yet prove to be the awaited black catalyst.

When the source of the creativity of black sects is perceived in the past, there is in it a clue to the potential creativity of these groups in the future. The revolution in black religious music was stimulated by unattached black Pentecostal and Holiness preachers who combined their baptism in the Holy Spirit with their baptism in the black realism of the streets. In the beginning, as well as in the present, these uneducated or "jackleg" exhorters were men of wide experience in the ghetto. Sometimes they moved from criminal activities, to singing the blues, to playing jazz, to preaching, though they seldom took the reverse route. But they always knew whereof they spoke, whether or not they were able to convey by the spoken word the meaning of that experience. They had been there and participated in all they later came to reject. They could speak with the voice of experience and be an authority to the prostitute, the dope addict, the adulterer, the thief, the murderer, the gambler, and the panhandler. In fact, they could set their experiences to music, or use the existing music of the people in verification of their spiritual rites of passage.

What is important in all of this has been neglected. The jackleg preacher, like the Pentecostal and Holiness movement he used to revolutionize black religious music, was an urban man. Holiness and Pentecostal churches were not the creations of rural migrants in search of cushion from the cultural shock. They were the creations of experienced urban life, stemming directly from the new mobility of Blacks. It was only in the urban milieu that one could put together Holiness dogma, Pentecostal answers, black music, and the deepest depression into a whole shape and sound limited neither by tradition nor fears of being put-down by wise fools or foolish wisemen. Only in the midst of urban depersonalization, alienation, statuslessness and the search for liberation could one create a new personality and a new black religion, which would be circumscribed only by the limits of ambition, charisma, imagination, and organizational powers. Only in the urban setting could one be so convinced of oneself, so sure that one had the answer, that he could seriously put that answer to whomever would listen. It was in the urban fire that strong personalities were molded. It was from these urban centers that they went out to the rural communities preaching their answers, sharing their vision, practicing their spiritual gifts, and selling their wares. They could not stay long in rural areas with their dreams and schemes, the community associations were too tight, the social controls too strong, the dependence upon white powers too restricting. The strong personalities had to move on, but they left behind in the rural areas a new religious nerve which created in ruralites a new need for dynamic religion. Thereby, ruralites came to the city seeking the religion of excitement, of dreams, of the answer. Long before ruralites reached urbanites, mobile Holiness and Pentecostal evangelicals had reached them. The urban man returned to the rural man a new form of the old religion.

The black ruralites moving to the urban South and North who joined the permanent sects did so for the same reason as the majority members of these sects who were urbanites. They did not wander helplessly into them, seeking an intimate fellowship or a primary-group experience, so much as they came determined to establish a new set of attitudes and values in an atmosphere of certainty. Joining a sect was an intentional act, not an accidental one. Often it was a facing up to a personal crisis or an awareness of their true condition as a black people that led these ex-ruralites and urbanites to become new persons. As a confirmation of that decision they joined a sect seeking strength. The religious quickening enabled them to be reborn as new creatures. The organization in its combative and nonconformist stance against churches and society engendered group consciousness, stability, and confidence. The sect thrived on controversy and its distinction from other religious groups united the members into an exclusive fellowship.

The earnestness and vitality of these sects, the intensity of religious feeling and belonging, led to a high sense of loyalty and urgency. The power produced in the past had been turned into the reorientation through religion of a previously disoriented people. Were it not for several factors, these sects would gradually have conformed to the world around them and become denominations like the independents. For one thing, instead of being in theological conflict with other black groups, Holiness and Pentecostal sects made a contribution to them in music and feeling. For another, these sects became objects of admiration by middle-class Blacks and whites, and this new vogue fostered pride. Thirdly, the economic and social distresses of Blacks kept them largely locked in the ghetto which not only guaranteed the permanency of these sects but their social liberality as well. Between the admiration of middle-class Blacks and whites and the distress of lower-class Blacks, the sects were brought to a new consciousness whereby the old encouragement of mere endurance in the face of adversity gradually gave way to the challenge of social crises. They became aware that satisfaction lies neither in the old religion, nor the old society, nor their new religion but in a new society. External forces impinging upon them prevented their simply living in the world and rejecting its influence upon them.

If black Holiness and Pentecostal groups reject the possibility of attaining their goals within the framework of religion and maintain their religious fervor, they may yet produce the emotional fire and stability so indispensable to leadership and cohesion of black people. They are the future and bear the burden of possibility which distinguishes permanent black sects from independents or the cults they have created but do not accept.

JOHN W. ROBINSON

This is a case study of the United House of Prayer for All People, a cult founded by "Sweet Daddy Grace" in Wareham, Massachusetts, around 1920 or 1921. Grace, who came from the Cape Verde Islands, soon attracted followers up and down the Atlantic seaboard and established "Houses of Prayer" in Providence, Washington, New York, Charlotte, and other cities. When he died in 1960 his followers were estimated in the hundreds of thousands. He left an estate of several millions of dollars.

Robinson has updated earlier work done on the Daddy Grace cult by Arthur Fauset. His study is particularly valuable in that it covers the period of the transition of leadership following Grace's demise and the investiture of Sweet Daddy McCulloch as his successor.

The strength and pervasiveness of the various cults in the black ghettos of America suggest both the flexibility and the vulnerability of black religion.

John W. Robinson is Pastor of Tremont Baptist Church in the Bronx, New York, and a candidate for the doctorate in clinical psychology at New York University.

A SONG, A SHOUT, AND A PRAYER

Source: First publication.

Origin

The "United House of Prayer for All People, the Church on the Rock of the Apostolic Faith" is an Afro-American cult founded by Bishop Charles Emmanuel Grace. The leader was born Marcelino Manoel da Graca on January 25, 1881, in Brava, Cape Verde Islands, a Portuguese territory off the West African coast. Of African ancestry, Bishop Grace was one of ten children. He journeyed to New Bedford, Massachusetts, around 1900, and worked as a short-order cook, salesman, and grocer.

A sister of the deceased Bishop Grace, Louise Gomes, and a niece cannot recall any of these jobs. They remember him only as a preacher and revere his memory. Mrs. Gomes recalls their mother's saying Marcelino was always "a different" child.[1]

The name "Sweet Daddy Grace" was not assumed by the bishop until after the growth of the cult. Catching attention with his one-to-three-inch fingernails (painted red, white, and blue), his shoulder-length hair, his colorful cutaways, and his flashy jewelry, Daddy was on the road about three hundred days a year.

[1] Phil Casey, "Whatever He Did Was Automatically Right," the Washington *Post*, March 7, 1960, p. B 1.

The "United House of Prayer for All People" began after Daddy's return from the Holy Land. Of his journey to Egypt and Jerusalem, he reported having converted hundreds of Mohammedans to the Christian faith:

> People with heads that had ached for years because of the turbans their heads were bound with, people with eye strain and inflamed eyes from the bright sun; they came lame, deaf, and paralyzed . . . and they were healed. But I could not be everywhere. I had to leave.[2]

Upon his return, the bishop established a mission in Wareham, Massachusetts, and one in New Bedford later in 1921. It was then that he received newspaper publicity with his remarkable statements. In January 1922, Daddy announced:

> People who have never spoken a word of any language other than English, all their lives, have come to the mission and the inspiration has come to them to speak in Chinese, Hindustani, Hebrew, or some other language of which they have absolutely no knowledge.
>
> We go back to the faith of the early Christians; we literally interpret the Bible. We believe that these are the last days and that what the world needs is greater faith in God's word.[3]

Within two years of his return from abroad, Daddy Grace had spread the cult from New Bedford south to Charlotte, North Carolina; Newport News; Norfolk; and other towns.

Organization and Membership

Until his death on January 12, 1960, Bishop Grace was the undisputed head of the United House of Prayer. Washington was the movement's official headquarters. Here Daddy maintained a lavish seventeen-room home and national headquarters at Logan Circle, conducted lively fire-hose baptisms, and was the "Holy Man" to thousands.

No board of presbyters appointed his preachers. Daddy reserved this prerogative for himself. In private he was even known to boast that he would not have any preacher serve in the United House of Prayer whom he might consider smart enough to question his undisputed authority.[4] Although Daddy did provide a constitution for the administra-

[2] Ibid., p. B 1.
[3] Ibid., p. B 1.
[4] Arthur Fauset, *Black Gods of the Metropolis* (Philadelphia: University of Pennsylvania Press, 1944), p. 23.

214

tion of the United House of Prayer, its provisions provided no check on the bishop's powers. Moreover, the constitution was not thorough in specifying the electral procedure for a successor to Daddy. Hence, turmoil erupted within the organization upon Daddy's death.

The task of the preachers was to carry out the instructions of the bishop, to conduct services and preach, and, perhaps most important of all, to raise money. All moneys were strictly accounted for and returned to Bishop Grace through his Washington office. On one night a week, the preacher of a given House of Prayer was permitted to claim for himself the moneys contributed.

Theoretically, membership in the United House of Prayer was limited to those who had had a special experience, but in actuality, the movement, as its name implies, was open to anyone who desired to join.

All of our meetings are conducted under the directions of the Holy Ghost. If we are directed to sing, we sing; and if we are called upon to exhort, we exhort. . . . We also have the power to heal, and the most devoted members of our congregation are those who have been healed.[5]

Daddy Grace claimed to have a following of three million, however, it was never possible to verify this figure. It is possible that the membership was under 100,000 or under several hundred thousand. Nevertheless, if the movement had but 50,000 members, contributing a half dollar per week, it still would have amassed a huge revenue. At the time of his death, Daddy Grace is said to have had several thousand followers in Washington, D.C. His largest area was Charlotte, North Carolina where his following was 12,000. In New Bedford, where the movement had an early start, there were but ten regularly active members.[6]

Finance

Sweet Daddy Grace had a flair for drama and money. His followers not only shoved dollar bills at him but also built for him money trees and money houses. Good paper money, from $1.00 to $20 was often pinned to replicas of trees and to miniature building fronts in his honor. In 1944, Arthur Fauset, an Afro-American anthropologist, performed a case study of the United House of Prayer in which he noted their

[5] Casey, op. cit., p. B 1.
[6] Phil Casey, "Daddy's Money Grew on Trees (Man-Made)," the Washington *Post*, March 11, 1960, p. B 12.

heavy emphasis placed on money. Fauset reported numerous collections taken in each service.

> Ushers who take up these collections in small aluminum pans vie with each other in their efforts to raise the largest amounts. They rush about the House of Prayer calling out, "Please put something in my pan!" "Please swell 'my' total!" Some special honor or favor of such as sitting on the right side of Daddy Grace when he comes to the local House of Prayer usually accrues to the person who collects the largest sum over a given period.[7]

The undue emphasis placed on money is further substantiated by the following extracts taken verbatim from the "General Council Laws of the United House of Prayer for All People"[8]:

> 6. There shall be no offering taken on the night that is set apart for Daddy Grace before his arrival to the mountain.

>   *

> 11. No pastor is to handle money. A sign shall be hung in each house of prayer to this effect.
>   a. All pastors must teach the same. Any secretary or member giving the pastor money or other moneys shall he come short, he also shall be found guilty with the pastor that handled it.
>   b. Each house must have a banking committee and a committee to pay bills unless there is a written order from Daddy Grace to do otherwise.

>   *

> 19. Ruled by the executive council each day and night during convocation where the Prophet is present there shall be an offering and a special sacrifice taken from the congregation for the extension of gospel. This occasion must be boosted and made a worthwhile occasion each night and day.

>   *

> 38. Pastors must be in knowledge of everything: every Penny raised and spent.
> 39. Each House must have representative a man besides the pastor to take note of everything and accompany the pastor at the time of checking.
> 40. All pastors must see to it that each member pays his convocation fee and substantial rallies put on for the upbuilding of the King-

[7] Fauset, op. cit., p. 24.
[8] Ibid., pp. 24–25.

dom of Heaven, and this is to be put in the hands of our General Builder to build as he sees fit without bounds.

*

48. All houses of prayer must raise money in a united drive to buy a car for our Daddy Grace. Each state must do its part.

*

50. The state that wins the convocation victory will have an elaborate banquet on the day appointed by Daddy Grace. (The convocation victory is determined by the amount of money turned in.) The convocation King, Prince, Queen, Princess and all of the honorable ministers, officers and members of the victory state will be the guests of Daddy Grace the Supreme. The banquet will be given at the expense of the losing states, Each losing state will have to pay a certain amount which will be named later. Money left over the expenses of the banquet will be presented to Daddy Grace which he will do with as he desires.

These extracts indicate that the members of the cult were divided into various clubs whose primary duty was to raise money which was later turned over to Bishop Grace. Usually in the Houses of Prayer, there was a large poster which listed those clubs and the amounts of money recently raised. As a means of arousing social rivalry and, at the same time, increasing the totals, frequent contests were arranged. These were usually King and Queen contests, in which men and women attempted to win the honor of representing the local House of Prayer or some special occasion. Here, garbed in crepe paper and tinsel, the victors would play the imperial roles ordinarily associated with characters in fairy tales.

Daddy Grace held separate convocations in different states and localities. In each of these convocations, sums of money were raised and turned over to the bishop. All of the district groups having met, a national convocation was called to which representatives from the East and South poured in. The scores of contributions from the local convocations were then augmented by one master contribution known as the national offering.

After his death, the Internal Revenue Service assessed the net worth of Daddy's estate at the end of 1956 as $4,081,511.62.[9] Immediately following his death, more than $300,000 was uncovered in New Bedford, Massachusetts bank accounts. At least ninety bank accounts were listed under Grace's name, including eight in Washington,

[9] News item in the Washington *Post,* June 16, 1960, p. B 3.

D.C. Daddy practiced assiduously his constant advice to never let one hand know what the other was doing. His New York real estate man, Edward M. Rogell remarked, "No one man knows everything about the Grace and church estate."[10]

Daddy's estate included 111 Houses of Prayer and missions in approximately ninety cities and towns. Many of these had a small membership of possibly only a few hundred people. His properties spanned fourteen states and the District of Columbia. They included apartment houses, stores and other commercial property, and his own homes and apartments—about a dozen. It is possible, however, that many of these buildings were merely partially owned.

The bishop's homes ranged from a $375,000 mansion of eighty-four rooms located in Los Angeles to less pretentious, less costly, but comfortable homes along the East Coast. He owned a mansion and a twenty-two-acre estate near Havana, and large homes in New Bedford; New Haven; Montclair, New Jersey; Philadelphia; Washington; Newport News; Charlotte; Detroit; and possibly elsewhere.[11]

Beliefs

Classified according to beliefs, the United House of Prayer has been equivalent to a Christian sect of the holiness type, believing in conversion, sanctification, and the intervention of the Holy Spirit, etc. Followers were not supposed to swear, smoke, drink, dance, or attend movies. Bishop Grace opposed these in addition to war, airplanes, and adultery.

In his study of the cult, Fauset asserted that the beliefs boiled down to a worship of Daddy Grace. He quoted Bishop Grace as heard admonishing his worshipers:

> Never mind about God. Salvation is by Grace only. . . . Grace has given God a vacation, and since God is on His vacation, don't worry Him. . . . If you sin against God, Grace can save you, but if you sin against Grace, God cannot save you.[12]

For Fauset, this and other often quoted scriptural references in which the word "grace" appeared convinced him that the cult believed Daddy Grace to be the spirit of God walking among men. This was also the view spread by the press.

[10] Casey, op. cit., p. B 1.
[11] Ibid., p. B 12.
[12] Fauset, op. cit., p. 26.

Contrary to this view, Daddy Grace never claimed to be God. He rarely if ever expressed his consciousness of his own identity. Parables served Daddy to evade direct replies. Followers, friends, and co-workers of Bishop Grace have denied that he played God. Sherman Jordan, a handyman in Grace's home, reported:

> I heard him say he wasn't God, so how could he be?
> He was our leader. Practiced what he preached.
> Gave us something we couldn't get anywhere else.[13]

A similar testimony was given by Elder David, a Washington man who had been a follower since the 1920s:

> We didn't think he was God. He said the word of God. He was our leader. Newspapers print what they want. Don't have to be the truth. The members may come and go. The House of Prayer will go on.[14]

Although not God, Daddy Grace was to his followers a holy man, a prophet who was infallible and possessed of supernatural powers. Early in his career he startled the crowd by reporting that he had raised his sister from the dead after she had been pronounced dead by a physician. Another sister, Louise Gomes, confirmed this. A chauffeur, Joshua Raynor, interviewed in New Haven in 1958, reminisced over Daddy's healing days.

> He used to heal by the laying on his hands, but now he's getting old, he doesn't do that anymore. He tells people they've got to believe if they want to be cured, though.[15]

Whatever his appeal, it is clear that Daddy sought and drew a rejected people, frustrated in their daily lives, and gave them a sense of acceptance, importance, and achievement.

> It was a place you could go no matter how you looked, or who you were. It was all right. Yes, I had a uniform too. I was a choir singer.[16]

[13] Phil Casey, "The Enigma of Daddy Grace: Did He Play God?", Washington *Post*, March 6, 1960, p. E 1.
[14] Ibid., p. E 1.
[15] Phil Casey, "Many Setbacks Failed to Deter Daddy Grace," Washington *Post*, March 8, 1960, p. B 4.
[16] Phil Casey, "The Enigma of Daddy Grace: Did He Play God?", Washington *Post*, March 6, 1960, p. E 1.

Grace would set up churches in blighted neighborhoods, provide for services nightly and all day Sunday, and offer titles, uniforms, and duties to his followers. Simple, humble people identified with him. They might live in slums but Daddy was rich and through him they could feel like big shots.

Ritual—A Typical Service

The most distinguishing characteristic of the worship practices of this cult has been the heightened emotionalism. In Grace's time, a typical service would begin with unison singing, accompanied by piano or band. Then there was testimony. The singing was interlarded with shrieks, handclapping, stamping, and frequently concluded with the wholesale spectacle of a number of followers advancing to the front of the auditorium where they danced on the sawdust-covered floor. Followers were encouraged to dance ecstatically but always with members of the same sex. Frequently the dancers fell to the floor where they lay for many minutes. The sawdust on the floor in the front of the auditorium served to break the fall.

After a member had fallen and lain prostrate for a time, she was likely to arise suddenly, weeping profusely, and to leap about singing and dancing through the House of Prayer. Gradually she became subdued, sitting down on a chair or bench. Soon thereafter, she might have been observed leaving the meeting room, chatting and laughing with friends as if nothing had happened to her all evening.

If Bishop Grace himself were present, many worshipers would march or dance to the front and grasp his hand. Frequently the worshipers would place a bill of sizable denomination in his palm. Often the mere touch of the leader's hand was sufficient to induce terrific contortions or to produce a state akin to catalepsy. Once in an interview, the bishop assured Fauset that there was nothing on his person such as an electric charge to account for this phenomenon. He claimed it to be the action of the Holy Spirit.

Oftentimes the leader, who might be an elder, a minister, or simply a brother or sister, would interrupt his speaking with a song, thus, giving the followers a chance to express themselves in a manner obviously most satisfying to them. All the while there would be much calling out in tongues, which has been said to be the Holy Spirit speaking through the human form but which to the uninitiated appeared to be a series of nonsense syllables.

The preacher would then read from the Bible with interpolating remarks. He would call on an elder to assist with the reading, and after each clause read by the assistant, he would repeat the clause and elucidate it. Usually the exposition was concerned with the spirit of "Grace" in the lives of the bishop's followers, or with the cardinal sins: fornication, adultery, lying, stealing, and backbiting. There would be frequent reference to the desirability of giving up everything, including all worldly possessions, to Daddy Grace.

At any point this extemporaneous preaching was liable to come to an abrupt halt, and the preacher would find some pretext for collecting an offering. The pastor might suddenly say, "Let us walk!" and, following him, the members would rise and walk to the platform (called "the holy mountain") on which was hung a picture of Daddy Grace. They might genuflect before this, then raise the right hand, say a prayer, and drop money in the plate on the platform. When the proper moment had arrived, the minister would announce the next service, and the formal part of the service would be terminated. By this time many of the followers had already left the auditorium, or were otherwise engaged in such pursuits as selling the *Grace Magazine,* eating, or talking to friends in the rear of the meeting hall.

Each House of Prayer contained a canteen where Daddy Grace products, an essential part of the spiritual exposition, were sold. Daddy Grace products included the following:

Daddy Grace soap—to cleanse the body, reduce fat, or heal according to the individual need.

Daddy Grace writing paper—to aid the writer in composing a good letter.

Grace Magazine—if placed on the chest, to give a complete cure of cold, tuberculosis, etc.

In addition there were Daddy Grace toothpaste, transcontinental tea and coffee, men and women's hair pomade, face powder, cold-water soap, talcum powder, shoe polish, lemon cream, cold cream, pine soap, vanishing cream, castille and palmolive soap, and even Daddy Grace cookies. There were numerous emblems, buttons, badges, banners, and, finally, elaborate uniforms with accessories of swords, batons, and walking sticks whose sale swelled the totals of funds garnered by the bishop in his United House of Prayer.[17]

Arthur Fauset reported frequent allusions to sex motives.

[17] Fauset, op. cit., p. 30.

In a moment of comparative tranquility, I heard a preacher call out to the followers, who were chiefly women, "Who has the best thing you ever did see? I mean the best feeling thing you ever did feel? You feel it from your head to your feet. You don't know what I mean? Makes you feel good. Makes everybody feel good."

Such allusions, like the dancing, cause weird cries to emanate from various parts of the house of prayer. "Sweet Daddy!" "Oh, Daddy!" "Daddy, you feel so good!" "Daddy, Daddy, Daddy!" are typical expressions.[18]

At this date, the report of sexual allusions is unverifiable. Nevertheless, the evidence does not appear to substantiate it. The cult has always been extremely conservative in its approach to sex and "worldly" issues. Moreover, followers continued to regard Daddy as a "superman" not subject to sexual gratification. This is obvious from their undeviating support of Daddy through his host of suits by various and sundry women.

How did Grace appear before his followers during worship services? He was a "divine presence." Grace was not a ranting evangelist. He sometimes barely spoke at all but looked over the throng, casually, and somewhat amusedly. At other times Daddy gave Bible lectures, or would have passages read so that he could explain them. His Portuguese accent prevented any great and understandable flow of eloquence, but this seemed not to matter.

Norman Eddy, one-time professor of human relations at Boston University, who knew Grace and has written about the man and his cult, has provided a vivid description of the bishop.[19]

He wasn't much of a preacher, seldom said anything. He was sort of a Buddha. Men such as Father Divine and Daddy Grace have a psychic power. The power was in his personality, not in anything he said or did.

He thought of himself as a Noah, warning of the wrath to come. He was a father image to his children.

Daddy Grace, a Charismatic and Colorful Personality

Enjoying the publicity from frequent news interviews, Daddy Grace was something of a jest to the press. He displayed obvious determination not to expose himself as a person. He has been described as in-

[18] Ibid., p. 29.
[19] Casey, op. cit., p. E 1.

scrutable, enigmatic and wary, imperturbable and unafraid, but gracious and somehow charming, with a whimsical sense of humor.

In interviews, Daddy talked freely about the love of his followers and his home possessions. When the subject turned to money, he quoted from the Bible or spoke in parables:

The love of money is the root of all evil.

Never let your left hand know what the right hand is doing.[20]

As long as the conversation stayed close to Daddy's success, his homes and work, and his "children," the followers, he would occasionally commit himself, but not often. Despite what must have been a lack of formal education, Daddy spoke several languages and had what seemed a verbatim knowledge of the Bible. He also seemed to know a good bit of history.

Many setbacks failed to deter Daddy Grace. In 1934, ten years after the inception of the cult, Grace was indicted for violation of the Mann Act, transporting a female across state lines for immoral purposes. Daddy won that case as he has won practically all court disputes. Upon his death, his first wife, Jennie J. Lombard, whom he married in New Bedford, Massachusetts, in 1909, claimed a stake in the Grace estate.

Jennie Lombard claimed that Daddy deserted her for another woman. Although she received aid from her family, Mrs. Grace said she was forced to work to support their two children. She denied that the bishop ever offered to aid his children. Mrs. Jennie Grace was left out of Daddy's will which provided $70,500 for relatives. She insisted that there was no divorce, but other relatives of the bishop said that they had been divorced and that Mrs. Grace had no legal claim to the estate. To the writer's knowledge, Mrs. Grace never sustained her case.

One of Bishop Grace's most widely publicized cases was the Royster case in Washington, when Mrs. Louvenia Royster, a schoolteacher of Waycross, Georgia, filed a non-support suit against the prelate. The case was aired in 1957. Mrs. Royster said that she was married to Bishop Grace on September 26, 1923, in New York City, when he was known as "John H. Royster." In 1925, they moved to Stanford, Florida, where a daughter was reportedly born in 1927. In January 1928, her husband deserted her and disappeared, she contended. It was not until 1933 that Mrs. Royster discovered that he was using the name of Bishop Grace.[21]

---

[20] Phil Casey, "Parables Served Daddy to Evade Direct Replies," Washington *Post,* March 9, 1960, p. B 1.
[21] Rufus Wells, "The Secrets of Daddy Grace," *Afro-American,* March 5, 1960, p. 5.

After twelve days of testimony, the judge ruled in favor of Daddy Grace. He explained that John H. Royster was a natural-born citizen, while Bishop Grace was a native of Portugal who had remained a citizen of that country. The marriage could not be validated. After winning this costly non-support trial, Daddy was sued by his attorney, Franklyn Yasmer, for $50,000. However, Daddy remained imperturbable throughout all of the proceedings.

> I have already given him some. He can have some more. If he and I sit down together, I can give him something to buy ice cream with.[22]

Again in 1957, Daddy Grace was arrested in Richmond, Virginia, on a charge of assault and striking a fourteen-year-old girl at his House of Prayer in that city. Again, he was cleared of the charge at a hearing in Juvenile and Domestic Relations Court. The Washington and Richmond cases were the last court victories for the aging religious leader who was even then suffering with a heart condition that was to lead to his death in Los Angeles, California, on January 12, 1960.

During the height of his career, Daddy wrestled year after year with the Internal Revenue Service which claimed more than $5.9 million upon his death. Nevertheless, he continued to buy property. In 1956, Daddy took over the Detroit property of Prophet Jones. Earlier in the 30s his most publicized purchase (and one of his least expensive) was Father Divine's "Heaven."

Father Divine had made a claim to being God which came to Daddy's attention. He did not like it and decided to evict Divine by buying Divine's "Heaven" on West 115th Street, New York City. Daddy went to Edward M. Rogell, his Jewish estate advisor, asked about buying the ramshackle building and was told that it belonged to the bank. Daddy later bought the building. It is reported that he had the money in his pocket when he first approached Rogell. Reporters went to him for feature stories about the purchase:

> I will not drive him out of Harlem. I will give him peace and pity. I'm a servant of man. Let him stay.[23]

Nevertheless, Divine left his "Heaven" and set up headquarters elsewhere, saying he had willed it anyway.

[22] Phil Casey, "Friends Say Daddy Didn't Need Money, He Had Everything," *Washington Post*, March 10, 1960, p. A 26.
[23] Phil Casey, "Many Setbacks Failed to Deter Daddy Grace," *Washington Post*, March 8, 1960, p. B 4.

In spite of his many purchases, Daddy Grace was foremost a religious leader, and not a promoter of Afro-American business or social action. A real estate man and business partner of Daddy's, Samuel H. Keets, pointed out to the bishop that many of his followers were dying, unable to pay for burials. Daddy established the Family Aid Association for the United House of Prayer. Followers paid a membership fee and small monthly dues; Daddy got 25 per cent off the top.

The association was growing; meanwhile, Keets was working without pay. He wanted to start a complete insurance program for the church which, he claimed, "would make the Metropolitan Insurance Company look like a pup." However, Daddy lost interest, claiming that the program was getting bigger than he was. In a similar vein, Daddy made no contributions to the NAACP and did not encourage his followers to support this and other social action organizations.

To many critics, Daddy Grace was a charlatan who was "out for" money and women. On the other hand, Daddy was respected by a number of men of standing for his "religious genius" and sincerity. He was admired by relatives, some of whom worked with him, as a hardworking holy man. In addition to fulfilling the needs of many downtrodden, the United House of Prayer was effective in reducing crime. According to Frank Littlejohn, former chief of police in Charlotte, North Carolina:

> He set up his church on "murder corner" and crime was reduced greatly. It was the rarest thing in the world to see any of his members in any criminal trouble. He was really an asset.[24]

Daddy Grace's Successor

Little descriptive information has been written concerning Daddy Grace's successor, Walter McCullough. A former elder under Bishop Grace, Walter McCullough appears to be between fifty and fifty-five years of age. Approximately six feet tall, and of light complexion, Bishop McCullough wears gold-rimmed glasses and makes a distinguished-looking appearance. "Sweet Daddy Grace McCullough," as he is most often called, operated a tailor and dry-cleaning shop at 817 S St. N.W., Washington, D.C., prior to assuming leadership of the cult.

Bishop McCullough has not the charismatic and colorful personality of Daddy Grace. He is married and, to the writer's knowledge, has one son. Whereas the national headquarters remains at 601 M St. N.W.,

[24] Phil Casey, "Daddy's Outstanding Miracle: Hold on Flock," Washington *Post*, March 13, 1960, p. B 5.

Washington, D.C., followers are encouraged to write Bishop McCullough at his Washington residence, 300 Allison St. N.W. Here the bishop maintains a semidetached, inconspicuous row house. This was obviously his residence prior to his election.

In October 1967, the bishop made a twelve-day trip to the Holy Land. He was accompanied by his immediate family, his general secretary, and senior minister among others. Upon his return he made little claim to conversions, healings, and cures as had his predecessor. McCullough's followers were out in full numbers and regalia to greet Sweet Daddy at Kennedy International Airport, New York City. However, his return received no publicity in the New York *Times* or other major New York papers.

In conducting religious services, McCullough carries himself in much the same style as did Daddy Grace. During fire-hose baptisms in Washington, McCullough has sat Grace-style on the back of a flat-bottomed truck, in a leather chair, under a terrace umbrella held upright by two retainers. Like Grace, he has looked impassively at the crowd of more than a thousand as an evangelistic orator roused the faithful. Like Grace, McCullough wears his hair long, and like Grace, who was renowned more as a "presence" and a "spirit," McCullough is not a powerful speaker.

Successor Inherits Legal Turmoil

Bishop McCullough assumed a host of legal difficulties when he took over leadership of the United House of Prayer. Upon the death of Daddy Grace, the elders deliberated on the interpretation of the Constitution and By-laws which stated that a bishop would be elected from among the regular ministers who would be the chief executive and spiritual advisor. The elders designated Walter McCullough, one of the chief elders and Chairman of the District of Columbia, to select the date, place, and time of the election.[25]

The election took place on February 6, 1969 at 10 A.M. in Washington, D.C. There were five nominees running for the office of bishop. When the final vote had been cast, the nominees received one, four, five, eighty-eight, and one hundred and seventeen votes respectively. Elder McCullough was victorious, polling more than half of all the votes cast.[26] However, dissident factions within the United House of

[25] Walter McCullough, "The Truth and Facts of the United House of Prayer," (Washington: United House of Prayer, 1966), p. 1.
[26] Ibid., p. 1.

Prayer took court action, claiming the election illegal. At the same time, the Internal Revenue Service sought back taxes from the Grace estate totaling $5.9 million.

Attorneys for the United House of Prayer argued that the IRS' estimates of the worth of the Grace estate included property that Grace held only as leader of the House of Prayer. The attorneys also filed protests to the tax liens, claiming that all tax deficiencies in the 1945–55 period was excused by the statute of limitations. Their motion protested many penalty charges for non-payment of taxes and noted that Bishop Grace's marital status between 1952 and 1954 was, at the time, still undecided by the court in Bristol County, Massachusetts.[27]

Meanwhile, Walter McCullough filed suit against James Walton of Philadelphia, and his lay followers to prevent them from using the church's name. Simultaneously, Walton had a suit going against McCullough demanding an accounting of the church finances. Within two months, John McClure, a former minister of the House of Prayer, filed suit, asking for a final court determination naming the legal heirs of Daddy Grace. One of eight defendants in the McClure suit was Walter McCullough who was charged with "usurping the bishopric" when Grace died.

District Court Judge George L. Hart called for peace in the legal battle besetting the House of Prayer. He referred to the case as a "can of worms" as attorneys argued over which faction of the United House of Prayer was frustrating settlement.[28] On August 25, 1961, Judge Hart issued a restraining order deposing Walter McCullough as head of the United House of Prayer. He froze the assets of the organization in the hands of a receiver, William Bryant. The judge noted that McCullough had removed at least $31,000 from Daddy's office closet to which he alone had a key, explaining later that it was in a safe place.

In the same ruling, the judge touched on the sale by McCullough of a huge New York apartment supposedly sanctioned by McCullough's election meeting. No indication of this was found. Attorney Bryant was to arrange a new election and to unshuffle the funds, properties, and investments of the Grace estate.

The restraining order was issued because the court contended the following:

a. The first election was invalid because only the Elders had voted and representatives were not sent from each congregation to vote.

[27] News item in the Washington *Post*, June 16, 1960, p. B 3.
[28] News item in the Washington *Post*, July 29, 1960, p. A 3.

b. The election should have been called and supervised by the Senior Minister.[29]

There had never been a Senior Minister in the House of Prayer serving under Daddy Grace. The General Council had appointed Walter McCullough to act as chairman, but they were told by attorneys that they had the power to appoint someone to act as Senior Minister. In addition to the restraining order, the judge ruled to bar the use of the title "Sweet Daddy" by any of Grace's successors. The government had placed liens and levies against all of the House of Prayer funds and properties and the operation of the organization was paralyzed.

The court ordered a second election to be held on April 7 and 8, 1962 under the supervision of the receiver. The General Assembly, consisting of all elders, pastors, and two representatives from each congregation met and voted. When the final count of the votes was completed, there were 462 votes cast. Four candidates ran for the bishopric. Bishop McCullough was elected by a landslide of 410 votes.

In early July 1962, Attorney Bryant issued a statement that more than $4.7 million remained of the Daddy Grace estate. He listed bank holdings of $1,576,000 and property valued at $3,110,000.[30] It was not until March 1963, however, when the court completed its ruling and handed over the control of more than $4.5 million in assets to Bishop McCullough as Daddy Grace's legal successor. Until this time, Bishop McCullough, now legally elected, was still involved in suing dissident factions.

Practices

The practices of the United House of Prayer have remained much the same as they were during the days of Daddy Grace. Services are still held nightly and all day on Sundays. The writer spent a number of nights observing the "mother" House of Prayer of New York City, located on the second floor at 2320 Eighth Avenue. This house consists of a meeting room seating approximately five hundred, several offices, including a lavish room at the rear of the auditorium for Bishop McCullough, and a large kitchen equipped with counters for sales.

The auditorium is dominated by a central platform, the holy mountain. At the rear center of the platform is a red-cushioned chair, the bishop's seat. There are lamps on each side of this chair and a huge mirror behind it. Red carpet adorns the platform which is enclosed by

[29] McCullough, op. cit., p. 2.
[30] News item in the Washington *Post*, July 4, 1962, p. C 3.

a wooden bannister painted red, blue, and white. The chair and two wooden podiums remain covered when the bishop is not present. At the base of the platform is written "One Man, One Baptism, One Way Eph. 4:5." A large picture of Bishop McCullough seated with robe and crown overhangs the central chair. The platform is lit by sparkling chandeliers. On either side of the platform, outside of the bannister, are two ordinary chairs, the seats of the local leaders.

The services do not differ greatly from the days of Daddy Grace. The typical night service begins whenever enough worshipers are present, usually between 7:30 and 8:00 P.M. The service consists of singing, testifying, extemporaneous preaching by the elders and minister, marching, and collection raising. Members are encouraged to call out and second the speaker. However, the singing most often arouses the members to jump and shout. At any point in the service, members are liable to make their way to the platform and to dance around it, but all services end by members gathering around the "holy mountain" singing and shouting and reciting a prayer of dismissal.

One night a week is "pastor's night," and the service assumes the form of a talent show. Members sing, shout, witness, and strut to the rhythm of the brass band. The pastor's salary consists of the collection taken one night a week, and it is probably on this night that he collects his money.

When Sweet Daddy McCullough is present, more of everything occurs. On one occasion when the writer observed Bishop McCullough in New York City, he remained seated for most of the service, holding a stack of money in his right hand. Photographers who made their way to the front had first to give a monetary contribution to McCullough's female platform attendants before they could photograph the bishop.

When Sweet Daddy left the platform, members lined the center aisle, shoving bills into his hands. All the time collecting money and occasionally giving some out, Daddy paused and listened to some, and touched others as if to heal. Given bags of candy, he tossed pieces to his followers who scrambled frantically to catch them.

People and Beliefs

The United House of Prayer continues to be patronized by low-income, downtrodden, uneducated Afro-Americans. Three-quarters of the followers are female. The average formal educational level of the followers of the Eighth Avenue House appears to be about the sixth grade. It was interesting to note much less emotionalism shown in the crowded service attended at the "mother house" in Washington, D.C.

than at the services of the Eighth Avenue House in New York. Whereas no written restrictions were put on dress under Daddy Grace, each house of prayer now contains a sign which specifies that men are to wear coats and ties to worship services. This regulation is not enforced, however.

The beliefs of the cult remain essentially the same as those of a holiness sect—that is, conversion, sanctification, the intervention of the Holy Spirit, etc. One unique characteristic of the cult is that its members did not believe in the word "church," as commonly used. For them there are not "churches" but Houses of Prayer which are open to all people. Only God's elect, those who speak in tongues and have had a conversion experience, belong to the "church," apparently an organization with no formal structure.

In addition, the religious identity of the present leader has been much better clarified. Although many members still appear to worship Sweet Daddy Grace McCullough, others will admit openly that he is not God, but a prophet, God's only messenger on earth. They maintain that Daddy Grace and Bishop McCullough are religiously equal, but that Bishop McCullough is Grace's son. The relationship is clarified by two identical murals on the rear wall of the temple in Washington, D.C., "God's White House." These murals depict God looking down on Jesus and Daddy Grace, who are standing on a par shaking hands. The setting is obviously heaven. With one hand Daddy points below to a bust-photograph of McCullough, and says, "This is my beloved son in whom I am well pleased." Daddy Grace and Bishop McCullough are thought to have been the only prophets on earth since Jesus. Apparently they are equivalent to Jesus.

Bishop McCullough is thought to be a prophet and a healer. On October 17, 1962, Daddy McCullough wrote a letter to every House of Prayer throughout the eighteen states claiming that he had been moved by the Holy Spirit and that it had been revealed to him by God that serious trouble was about to shake the world. He urged his followers to go to the "holy mountain" no later than 10 P.M., on October 22, 1962, and "let the spiritual wind blow its breeze of blessings from on high on them. He was speaking of the same wind that was felt on the day of Pentecost."[31]

On October 22, the Cuban crisis had the world upset. Followers of Bishop McCullough maintain that it was their prayers which kept war and destruction from American soil. This gave rise to the "Spiritual

[31] "Welcome to God's House and Vineyard," Throw-away, United House of Prayer, (undated), p. 6.

Hurricane" services which are held every Thursday, Friday, and Saturday nights at 10 P.M.

> Many souls have been saved, bodies healed, and troubles cast away in the Spiritual Hurricane. The Spiritual Hurricane will bring peace to those who are in sorrow, consolation for those who are in trouble, healing for the sick, and salvation and life for the sin sick and spiritually dead.[32]

The United House of Prayer's solution for the ills of the world is summarized in the formula: singing, shouting, and praying.

Unlike Daddy Grace, Bishop McCullough apparently does not heal by the laying on of hands. His remedy is faith in Daddy, singing, shouting and praying.

> I got on the telephone and I called Madam and she relayed the message to Daddy. I told her the doctor told me he wanted me to go to the hospital. And, a few minutes later, my telephone rang and it was Madam McCullough giving me a message from Precious Daddy telling me to pack my clothes, get on the road with him, as he was en route to Miami, Florida. And that as I went along the road singing and shouting nightly that I would be healed.

> . . . After the House was turned over to Sweet Daddy McCullough, he began teaching. The (man) that shouts the most, the one that speaks in tongues the most, that one has the most God. He further taught about glorifying God. One lady was shouting after all the others had stopped and Dad said that that Sister had more God than anyone in here. Something went over me and I shouted out of my shoes. I shouted and shouted and cried after hearing the Man of God speak. And that night for the first time in three and one half months, I Slept All Night Long. . . .[33]

Developments and Innovations

Although Bishop McCullough lacks the charism of Daddy Grace, he is an organization man. Between 1961 and 1965, he built at least a dozen new Houses of Prayer and made improvements in old facilities. He purchased approximately nine buildings to be converted into Houses of Prayer and bought land in at least four states for future development.

[32] Ibid., p. 10.
[33] Louise Wilkerson, "Testimonial," *Grace Magazine*, August 1967, p. 5.

Bishop McCullough designed the marble mausoleum which he had erected in the Pine Grove Cemetery in New Bedford, Massachusetts, where the body of Daddy Grace is interred. He effected the building of the main temple in Washington, D.C. which was dedicated on November 28, 1965. The temple is constructed of white split stone with three domes on the top of the building as a symbol of the Capitol. Prior to the dedication ceremony, McCullough said:

Just as the President of the United States has a White House, so must God have a White House.[34]

Daddy Grace McCullough replaced the old "General Council By-Laws" by a revised edition called the "Supreme Laws for the Government of the United House of Prayer for All People on the Rock of the Apostolic Faith." These laws make provisions for the election of a successor to the bishop. They require that an account be given for every penny of money raised at Houses of Prayer. However, neither regulations are applicable to, nor commitments required from, the bishop. The By-Laws are paternalistic and legalistic in their treatment of members.

Article XVII (17)

. . . Section A. All members of good standing must first consult the Bishop before marriage and give full respect to his decision, as the Constitution states, "His decision is final."

Section B. No member of this Organization, regardless to his standing, should marry without consulting his Pastor, as the Bishop's rule that this Organization does not approve of a mixed-faith marriage.

Section C. Any Minister or Elder of this Faith and Organization who marries without consent of the Bishop has disrespected the Bishop and will be discharged from the Elder Board.

Section D. Any Minister or Elder who is caught marrying a couple without consent of the Bishop will be discharged from the Elder Board.[35]

[34] News item in the *Afro-American,* August 27, 1966, p. 6.
[35] Walter McCullough, "The Supreme Laws for the Government of the United House of Prayer . . . ," Washington: United House of Prayer for All People, 1962, pp. 11–12.

Madam McCullough assists the bishop by visiting a number of houses herself. She does not work for individual organizations, but only for a house, city, district or state. Another development of the bishop's is the Back the Attack Club. This club reports to Washington monthly. It was set up by Daddy McCullough to assist the organization and members from any attack by enemies. A special fund is set up to assist the organization in its legal battles.

Bishop McCullough's latest development has been the establishment of a ministerial school in Richmond, Virginia. During 1967, he issued a call for five hundred ministers which terminated at the end of the year. The course of study is set up to train ministers to interpret the Scripture, the rules and regulations of the organization, and to perform ceremonial rites such as marriages, funerals, etc. One does not have to be a member of a House of Prayer to sign for the training. Moreover, one merely has to give his name to a secretary to become a member of a House of Prayer. This is the primary reason for the impossibility of ascertaining the cult membership. The training will prepare elders to become pastors at the completion of their course. While engaged in their studies, they will be provided free room and board, with transportation their only expense.

Conclusion

The present United House of Prayer has retained the basic beliefs and ritual from its administration under Daddy Grace. Heightened emotionalism and money raising remain unique characteristics of the cult. Yet they are not practiced to as intense a degree as under Daddy Grace. Bishop McCullough has tightened the organization by means of his "Supreme Laws . . ." The bishop's powers have been thereby increased; nevertheless, he has given the organization more of an institutional structure. In order to continue to operate as an unchallenged dictator, the bishop must now be more shrewd than in the days when there were no checks and balances within the organization—the days when he was religious leader and administrator.

It is common for cults to disintegrate upon the death of their leader. However, the genius of Daddy Grace provided, even though ambiguously, for a successor. Although Bishop McCullough, the successor, lacks the religious charism and originality of Daddy Grace, both his tenacity in pursuing legal action and his organizational ability have given stability to the movement. His organization of a formal ministerial school is unprecedented in cult leadership. If Bishop McCullough continues to operate in the same style, his successor will inherit not a "man-worshiping" cult, but a holiness sect with a powerful bishop.

This transformation will not in itself promise a successful future for the United House of Prayer or for any other black Christian institution for that matter. The level of discontent is uncontrollable within the ghetto. More and more the black Christian minister and the black church are attacked by black militants and more conservative youth for their pacification of exploited blacks and their general irrelevancy.

The other-worldly singing and shouting religion of the United House of Prayer was the norm among black churches of free-worship pattern during Daddy Grace's heyday. Many of these churches still exist, especially in the core of the black ghetto. However, the better established black Christian churches of today are being forced to update their theology, and to become involved in the liberation of their people and in other social action projects.

If the United House of Prayer is to continue to be of any great attraction, it might well retain its soulful singing, many organizations, evangelistic testifying, and preaching patterns, but it must develop a relevant theology and become involved in the spiritual and secular problems of its followers.

BIBLIOGRAPHY

Afro-American, August 27, 1966, p. 6.

Casey, Phil, "The Enigma of Daddy Grace: Did He Play God?", Washington *Post*, March 6, 1960, p. E 1.

Casey, Phil, "Whatever He Did Was Automatically Right," Washington *Post*, March 7, 1960, p. B 1.

Casey, Phil, "Many Setbacks Failed to Deter Daddy Grace," Washington *Post*, March 8, 1960, pp. B 1, B 4.

Casey, Phil, "Parables Served Daddy To Evade Direct Replies," Washington *Post*, March 9, 1960, pp. B 11, B 12.

Casey, Phil, "Friends Say Daddy Didn't Need Money, He Had Everything," Washington *Post*, March 10, 1960, p. A 26.

Casey, Phil, "Daddy's Money Grew on Trees (Man-Made)," Washington *Post*, March 11, 1960, pp. B 11, B 12.

Casey, Phil, "Daddy's Outstanding Miracle: Hold on Flock," Washington *Post*, March 13, 1960, p. B 5.

Fauset, Arthur. *Black Gods of the Metropolis*. Philadelphia: University of Pennsylvania Press, 1944.

McCullough, Walter, "The Supreme Laws for the Government of the United House of Prayer . . . ," Washington: United House of Prayer for All People, 1962.

McCullough, Walter. "The Truth and Facts of the United House of Prayer," Washington: United House of Prayer, 1966.

United House of Prayer, "Welcome to God's House and Vineyard," undated, p. 6.

Washington *Post*:

June 16, 1960, p. B 3.

July 12, 1960, p. B 3.

July 29, 1960, pp. A 3, B 11.

August 26, 1961, p. A 3.

August 28, 1961, p. A 11.

August 31, 1961, p. B 7.

April 9, 1962, p. A 1.

May 9, 1962, p. B 3.

July 4, 1962, p. C 3.

August 14, 1962, p. A 3.

September 1, 1962, p. D 1.

October 18, 1962, p. D 1.

March 7, 1963, p. B 7.

Wells, Rufus, "The Secrets of Daddy Grace," *Afro-American*, March 5, 1960, p. 5.

Wilkerson, Louise, "Testimonial," *Grace Magazine*, August 1967, p. 5.

C. ERIC LINCOLN

The new wave of black ethnicity which dominated the 1960s brought new acceptability for the Black Muslims. As "black people" they were welcomed into the ranks of "Blackamerica" with unaccustomed fervor. Religious differences were brushed aside by Blacks who had finally discovered an acceptable identity (but not by the Muslims, who already knew who they were)! Ironically, the Black Muslims had been trying to teach the values of ethnicity to a sceptical black community, who, bent on integration, had found little in Muhammad's doctrines to attract them. The pattern has changed now, and the prosperous Black Muslims are now often pointed to with pride, and sometimes with envy.

The Muslim acceptance outside the ghetto is less certain. While they enjoy all of the legal privileges of other religions, their legitimacy is still suspect and they are largely ignored by mainstream religion. This is nettlesome to the Muslim leadership, which, while it does not especially want to be identified with orthodox Islam, does want recognition as being legitimately Islamic.

The Black Muslims (or the Nation of Islam) are an important segment of self-conscious black religion in America. Their notable success

235

in making their religion a total way of life, and thus integrating their economic, political, social, and even dietary interest into their religious understanding, has had a marked effect upon their effective adjustment to minority status in America.

C. Eric Lincoln is Chairman of the Department of Religious and Philosophical Studies at Fisk University and editor of the C. Eric Lincoln Series in Black Religion.

THE BLACK MUSLIMS AND BLACK ACCEPTANCE

Source: C. Eric Lincoln, *The Black Muslims in America* (Boston: Beacon Press, 1973), (Revised Edition), pp. 232-50.

A major goal of the Muslim leadership a decade ago was the general acceptance of the Movement as a legitimate religion—specifically, as a legitimate sect of orthodox Islam. This is no longer considered necessary: the Muslims' self-respect does not hinge on such acceptance. Muhammad has stated that the Muslims *are* legitimate and Islamic, and so far as the Muslims themselves are concerned, this settles the matter. Nor is it an expedient directed at the black community any longer, for the aegis of orthodox Islam means little in America's black ghettos. So long as the Movement keeps its color identity with the rising black peoples of Africa, it could discard all its Islamic attributes—its name, its prayers to Allah, its citations from the Quran, everything "Muslim" without substantial risk to its appeal to the black masses.

In pressing their demand for complete acceptance as a legitimate religion and a Moslem sect, the Muslims had their eye primarily on the white community. In many ways, America does live up to its democratic ideal in the elaborate safeguards it provides for freedom of worship. Religious groups in America are unfettered; only in the most extreme cases is certain behavior in the name of religion construed as against public policy and, as such, prohibited. The Black Muslims know that, as they prosper, they will encounter repression and reprisal. The more swiftly and securely they become acknowledged as a legitimate religion, the more securely they could rely upon the counterpressures of democratic toleration and constitutional immunity to protect them from harassment. Malcolm X was a strong advocate of the internationalization of the Nation of Islam. Elijah Muhammad never was. While he may have wanted the legitimacy of orthodoxy, the possibility of his black nation losing its identity in the vast configurations of international Islam was not a notion he ever entertained seriously. What he wanted was recognition as a legitimate religious leader presiding over a legitimate religion.

The Muslims have generally been given the benefit of the doubt. They have been treated, if only provisionally, as a legitimate religion. Except in prisons, their meetings have never been barred by any agency of the government. The Universities of Islam are legally approved as parochial schools. And the temples and school properties are tax exempt in all states where they exist, under the same regulations that govern the church properties of all other religious bodies.

But this provisional acceptance is not enough. The Black Muslims are not generally included in the national gatherings of religious leaders, and Muhammad, who frequently equates himself with "the pope of Rome," resents being snubbed. Beyond that, the FBI keeps the Movement under as close surveillance as it would a political terrorist organization. And in some instances, the Muslims' status as a religion has been flatly denied by government officials. Perhaps the most significant of these denials to date have occurred in prisons, which are among the Muslims' most fertile recruiting grounds. In some prisons, the Muslims are permitted to hold services, but in others they are denied the right of assembly. A case in point is Clinton State Prison at Utica, New York, where four inmates were allegedly placed in solitary confinement when they sought to practice their new faith. (The warden described three of the prisoners as "Protestants a year ago"; the fourth had been a Catholic.) Prison officials did not dispute that discipline improves markedly among those converted to Islam, but they protested that the Muslims have "ulterior motives," aimed at "forcing supremacy over whites, although they do not express it."

To defend themselves against such harassments, now and in the future, the Muslims are pressing hard for complete recognition as a legitimate religion, on equal terms with the reigning triumvirate of Protestants, Catholics, and Jews, but they do not want to be identified with "white orthodox" Islam. The orthodox Muslims are denounced for currying favor with the (white) enemy. The Asiatic origin of the Nation is now down-played: "The Black African, the Aboriginal Black People of the earth are our real brothers," says Muhammad. "The Black Man of America and the Black Man of Africa must unite again. We are a part of, and belong to, each other." Hence, the Muslims want to be "Islamic" but not "orthodox," because orthodoxy is contaminated with the implications of whiteness. Just how this goal is to be accomplished is not exactly clear, but Muhammad speaks of a "New Islam" to be ushered in after his death:

It will be a New Islam to what the old Orthodox is today. It will be altogether a New One. . . . The Old Islam was led by white people, white Muslims, but this one will not be. This Islam will be established and led by Black Muslims only.

Who will rule over the new Black Islam? Allah. Once the truth has been established, there will be no need for human intermediaries:

There will be no successor. There will be no need for a successor when a man has got the divine truth and has brought you face to face with God. . . . When we are face to face with God, that is the end of it, and so what would another one do? There is nothing for him to do.

In fact, Muhammad sees himself as the last Messenger the Black Nation will ever have, or need. He has brought his people to the point where they, if his teachings are followed, will be able (to use his own famous aphorism) to go for self. As for the material wealth gathered by the Nation, it will be looked after in terms of instructions already laid down. The whole Nation will be responsible:

That will be carried on by the Nation. After setting up the Nation on the right way, or right path, to take care of themselves, they do not need any more instruction on that. They will follow it as the Constitution of America will be followed.

It is commonly accepted among the faithful that in lieu of ordinary death, Muhammad will "go away for a period," after which he will return with Allah himself—"in person of Fard Muhammad." Hence the Messenger's reference to bringing them "face to face with God." Following the Messenger's lead, the Black Muslim rank and file have taken up the task of distinguishing between themselves and the "spooky-minded" orthodox Muslims. Orthodox Muslims are "spooky minded" because "they believe that Allah is some immaterial something, but yet he made a material universe!" (Alas! Most Christians must also be "spooky minded!") The Blacks are the true Muslims:

. . . every Black Man under the sun is born a Muslim by nature. . . . There are some of the white race who are Muslims by faith. The white race is the only people on Earth that are not real Muslims, or Black Muslims by nature. . . . These poor Orthodox or Conventional Muslim brothers fail to understand our Leader . . . the Honorable Elijah Muhammad. . . . 99% of our Muslim brothers from the East have been deceived one way or another. . . .

The notion that Black Muslims are seeking indiscriminate solidarity with the world of orthodox Islam is further shattered by Ali Baghdadi's attack on Iran in his column "Middle East Report" in *Muhammad Speaks*:

> The 2500 year birthday celebration of the so-called Persian empire, destroyed by Alexander the Great, is just one of the many reasons for which the Shah of Iran, "King of Kings, Light of the Aryans, Shadow of God, and Center of the Universe," should be brought to trial as one of the most wanted world criminals. This party unmatched in history cost the impoverished people of Iran over $80 million. Some say the total cost is closer to $2 billion.

Iran's foreign policy fares no better:

> The Shah's reactionary policy, which is in agreement with the Nixon doctrine, simply means that Asians equipped by the U.S. government will be used to suppress other Asians seeking national liberation and progress.
> The Shah has made it clear that he intends to secure the colonial interests of the United States and to guarantee the flow of oil to his imperialist masters.

At the moment, orthodox Islamic groups in the United States do not acknowledge the Black Muslims as in any way related to world-wide Islam. The response from Arab and other Moslem nations is more ambiguous. There seems to be no good reason to doubt that the Black Muslims will eventually find the acceptance they want in international Islam, and this despite their insistent parochialism. In rejecting orthodoxy, Muhammad has been careful not to reject Islam, nor for that matter does he reject all Moslems who are orthodox. His adulation of the late President Nasser of Egypt is undiminished, and apparently the whole Arab bloc (which is considered "black" by many Blackamericans, Muslim and non-Muslim) is excluded from the worst implications of the "spooky minded."

A Legitimate Religion?

The line that separates a purely social organization from a purely religious communion is seldom well defined. Religion is, in part, a facet of man's social life; and social concerns are at times invested with an almost religious aura. Some great religious movements developed originally out of social concerns (Methodism is a well-known example), and social movements ranging from communism to the Townsend Plan have exhibited marked religious overtones. An incipient mass movement such as the Black Muslims, therefore, may be *both* "social" and "religious," though its emphasis will be weighted in one direction or the other.

America has always been wary of definitions which claim to draw a precise line between the religious and the secular. Such definitions tend to be either too nebulous or too subjective; in either case, they are unreliable guides for a democracy intent on safeguarding an absolute freedom of worship. The American public, as a result, eschews all rigid criteria of orthodoxy and maintains an historically unique tolerance of religious deviation. Americans may reject and even combat an organization which claims to be a religion, but they are not likely to deny that it *is* a religion.

Within the American tradition, then, it is not necessary for the Black Muslims to prove that they are a valid religious communion. The question is whether it can be proved that they are *not*. If the negative cannot be proved, a general acceptance of the Movement as a legitimate religion is assured.

Emile Durkheim, one of the most critical observers and students of the sociology of religion, insists that any attempt at a definition of religion must derive from the existential phenomenon, from "the reality itself . . . for religion cannot be defined except by the characteristics which are found wherever religion itself is found." At an irreducible minimum, he suggests, these characteristics are *beliefs* and *rites*.

> Religious phenomena are naturally arranged in two fundamental categories: beliefs and rites. The first are states of opinion, and consist in representations; the second are determined modes of action.

A religious rite is distinguished from its secular counterpart by the sacred nature of its object. A moral rule or a legal statute, for example, may prescribe behavior identical to that of a religious rite; but the religious prescription refers to a different *class of objects*. The religious object is "sacred"; the secular object, even when of the highest social value, is "profane." There is no necessary relationship, however, between the sacred and either "deity" or the "supernatural." Neither the divine nor the supernatural is necessary to a religion.

> The circle of sacred objects cannot be determined . . . once for all. Its extent varies infinitely, according to the different religions. That is how

Buddhism is a religion: in default of gods, it admits the existence of sacred things, namely, the four noble truths and the practices derived from them.

Indeed, the "circle of sacred objects" cannot be rationally defined at all. That is sacred which the believers of a particular faith *feel* is sacred. And this feeling is at once the most subjective and most widespread, the most familiar and most elusive of phenomena. It evades definition, yet its presence is the identifying mark of a legitimate religion. In pragmatic terms, wherever a body of men shares the feeling that a specific group of objects is sacred and has elaborated this feeling into specific beliefs and rites, there a religion must be said to exist.

It must be granted, then, that the Black Muslim Movement constitutes a legitimate religion within the definition of the sociology of religion. But there are many kinds of religion; and while all enjoy a nearly unrestricted freedom of worship in America, they are not all granted equal deference and respect by the community at large. Mere cults, for example, like the followers of Father Divine and "Daddy Grace," are not taken as seriously as Presbyterians, say, or as Jews. But the Black Muslims want and are determined to achieve the respect of all Americans, even of the "blue-eyed devils." Their success will depend, in large part, on the *kind* of religion they are—that is, on the degree of religious stability and respectability they can be said to have achieved.

Perhaps the best-known analysis of religious groups into broad categories is that developed by Ernst Troeltsch and refined by J. Milton Yinger. This system of categories, like all others familiar to Americans, is based on Christian groups, and there is no real assurance that it is valid when applied to non-Christian religions such as the Black Muslims. It is, nevertheless, the system by which the Muslims will be evaluated by most Americans; it is the scale against which the Muslims will actually be measured in their demand for deference and respect.

Troeltsch divides religious groups into two types: the *church* and the *sect*. The leader of a church is characteristically a "priest"; the leader of a sect is characteristically a "prophet." In broader terms:

> The Church is that type of organization which is overwhelmingly conservative, which to a certain extent accepts the secular order, and dominates the masses; in principle, therefore, it is universal; i.e., it desires to cover the whole life of humanity. The sects, on the other hand, are comparatively small groups; they aspire after personal inward perfection, and they aim at a direct personal fellowship between the members of each

241

group. . . . Their attitude towards the world, the State, and Society may be indifferent, tolerant, or hostile since they have no desire to control and incorporate these forms of social life; on the contrary, they tend to avoid them; their aim is usually either to tolerate their presence alongside of their own body, or even to replace these social institutions by their own society.

The church, in short, attempts to include the whole society in its outlook and thus inevitably becomes an integral part of the social order. It may even become a determining force, providing stability and sanction; but to the same extent it becomes a captive of the upper classes and dependent on them. The church may thus defeat its own ends, for as the lower classes find themselves abandoned, schisms will occur, and the social order will again be threatened. New religious groups, or sects, will then coalesce in response to various middle- and lower-class needs not met by the church—needs which center at times on theological or ritual disagreements but more often on questions of economic or political enfranchisement, racial or ethnic status, social mobility or social change. The church, to the extent that it is a balance wheel of the status quo, is impotent to cope with such revolutionary tensions.

The sect, by contrast, draws primarily upon the disinherited, the unchampioned, and those opposed to the existing social order. It repudiates the compromises the church has made with secular institutions, and it resents the church's failure to assert itself against social abuses. The sect may respond to worldly evil by withdrawing from society, hoping to avoid present injustice and ultimate perdition, or by embracing a radicalism intended to establish in the social order its own ideals and sense of justice.

Not all sects (as Yinger points out) originate in the lower classes. The Methodist movement, for example, "remained throughout its history in the control of men who had been born and bred in the middle class," although it was substantially a lower-class movement until recent times. The Bahais, Christian Scientists, Theosophists, and numerous other familiar sects have been predominantly middle class from their inception. Middle-class sects are not characteristically in protest against the social order, for they have usually been favored by it. They are more often disenchanted with the institutionalized churches, which seem to them to be neglecting essential human values.

Lower-class sects, on the other hand, are most often spawned in poverty, disprivilege, depression, and despair. They are the refuge of those who are without power and who lack even an effective advocate in the circles where power resides. The existing society has been unjust to them, so they will reorganize the social order—usually along lines that those in power construe as "radical." But sects of this type tend to elicit concerted opposition and are thus predisposed to failure. They incur the hostility not only of the power elite but also of the less radical sects, which are potentially more mobile and which stand to suffer if the power structure, feeling threatened, becomes more rigidly exclusive. The usual history of a radical sect is therefore short.

The Black Muslim Movement is clearly a sect, in Troeltsch's broad definition of that term. Appealing to an almost exclusively Christian black community, the Movement repudiates the Christian church not only in particulars but *in toto*. It insists upon the separations of black men from white society, leaving that corrupt edifice to crumble under the weight of its own iniquity. And where the Movement is forced into contact with the white community, it reacts with a radicalism which is—from the Muslim point of view, at least—idealistic and just. But to categorize the Muslims as a sect is not quite so simple as Troeltsch's terms suggest, for Yinger's modification introduces a new element that must be carefully reckoned with.

As part of his refinement of Troeltsch's categories, Yinger points to the existence of a third type of religious group which, while it somewhat resembles the sect, is in fact quite dissimilar. This type is the *cult*, a small group of people unrelated to any other religious institution and "tied together only by common religious emotions and needs." Yinger seems to consider the Black Muslims a cult, pure and simple:

> Pure cult types are not common in Western society; most groups that might be called cults are fairly close to the sect type. Perhaps the best examples are the various Spiritualist groups and some of the "Moslem" cults among American Negroes.

The cult, as Yinger defines it, is characteristically organized around a charismatic leader (such as Muhammad), in whom are centered the loyalties of the rank and file. As a result, the cult usually is confined to a small area and dies with its founder: problems of succession are not effectively anticipated, and the bereaved cult disintegrates into splinter groups, which eventually fade into oblivion. But while it exists, the cult deviates even more sharply than the sect from the dominant church and the established social order, and its "implications for anarchy are even stronger." It takes individual problems, especially the "search for a mystic experience," as its total concern and shows little or no interest in problems of social justice. Cult members are typically indifferent to their status and prospects in the developing society.

On the surface, the Black Muslim Movement might seem to merit Yinger's designation of it as a cult. It is (1) a relatively small group of people, (2) under strong charismatic leadership, (3) deviating sharply from the established social order and, (4) diverging absolutely from the dominant church of its society. But on close inspection, a number of significant differences appear. (These differences were perhaps not familiar to Yinger when he wrote in 1957, for there had been no serious published study of the Black Muslims in almost twenty-five years.)

The Muslims originated as a small, local group, but in their period of greatest growth—the middle 1950s to 1964—their membership may have reached between 50,000 and 100,000. No one outside the movement can be certain, and only the inner circle of the inner circle of the Chicago headquarters of the Nation would have the inside information on membership. There are still more than fifty mosques stretching across the country and many of these have satellite units identified only as "A," "B," "C," etc. While still relatively small compared to the nation's major religious bodies, they are larger than *most* American denominations, sects, and cults. More than fifty Protestant denominations, for example, have fewer than ten congregations each, and more than half the sects in the nation have only 7,000 members or less.

The impressive cohesion of the Black Muslim Movement today is certainly due to the charismatic leadership of Elijah Muhammad. True, he is not the founder of the Movement but only the Messenger of Allah; the Muslims passed through their first crisis of succession when, under extremely divisive conditions, the mantle was passed down from Wallace Fard to Muhammad. Yet the Muslims' absolute loyalty to Muhammad and their uncritical faith in his wisdom and leadership suggest a simple continuity of charisma, which has postponed the problem of succession without really solving it. On the other hand—and perhaps of decisive importance—the Movement is rapidly developing a firm organizational structure. Under the direction of an aggressive clergy and inner council, the Movement continues to expand vigorously in all parts of the country without the physical presence of the Messenger.

The Muslims do deviate sharply from the established social order, and their call for separation in some ways resembles the withdrawal characteristic of the cult. The Muslims consider futile any attempt to reform American society; they plan simply to retire from it, cultivate the Black Nation and wait. The white devils, lacking black victims, will then presumably turn on each other and destroy themselves, and the Black Man will inherit the earth. Yet the driving force of the Movement is not separatism *per se*, but a sense of the unique manifest destiny Allah has decreed for the Black Man. In the Black Muslim's understanding of ultimate reality, the white man simply *isn't!* His present temporary existence is an anachronism, a physical and social aberration foisted upon human society by a mad devil named Yacub. The devils now have the upper hand over Allah's Black Nation; hence, the torrent of racial condemnation which fills its sermons and publications is undeniably social protest, all the more so for its bitter rejection of any hope for reform. There is no trace among the Muslims of that mystical absorption and indifference to social injustice which mark a cult.

Finally, the Muslims are unequivocal in their repudiation of the dominant church in American society. Their beliefs and rites are almost totally deviant from those of the Christian tradition, and within this frame of reference a case might be made for labeling them a cult. But the Muslims do not claim to be a Christian sect. They have declared themsleves an integral part of Islam, which they consider the church of the Black Nation. Muslim leaders are now working skillfully and hard to establish the Movement's authenticity as a legitimate Moslem sect. If they succeed—and it seems virtually certain that they will—the last realistic argument that would relegate the Movement to the status of a cult will have been answered.

The massive weight of all available evidence, in short, suggests that the Black Muslim Movement is not a cult but a sect. It is not local, ephemeral, or isolated; it will be shaken by, but will probably not collapse at Muhammad's death; and it may soon be able to draw upon the vast prestige and power of international Islam to defend it in case of harassment by the white community, despite its repudiation of orthodoxy. To shrug it off, in the manner of some observers, as "just another cult" would be a tragic error. The Muslims today are powerless children of despair and poverty in revolt against a social order they have found unjust. But they will not remain powerless, and it is likely that they will be with us a long time to come.

A Moslem Sect?

The Muslim dream is to have a solid Black Muslim community in the United States, recognized and supported by Moslems throughout the world as an accepted part of Islam. This is not sheer expediency: from the earliest days of the Movement, the Black Muslims have considered themselves devout adherents of the Moslem faith. They recognize Allah as the one true God (though they see Him not as a unique deity but as the Supreme Black Man among Black Men, all of whom are divine). They base their services on both the Quran and the Bible, and they are learning Arabic so as to be able to rely entirely on the original Quran. They observe the classic Moslem prayer ritual and dietary laws, and they hold in high esteem the traditional pilgrimage to Mecca.

On certain fundamental points of doctrine, however, the Black Muslims have departed widely from the orthodox Moslem tradition. Partly for this reason, and partly from an instinctive militancy toward newcomers, the official representatives of orthodox Islam in the United States have refused any recognition of the Black Muslims. The Movement has not been admitted as an affiliate of the official Federation of Islamic Associations in the United States and Canada, nor has it been recognized as legitimate by any affiliate of the federation. It has, in fact, been vigorously denounced by several Moslem groups, including the rival Muslim Brotherhood of America.

Muhammad readily admits that some of the teachings and practices of his Movement are at variance with those of other Moslem groups, but he presents these as differences of *interpretation* within a unity of belief. Blackamericans, he argues, have been the victims of a harsh and cynical oppression, and the Islamic faith in its pure orthodox form is not appropriate to their needs:

> My brothers in the East were never subjected to the conditions of slavery and systematic brainwashing by the Slavemasters for as long a period as my people here were subjected. I cannot, therefore, blame them if they differ with me in certain interpretations of the message of Islam.

He is not troubled by the rejection of the handful of orthodox Moslems in the United States; his hopes are staked on recognition by the more important (and more flexible) officials in the Moslem nations of Africa and Asia.

Two of the Black Muslims' basic doctrines are at the heart of the controversy: their insistence that the black man must separate himself from the abhorrent and doomed white race, and their belief that it is the manifest destiny of the Black Nation to inherit the earth. These doctrines are in flagrant contrast to the orthodox Moslem ideal of an all-embracing brotherhood of man. Moslems have, throughout their history, shown a rare and admirable indifference to boundaries of race; and any tinge of racial bigotry in an acknowledged Moslem group would cause the orthodox acute embarrassment and anguish. The Black Muslims, however, refuse absolutely to moderate or compromise their racial doctrines. Muhammad is convinced that a belief in panracial brotherhood would leave his followers with no more dignity and hope than they can now find in the Christian church.

Are these contradictions so extreme that the Black Muslims must be said to have exluded themselves from Islam? The question will have to be answered, of course, by Moslem theologians, but it seems likely that they will find the Black Muslims to be within the pale—a legitimate if somewhat heretical Moslem sect. Every faith has its deviates, and every international faith makes broad allowances for interpretations of doctrine to fit local conditions. The fact that orthodox Moslems in America reject the Movement has no real significance: most Christian sects and denominations were likewise spurned by the orthodox in their founding years. And a clear precedent exists in Islam itself for the ultimate recognition of heretics as a sect despite major doctrinal differences. This precedent is the Ahmadiyah movement, a small Moslem group of India and Pakistan, with an increasing number of black adherents in the United States.

> The "prophet" of the movement was the pious Mirzā Ghulām Ahmad (1839–1908) . . . [who] was accepted by many, including orthodox religious, as a great [Moslem] reformer. Suddenly, in 1889, his popularity gave place to extreme denunciation, when he announced that he had received a revelation authorizing him to receive men's allegiance as the promised Messiah and *Imām Mahdi;* that is, Jesus returned to earth and the apocalyptic saviour who [Moslem] tradition has held will appear at the last day. The general (Moslem) community, and particularly the divines, outraged by this blasphemy, attacked him relentlessly. . . . Despite intense persecution, the community grew, in numbers and in faith.

There are still intermittent quarrels between the Ahmadiyah and the orthodox, but the Ahmadiyah are now generally accepted as a legitimate sect of Islam.

The open assertion by the Black Muslims that it is their destiny to inherit the earth and that the present rulers of this world will soon fall upon evil days is certainly not unique in the history of religions. Such a religious philosophy is at least as old as the ancient Hebrews and at least as recent as the newest adventist Christian sect. The characteristic orientation of all religions has been the expectation that God's first pleasure is His own elect, the elect being those who are pure in doctrine, correct in ritual and, oftentimes, racially or ethnically select. The multiple fractures within the Catholic and Protestant communions respectively, and the sects which elaborate every other major religion, provide ample, if disheartening, evidence of this universal assumption.

Islam itself, although it claims no significant racial bias, does share this pronounced intolerance for the non-believer. To this extent, the ground is prepared for understanding and perhaps even tolerating the Black Muslims' racial exlusiveness. A Christian writer, while praising Islam's record of racial inclusiveness, has suggested that racial lines might be drawn and held even by orthodox Islam "if it got a foothold in Europe or America, where the deeper racial prejudices seem most to flourish." He cites the case of a Moslem missionary in this country meeting separately with white and black members "because of the Christian background of the white people."

Racial hatred, wherever it is taught or practiced, reflects a social depravity. It debases the hater, alienates the hatred and usually impairs the creative capacities of both. Yet history offers almost no instance of a religious subgroup being expelled from the parent communion because it teaches hatred of the outsider. The Christian church, for example, was divided in its early years over the issue of whether to admit gentiles; today it is in controversy over the status of its black members. Yet never, in all its turbulent history, has the church developed a tradition of excluding those whose racial views are repugnant to the mainstream of Christian thought. Instead, the church has sought to preserve its ties, hoping that time and circumstance, interpreted through the spiritual emphases of the church, might work reform.

The most pertinent example, perhaps, is the split within American Protestantism over the question of slavery. The southern churches taught—and many still teach—that some races are superior to others and that men's social destinies are divinely predetermined by race. These churches formally withdrew from communion with the Northern churches when they could reach no agreement on the slavery issue, yet their status as Christian churches was never in dispute. Even today, a number of southern Protestant churches proclaim the inferiority of black people whose role as "hewers of wood and drawers of water" is said to be preordained by God Himself; and in the Mormon Church, racial bias categorically excludes blacks from full membership. Yet these churches have not been expelled from the Christian communion, nor are they even held in suspicion of heresy by their brothers in Christ.

Shall we expect any other religion, even Islam, to be more insistent on brotherly love than we are ourselves?

In 1959, Malcolm X made a special trip to Egypt and other Moslem countries to test the acceptability of the Black Muslims abroad. He was received cordially as a "Moslem brother." Later that year, Muhammad and two of his sons made a tour of several Moslem countries. The Messenger was recognized as an important leader and was permitted to make the traditional Moslem pilgrimage to Mecca. He wrote to his followers in the United States:

> On my arrival in Jeddah, Arabia, December 23, 1959, it was almost a necessity that I go to Mecca. The next day . . . the authorities made ready a car to take me and my two sons over the forty-mile distance from Jeddah to that ancient city which is the glory of the Muslim world of Islam.

In Cairo, Muhammad reported that:

> Here . . . I met the Great Imam. He invited me to visit him, and I have experienced great happiness . . . with him. He is over all the Imams in . . . Egypt. He placed a kiss upon my head, and I placed a kiss on his hand.

Back in the United States, the Muslim leader described his Islamic tour to some ninety-five hundred Blacks who gathered to hear him in Los Angeles. In Boston and New York, meanwhile, Malcolm X announced that the question of the Muslims' orthodoxy is "a closed issue," because "those who are not orthodox do not go to Mecca."

The Political Implications

Like Christianity and Judaism, Islam is more than a religion: it has served also as a political force, drawing together coalitions of states for various purposes at various times. Today it is dynamically important in shaping political alignments among Moslem nations from Morocco to Indonesia—that is to say, across the entire span of the African-Asian land mass. If Islam could establish a large and influential body of believers in the United States, the Moslem brotherhood would circle the earth.

Apart from the followers of Muhammad, there are scarcely 33,000 Moslems in the whole of North America—compared with 345,000 in South America, 12.5 million in Europe, and more than 400 million in

Africa and Asia. This disproportion is due not so much to the vitality of the Christian church as to America's immigration policies, which discriminate against Africans and Asians. To build an effective bloc in the United States, therefore, the Moslem states would have to convert large numbers of American citizens to Islam—and this the Black Muslims are doing with evident success. The orthodox Moslem bodies in America are dwarfed by Black Islam, and their cries of protest are likely to fall upon apathetic ears in the important Islamic capitals of the East.

Much has been made of an alleged link between the Black Muslims and the United Arab Republic. The Muslims are accused of accepting financial support from the Egyptians and of being "pro-Nasser." There is no known evidence to support the allegation of financial support, and Muhammad has vigorously denied these allegations:

Now it has been charged that I am receiving aid from some alien government or ideology. These charges, of course, come from those who resent the progress we have made toward enlightening our people. I want to say here and now that these charges are absolutely false. I do not receive any aid from the United Arab Republic; I do not receive aid from the Communist party; there is not one dime that comes to us from any source other than our own followers.

But political favors do not always turn on money. The UAR has shown little public recognition of the Movement, but Muslim leaders have been welcomed enthusiastically abroad, and the Movement has received important encouragement and advice from Egyptian nationals in this country. The Muslims have responded by considering themselves specifically "anti-Zionist" rather than "anti-Semitic," and they were proud to identify themselves with President Nasser, whose picture still graces the walls of many Muslim homes and temples.

Malcolm X made a frank bid for UAR support, offering the growth potential of the Movement as a prime incentive. "The Arabs," he asserted, "as a colored people, should make more effort to reach the millions of colored people in America who are related to the Arabs by blood." The Arab leaders' response to this appeal is not known. But Malcolm's pledge that "these millions of colored peoples would be completely in sympathy with the Arab cause" was undoubtedly received with quiet appreciation.

In January 1958, Muhammad sent the following cablegram to President Nasser, who was then host to the Afro-Asian Conference:

Lt. President Gamal Abdel Nasser
President of the Egyptian Republic, and
Host to the Afro-Asian Conference

In the name of Allah, The Beneficent, The Merciful.
Beloved Brothers of Africa and Asia:

As-Salaam-Alaikum. Your long lost Muslim Brothers here in America pray that Allah's divine presence will be felt at this historic African-Asian Conference, and give unity to our efforts for peace and brotherhood.

Freedom, justice and equality for all Africans and Asians is of far-reaching importance, not only to you of the East, but also to over 17,000,000 of your long-lost brothers of African-Asian descent here in the West. . . . May our sincere desire for universal peace which is being manifested at this great conference by all Africans and Asians, bring about the unity and brotherhood among all our people which we all so eagerly desire.

All success is from Allah.

As-Salaam-Alaikum:

> *Your Long-Lost Brothers of the West*
> *Elijah Muhammad*
> *Leader, Teacher and Spiritual Head of*
> *The Nation of Islam in the West. . . .*

The *Pittsburgh Courier* carried President Nasser's purported reply:

Mr. Elijah Muhammad:

Leader, teacher and spiritual head of the Nation of Islam in the West.

I have received your kind message expressing your good wishes on the occasion of the African-Asian Conference. I thank you most heartily for these noble sentiments.

May Allah always grant us help to work for the maintenance of peace, which is the desire of all peoples. I extend my best wishes to our brothers of Africa and Asia living in the West.

> *(Signed) Gamal Abdel Nasser*

In the summer of 1959 came Malcolm X's visit to the United Arab Republic. The invitation was originally extended to Muhammad, who then appointed Malcolm to make a preliminary tour as his emissary. Malcolm was warmly received in Cairo and Saudi Arabia by Arab officialdom, and he met all of the important people in the Moslem Con-

gress, thus insuring Muhammad's impending visit against embarrassment. The Black Muslims were taken as Moslems, and the Egyptians
were delighted by the throngs of black worshipers they saw on the
11"×20" photographs Malcolm carried in his briefcase. They were
also properly appalled at his descriptions of the oppression of the black
man in America.

During his tour, Malcolm found that:

> The people of Arabia are just like our people in America . . . ranging
> from regal black to rich brown. But none are white. It is safe to say that
> 99 per cent of them would be jim-crowed in the United States of Amer-
> ica.

From Africa, he wrote:

> Africa is the land of the future . . . definitely the land of tomorrow, and
> the African is the man of tomorrow. . . . Africa is the New World, a
> world with a future . . . in which the so-called American Negroes are
> destined to play a key role. . . . Like the Asians, all Africans consider
> America's treatment of Negro Americans the best yardstick by which to
> measure the sincerity of America's offers on this continent. . . . The veil
> of diplomatic art does not obscure the vision of African thinkers when
> abuse of black Americans still obtains.

A few months later, Elijah Muhammad went to Cairo and thence to
the Holy City. Muhammad is not fluent in Arabic, but on the counsel
of his advisors, he learned the various Moslem prayers and creedal
affirmations before setting out on his trip. On his return to America,
he declared: "The whole world of Islam is behind me. I was received as
a brother and a leader. I did not have to ask for a visa to make the Hajj
[pilgrimage] to Mecca, the Holy City. They asked me to go."

That these visits of top Muslim leaders to the Islamic countries have
political implications is taken for granted by most observers. The precise weight of these implications remains open to speculation. However, it is reasonable to conclude that the controversial Muslim leader
could hardly have been admitted to Mecca in the face of the opposition
of American Moslems unless he had powerful friends abroad to sponsor
and receive him. Because of his heterodoxy, that sponsorship is unlikely
to have been primarily religious. It seems possible that some Moslem
leaders, at least, found the political possibilities sufficiently impressive
to overbalance the religious risk.

Thus does the Messenger maintain his spiritual liaison with the wider world of international Islam. They have their Mecca; and they have Medina. But Elijah has Chicago. And New York. And Los Angeles. The block lettering on the façades of his many temples always proclaim: *MUHAMMAD'S* MOSQUE OF ISLAM, or *MUHAM-MAD'S* UNIVERSITY OF ISLAM. *Elijah* Muhammad is what is meant—not some other. And wherever his name appears, *he* is the Leader, the Teacher, the Prophet, the Messenger, the One-Who-Knew-Allah (in the Person of Master Fard Muhammad), and who raised the Dead Nation, indeed, the *Lost* Nation from low to high degree, bringing them face to face with their own black destiny. Muhammad does not want orthodoxy. Paradoxy will do.

DEANNE SHAPIRO

The failure of the Black Church to take care of the total needs of the black masses in the cities influenced the existence of Black Judaism. The Black Church is itself, in some sense, an aspect of the general failure of Christianity in America, for slavery and Christian morality were obviously incompatible, and the segregated White Church precluded the possibility of reasonable religious fulfillment for black Christians, forcing them to establish their own traditions. Blacks were probably influenced also by the "strong communal bond" existing among Jews, and by their high level of economic success. Even Booker T. Washington urged his followers to "imitate the Jew" if they hoped to overcome their racial and economic obstacles. Black religion's affinity for the Old Testament and the black man's felt need of some kind of deliverance such as the Jews experienced in the Exodus have helped to make Judaism attractive to some Blacks. The "Suffering Servant" theme is also a prominent notion with which Black Judaism has been identified. "Ethiopianism," a form of black nationalism, influenced the Black Jews through "the development of a climate of black self-awareness and race pride . . ."

The re-examination of black Judaism would seem to be particularly urgent at this time when traditional relations between Jews and Blacks in America are in a state of flux. The Black-Jewish coalition in civil rights has suffered significant erosion, and the Third World ideology attractive to some Blacks is often inclined to see American Capitalism, American Jewry, and Zionism as part of the same cloth. The black

Freedom movement contributed to the freedom of Blacks largely through the *trickle-down effect,* which is to say that before Blacks (who were at the bottom of the socioeconomic pyramid) could be benefited, every group above them suffering similar disabilities would be benefited first. The Jews who were long involved in the support (and sometimes the invisible leadership) of black protest were early beneficiaries. Once the restrictions on Jewish mobility were removed or substantially reduced, the attitudes Blacks (who were still suffering) and Jews (who no longer needed to make common cause with Blacks) had for each other were inevitably modified.

The persistence of an established cult of Black Jews, the fact that the cult is growing, and recent emergence of other black movements, associating themselves with the Hebrew or Jewish tradition, raises interesting questions which give added significance to this selection.

Deanne Shapiro is a doctoral candidate in the Sociology of Religion at Columbia University.

FACTORS IN THE DEVELOPMENT OF BLACK JUDAISM

Source: Deanne Shapiro, *Double Damnation, Double Salvation: the Sources and Varieties of Black Judaism in the United States.* (Unpublished Master's Thesis, Columbia University).

Social Factors

The first of the social influences upon Black Judaism may be observed in considering the consequences of the Negro Church's failure to fulfill adequately the needs of the black masses in the cities. This failure did not occur in a moral vacuum but was preceded by the failure of the Christian message, as mediated by whites, to account for the suffering of blacks under the strictures of the slavery and Jim Crow systems.[1] The ethical incompatibility of Christianity and slavery was heightened and highlighted by the development of Jim Crow practices, wherein the southern white churches acted as an "avant-garde" of racism, helping to prepare the South for its later complete capitulation to it. The white southern Protestant churches were fully segregated by the end of Reconstruction, far in advance of the segrega-

[1] For a general account of the Jim Crow system, see C. Vann Woodward, *The Strange Career of Jim Crow* (2nd ed. revised. New York: Oxford University Press, 1966).

tion of many public areas. By the time of total segregation in the South, in the 1890s, white churchmen were condoning southern racism and, at times, aiding it by their concentration on improvement of the "lowly" individual black through education and moral training.[2]

One may thus find, as does Joseph Washington, Jr., that the forces excluding blacks from full participation in society also excluded them from any real participation in the Christian faith[3] as defined and delimited by whites. This exclusion may well have made some black people receptive to other religious traditions and modes of expression, as they realized, with Washington, that

> A religious life which is not rooted in the structure of society is ultimately transitory and ineffective . . . Negroes have yet to learn that the Christian faith is the warp and woof of the Western world, and to be excluded from this sphere is to be pre-empted of full participation in its ethos. Participation in the Christian community is the sine qua non of contributing to that society.[4]

If one accepts this observation as true, at least in part, one might be inclined to see both blacks and Jews as the victims of exclusion from effective participation in and contribution to Western society. While in reality, this is not necessarily the case, the perception by members of the two groups of such exclusion might have generated a bond between them. Blacks may have been encouraged to look elsewhere for a religious identity which would permit full participation in a non-Christian ethos, such as Judaism. Ironically, those who wished to identify as Black Jews, were not allowed full participation in Judaism either, as the doors of the synagogues remained closed to them until the twentieth century and are even now only opening slowly. Not having been tested in the crucible of Jewish religious life, then, these potential Black Jews may have simply created their own version of the Jewish religious experience in order to gain entry back into Western society through some aspect of the Judaeo-Christian tradition.

A further similarity between black and Jewish religious communities,

---

[2] David Reimers, *White Protestantism and the Negro* (New York: Oxford University Press, 1955), p. 133. Reimers provides an expanded treatment of the churches' role in Jim Crow, which is briefly noted in the above observation.

[3] Washington, *Black Religion*, p. vii.

[4] Ibid., p. 290. Washington has altered his views on black religion in a later work, but the comments cited here and in n. 52 from his earlier book provide an interesting insight into the developing attitude towards Christianity of a black theologian.

in addition to their shared exclusion from Christian-dominated white society at times, appears in their response to such oppression throughout their respective histories. Each group has, to some extent, turned in upon itself so as to strengthen internally its emotional and structural bonds of cohesion. Thus, as Gerhard Lenski has noted in *The Religious Factor*, Jews and black Protestants are alike in the strength of the communal aspects of their religious behavior. They are both bound together as religious communities, based on kinship or friendship relations, as well as religious associations, based on the highly specialized and formal relationships of the ecclesiastical body itself.[5] Both Jews and blacks, then, form a tightly knit social structure within their respective religious groups which sustains their existence, a parallel which might easily have attracted blacks alienated from the traditional black religious community and social structure.

The strong communal bond between Jews had perhaps another impact on black affinity for Judaism. This bond has been one source of Jewish socioeconomic success in the United States, a fact which blacks oriented towards social mobility no doubt perceived. They were encouraged in this orientation by various black leaders who urged blacks to pattern themselves after the Jews. One of these leaders was Benjamin Tucker Tanner, editor of the leading black magazine, the *African Methodist Episcopal Church Review*, from 1868–84, who encouraged his readers to imitate the Jews who, having been persecuted and thrown back upon themselves like blacks, became "the master of Europe" through economic advances.[6]

Foremost among the "self-help" advocates was Booker T. Washington, who suggested that blacks model themselves after Jews in several aspects, particularly in their mutual supportiveness and inward pride as these had been successfully maintained throughout their troubled history. In Washington's view, Jews were similar to blacks in the extent of social oppression they had experienced and in their cultural uniqueness, both features providing a natural basis for black emulation of Jews. Commenting on the struggles of the Jews, Washington observed that,

We have a very bright and striking example in the history of the Jews in this and other countries. There is, perhaps, no race that has suffered

[5] Gerhard Lenski, *The Religious Factor* (Revised ed. Garden City: Doubleday, 1963), pp. 36–41.
[6] August Meier, *Negro Thought in America, 1880–1915* (Ann Arbor, 1963).

so much. . . . But these people have clung together. They have had a certain amount of unity, pride, and love of race; and as the years go on, they will be more and more influential in this country—a country where they were once despised, and looked upon with scorn and derision. It is largely because the Jewish race has had faith in itself. Unless the Negro learns more and more to imitate the Jew in these matters, to have faith in himself, he cannot expect to have any high degree of success.[7]

In discussing the parallel uniqueness of Jewish and black cultures, Washington noted that

> In the Bible one finds over and over again the words "a peculiar people." Reference is made to the Jews as "a peculiar people"—a people differing in thought and temperament and mode of life from others by whom they were surrounded. Now the race to which Americans of African lineage belong is often described as "a peculiar people," having had, as we know, a peculiar history. They differ in color and appearance, and in a very large degree their temperament and thought differ from that of the people about them. Now the Jews because they were different from the peoples by whom they were surrounded, because of their peculiar religious bent, were able to give to the world the doctrine of the unity and Fatherhood of God, and Christianity, the finest flower of Jewry. It is then, I think, not too much to hope that the very qualities which make the Negro different from the people by which he is surrounded will enable him, in the fulness of time, to make a peculiar contribution to that nation of which he forms a part.[8]

In the popular understanding, such counsel was translated into encouragement to follow the Jews' lead in material success.[9] In either form, however, these suggestions may well have facilitated the identification of a small group of blacks with the Jewish tradition and community.

Some black leaders also understood an additional appeal of Judaism for black people, the simple psychological effect of being excluded initially from Jewish religious observance as slaves, and the subsequent impact of their attack upon such exclusion. With a keen perception of the religious appeal of "forbidden fruit," black leaders such as Bishop Crowdy of the Church of God and Saints of Christ, Prophet Cherry of

[7] Booker T. Washington, *The Future of the American Negro* (Boston: Small, Maynard and Co., 1902), pp. 182ff, cited in Brotz, *Black Jews*, p. 8.
[8] Booker T. Washington, "On Making Our Race Life Count in the Life of the Nation," cited in *Negro Social and Political Thought, 1850–1920*, Howard Brotz, ed. (New York: Basic Books, 1966), p. 379.
[9] Brotz, *Black Jews*, p. 7.

the Church of the Living God, and Rabbi Matthew of the Ethiopian Hebrews seem to have committed themselves to breaching the doors which the Jewish community had held so firmly closed against them. Since Jews did not wish to convert them, these blacks began to preach what was, in effect, a new Jewish eschatology in which the real Jews were black and the white Jews merely pretenders to the throne of David. They were, in reality, creating their own conversion experience. As Howard Brotz has described it,

> What was common to all these groups . . . may be termed an "explosive" sense of the past, experienced as a conversion, transmitted by dynamic, prophetlike leaders outside of kinship groups or other traditional social relationships. It is thus not subject to the restraints of institutionalized expectations and aspirations in the extent of its demands upon the present.[10]

Ideological Factors

A basic ideological source of the Black Jews' religious identification may be observed in the traditional sympathy within black religion for the Old Testament, particularly its account of the persecution and election of the Jewish people. This sympathy was manifest during slavery in the slaves' songs and spirituals, although in indirect fashion. It was heightened at the turn of the twentieth century by black preachers travelling in the South, who affirmed that the "so-called Negroes" were actually the lost sheep of the House of Israel. As Brotz notes, this identification with the Old Testament was not unique to blacks but was an inherent aspect of the religious indoctrination they received from white Protestants[11]:

> The type of radical Protestantism which became the religious tradition of the slaves, and which, in its essence, conceived of itself as a return to the literal word of God, revealed in both Testaments and accessible in the vernacular to all who could read, elicited on its fringes an eccentric tradition in which the Old Testament not only became held in honor equal to that of the New but in fact became more venerated and even opposed to the New Testament when they came into conflict.

[10] Brotz, "Negro 'Jews' in the United States," *Phylon* XIII (1952), 324–25. This comment, while appearing relevant to the writer of the present essay, must be read somewhat critically in the light of Brotz' counsel to disregard the *Phylon* article. Letter from Brotz to present writer, May 19, 1969.
[11] Brotz, *Black Jews*, p. 6.

A further aspect of this "eccentric tradition" on the fringes of radical Protestantism, in addition to the free use of the Bible, was the rejection of the established political order. This aspect was reinforced in the case of the blacks by the difficulties of their situation and appeared as both a frequent theme in the black slave songs and, no doubt, an added impetus to the formation of other-worldly or nationalist sects. Thus, the dual influence in this tradition of sympathy for the Old Testament and antipathy towards society provided a "new world" for blacks,

> a world centered upon a veneration for the Bible as the literal word of God [in which] lay both the contents of and the freedom for . . . innovation by Negroes in America . . . specifically the freedom to move from an admiration of the Old Testament patriarchs to the view that they were one's very own ancestors.[12]

Although this "Judaistic idiosyncrasy," as Brotz calls it, was fairly widespread among fringe Protestant groups and black people, it was particularized by potential Black Jews through the frequent reference to two biblical themes. The first, the idea of the Chosen People of God, was articulated by these blacks as a counterpoint to the popularized racism of the Jim Crow South.[13] In identifying themselves, however momentarily, as a chosen people like the Jews, they provided themselves a new basis for pride, self-sufficiency, and a moral reordering of family and community life.

The Suffering Servant theme, the second of the two popular biblical concepts with which the new Black Jewish followers identified, operated as a built-in corrective for the first idea. For most blacks, of course, the Cross of the New Testament provided a deeply meaningful symbolic expression of human suffering. There were, however, some blacks, including those of pronounced sympathy for the Jewish tradition who were most likely to become Black Jews, whose attempts to remain faithful to the Christian Gospel were often thwarted by their need for a more immediate expression of their daily suffering than the Cross. The few political pronouncements by Jesus moved these blacks to look to the Old Testament prophets for comfort in their troubles. They did not, however, view the suffering of their people as that of an elect people unfaithful to a covenant with God, as did the Hebrew prophets. Rather, they saw themselves as chosen to suffer because of their color. This racially based understanding was well articulated in the adaptation of the

[12] Ibid.
[13] Brotz, "The Negro-Jewish Community and the Contemporary Race Crisis," *Jewish Social Studies*, XXVII (1965), 12.

Suffering Servant theme to the immediate, individualistic expression of biblical influence reflected in the slave songs[14]

The sympathy for the Old Testament tradition of many blacks and their consequent ideological identification with God's Chosen People and Suffering Servant, the Israelites, was manifested in many slave songs, although in a pragmatic and individualistic manner. As Miles Mark Fisher notes, these songs[15] represented the immediate, historical experience of the slaves, rather than their Christianization and subsequent turning to the Bible under this influence in the nineteenth-century revivalist period.

In the songs, the slaves created their own vocabulary and symbol system to express certain of their basic concerns and desires in the only form of historical document they were able to produce. Thus, some of the spirituals provide evidence of the slaves' active concern with freedom and justice, strategy plans, self-improvement, and above all their longing to be returned to Africa, the "Heaven" so often referred to in the songs. Rather than manifesting an other-worldly orientation, the words of these songs represent specific realities of the slaves' existence. The "Lawd" was the slavemaster, "Babylon" or "bondage" was slavery, "Hell" was being sold farther south, the "Israelites" who were so oppressed were the slaves, and the cruel "Egyptians" were the harsh slaveholders.

Fisher offers an extended interpretation of several popular spirituals. The song "Go Down Moses" evoked the person of Bishop Asbury of the Methodist Church, who was seen as a benefactor of the black man. It was sung to call together meetings of the secret "African cult." The words of "Swing Low, Sweet Chariot" spoke of a sledlike vehicle, like those used for carrying tobacco, which would swing out of the sky and carry the slaves back to Africa.

Several of the figures in the songs evolved along with the changing form of the songs. Thus, "Moses" was successively interpreted as Bishop Asbury, as a well-known black who frequented the camp meetings, as

[14] I am indebted to Dean Laurence Jones of Union Theological Seminary for this understanding of black concern with the Suffering Servant theme, a concern he finds relevant to contemporary black theology. These comments were made in a seminar entitled "The Negro in American Church History," conducted by Professor Robert T. Handy and himself at Union in Fall 1968.

[15] Miles Mark Fisher, *Negro Slave Songs in the United States* (Ithaca: Cornell Press for the American Historical Association, 1953). The discussion of the songs which follows in the present essay is adapted from Fisher's account. One should note, however, that other accounts stress the other-worldly orientation of the songs, as in Benjamin E. Mays, *The Negro's God* (New York: Atheneum, 1968) and LeRoi Jones, *Blues People* (New York: William Morrow, 1963), both of which also emphasize the analogy with Jewish suffering made in the songs.

an emigré to Africa, and, finally and symbolically, as the recipient of entreaties by slaves to return to the United States in order to tell the slavemaster or "Pharaoh" to let the slaves go to the promised land of Africa and in order to stretch out his rod that they might walk there on dry land. Similarly, "Weeping Mary" was first seen as the woman who was ejected from the white churches for "shouting," then as an African colonizer, later as one who returned mysteriously to the secret meetings of American slaves, and still later as the woman Mary at the tomb of Jesus on the morning of the Resurrection.

Thus, it becomes increasingly clear that the identification of blacks with the Old Testament was at best indirect. Most black people did not conceive of themselves as the Israelites in actuality, as really the Chosen People or the Suffering Servant of God, but used these and other biblical themes to represent and to protest allegorically what could not be said otherwise. While not providing a direct source for the religious identification of the Black Jews, then, it may well be that such common usage of biblical images strengthened their identification. It does represent clearly, at least, a basic sympathy for the Jewish tradition and its historical figures, a sympathy which was both a necessity for incorporating them in their forms of self-expression and, no doubt, a significant ideological influence upon future black Jews.

One last source of the Black Jews' elective affinity was the broad movement of "Ethiopianism" among American and African blacks. Leaders and followers of this movement identified the "Ethiopia" referred to in such biblical verses as Psalm 68:31 (R.S.V.), "Let Ethiopia hasten to stretch out her hands to God," as the whole of the African continent. Ethiopia thus became a symbolic representation of African nationalism, as it was expressed by two groups of native African churches.

As described by George Shepperson, the term "Ethiopianism" was subject to two interpretations.[16] Strictly defined, it indicated certain aspects of the African Independent Church movement going back to the establishment in the 1870s in South Africa of "Ethiopian Churches" among quasi-respectable secessionist groups from non-conformist European churches, usually Wesleyan, Baptist, or Free Church. Another usage of the term, however, was to describe what might be better called Zionism, the development of apocalyptic-type churches which originated in the missionary efforts of black and white American denominations, first appearing in South Africa in 1904 when Africans

[16] George Shepperson, "Ethiopianism and African Nationalism," *Phylon*, XIV (1953), 9–18.

were baptised as members of the Christian Catholic Apostolic Church in Zion, a United States based group. One example of this type of Ethiopianism was the widespread impact of the Watchtower movement, a blend of African nationalism and American apocalyptism. This impact was manifested in the wave of pentecostal revivalism stirred up by Elliot Kamwana in Nyasaland and suppressed by the authorities there.

Both varieties of Ethiopianism were characterized by governmental persecution, which ultimately forced a divergence of the religious and political ends of the movement, and by the role of Americans, particularly blacks whose missionary work reflected the post-Reconstruction concern of the Negro Church with its "manifest destiny" to spread the Gospel to Africa. Ethiopianism has now been replaced as a political force by secular politics and as a religious force by the gradual demise of traditional Christianity and the development of African tribal ideologies. It now persists only as a sentimental, nebulous symbolic term occasionally utilized to restir racial hostilities.

The Ethiopianism movement has, however, had a significant ideological influence in the Western Hemisphere. One area which felt such impact was Jamaica, West Indies, where the Ras Tafari movement continued the representation of Ethiopia as the symbol of black dominance and African nationalism.

Ras Tafari, as described by George Eaton Simpson,[17] is a verbally violent, anti-white cult which originated in Jamaica in 1930 claiming Marcus Garvey's movement as its spiritual forerunner. The Ras Tafari creed declares that Haile Selassie, emperor of Ethiopia, is the living God, the invincible Lion of Judah, before whom all the peoples of the world will someday bow. It states that there is no hope in the West Indies for blacks, who should rather look towards an early return to their homeland in Ethiopia. All blacks are considered to be Ethiopians, the true Israelites, and more specifically, black Jamaicans are reincarnations of the ancient Hebrews, such as David, Solomon and Sheba, who were themselves black. The black man is known to be superior to the white man, who is a murderer and thief, and who has defrauded blacks through religion and politics. As a result, the Jamaican situation of the blacks is understood as hopeless, but in Ethiopia, it is affirmed, blacks will revenge themselves upon whites in the black homeland, their Heaven and their only hope.

In the United States, Ethiopianism, broadly defined, has influenced

[17] George Eaton Simpson, "The Ras Tafari Movement in Jamaica: A Study of Race and Class Conflict," *Religion, Society, and the Individual,* Yinger, ed. pp. 507–17.

various black nationalist groups, including the Nation of Islam or "Black Muslims" which resembles Ras Tafari in many of its ideas.[18] Both of these movements, the Muslims and Ras Tafari, were preceded in time and influence by Garveyism, perhaps the most important expression of Ethiopianism in the Western Hemisphere. The most general aspect of nationalist influence upon the Black Jews was the impetus it gave to the development of a climate of black self-awareness and race pride, which was also manifest in the black cultural renaissance of the turn of the twentieth century, its concomitant image of the "New Negro," and a growing body of black literature including works which claimed that all the Near Eastern peoples of ancient and biblical history were in fact of black origin.

An additional feature of the Ethiopian or Garveyite influence may well have been the orientation of some black leaders, particularly among Black Jews, towards the observation of a loose parallel between Jewish Zionism as formulated by Theodor Herzl and Garveyism, based on certain similarities between the careers of the two leaders.[19] Neither Herzl nor Garvey grew up with much experience of prejudice but came in contact with it in depth only in his adult years, reacting by the development of a philosophy and strategy for the establishment of a national homeland for his beleaguered people. Both movements which followed upon their leadership took on the coloration of a religious, and frequently chauvinistic, nationalism which developed a certain fanaticism in the quest for a better life for the peoples involved. Yet there is no evidence of Garvey's being familiar with Herzl's specific proposals which preceded his own by many years, while there is material in Garvey's writings which suggests his strong antipathy to the Jews.[20]

The net effect of the possibly perceived similarities of the two nationalist ideologies ultimately, then, may have been the social and psychological impact of the fact that while Zionism continually gained intellectual and financial support from the international Jewish community, Garveyism gradually lost its initial impetus as its appeal increasingly was restricted to the personal charisma and foibles of its leader. Thus, Jewish Zionism, in giving still further support to the already

[18] For an excellent treatment of the Black Muslims, see C. Eric Lincoln, *The Black Muslims in America* (Boston: Beacon Press, 1961).
[19] These similarities and this parallel have been discussed by Arnold Rose, *The Negro's Morale: Group Identification and Protest* (Minneapolis: University of Minnesota Press, 1949), pp. 43–44, cited in Cronon, *Black Moses*, pp. 199–200.
[20] An example of such material may be found in Marcus Garvey, "The Jews in Palestine," *Black Man*, II (July-August, 1936), 3, as noted in Cronon, ibid., p. 200.

well-established image of Jewish successes, and in emphasizing certain themes familiar to black nationalists and their listeners, may have provided an additional basis for black identification with Jews.

Commenting further on this parallel, Edmund Cronon, Garvey's biographer, notes that

> like their Jewish counterparts, most American Negroes would watch with eager interest the building of a free Zionist state in Africa. They could be counted upon for generous financial support and enthusiastic moral encouragement. But only very few would be ready to undertake the hard and thankless pioneer work needed to create a Black Israel in the African jungle.[21]

Thus, too, for black as for Jew in America, the ideal of the ancestral homeland proved more a motive factor for sympathy than for strenuous effort towards achieving its reality. This and the other similarities of the two nationalisms discussed above may have furthered a confluence of interests between the black and Jewish communities. Perhaps, as a result, the ultimate impact of early black nationalist thought and action upon the Black Jews was to encourage the creation of a Black Israel in the only homeland most American blacks were likely to know.

The more specific influence of Ethiopianism, particularly Garveyism, upon Black Jews may be observed in reviewing the development of Black Jewish groups which appeared in the late nineteenth and early twentieth centuries but which have not persisted to the present day. Two accounts of such early groups are available, but they conflict in certain details.[22]

According to the more reliable account of Ruth Landes, writing in the 1930s originally, Black Judaism was largely a response to urban anomie by former Garveyites. As Landes notes, however, there existed two separate types of Black Judaism in Harlem in this period, differentiated by national background and orientation although crossing paths from time to time.[23] The Black Jewish groups led by former West Indians were, on the whole, concerned with the total racial situation of the American black man and with political remedies for this situation.

[21] Cronon, ibid., p. 128.
[22] The better of these accounts is by Ruth Landes, "Negro Jews in Harlem," *Jewish Journal of Sociology*, IX (December, 1967), 175–89, based on her 1933 study. Less impressive, but more up to date, is Arthur Dobrin, "A History of the Negro Jews in America" (unpublished paper, City College of the City University of New York, 1965, Schomburg Collection, New York City Public Library).
[23] Landes, "Negro Jews," p. 175.

American Black Jewish leaders and their adherents were largely other-worldly in orientation, transporting their already well-established evangelical mode of worship to the cities and taking shelter there in devotion to Jesus Christ and in a loose identification with Judaism.

The sporadic reports of blacks identifying themselves as Jews which appeared in late nineteenth century newspapers, in the same period that saw the more permanent emergence of the Church of God and Saints of Christ and the somewhat different Church of the Living God Black Jewish groups, were too infrequent to be classified as either of these early types of Black Judaism. In 1895, various news articles reported the existence of self-converted Jews, like William Ephraim of Philadelphia, in several northern cities. A prisoner in the Newark, New Jersey jail in 1908, Samuel Johnson, claimed to be a Jew named Klowsky. In 1912, Rufus L. Perry, a prominent black New York attorney, converted to Judaism.

More important than these few individual instances was the establishment in 1899 of what one writer considers the first Black Jewish congregation in the United States,[24] the Moorish Zionist Temple. Rabbi Richlieu, the founder of this integrated group, stated that he was born in Ethiopia and was ordained by three recognized rabbis. It was further claimed that both Arnold Ford and Rabbi Wentworth Matthew of the later Ethiopian Hebrews were members of his group, which is doubtful, it being more likely that Ford became involved in the Moorish Zionist Temple only in its later reorganization and that Matthew was not involved at all.

Prior to the re-emergence of the Moorish Zionist Temple, a group, which fit the American pattern of Black Judaism as described by Landes, was established by a southern migrant evangelist, Elder Warren Robinson, or Roberson, who claimed it to be Jewish in religious affiliation. This claim is accepted by Landes, who calls the group the most powerful of American Black Jewish groups extant in 1933, while Arthur Dobrin rejects the claim as invalid.[25]

The cult was at best nominally Jewish, with no Jewish observances and a basically Christian orientation. Its claim was based on the syllogism, "We who are black worship Christ; Christ was a Jew; therefore we are black Jews," and on the usage of Jewish symbols on letterheads appealing for financial support from white Jews, particularly for a non-

[24] Dobrin, "Negro Jews," p. 37. Dobrin discounts the earlier organization of the Church of the Living God and the Church of God and Saints of Christ because he does not view them as Jewish.
[25] Landes, "Negro Jews," p. 178; Dobrin, "Negro Jews," p. 47.

existent Black Jewish orphan asylum. The simple creed of this "holy roller" group stated, "Believe in Jesus; believe that Robinson is the Messiah, the Christ; then you are saved and will never die."

The cult served as a total community for its members, all of whom lived in group-owned homes in a communal pattern and worked in group-owned shops. Marital ties were forsworn, all women belonging to Robinson and reportedly being sent to a "baby farm" in New Jersey when pregnant. The high mortality rates and reputed sexual exploitation occurring in the group brought Robinson under investigation and in 1922, he was imprisoned by the Federal government for violation of the Mann Act, which heightened his prestige. He died in 1932, having promised that he would arise again, and for a time thereafter, his followers hid his body so that it might not be buried. The group largely disappeared after the demise of its charismatic leader and left an unfavorable image of the Black Jews, as noted in Rabbi Wentworth Matthew's statement that "It sure took a long time to live that one down."[26]

In 1921, the Moorish Zionist Temple was reorganized by Mordecai Herman, a peddler of Jewish religious articles, who professed Judaism and spoke Yiddish. Herman came to Liberty Hall, Garvey's headquarters in Harlem, at this time to secure pupils for Hebrew lessons, although he was not very familiar with the language. There he met Arnold Ford, who was to be expelled three years later, in 1924, from his position as choirmaster in the Universal Negro Improvement Association and from the Association itself, at which time he joined with Herman in the Moorish Zionist Temple. According to Landes, Ford was a cofounder of the reconstituted group with Herman, while in Dobrin's view, Herman joined Ford in the Beth B'nai Abraham after the collapse of the Moorish Zionist Temple.[27] It seems more likely, if one accepts the dates of these various developments as correct, that Ford did affiliate with the Moorish Zionist Temple as Landes says, but only after it was a going concern and not as an original founder.

The group which he joined was oriented like West Indian-led Black Jewish groups towards a nationalistic solution to the black man's situation, favoring the establishment of a Palestinian homeland for all Jews, including Black Jews. In a pamphlet prepared by the Moorish Zionist Temple Society of East New York, Brooklyn, Rabbi Herman wrote[28]:

[26] Rabbi Wentworth Matthew, cited in Brotz, *Black Jews*, p. 11.
[27] Landes, "Negro Jews," p. 181; Dobrin, "Negro Jews," p. 40.
[28] Rabbi Mordecai Herman, cited in Dobrin, ibid.

Dear Sirs and Brothers,

It is my present belief that Palestine will be free. For reasons, however, which cannot be explained by the world, the fact is that our Jewish brothers in America and Europe cannot uphold and protect Palestine; but our black Jewish brothers in India, China and Abyssinia have a little bit more skill in war and manly heroism than the usual Jewish man.

Fast work is being done by the Moorish Zionists to bring together all the black Israelites in one place in Palestine for military reasons, and for that purpose funds are being gathered to feed the hungry, clothe the naked, and provide a home for the homeless. Also, Jewish schools are being built to instill in the youth the Jewish religion and tradition.

Fairly soon after Ford joined Herman's group, the Moorish Zionist Temple began to experience dissension between the two prominent figures. Ford insisted on being called "Rabbi" and expected freedom to tour with his singing group, while Herman did not have Ford's popular appeal and claimed that Ford took advantage of him. Finally, in 1925, Ford and the choir split off from the group and formed Beth B'nai Abraham.

Reports vary on the outcome of this conflict for the Moorish Zionist Temple.[29] Dobrin claims that Herman also left the group and joined the Beth B'nai Abraham (B.B.A.), but after further conflict with Ford over B.B.A. Progressive Corporation stock, he disappeared in 1930. Furthermore, Dobrin asserts, the Moorish Zionist Temple continued under the leadership of a white Jew named Max Glickstein, until its almost total disappearance in the late 1930s. Landes' account seems more probable, in finding that Herman carried on the Moorish Zionist Temple with a southern black named Sledge, who later changed his name to the more Jewish-sounding name Mordecai. Although Herman and Sledge claimed to have established Hebrew schools and services in Harlem and Newark, no evidence exists of these institutions. The group did, however, secure financial support from white Jews who believed the members' claims to be either Ethiopian or Egyptian Jews and who accepted as proof of their Jewish identity such practices as the wearing of skullcaps, the circumcision of Herman's son, and the denouncement of the "so-called Negro."

Although Ford had been expelled from the Universal Negro Improvement Association (U.N.I.A.) in 1924, after clashes with Marcus Garvey, he adhered to its basic political program and ideas in reorganizing his followers in the B.B.A., the group which most strongly manifested the influence of Garveyism, and more generally, Ethiopianism,

[29] Dobrin, ibid., p. 40; Landes, "Negro Jews," p. 182.

upon the Black Jews. Ford understood himself as the destined leader of the black man's political future after Garvey was convicted of fraud. While he shared Garvey's view on politics and religion, Ford, who was raised by his father, the leader of an evangelical sect in Barbados, repudiated all Christian doctrine in the B.B.A. Such anti-Christian feeling was a logical outcome of the anti-white sentiments of Garveyism, for which Ford found partial vent in Judaism, cued in part by the success of Elder Robinson's group and in part by contact with prominent philanthropic Jews in Harlem. Thus, it was not unnatural for him to find that the "only true Jews were blacks; white Jews were only European offshoots of the original black African Hebrews,"[30] Yet his "Hebraism" was nonetheless secondary to a type of African nationalism very similar to that of the U.N.I.A.

The organization of the B.B.A. provided an opportunity for the systematic articulation of the idea that its members were blood Hebrews. Ford held that Blacks were born Hebrews by virtue of being Africans, because Africans were traditionally Hebrew. He stated that fragments of such Hebraism had persisted but were virtually destroyed by slavery. A correct reading of the Old Testament, Ford asserted, proved that the "true religion" of the blacks was that of the Hebrews, and in fact, "old time" black religion stressed the continuity of black tradition with that of the Hebrew.

One constant theme of Ford's preaching was the unique superiority of Judaism and the Jews, who had come from North African ancestors who were, through intermarriage, indirectly responsible for the growth of Europe and of all Western civilization. He rejected the use of the word "Jewish" and insisted on calling his followers "Hebrews," finding that "Jewish" was a term which applied only to Western whites who had been converted to Judaism by blacks. A concomitant emphasis was Ford's dislike for whites and for the "so-called Negro." In accord with this view, he stated that each member of his group had another, Hebrew, name which would be revealed to him in the B.B.A., in addition to his Christian name received in slavery. He affirmed his anti-Negro feeling in saying that

> All I recognize by "Negro" is an African or person of African descent whose mind is a byproduct of European civilization, but has no traditions of its own. Hebrews are not Negroes.[31]

[30] Arnold Ford, cited in Landes, ibid., p. 180.
[31] Ford, cited in ibid., p. 185.

Ford offered various evidence of the African origin of the Jews. He noted the persistence of elements of Hebrew culture in Africa, such as the motif of the shield of David which was used in West Africa and the facial markings upon tribal Nigerians of the Ten Commandments. Further, he asserted his traditional and hereditary right to the office and title of "Rabbi," a claim which he based on several often contradictory sources. The first of these was his account of the migration of the ancient Jews from Nigeria east to Egypt and then Palestine. Later, Ford identified Hebrew history with that of Carthage, stating that his mother, of Carthaginian descent, had passed on the Hebraic tradition to him, a tradition which could only be transmitted orally because it was "cabalistic" and contained knowledge lost to white Jews. He held, as part of this view, that northern Mediterranean peoples had intermarried with the Carthaginians, producing the "white" Jews who were in actuality mixed bloods. Still later, Ford found the roots of Judaism to be in African concept of *Sinye*, the native law of the Sudan which his Mende mother had identified with the Arabic word for Sinai, and thus was the law of the Torah.

The last claim which Ford made as to the origin of Black Judaism seems the most probable historically of all these manifold sources. Some West Indian blacks, Ford held, had become Jews following upon the intermarriage of blacks with 800 white Jewish migrants who fled the Spanish Inquisition and came to the Western Hemisphere. Yet, while his people had traditionally been Jewish for several centuries, Ford said that he did not realize his own tendencies until he observed white Jews in Harlem.

Like the Garvey movement from which it developed, the B.B.A. was not without its problems. For its first five or six years, however, it was quite successful, receiving support and frequent visits from white Jews. The B.B.A. Corporation, or Progressive Corporation, was established as a "secular limb" of the group, selling stock to further industry and commerce in and with West Africa, thus realizing the group's Garveyite inclinations towards African nationalism. Many members, most of whom were former British West Indians who had supported Garvey, bought stock and went to Africa as laborers. Among the features of the group, which developed in support of this nationalist impulse, were the utilization of turbans and old U.N.I.A. songs and the establishment of classes in mechanics, mathematics, Arabic, Hebrew, and the Bible as preparation for migration to Africa.

Gradually, however, the internal tensions within the group came to the surface. Criticism of Ford, petty jealousies, and conflict between natives of different West Indian islands were among the problems affecting the group. More important, there was a growing schism between the Hebraic-African sympathizers and those who wished to be identified simply as Jewish. Ford opposed the use of the Yiddish language because it was not African in origin, while others wanted to use it to evoke the sympathy of white Jews.

A group of Jamaicans, more class-conscious than others in the B.B.A., including the Barbados faction, broke off and formed their own group, its only concrete result being that some of its members sent their children to white Hebrew schools in Harlem and the children returned home with a systematic knowledge of East European Jewish practices, previously unknown to B.B.A. members. The father of one of these students evidenced his concern with social mobility and the success of the Jews in commenting that,

> We think the Jews are a great people! They have gone so far in spite of persecution. They own all the money in the country. Their religion did that for them, and maybe it will do the same for us. They may help us to get jobs; Jews should help one another.[32]

Within the B.B.A. itself, acute financial trouble developed at this time. Many others left the group, and after brief membership spurts, it collapsed totally in 1930. All property was lost, and Ford left the United States, migrating to Africa and very possibly, to an encounter with Islam. The few of his followers who remained loyal reorganized, under a former U.N.I.A. man whom Ford designated, into a loose group based on U.N.I.A. nationalism which was not destined to last very long. Thus, one may agree with the first part of Landes' judgment on the group, when she says that such nationalism was its essential matrix and that,

> Judaism had touched the B.B.A. only as an arabesque, a signature of Ford's genius. It took no hold, although the B.B.A. had carried its pretensions further than any Negro Jewish cult preceding or following it. . . . Black Judaism is now almost an exhausted theme in Harlem. . . . But its mainsprings are still active.[33]

One must, however, question the latter part of this observation, keeping in mind the very lively theme of Black Judaism, as manifest in the three types of Black Jewish groups considered in the present essay, each of which have articulated their Jewish sympathies more positively than did the B.B.A.

One last aspect of the specific influence of Ethiopianism upon

[32] Cited in Landes, ibid., p. 186.
[33] Landes, ibid., pp. 186–87.

One last aspect of the specific influence of Ethiopianism upon Black Jews is evidenced in the claim by one of the three groups, the Ethiopian Hebrews, to be descended from the Falasha Jews of Ethiopia. Other suggestions as to the African sources of Black Judaism have also appeared frequently. Among these are the opinions of Arnold Ford discussed above; the descriptions by one writer of a West African native group called Judaeos, who professed and observed a basic Judaism, of a black sect in Madagascar called the Zafy Ibrahim (descendants of Abraham), and of a general infusion of Negroid blood among Jews in North Africa[34]; author Roi Ottley's assertion that Jews were numbered among the black Africans brought to America on slave ships[35]; and Father Joseph Williams' discussion of a general movement of "Hebrewisms" from Ethiopia and east Africa, even before the Falashas, to the Ashanti people in West Africa and then on to Jamaica.[36]

In any case, however, it was unlikely that the slaves were originally Jewish and continued this identification in America, as the numbers of those on the slave ships who might have been Jewish were minuscule and, further, as it was most improbable that they would have retained their Jewish heritage when faced with the pressures of the plantation. Thus, some explanation of a later "return" to the Jewish tradition by Black Jews is needed, regardless of which of these many sources one looks to for evidence. The Ethiopian Hebrews' account of their "lost" heritage is perhaps the most significant explanation and utilization of the African past and the Ethiopian impulse to appear among American Black Jews, although their claim is not substantiated by any real correspondence between their practices and those of the Falashas.

The renewed awareness of their origins by the Ethiopian Hebrews was heightened by contact with the white Jewish Pro-Falasha Committee, led by Jacques Faitlovich, who found the original Falashas to be "worthy sons of our people . . . [who] have demonstrated that they possess the characteristics of our race, the vivifying force of the existence of Israel."[37] His efforts to establish their connection to the American group proved fruitless, however, as may be observed in a brief review of his description of the Ethiopian Falashas.[38]

[34] Sherry Abel, "Negro Jews," *Universal Jewish Encyclopedia*, VIII, 145, reprinted in vertical file under "Black Jews," Jewish Theological Seminary Library.

[35] Roi Ottley, *New World A-Coming* (Boston: Houghton-Mifflin, 1943), p. 141, cited in Dobrin, "Negro Jews," p. 1.

[36] Father Joseph Williams, *Hebrewisms of West Africa* (New York: Biblo & Tannen, 1967).

[37] Jacques Faitlovich, "The Falashas," *American Jewish Yearbook* (1920–21), p. 80.

[38] Ibid., pp. 80–100.

The Falashas, now numbering about 20,000 but nearer to 50,000 when Faitlovich wrote, are a people of non-African stock who call themselves *Beta Israel,* the House of Israel, and represent a peculiar form of Judaism. They trace their roots back to the union of King Solomon and Sheba, as recounted in I Kings 10 and II Chronicles 9. According to the national legend of Ethiopia, with which the Falashas particularly identify themselves, Menelik I, the offspring of this royal union, was sent back to Ethiopia by Solomon with a retinue of thousands. In departing, Menelik stole the original Tables of the Mosaic Law in place of the copies his father had given him. He returned home to establish a dynasty of Jewish kings and to make Judaism the national religion of Ethiopia for centuries. While various and conflicting historical accounts of their origin exist, the Falashas accept this historical fiction as definitive and in so doing, "rationalize" their existence in much the same way as do the American Ethiopian Hebrews.

The Falashas are completely dependent upon the Pentateuch for their religious observances, having no knowledge of Hebrew, the oral law, post-Exilic history, or the Talmud. All worship centers around the *mesgid* or place of prayer in each village. In the mesgid, observances are presided over by the *Kohan,* or priest, while the *Debteras,* or learned men, provide religious instruction. The Falashas observe all the revealed Law, paying particular attention to the Sabbath, to all Jewish festivals except the post-Exilic ones, to several half-holidays and fast days which they observe as reminders of the annual holidays, to circumcision, and to ritual cleanliness.

There is, thus, little observable connection between the rather esoteric Judaism of the Falashas, which resembles an early Jewish sect, and the very Americanized Ethiopian Hebrews' type of Black Judaism. Yet the American group continually reaffirms their identity, which functions both as a mystique and as a rational theology for its clergy and members, making explicit the ideological impact of Ethiopianism upon many Black Jews. The Ethiopianism movement cannot be claimed as a direct source of this particular Black Jewish group's religious identification nor even as indirect source for the two Black Jewish groups herein considered who do not claim to be descended from Ethiopian Jews. Yet the influence of Ethiopianism upon this one group has been articulated in the context of a growing black self-awareness and pride which is itself an intrinsic part of the historical and cultural ethos of the black man, and thus of all Black Jews in the United States.

CHAPTER V

BLACK RELIGION: AFRICA AND THE CARIBBEAN

Recent anthropological studies in East and Southern Africa have shed important new light on the long prehistory of the human race. When the data are all in, and the tangled skein of evidence is unraveled, science will undoubtedly confirm what the traditions and wisdom of the people have always taken for granted: that Africa is the womb of human development and the mother of civilization. But we need not wait the validation of science to recognize that for thousands of years countless civilizations have turned to Africa for the *nurture* they needed, in one form or another, to sustain their viability and to stay the decline of their power and influence.

Following the discovery of the New World, the maritime civilizations of Western Europe embarked on a strategy of conquest and redeployment unequaled since the time of Alexander. What they wanted from Africa this time was labor, *free* labor, and to supply that commodity for their military and economic adventures in the Americas, the Europeans developed a highly sophisticated system of human procurement and disposal—unmatched for its magnitude, its commercial efficiency and its wastage of human lives by any similar slavery enterprise in history. We shall never know with certainty how many tens of millions of Africans were torn from that ancient land and transplanted in the two Americas and the islands of the Caribbean. We only know that their numbers were legion and that their mark on the host cultures is certain and ineradicable. Their names are known only to the gods who keep their souls. Their numbers remain the secret of the logs of a million ships, the ledgers of a thousand counting houses, the memories of a vast array of sea captains, factors, agents, auctioneers, overseers, and plantation entrepreneurs—all of whom have long since drunk their cup . . . and sought their rest. But Africa lives on and flourishes, in the Americas and in the Caribbean; for Mother Africa, whose fructiferous womb cast forth the chiefs and warriors, the fishermen, the drummers, the priests and the doctors who reached the new world as slaves, is projected upon the cultures of the New World through this involuntary black diaspora.

Religion is an important element of the African projections in America—most especially in the Caribbean where the religions of Africa were not so vigorously repressed as in the United States. Hence, in Haiti, "Voodoo" flourishes, and in Cuba and the West Indies, Guyana, Brazil and Panama, religious attitudes based on the West African heritage are quite common and take on a variety of ritualistic and doctrinal expressions.

A prominent interest of the contemporary study of black religion ought to be to rediscover the linkages between the religions of West Africa and the religious expressions of the African diaspora in the West. There are no surer signs of a common heritage. While three centuries of slavery and its natural sequence of cultural accommodations have indeed obliterated much of what was African with a patina of Western culture, the African experience is measured in millennia not in centuries. Chances are, if it is rubbed hard enough, it will glow through the gloss of more recent cultural accretion.

JOHN S. MBITI

The notion of God as the Supreme Being is found in all African societies. Knowledge of God is expressed in proverbs, songs, prayers, stories, and religious ceremonies and, through these media, is passed on from one society to another. Concepts of God are influenced by history and sociocultural factors. God is omniscient, almighty, transcendent, etc. He is also immanent, available to men. He is uncreated, self-dependent, and unchanging. God is also Spirit, and He is eternal. The moral nature of God is shown by his giving fertility to the people, averting calamities, etc. God has a personality, but the nature of God is beyond human comprehension.

John S. Mbiti is a native of Kenya. Educated in England and in the United States, he is Professor of Religious Studies at Makerere University College in Uganda.

THE NATURE OF GOD

Source: John S. Mbiti, *African Religions and Philosophies* (New York: Anchor Books, 1970), pp. 37–49.

Expressed ontologically, God is the origin and sustenance of all things. He is "older" than the Zamani period; He is outside and beyond His creation. On the other hand, He is personally involved in His creation, so that it is not outside of Him or His reach. God is thus simultaneously transcendent and immanent; and a balanced understanding of these two extremes is necessary in our discussion of African conceptions of God.[1]

In my larger work, *Concepts of God in Africa* (1969), I have collected all the information available to me concerning the traditional concepts of God. The study covers nearly 300 peoples from all over Africa outside the traditionally Christian and Muslim communities. In all these societies, without a single exception, people have a notion of God as the Supreme Being. This is the most minimal and fundamental idea about God, found in all African societies. Obviously there are many who have much more to say about God than this; but apart from a few comprehensive studies, our written information about the concepts of God held by individual peoples is incomplete.

African knowledge of God is expressed in proverbs, short statements, songs, prayers, names, myths, stories and religious ceremonies. All these are easy to remember and pass on to other people, since there are no sacred writings in traditional societies. One should not, therefore, expect long dissertations about God. But God is no stranger to African peoples, and in traditional life there are no atheists. This is summarized in an Ashanti proverb that "No one shows a child the Supreme Being." That means that everybody knows of God's existence almost by instinct, and even children know Him.

African concepts of God are strongly colored and influenced by the historical, geographical, social and cultural background or environment of each people. This explains the similarities and differences which we find when we consider the beliefs about God from all over the continent. It is this which partly accounts also for the beliefs parallel to those held by peoples of other continents and lands, where the background may be similar to that of African peoples. This does not rule out the fact that through contact with the outside world, some influence of ideas and culture has reached our continent. But such influence is minimal and must have operated in both directions. There are cardi-

[1] Those wishing to get a more detailed and comprehensive account are referred to J. S. Mbiti, *Concepts of God in Africa* (S.P.C.K., London, 1969; Praeger, New York, 1969), available in hard and paperback covers. This and the next two chapters draw considerably from that work, for which I am grateful to the publishers, the Society for Promoting Christian Knowledge (S.P.C.K.).

nal teachings, doctrines and beliefs of Christianity, Judaism and Islam which cannot be traced in traditional religions. These major religious traditions, therefore, cannot have been responsible for disseminating those concepts of God in traditional religions which resemble some biblical and Semitic ideas about God, while at the same time omitting their infinitely more important aspects of belief and practice. I maintain that African soil is rich enough to have germinated its own original religious perception. It is remarkable that in spite of great distances separating the peoples of one region from those of another, there are sufficient elements of belief which make it possible for us to discuss African concepts of God as a unity and on a continental scale. But obviously the situation is more complex than the impression which that unity might give here. This is a task I have attempted to accomplish elsewhere; there are also other writers who deal with individual people's concepts of God, but we need not trace here ground which has been covered elsewhere.

[a] The Eternal and Intrinsic Attributes of God

These attributes are difficult to grasp and express, since they pertain more to the realm of the abstract than concrete thought forms. Broadly speaking, African thought forms are more concrete than abstract. We find, however, considerable examples of how African peoples conceive of the eternal nature of God.

A number of societies consider God to be omniscient, that is, to know all things, to be simultaneously everywhere (i.e., omnipresent), and to be almighty (omnipotent). These are essential aspects of His being; they are part of His unique nature and no other being can be described in the same terms. It is these and other eternal attributes discussed below, which distinguish God from His creation and which make Him not only the genesis but also the sustainer of all things.

When African peoples consider God to be omniscient, they are at the same time conferring upon Him the highest possible position of honor and respect, for wisdom commands great respect in African societies. In so doing, people admit that man's wisdom, however great, is limited, incomplete and acquired. On the other hand, God's omniscience is absolute, unlimited and intrinsically part of His eternal nature and being. To the Zulu and Banyarwanda, God is known as "the Wise One," and to the Akan as "He Who knows or sees all." It is a common saying among the Yoruba that "Only God is wise" and they believe that God is "the Discerner of hearts" Who "sees both the inside and outside of man."[2]

The metaphor of seeing and hearing explains the concept of God as ominiscient in a concrete way which is easy to grasp. So we find examples from many areas of Africa, in which God is said to be able to see or hear everything. One name for Him among the Barundi is "the Watcher of everything"; while the Ila say that His "ears are long."[2] Other peoples visualize God as "the Great Eye" (like the Baganda), or "the Sun" which beams its light everywhere. Whether or not people literally think of God as having one or more eyes, or long ears, is immaterial: the point is that they regard Him as the omniscient from Whom nothing is hidden, since nothing can escape His vision, hearing or knowledge. He knows everything, observes everything and hears everything, without limitation and without exception.

When the Ila say that "God has nowhere or nowhen, that He comes to an end," they are speaking about His nature of omnipresence. The Bamum express the same concept in their name for God (*Njinyi* or *Nnui*) which means: "He Who is everywhere." This idea comes out among other peoples who say that God is met everywhere (e.g., Barundi and Kono); that the presence of God protects people (e.g., Akamba); that wrong-doers cannot escape the judgment of God (e.g., Yoruba, Kono); or that God is like the wind or air (e.g., Shilluk, Langi). These are attempts to describe another intrinsic and eternal attribute of God, His omnipresence.

That God is almighty is a concept easier to grasp than the attributes discussed above. Consequently we find many concrete examples from all over Africa, in which people speak of God as omnipotent. Among some peoples, like the Yoruba, Ngombe, Akan and Ashanti, one of the names for God describes Him as "the All-powerful" or "the Almighty." His power is seen in practical terms. The Yoruba might say of duties or challenges that they are "easy to do as that which God performs; difficult to do as that which God enables not."[3] The Zulu conceive of God's power in political terms, which for such a powerful nation is full of meaning. They describe Him as "He Who bends down . . . even majesties," and "He Who roars so that all nations be struck with terror."[4] The Ngombe who live in the extremely thick forest in the Congo see God's omnipotence in relation to the forest and praise Him as "the

[2] Danquah, p. 55 (Akan); Idowu, p. 41 (Yoruba); Guillebaud in Smith, p. 187 (Barundi); Smith and Dale, p. 208 (Ila).
[3] Idowu, p. 40f.
[4] Smith, p. 109.

One Who clears the forest."[5] For these people, the forest is the symbol of power, and no doubt they struggle constantly to keep it under some form of control. Yet this is no problem with God: He can clear the forest without difficulties, therefore He is omnipotent.

Among many peoples, God's omnipotence is seen in His exercise of power over nature. A few examples will illustrate this. In two proverbs the Banyarwanda say that "the plant protected by God is never hurt by the wind" and that "God has very long arms."[6] The Kiga refer to God as "the One Who makes the sun set"; and when the Gikuyu make sacrifices and prayers for rain, they address God as the One Who makes mountains quake and rivers overflow. The wind, the sun and the rain are beyond human power of control, but not beyond God's power Who works through them and other natural phenomena or objects. There are those peoples, like the Akamba, Gikuyu, Teso, Vugusu and others, who see God's omnipotence in terms of His being able to deal with, or control, the spirits—these being more powerful than men.

So in this context, power is viewed hierarchically in which God is at the top as the omnipotent; beneath Him are the spirits and natural phenomena; and lower still are men who have comparatively little or no power at all.

The attribute of God's transcendence must be balanced with that of His immanence, since these two are paradoxically complementary. This means that He is so "far" (transcendental) that men cannot reach Him; yet, He is so "near" (immanent) that He comes close to men. Many foreign writers have gone astray here, in emphasizing God's remoteness to the exclusion of His nearness.

In terms of time, God "stretches" over and beyond the whole period of *Zamani*, so that not even human imagination can get at Him. He not only fills up the *Zamani* period, He also transcends it. This is what the Akan are attempting to express when they praise Him as "He Who is there now as from ancient times"[7]; and when the Tonga refer to Him simply as "the Ancient of Days." The Ngombe compare this essential nature of God to the forest, for which reason they speak of Him as "the everlasting One of the forest."[8] As far back as they can imagine, the forest has always been in existence; but God antedates it since He made it.

It is, however, in spatial terms that people more readily conceive of

[5] Davidson in Smith, p. 167.
[6] Maquet in Forde, p. 169.
[7] Danquah, p. 55.
[8] Davidson in Smith, p. 166.

God's transcendence. God is thought of as dwelling far away in the sky, or "above," beyond the reach of men. Obviously the sky in its great immensity invites people to gaze in it, both with their eyes and imagination. Practically all African peoples associate God with the sky, in one way or another. Some have myths telling of how men came from the sky; or how God separated from men and withdrew Himself into the sky, whence nobody could directly reach Him.

The concept of God's transcendence is summarized well in a Bacongo saying that "He is made by no other; no one beyond Him is."[9] There cannot be, and there is no "beyond" God: He is the most abundant reality of being, lacking no completeness. He transcends all boundaries; He is omnipresent everywhere and at all times. He even defies human conception and description; He is simply "the Unexplainable" as the Ngombe like to call Him. Ontologically He is transcendent in that all things were made by Him, whereas He is self-existent. In status He is "beyond" spiritual beings, the spirits, men and natural objects and phenomena. In power and knowledge, He is supreme.

Yet, in spite of all this transcendence of God, He is immanent so that men can and do in fact establish contact with Him. One of the best-known praise names of God among the Ngombe describes Him as "the One Who fills everything." It is, however, in the many acts of worship that men acknowledge God to be near and approachable. Such acts include sacrifices, offerings, prayers and invocations. Men also associate God with many natural objects and phenomena, indicating their belief that God is involved in His creation: there is no space where, or time when, He cannot be found since He is contemporaneous with all things. This is not pantheism, and there is no evidence that people consider God to be everything and everything to be God.

For most of their life, African peoples place God in the transcendental plane, making it seem as if He is remote from their daily affairs. But they know that He is immanent, being manifested in natural objects and phenomena, and they can turn to Him in acts of worship, at any place and any time. The distinction between these related attributes could be stated that in theory God is transcendental but in practice He is immanent.

A number of African peoples think of God as self-existent and pre-eminent. From the Zulu we get a clear expression of this concept. They give one name to God which means: "He Who is of Himself" or "He Who came of Himself into being."[10] The Bambuti think that God "was

9 Claridge, p. 269.
10 Smith, p. 109.

the First, Who had always been in existence, and would never die."[11]
These are theological and philosophical expressions; but there are
others of a biological nature. Thus, the Gikuyu believe that God has

> *No father nor mother, nor wife nor children;*
> *He is all alone.*
> *He is neither a child nor an old man;*
> *He is the same today as He was yesterday.*

They go on to point out that He does not eat and has no messengers.[12]
In almost identical words, the Herero say that God has no father and
is not a man. These statements indicate that God is self-sufficient, self-
supporting and self-containing, just as He is self-originating. In human
terms, it is clearly emphasized that God is uncreated, without parents,
without family, without any of the things that compose or sustain human life. He is truly self-dependent, absolutely unchangeable and unchanging.

From this it follows that God is pre-eminently great and supreme.
Many societies, like the Akan, Baluba, Ngoni, Tonga and others, speak
of Him as "the Great One," or "Great God," or "the Great King," or
"the surpassingly great Spirit." The main Zulu name for God, *Unkul-
unkulu,* carries with it the sense of "the Great-great-One" and the same
name is used by neighboring peoples, such as the Ndebele for whom
it means "the Greatest of the great."[13] The attributes of transcendence
and self-existence also point in this same direction of the supremacy
and pre-eminence of God.

It is commonly believed that God is Spirit, even if in thinking or
talking about Him African peoples may often use anthropomorphic
images. As far as it is known, there are no images or physical representations of God by African peoples: this being one clear indication that
they consider Him to be a Spiritual Being. The fact that He is invisible also leads many to visualize Him as spiritual rather than physical.
To grasp this aspect of God, some societies like the Ga, Langi and
Shilluk compare Him with the wind or air. There is no information
available to indicate that anyone has ever seen God; though there are a
few vague accounts of theophanies, i.e., physical manifestations of God,
but it is possible that these are hallucinations rather than external
experiences.

[11] Schebesta, II, p. 171f.
[12] Routledge, p. 225f.; Kenyatta, p. 233.
[13] Smith, p. 103; and Hughes and Velsen, p. 103.

One of the most explicit descriptions of God as Spirit occurs in a traditional Pygmy hymn which says:

> *In the beginning was God,*
> *Today is God,*
> *Tomorrow will be God.*
> *Who can make an image of God?*
> *He has no body.*
> *He is as a word which comes out of your mouth.*
> *That word! It is no more,*
> *It is past, and still it lives!*
> *So is God.*[14]

In a Shona traditional hymn, God is addressed as "the Great Spirit" Who piles up rocks to make mountains, causes branches to grow and gives rain to mankind.[15] Thus, God is pictured as an active and creative Spirit.

It is particularly as Spirit that God is incomprehensible. So the Ashanti rightly refer to Him as "the fathomless Spirit," since no human mind can measure Him, no intellect can comprehend or grasp Him. To the Bacongo, He is "the Marvel of marvels," and anything which seems beyond their understanding is attributed to Him as "a thing of God." Many people readily admit that they do not know what God is like, and that they do not possess the words of God—since words are vehicles of someone's thoughts and to a certain degree they give a portrait of the speaker. Some even say that God's proper name is unknown; or give Him a name like that of the Lunda, which means or signifies "the God of the unknown," or that of the Ngombe which means "the Unexplainable," or of the Maasai which means "the Unknown."[16] A person's name in African societies generally has a meaning descriptive of his personality and being. In the case of God, people might know some of His activities and manifestations, but of His essential nature they know nothing. It is a paradox that they "know" Him, and yet they do not "know" Him; He is not a Stranger to them, and yet they are estranged to Him; He knows them, but they do not know Him. So God confronts men as the mysterious and incomprehensible, as indescribable and beyond human vocabulary. This is part of the essential nature of God.

[14] Young, p. 146, without specifying which group of Pygmies.
[15] Smith, p. 127.
[16] Lunda name is *Njambi-Kalunga* (Campbell, p. 245); Ngombe name is *Endalandala* (Davidson in Smith, p. 167); Maasai name is *Ngai* (Hinde, p. 99; cf. other writers claim that it means "rain and sky").

Ideas of God's eternal nature are expressed variously by different peoples. The Ngombe, for whom the forest symbolizes agelessness, regard God and praise Him as "the everlasting One of the forest." The Ila, Baluba and others liken God's eternal nature to the apparent endurance of the sun, calling Him "He of the suns," or "He of many suns." God's eternity is here compared to the sun of many suns: He endures forever, and His eternal nature makes Him impervious to change and limitation. The Baganda and Ashanti address Him as "the Eternal One." The Yoruba, on the other hand, consider God to be "the Mighty, Immovable Rock that never dies."[17] This metaphor of immortality is used also by the Tonga in their saying that "Heaven never dies, only men do!"[18] (where "Heaven" stands for God). The same idea is emphasized by the Yoruba in a popular song that "one never hears of the death of God!"[17] God is eternal, beyond the effect or influence of change; He endures for ever and ever, as He was He continues to be, so that He cannot be other than being God.

Every African people recognizes God as One. According to some cosmologies, however, there are, besides Him, other divinities and spiritual beings, some of whom are closely associated with Him. These beings are generally the personification of God's activities, natural phenomena and objects, or deified national heroes, or spiritual beings created by God as such. In a few cases, such as among the Bari, Lugbara and Turu, dual aspects of the One God are recognized, as an explanation of the transcendence and immanence of God, and of the problem of good and evil. A form of trinitarian concept of God is reported among the Ndebele and Shona peoples, according to which He is described as "Father, Mother and Son."[19] This is probably a logical convenience, rather than a theological reflection, to fit God into the African conception of the family.

[b] The Moral Attributes of God

Of the moral attributes of God we have little information. Many peoples, such as the Akamba, Banyarwanda, Ila, Herero and others, consider God to be merciful, showing kindness and taking pity over mankind. For that reason He is referred to as "the God of pity," "God is kind," or "God is merciful." The mercy or kindness of God is felt in situations of danger, difficulty, illness and anxiety, when deliverance

[17] Idowu, pp. 36, 43.
[18] Junod, p. 135.
[19] Hughes and Velsen, p. 104f.; and Merwe, p. 11f.

or protection is attributed to Him, or He is called upon to help. Even when sorrows have struck, God may be called upon to comfort the people, as is done, for example, by the Nuer; and some societies like the Akamba and Akan, speak of Him as "the God of comfort."

The majority of African peoples regard God as essentially good, and there are many situations in which He is credited with doing good to His people. Some, like the Akamba, Bacongo, Herero, Igbo, Ila and others, say categorically that God does them only what is good, so they have no reason to complain. The Ewe firmly hold that "He is good, for He has never withdrawn from us the good things which He gave us."[20]

For some, the goodness of God is seen in His averting calamities, supplying rain, providing fertility to people, cattle and fields. Thus, the Langi consider rich harvests to come from God; the Vugusu believe that material prosperity comes from God; and the Nandi invoke God daily to grant fertility to their women, cattle and fields. Believing that God is essentially good, the Barundi do not wish to thank Him since it is His right to do good things to them.

There are, however, situations when calamities, misfortunes and suffering come upon families or individuals, for which there is no clear explanation. Some societies would then consider these to be brought about by God, generally through agents like spirits or magic workers, or as punishment for contravening certain customs or traditions. By so doing, they do not consider God to be intrinsically "evil" as such: that is simply a rational explanation of what may otherwise be hard to explain. This dilemma comes out in a saying of some Katanga peoples, that God is "the Father Creator Who creates and uncreates."[21] The Ila show similar difficulties when they consider God to be responsible for giving and causing to rot. Some peoples hold that God is capable of showing anger; and death, drought, floods, locusts and other national calamities are interpreted to be manifestations of His anger. A few, like the Tonga and Tiv, look upon thunder and lightning as resulting from God's anger; while the Barundi fear that adultery will arouse His anger and cause Him to punish them with misfortune.

A number of peoples consider God to have a will which governs the universe and the fortunes of mankind. When the Bambuti Pygmies fail to kill game in their expeditions, they take this to be God's will against which they can do nothing. On the other hand, the Banyarwanda believe that only through God's will does one find a wife (or husband),

[20] D. Westermann, *The Shilluk People* (Berlin/Philadelphia, 1912), p. 197.
[21] Campbell, p. 245.

wealth, job, or is restored to good health. When planning to do something, the Akamba add the words "if God wills"; and some like the Mende end their prayers with the phrase "God willing." Misfortunes, especially death, are accepted by some, such as the Gikuyu, Lugbara and Nuer, to be God's will, whatever other explanations may be advanced.

God has a personality, and in this personality there is a will which governs the universe and the life of mankind. It is an immutable will, and man generally has to invoke it or accept it in situations that seem beyond human power. This will of God is exercised, however, in a just way, and African peoples consider Him to be just. No matter what befalls them, the Nuer believe that God is always right. They hold that "God evens things out," rewarding good to those who follow good conduct, and evil to those who follow evil conduct, and overlooking breaches done accidentally or in error.[22] The justice of God is felt or invoked often in judicial situations, taking oaths, and pronouncing formal curses, all of which are taken seriously by African peoples. He is the ultimate Judge, and He executes judgment with justice and without partiality.

Concerning the holiness of God, little is said directly by African peoples as far as our records show. The Ila hold that God cannot be charged with an offence, since He is above the level of "fault," "failure," "wrong," and "unrighteousness." In the eyes of the Yoruba, God is "the pure King . . . Who is without blemish."[23] The concept of God's holiness is also indicated from the fact that many African peoples have strict rules in performing rituals directed to God. Sacrificial animals, for instance, have to be of one sacred color, and priests or officiating elders must refrain from sexual intercourse and certain foods or activities before and after the ritual. These ritual formalities clearly show that people regard God as holy.

As for the love of God, there are practically no direct sayings that God loves. This is something reflected also in the daily lives of African peoples, in which it is rare to hear people talking about love. A person shows his love for another more through action than through words. So, in the same way, people experience the love of God in concrete acts and blessings; and they assume that He loves them, otherwise He would not have created them. Whereas manifestations of evil, such as sickness, barrenness, death, failure in undertakings and the like, are attributed to malicious human (and occasionally, spiritual) agents,

[22] Evans-Pritchard, II, pp. 12, 19.
[23] Idowu, p. 47.

the manifestations of good, such as health, begetting many children, fertility, wealth, plenty and the like, are attributed to God: they are the tokens of His love to mankind. People experience the love of God, even though they do not speak of it as though it were detached from His activities.

The Nature of God escapes human comprehension. We have here presented only a few glimpses of it as seen in different parts of Africa. It is, however, in the realm of God's activities that we find the greatest number of examples of what people think and say about God. These activities are an essential dimension of God and reflect, ultimately, the nature of God—or, more accurately, what people imagine Him to be and to do.

KOFI ASARE OPOKU

To understand the Akan, one must understand Akan religion, for much of the activity of the Akan's life is centered around worship which involves divinities and their cults, corporate religious festivals, prayers, pouring of libations, sacrifice of animals, and offering homage to the Akan Supreme God, Onyame. Worship is not an intellectual submission to rules based on God-consciousness. Rather, for the Akan, worship means acting out one's dependence upon a force superior to man.

Opoku describes the two categories of divinities (the Tete Bosom and the Bosom Brafoo) and says that the Tete Bosom gods are community gods while the Bosom Brafoo gods are put to individual use. Corporate worship is very important to the Akan community. It takes place at a shrine during sacred days of a certain deity and may last an entire day or night. Its purpose, says Opoku, ". . . is to contribute to the spiritual edification and renewal of faith of devotees, as well as dedication of converts."

Since Akan religion is both ritualistic and liturgical, its ritual follows a determined pattern and a proper procedure.

Other aspects of Akan worship which Opoku described are the relationship of the revered dead ancestor to certain religious practices; the nature of the Akan's worship of Onyame, the practice of incorporating a god's name into that of a child, and the importance of proverbs in the expression of Akan religious thoughts.

Kofi Asare Opoku is a member of the Faculty of the Institute of African Studies at the University of Ghana.

ASPECTS OF AKAN WORSHIP

Source: First Publication.

The phenomenon of religion is so pervasive in the life of the Akan, and so inextricably bound up with their culture, that it is not easy to isolate what is purely religious from the other aspects of life. It may be said, without fear of exaggeration, that life in the Akan world is religion and religion is life, and to understand the Akan, a thorough knowledge of his religion is imperative. The general applicability of this assertion was stressed by Professor E. Bolaji Idowu when he wrote ". . . a study of African Traditional Religion is the master key to the understanding of Africans who *in all things* are religious."[1]

Worship refers to what is done in the cultic sphere, but a more accurate designation of worship is an imperative or commanding response to the spiritual world, or to a power which is greater or other than man. This imperative response is not exclusively confined or limited to cultic activity, as Akan worship clearly illustrates.

The Akan uses the word "ɔsom" to describe this response. The verb "som" means to serve or be a servant to a (master, a king, God or an idol or fetish), according to Christaller.[2] Thus "ɔsom Nyame" means he worships God or the Supreme Being; and "ɔsom Ɔbosom" means he worships a god or deity; but this "ɔsom," or worship, involves far more than a call to cultic performance; it embraces all that the Akan does in his response to God or a deity. Worship in the context of Akan religion is a very concrete expression of religiosity and not an intellectual submission or assent to a set of propositions in response to an awareness of a deity. Through his worship, whether it is a purely cultic performance or otherwise, whether in word or deed, the Akan acts out his dependence on a power superior to himself, and each act of worship becomes a reaffirmation of man's creatureliness and his dependence.

In Akan religion, the multitude of divinities and their various cults which are seen everywhere seem more prominent to the casual observer than the Supreme Being, for whom no such visible evidence of worship

---

[1] "The Study of Religion with Special Reference to African Traditional Religion," *Orita*, Vol. 1, No. 1, June 1967, p. 11.
[2] Dictionary of the Asante and Fante Language, p. 468.

may be found. But the absence of shrines, or other places of worship, solely dedicated to the Supreme Being is, in fact, a manifestation of the special regard the Akan has for Him, as well as a pointer to what the Akan's conception of Him is: a Being, who is everywhere and is invisible, and that if one wants to speak to Him, he should tell it to the wind. The ancient Yoruba, who replied to the question as to why he had no temples for Olorun by saying that since He (Olorun) was everywhere it was foolish for him to try to confine him to one place, also spoke for the ancient Akan.[3]

The absence of temples, etc., does not mean that the Supreme Being has little or no place in Akan religiosity. His position is without question. He is the Final Authority and Overlord of society, with power over life and death—"if God has not decreed your death, you do not die"—as well as the Creator, "Ɔdomankoma Ɔbɔadeɛ," and Sustainer of the Universe. The divinities and the ancestors,[4] or living-dead,[5] all derive their powers from Him, and may serve as intermediaries between men and the Supreme Being.

We shall start with the divinities and their cults. The Akans call the divinities "abosom" (ɔbosom—singular), and there are two categories of these. The first is *"tete bosom,"* the ancient tutelar deities whose main function is to protect the villages, towns, and states from harm; they belong to the whole community and are believed to be the children of the Supreme Being and are benign, such as Tano and Pra. The second category is *"bosom brafoɔ"* or "suman brafoɔ," which are of more recent origin. These are of northern Ghana origin, such as Tigare, Kune, and Nana Tongo. In contrast to the "tete bosom," the "bosom brafo" can be influenced to kill or bring sickness upon one's enemies. The shrines of the "bosom brafo" are owned privately by individuals and it appears that they were brought in as additional protection, alongside of the old tutelar deities.

In the worship of the divinities or "abosom," there is both individual and corporate worship. An individual may attach himself to a shrine and place himself under the protection of a particular deity. He may be given a "suman," or any visible representation of the deity, to be taken to his house if he visited the shrine of a "bosom brafo." And before

[3] The Akan, of course, had the Onyamedue—God's tree—specifically dedicated to the Supreme Being. See page 19.

[4] The Supreme Being Himself is called "Nana" or Grand Ancestor.

[5] John Mbiti prefers to call the ancestors living-dead in his book, *African Religions and Philosophy*, Praeger, 1969.

this suman he may be expected to perform daily acts of worship which may take the form of prayers or libation, the offering of kola nuts or the sacrifice of an animal and the sprinkling of its blood on the object of worship. These acts are meant to ensure the continued protection of the devotee by the deity. Normally moral uprightness and ritual cleanliness are a prerequisite; the devotee has to observe certain taboos and adhere to specific rules and regulations, the infringement of which may render the "suman" ineffective, or bring punishment on the offender.

In addition to individual worship at home, the devotee may also go to the shrine for an interview[6] with the priest, for it is only the priest who can communicate directly with the deity. The suppliant may present his request to the priest who in turn passes them on to the deity for an appropriate answer or solution. Suppliants at the shrine may ask for special favors and blessings such as children, prosperity in certain undertakings, and victory over enemies. The purpose of the interview with the priest may also be to present a thank offering to the deity for specific favors received, and on such occasions votive offerings are made to the deity through the priest. This may be in the form of money, fowls, or sheep.

Such interviews are strictly private and only the priest and the suppliant may be present. The interviews normally take place at the sanctuary and both the priest and suppliant remove their footwear before they enter the sacred room.

Corporate Worship

Occasionally public worship takes place at the shrine. It either falls on the sacred days of the particular deity or on "dabɔne" (unlucky days), when the Adae festival is held. Corporate worship also takes place during the state festivals such as Ohum, Odwira, and Ahobaa, which are occasions for thanksgiving and rejoicing, or at the annual festivals of the gods, such as Apoɔ.

Corporate worship is accompanied by singing, drumming, and dancing and the principal actor is the priest or priestess, assisted by attendants. The music is provided by the drummers and the singing by the worshipers (spectators). The Ɔkɔmfo stands in the middle of the

[6] This session with the "Ɔkɔmfo" (priest) in which the supplicant tells of his problems and makes his requests known is called "abisa," from the verb "bisa," meaning to ask.

gathering, while the singers with the aid of the drummers pick up song after song. Each deity or "ɔbosom" has a set of songs and hymns which tell of his origin, prowess, and dependability.

The Ɔkɔmfo begins his preparations several hours before the congregation arrives, and included in these is abstention from sexual relations the night before, in order that he may remain ritually pure. By the time the actual worship begins, the Ɔkɔmfo is in a state of possession. Most of the time during public worship is taken up by the performance of "akɔm," or religious dance. The Ɔkɔmfo, dressed up appropriately for the occasion, wearing either a "dɔsɔ," raffia skirt, or a "batakari," smock, enters the circle of worshipers and musicians (drummers). He then throws "hyirew" (white clay) skyward and looks up, to show his dependence on, and give recognition to, God; then he throws some on the ground, to give recognition to Asase Yaa (Mother Earth), on whom also human beings depend. On other occasions when the Ɔkɔmfo dances with a knife or sword, he begins by pointing it skyward and downward, to indicate the same sentiment. After this he marks out a circle, with white clay, within which he will dance.

It must be pointed out at this stage that the akɔm, or ritual dancing, which is performed on occasions of public worship is not simply an emotional response to the drumming and singing, neither is it a set of haphazard movements and wild and random gesticulations without meaning or significance. On the contrary, each dance has a symbolic meaning, and may re-enact some period or incident in the sacred history of the deity or the tribe. The dance may also depict the characteristics and idiosyncrasies of the deity which distinguish him from others. The dance is an important feature of formal worship among the Akan, for there is a crucial element of communication involved, which gives the whole exercise its *raison d'être*. There is communication between the priest and the deities as well as between the worshipers and the priest. Through the dance movements the priest communicates, and the movements say more than verbal utterance. The dramatic element is very strong and is the most distinguishing aspect of our formal worship, as opposed to other aspects of worship described in this paper. And precisely because formal worship involves so much drama, participation (worshipers' response) is greatly emphasised. Thus communication through movement (dance) becomes very important, and the contrast between formal Christian worship and Akan formal worship should be noted.

The "akɔm" usually opens with "ntwaaho," in which the priest spins round and round, while the singers call on God, the Creator, Mother Earth, or the particular deity being worshiped. A typical song may be:

Ɔbɔɔnyame ee,	Hail God, the Creator
Asase oo nyee.	Hail the Earth.
Ɔbɔɔnyame aboa me.	God, the Creator has helped me.
Asase aboa me,	Earth has helped me,
Akɔm ba.	Child of cult.[7]

The next dance, "adaban," is usually accompanied by songs of invocation and supplication. In this dance the priest dances straight backward and forward and his dancing may be accompanied by a song such as this:

Nyee ee!
Yee Akyena e, bra oo.
Bribi reyɛ me oo,
Nyee, nsuo a snyaa agyinaeɛ,
Tanɔ, bra oo.
Bribi reyɛ wo mma.
Nyee ee!
Yee Akyena e, bra nnɛ oo.
Bribi reyɛ yɛn oo.

All hail.
Yes, Akyena, come along,
Something is happening to me.
Hail the water that found a stopping place.
River god, Tanɔ, come along:
Something is happening to your children.
All hail.
Yes, Akyena come today,
For something is happening to us.[8]

In the "abɔfoɔ" dance, which usually follows the "adaban," the priest imitates a hunter tracking down an animal. This dance is symbolic of the deity, who, like a hunter, hunts down evil. The "abɔfoɔ" may in turn be followed by "abɔfotia," which is similar to "abɔfoɔ."

There are numerous dances,[9] all of which are symbolic, and at every

[7] Quoted from J. H. Nketia, *Drumming in Akan Communities*, 1963, p. 94.
[8] Ibid., pp. 94–95.
[9] Nketia recorded twelve such dances during his field work for his book:

public worship, most, if not all the dances would be performed. The Akan priest is certainly a "dancing priest," as Nketia correctly asserts, and this is clearly in evidence on occasions of public worship.

It should be mentioned that at such gatherings for public worship, it is not only the deity being worshiped who makes his appearance; other deities, who are believed to be attracted by the music, descend on the priest, who at once changes his dress and varies his steps to portray the characteristics of the visiting deity. Nketia wrote: "The dance motions are interesting to watch, but the combination of these with trembling motions, leaps and gesticulations instills awe and terror into the onlookers. For believers, there is assurance of the divine presence in all these, for while trembling and falling into ecstasy a priest is no longer himself but the embodiment of the spirit of his god working through him. The words that fall from his lips, his suggestive gestures, and any features he introduces into the drama such as impersonations of creatures, climbing of trees, etc., are carefully noted."[10]

There are periods of rest during public worship when the priest may deliver messages from his deity through an "ɔkyeame," interpreter. He may walk round the circle and shake hands with worshipers and onlookers. The sick may be brought to him so that he may touch them or prescribe some medicines for them.

At the end of the performance, when the deity takes his leave of the priest, the latter collapses into the arms of attendants and is carried into the sanctuary. Later on, his personality, which had been displaced by the god during the time the priest was under possession, returns and he is usually unaware of what had transpired, having been simply a medium who spoke and behaved as the deity wanted him to.

After the departure of the priest, the drummers and singers may continue while the congregation may then dance. The period of such public worship may last for a whole day or a whole night; and the pur-

1.	Ntwaaho	whirling
2.	Adaban	circling
3.	Abɔfoɔ	hunters' dance
4.	Abɔfotia	minor hunters' dance
5.	Ta ksse bekɔ Takyiman	the great Ta will go to Techiman
6.	Akamu	outburst
7.	Sapa	dance of enjoyment
8.	Dwenini katakyi	valiant ram
9.	Denkyemkye	hat of the crocodile
10.	Asɔnkɔ	—
11.	Ɔkwaduo bedi mprem	the antelope will receive shots
12.	Samrawa	—

[10] Op. cit., p. 99.

pose is to contribute to the spiritual edification and the renewal of faith of devotees, as well as dedication of converts. It is not only officials who perform at public worship, the whole congregation participates. Usually at public worship, drinks and meals are served, and this provides an opportunity for communion between the deity and his "children," and between the members of the congregation and each other.

Worship in Akan religion is both ritualistic and liturgical. In the case of ritual, it follows a set pattern, "the way it is done," and adherence to properly established procedures ensures the efficacy of the ritual performed. The liturgy is embodied in the songs, prayers, and praises sung to the deities and also in the language of the drums.

Prayers

As a result of the Akan's awareness and acceptance of the fact of his dependence on a power superior to himself, the power which determines his destiny, the Akan offers prayers through which he makes his petitions known. Prayers are usually made up of petitions and requests for material blessings—health, longevity, prosperity, children, protection from enemies and death, blessings and prosperity on the town, more money, more produce from farms, prosperity and blessings on all well-wishers, and condemnation to all who wish others ill.[11] As the officiant prays, the onlookers express aloud their concurrence with, or approval of, the contents of the prayer, after each pause by saying "Ampa ara" (It is just the truth) or "Yonn" (Yes indeed!).

The petitions may be an expression of the will of man who asks favors for himself and those who wish him well and damnation for his enemies. But the true nature of Akan prayers will be appreciated if it is borne in mind that the petitioner addresses his requests to the Determiner of Destiny upon whose will alone depends the answer to his requests. So that the ultimate outcome of the prayers does not depend on the will of the petitioner but rather on the will of the One to whom the petition is addressed. If it were a matter of the will of man prevailing, there would be no need to ask a superior power to do it, man could just exercise his will and have it come to be as he wished. Prayers, therefore, are a symbol of man's dependence on some power beyond himself.

As a general rule, prayers may be said at any time and at any place, as the occasion demands. Normally before the start of any venture, or even the conclusion of a venture, prayers may also be said. There are

[11] For further reading see Kofi Antubam, *Ghana's Heritage of Culture*, Koehler and Amelang, Leipzig, 1963, pp. 40–43.

brief ejaculatory prayers calling on a deity for help, such as "agya ei!," or "Tanɔ," in the face of some danger or crisis; and then there are the elaborate ones which follow a fairly set pattern, as we find in libation.

Libation

Prayers are often accompanied by the pouring of libation, usually of palm wine or some other alcoholic beverage. The normal procedure for the officiant is to bare his chest and take off his sandals and call on the Supreme Being, by raising the container (calabash or glass) skyward and first offering Him a drink, then to Mother Earth, and afterward the ancestors and the gods, before the petitions are made.

Next to the Supreme Being in importance, in Akan religion, are the ancestors, for the Akan always holds the Supreme Being and ancestors in deep reverence, while the gods may be ridiculed and treated with contempt if they fail their devotees.[12]

Most libation prayers are addressed to the ancestors who are believed to live close to God in their spiritual state of existence. The ancestors are our elders and the reverence given to them is reminiscent of reverence and homage paid to saints and angels in the Catholic Church. It is generally believed that the ancestors need food and drink to sustain them in their spiritual existence, and so occasionally these are offered to them. People normally make sure that there is water in their houses before they go to bed, believing that the ancestors would come round at night to drink; or they may pour a bit of water on the ground when they drink, and this is meant for the ancestors. They may also throw a morsel of food on the ground when eating, and that too is a food offering to the ancestors.

The relationship between the living and the ancestors is symbiotic, the living have their part to play in providing for the ancestors and the ancestors have their part to play in protecting and pleading for their relatives at the court of the Supreme Being; as Dr. Danquah put it: "They act as friends at court to intervene between man and the Supreme Being and to get prayers and petitions answered more quickly and effectively."[13]

The ancestors are constantly kept in mind and informed of whatever is happening, as "living" members of the family. They are informed

[12] See K. A. Busia, "The Ashanti," in *African Worlds*, Cyril Daryll Forde, ed., Oxford, 1954.
[13] "Religion in the Ghanaian Society," speech at the 1963 Student Christian Movement Conference at Aburi.

of what is going on in the family, and requests and petitions are addressed to them. The same petitions listed above are addressed to them as people who live in "Uumbwardo" (God's House), to use a Konkomba word. The ancestors are not the source of the blessings showered on their relatives; they serve as intermediaries between the Supreme Being and the living. They have a keen interest in what is happening among the living and serve as guardians of the family, its activities and ethics.

It is not just any dead relative who becomes a revered ancestor. Only those who have fulfilled certain conditions. Those who lived exemplary lives and lived to a ripe old age. Those who died natural deaths, i.e., deaths not caused by accident, or those whose death was not caused by such an unclean disease as leprosy. Those who fulfilled these conditions are constantly remembered, and regular communication is held between them and the living. Children are also named after them.

There are also stool ancestors who have blackened stools at the stool houses. These stools are fed periodically at the Adae festivals when the spirits of the departed stool ancestors are given food and drink, twice every forty-three days.

Sacrifice

Sacrifice constitutes the essence of Akan religion, as indeed, of all religions. Through sacrifice (which involves the killing of an animal) and offerings (which involve the presentation of food, drinks, and money), the Akan endeavors to maintain a right relationship between himself and his deity. The nature of the deity in question determines the kind of sacrifice offered. The ancestors normally receive food and drink offerings, and occasionally a fowl or sheep may be sacrificed to them.

The various deities in the Akan world who have their particular tastes receive numerous sacrifices. These include:

(1) Food and drink offerings made to the deities at the shrine. This is a normal daily practice, but in addition there are the big periodic sacrifices which involve elaborate preparations, such as at festivals or on sacred days.

(2) Suppliants who have received special favors or blessings, or those who have had their requests granted bring offerings to the deity to show their appreciation. A barren woman, for example, who consults a priest at the Tanɔ shrine, would, when she is able to bear a child, present gifts to the deity at the shrine. This may be made up of money,

drinks, food, clothes, etc., and it is also not uncommon to have the child named after the deity in grateful appreciation for this particular act of kindness on the part of the deity.

(3) Sometimes votive offerings are made. A votive offering is the honoring of a vow a suppliant made when he or she asked for a special favor. It could be in the form of money or an animal.

(4) There is also sacrifice of appeasement which is made in the case of the infringement of the deity's rules or taboos. Such a sacrifice is meant to avert the anger of the offended deity and to restore normal relations between deity and devotee.

(5) Oftentimes it becomes necessary to offer sacrifices to ward off evil or misfortune, not only for an individual but also for a whole community. An individual plagued by a succession of misfortunes may go to the priest to consult him. The priest in turn consults the oracle and then tells the suppliant what to do to reverse the misfortunes.

In the case of epidemics, which affect a whole community, a sacrifice, as the oracle prescribes, is made on behalf of the whole community. The sacrificial animal is killed and its blood sprinkled in specific areas of the town or it may be buried on the outskirts of the town.

In the case of witchcraft, for instance, it is not uncommon to find palm nuts and raw meat placed at the entrance to a town or village, and it is believed that the witches will eat the raw meat and palm nuts on the outskirts of the town or village and will not bother to enter to trouble the inhabitants.

(6) In the founding of villages, or the building of houses, usually a sacrifice of appeasement to Mother Earth[14] is made. Normally the oracle prescribes what sacrifice should be made and it is buried in the ground both to appease the Earth and also to prevent misfortune. It is a common practice even for Christians who, in laying the foundation for a house, bury a Bible and some money under the foundation, but it is the same idea which is being expressed.

Human Sacrifices

In the olden days human beings were sacrificed in extreme cases. Human sacrifice was the maximum sacrifice and it was offered in situations affecting the whole tribe or nation. It was the gravity of the situation which called for such a supreme sacrifice. For ordinary situations, animals were sacrificed instead of humans.

[14] Also, before a grave is dug, permission is sought from Mother Earth before the hole is dug. "We have come to beg you for this spot, so that we may dig a hole."

Human sacrifices were not unknown in the early religions of mankind. Abraham was about to sacrifice Isaac, his only son, to God to show his gratefulness; Jephthah (Judges 11:29–40) made a votive offering of his daughter to God for delivering the Ammonites into his hands.

But with the development of religion, man came to a better knowledge of the will of the deity, and animals, instead of humans, came to be sacrificed. An example of this is the annual "Aboakyer" Festival of Winneba, popularly called the Deer Hunt Festival. Tradition has it that in the olden days a member of the royal family was sacrificed annually. After some time the people consulted the deity, Pɛnkyɛ Otu, who requested that a leopard should be sacrificed instead of a prince. Later on, the people consulted the deity again who said that he would from then on settle for the blood of a bush buck (Ɔwansan), and that is how we came to have the "Aboakyer."

In addition to the sacrifice of humans to deities in the olden days, there was also the sacrifice of human beings on the death of kings and chiefs.[15] This kind of sacrifice was quite different from the first category discussed above, for here the main purpose was not appeasement of a deity but rather that the king or chief may have servants and wives to accompany him to the land of the spirits so that they may serve him. There is an Akan saying that in the realm of the dead there are kings as well as servants (slaves). This practice came into being as a result of the conception which was held of life beyond the grave. It was believed that after death people continued to live the same kind of life as they lived on earth, and the idea was not just to spill as much blood as possible on the death of a king or chief but rather to make it possible for the king or chief to continue to live as he did in the world.

This practice has been stopped without much damage to the ideas of the afterlife which is held among the Akans, for the idea of the afterlife did not need such a practice to sustain it.

Worship of God

Onyame (God) featured prominently in Akan religion and yet the casual observer who saw shrines of the many divinities would be tempted to conclude that the lesser deities and spirits were more prominent than the Supreme Being.

In the religion of the Akan there were no shrines dedicated to

[15] For further reading see B. S. Akuffo, *Kontonkrowi*, which contains accounts of fourteen Akan funerals, published by Bureau of Ghana Languages, Accra, 1964.

Onyame. The only visible symbol of worship for Onyame was the "Onyamedua" (tree of God), which stood outside houses, shrines, and palaces, and served as a visible symbol of the people's dependence on him. A pot was put in the forked branch of the "Onyamedua" and rain water gathered in the pot. This water, "Nyankonsu"—God's water—was used by the head of the household to sprinkle the inmates of the house daily, or as the occasion demanded it, and bless them. Women who had to leave the houses during their monthly period would be purified at the end of the period before they returned home, by having the water in the pot sprinkled on them. At the "Onyamedua" sacrifices of food and palm wine were made to Onyame occasionally. The following points may be noted about worship of God:

(1) The ultimate Recipient of the sacrifices and offerings is God whether the people who make them are aware of it or not.[16] As overlord of society, it is from God that all the other spiritual beings derive their power, and He is the Final Authority.

(2) Prayers are often addressed to Him by individuals. The common prayer: "Onyame boa me," is uttered by many at the start of any enterprise or undertaking.

(3) The expression, "Onyame pε a. . . . ," which is constantly on people's lips, is a recognition of God as the Controller of Destiny, and things happen according to His wishes. A cultured or well-bred Akan will not fail to precede his, or her, plans with this statement. Also in response to the question "How are you?" the cultured Akan replies, "Onyame adom me ho ye," by the grace of God I am well. The idea is that well-being is a gift from God.

(4) An herbalist or a priest at a shrine would, when consulted in the case of illness, always say, "If God permits I shall cure you." God is regarded as Healer and Giver of health. A priest, whose life and work we studied, stated that in the case of barrenness, for instance, he could treat all cases except those ordained by God to be barren.[17]

(5) Another expression of worship is when parents incorporate the name of God in their child's name, e.g., "Nyamekyε," Gift of God, after many years of childlessness. This means that the child is an answer to a prayer, and by naming the child "Nyamekyε," the parents are praising God through the name and giving concrete proof of the belief that God is the Giver of children. It is common among the Akans to say of a barren woman that "Onyame amma no ba," or "Onyame amma no

[16] See John Mbiti, *African Religions and Philosophy*, pp. 58ff.
[17] See *"Akɔm Ho Hkɔmmɔbɔ,"* Kofi Asare Opoku and K. Ampom-Darkwah, Institute of African Studies, 1969.

yafunu," God did not give her a child, or literally God did not give her a womb.

Another name which parents may give to their child is "Famenyame," Give to God. This name is a concrete expression of faith in God as the One who answers all prayers and the One to whom we must refer all our problems.

(6) Mention must also be made of some salutations and words of farewell which are couched in the form of a prayer to God. The person of whom leave is being taken says, "Wo ne Onyame nkɔ," Go with God; and the one who is departing says, "Mede Onyame gyaw wo," I leave you with God (or in God's hands). Both persons are saying in the farewell greeting that God is their Protector and they can leave each other in His safe hands. Oftentimes a person escapes from danger or injury or survives a serious illness, and when he is out of danger he says, "Sɛ Onyame ampata a . . .", "if God had not intervened (on my behalf). . . ." This means that it is God who has kept, and is still keeping, him alive.

(7) Through proverbs, the Akan expresses his thoughts about God. The proverbs contain the wisdom of the ages and are a reflection of the philosophical and religious ideas of the Akans. All this wisdom, the Akan believes, comes from God, and the Akan expresses this by saying "Nsɛm nyinaa ne Nyame," God is the source of all wisdom.

The proverbs play a very prominent part in the everyday language of the Akans, and the richness of the language is due, in no small measure, to the countless pithy proverbs which a speaker can fall upon to adorn and add considerable flavor to his speech.

Some proverbs tell of the nature of God. His existence has never been doubted and, in fact, so immediate and self-evident is knowledge of Him, that the Akan says, "Obi nkyere abofra Nyame," no one points out God to the child. Thus, to the Akan, even a child knows of the existence of God, and the logical extension of this maxim is that all men know of the existence of God, for "He did not leave himself without witness." At the same time God is everywhere and is invisible and the Akan expresses this by saying, "Wopɛ sɛ woka asɛm (kasa) kyerɛ Nyame a, ka kyerɛ mframa," If you want to talk to God, tell it to the wind.

Other proverbs speak of the attributes of God. It is firmly believed that the providence of God is constant and unfailing and that "if God gives you a cup of wine and an evil-minded person kicks it over, He fills it up again,"—"Onyankopɔn hyɛ wo nsa kora-ma na ɔteasafo ka gu a,

ohyla wo so bio." God is said to be full of love and compassion for all
His creatures: He is the help of the afflicted, and the Akans say:
"Onyame na ɔwɔw ɔbasin fufu ma no," It is God who pounds fufu for
the one-armed person. He even takes care of the animal without a tail
by driving away the flies for it, "Aboa a onni dua, Onyame na ɔpra ne
ho"; and He has not left any of His creatures without some talent or
special gift, and this idea is expressed by the proverb: If God gave the
swallow no other gift, He gave it at least nimbleness or agility,
"Onyankopɔn amma asomfana bribi a, ɔmaa no ahodannan."

Through proverbs, the Akan worships God by giving recognition
to His Power: "Asase trew, na Onyame ne panyin," the earth is large
(wide) but God is the Creator; and by telling of His many attributes
of love and care for His creatures, of His dependability, of His
omnipresence and invisibility, of his role as Creator and Sustainer of
the universe, of His love of justice and fairness, "Since God does not
like wickedness, He gave every creature a name," and of His omnipotence.

We see from the foregoing, some of the general aspects of worship in
the religion of the Akan. The formal aspect of worship must be distinguished from the other aspects of worship discussed. However both
aspects, formal and informal, point to an awareness of the creatureliness
of man and his consequent dependence on a power superior to himself,
and it is this commanding response to the spiritual world which is the
quintessence of Akan worship, as indeed, of all worship.

MARJORIE R. BOGEN

Yoruba art teaches a great deal about the history and the religious life
of the Yoruba people. Taken into particular account here are the art of
Ife and Benin courts, and the art which arose from the cults of Sango,
Orisa Ibeji, and the Ogboni Edans.

The Yoruba story of creation is linked with the history of Yoruba,
which makes the dating of the art debatable.

Ife art, the classical period of which was around A.D. 1300, shows
marked resemblance to Nok art (dating from 900 B.C. to A.D. 200),
which was characterized mainly by terra cottas. Ife art also produced
brass court objects, particularly heads.

Among the deities (Orisas), Sango is particularly important for art, for he is represented by a dance staff carried by his believers. Another important Orisa was Ibeji, the deity of twins. Twins were considered to be an unusual phenomenon in Yoruba society and special rules and behavior were observed in reference to them.

The Oshogbu Ogboni Society was a cult which held some political powers. It is represented by brass staffs called Edans.

Ife art influenced the art of Benin. Brass casting flourished there between A.D. 1500 and 1900.

The changing nature of society and the world has made the traditional gods and practices obsolete, and the art objects connected with the old religion have disappeared as a consequence. Internecine warfare has also destroyed the courts, and the kings who used to be remembered through statues and brass carvings are long gone.

Marjorie R. Bogen has studied and traveled extensively in Africa. She is completing her dissertation on African religions at the University of California at Los Angeles.

THE INTERACTION OF ART AND RELIGION IN THE CULTURE OF THE YORUBAS

Source: First publication

Yorubaland encompasses southwestern Nigeria and spills over into present-day Togo and Dahomey.[1] The region now occupied by the Yoruba has been one of shifting boundaries for perhaps the last one thousand years. The inhabitants are a combination of Yoruba-speaking people who still reflect characteristics of the composite culture groups.[2] The population today has been estimated at around eleven million. These being the survivors of Yoruba who have moved about, settling and resettling, as a result of land-grabs, civil wars, slavery, colonialism, and industrial technology.

Despite the Westerners' preoccupation with "how times have changed," the rich traditions of Yorubaland continue, as does faith in the traditional beliefs, interest and creativity in their art, and certainly,

[1] Robert Thompson, *Black Gods and Kings.* (University of California, Los Angeles, 1971), p. CH 1/1. G. J. Afolabi Ojo, *Yoruba Culture* (University of Ife, Nigeria, 1966), p. 18.

[2] J. A. Ademakinwa, *Ife, Cradle of the Yoruba, Part I* (Yoruba Research Scheme, Ibadan, Nigeria). Also, remarks by Jacob Ajayi, U.C.L.A. "Africa Week," Tuesday, April 27, 1971. Cecil Niven, *A Short History of the Yoruba Peoples* (Longmans Green, London, 1958), pp. 7–10.

adherence to the Yoruba value systems.[3] Although Yoruba art per se includes wood carving, statuary, masks, brass casting, terra-cotta works, fabric design, etc., I have chosen to deal specifically with the religious and functional aspects of Ife and Benin Court art, the Cult of Sango, Orisa Ibeji, and the Ogboni Edans.

Yoruba art is both an extension of, and a basis for learning about, the Yoruba's religion and history. Their art stems from their traditional religious beliefs, and so I have tried to examine the art within that context. Through Yoruba oral tradition we are told that all life was begun by the Creator God.[4] God, Olodumare (or Olorun), summoned Orisanla and directed him to create earth. Orisanla was given a snail's shell filled with dirt, a five-toed hen, and a pigeon. Orisanla threw the dirt over a stretch of the "watery waste. Then he let loose the hen and the pigeon; and these immediately began the work of scattering and spreading the loose earth. . . ."[5] Orisanla rejoined Olodumare. Olodumare then sent a chameleon to check on the work. After the chameleon reported that the earth was wide and dry enough, the town of Ife (also referred to as Ile-Ife, meaning the original Ife) was established. Orisanla returned to earth with his counselor, Orunmila. Together they oversaw the provision of trees, fowl (for meat), and rain (for crops). Orisanla's final task was to deliver lifeless forms to earth, where Olodumare breathed life into them. For his part in delivering the forms of life, Orisanla has become the sculptor's divinity.[6]

There is one other name that should be mentioned here. A variation on the creation myth relates that Orisanla did not complete all of his tasks. Before he began to work, he became thirsty and drank too much palm wine. After wondering why the work was taking Orisanla so long, Olodumare sent Oduduwa to check on Orisanla. Oduduwa, according to the variation, completed Orisanla's work, and hence he is often supplanted as the one who actually accomplished the creation of the Earth.[7] Although the Yoruba may assume that Oduduwa arrived at a lonely spot on which to build Ile-Ife, some of the Oral Traditions speak of people being at Ile-Ife when Oduduwa arrived to take charge.[8] However we choose to accept the creation myths, Ile-Ife is

[3] Thompson, op. cit., Chapter 1/1. Also, Ajayi, op. cit., April 27, 1971.
[4] Idowu, E. B., *Olodumare, God in Yoruba Belief* (London, 1962), pp. 19–20. Niven, op. cit., pp. 5–7.
[5] Idowu, op. cit., pp. 20–21. Frank Willet, *Ife in the History of West African Sculpture.* (Homes & Hudson, New York, 1967), p. 121. Nivens, op. cit., p. 7.
[6] Idowu, op. cit., p. 21.
[7] Ibid., pp. 21–22. Willet, op. cit., p. 121.
[8] Niven, op. cit., pp. 7–8. Idowu, op. cit., p. 23.

still regarded as the original home of the Yoruba-speaking people.[9] The implications of Ile-Ife as the center of the earth pervades all of art to be discussed below.

As the political influence of Ile-Ife spread over Yorubaland (and later into Benin), so too did the religion spread, and as it did, the number of religious deities (Orisas) increased to deal with the needs of the people. As various elements of life came to be acknowledged as important, Yoruba artists created styles and techniques necessary to concretize the life forces to the people. For example, wood, stone, terra cotta, brass, beaded and woven objects are still in use to gain assistance from such Orisa as Eshu, the trickster god; Ifa, the power of divining one's future; Sango, god of lightning and thunder; Olokun, goddess of the sea; Oko, god of the harvest; Oya, goddess of the river; Osanyin, god of healing; Ogun, god of war; Ibeji, god of twins, etc.[10] As elements of nature, and conflicts among humans sorted themselves out, the development of Yoruba art took several paths. Perhaps the best-known path was that which led to the court art of Ife.

Oral tradition holds that the first Oni (king) of Ile-Ife was Oduduwa.[11] He married Olokun, the goddess of the sea. They had two children. One son, Okanbi, left seven children who became the ancestors of the Yoruba people.[12] The third of these seven children later became the first Oba (king) of Benin.[13] The art of Ife, for our purposes, is exemplified in the form of terra-cotta heads and figures, and brass (called "bronze" by many writers) heads of the Onis and their relatives. The Onis of Ife were considered divine in that they traced their lineage from Oduduwa, sent from the Creator God. If that be so, then the Oni would probably wish to be worshiped and remembered by his people. Ademakinwa tells us that the Onis lived to be quite old and did not want their people to think that they ever died.[14] In order to perpetuate the idea that they had great powers of survival, the Onis had stone images made of themselves. "Eventually, when people wanted to speak of the long age of any of the people who had so cleverly deceived others into the idea of being magically turned into

[9] Ademakinwa, op. cit. William Fagg, *Nigerian Images* (Frederick A. Praeger, New York, 1963), p. 26.

[10] Idowu, op. cit., p. 70. Ladislas Segy, *African Sculpture Speaks* (Hill & Wang, New York, 1969), pp. 190–93.

[11] Idowu, op. cit., p. 25, Nivens, op. cit., p. 9. Willet, op. cit., p. 122.

[12] Nivens, op. cit., p. 9.

[13] Jacob Egharevba. *A Short History of Benin* (Ibadan University Press, Ibadan Nigeria, 1960), p. 3.

[14] Ademakinwa, op. cit., pp. 40–41.

stone, they used to express it hyperbolically thus: "O gbogbo, O di ota," i.e., "He was so old that he eventually became a stone."[15] If this be related to the origin of terra-cotta and brass heads of Onis, it would support the notion that those heads were commemorative. Either the brass (made of copper, lead, or zinc and tin as an impurity) works were tributes to outstanding Onis, or they were made to serve at a second, or official, funeral for the deceased. In regards to the latter, an Oni would be interred promptly after his demise,[16] but since the populace needed time to organize proper services, a second corpse was needed. To this end the court artist would cast a head to the memory of the departed, which would then be attached to a temporary form, carved of wood. To support this hypothesis, Willet has reported that in another Yoruba town, Owo,[17] the carved "corpse" of Queen Olashubude was done twice, and the first carved corpse (not deemed accurate enough) can still be seen in the king's palace at Owo.

The brass heads of Ife, in general, have several features which make this funerary function plausible. First, there are holes along the foreheads of several of them, suggesting that a crown could have been placed on the head. Second, several of the male heads have holes around the mouth and along the jawbones to the ears. Perhaps these holes were used to secure hair and to give the head a lifelike appearance.[18] Another interesting feature of many of the brass heads, and some of the terra cottas as well, are full-face scars. Does this mean that the royal family was so marked? Or does the scarring on the "faces" serve to remind us of the veils of bead or cloth that the Onis are said to have worn when they appeared in public?[19] In discussing the practical reasons for scarring one's face, Ademakinwa refers to the Yoruba who long ago used facial markings to identify each other, should children be separated from their parents by slave catchers.[20] Ojo, in describing Yoruba women's use of scarring for beautification, noted that "the pattern was

[15] Ibid., p. 41.

[16] Willet, op. cit., p. 26. Second burials were probably done in other parts of West Africa as well. Due to the climate, and lacking the art of embalming, time was of the essence. Or, according to Segy (*African Sculpture*), p. 8: "Among certain tribes, two burials were performed. The first burial was performed soon after the African died. The second burial, which was called the ceremonial burial, took place later, sometimes months later. The reason for delay was usually financial."

[17] Willet, op. cit., p. 34.

[18] Ibid., pp. 35-36. W. Fagg, op. cit., pp. 46-47. Also, Lucie B. McCandless, *African Art and Culture* (Warren Scholat, New York, 1968), p. 19.

[19] Willet, op. cit., p. 23.

[20] Ademakinwa, op. cit., pp. 24-26.

more a network of slanting lines which, for deep cutting, was more manageable than the intricacies of tattooing."[21]

A final note on the religious influence upon Ife court art is sounded by Ojo, "Many of the brass works were kept in, and discovered at, groves, or were in the possession of the divine ruler, the recognized link with the ancestors."[22]

The most often used adjectives for the Ife heads are "naturalistic" or "idealized." The use of these adjectives has caused one of the longest controversies about the source of Ife court art. African sculpture, in West Africa, is generally thought of as being symbolically styled, abstract, or non-naturalized. In terms of Western art, the African artist has had a penchant for not designing works that replicate nature. Some critics maintain that this is out of respect for god's ability to make things look as they do in nature.[23] It is not a lack of skill, therefore, but almost a taboo for the African artist to copy life.[24] Along these lines, many writers remind the viewers that what therefore appears to be "distorted" is actually a style that has meaning (politically, religiously, and culturally) to the African artist, and that reflects a traditional way of designing their creations.[25] Due to the abundance of abstract African art, and because Ife heads in particular are no longer being made—for their purposes—in Yorubaland, the earliest reports on the Ife heads asserted that the Africans could not have made them, that they must have been left by some itinerant group of European artists.[26] The dating of the Ife heads puts their manufacture out of the time during which Europeans could have done them.[27] Also, the "clothing styles" found on the full figures display garments typical of Africa, not of Europe. The fact that the Yoruba brass casters of today are not making heads in the

[21] Ojo, op. cit., p. 261.

[22] Ibid., p. 255.

[23] Lucie B. McCandless, *African Art and Culture* (Warren Scholat, New York, 1968), pp. 24–25.

[24] Delafosse wrote, in *Les Nègres,* that Africans "are among the most religious people in the world"—see Segy, op. cit., p. 7. The African artist would not wish to challenge God's power of making things too natural. What, then, of the naturalism of the Yoruba? See Elsy Leuzinger, *The Art of Africa* (Crown Publishers, New York, 1967 ed.), pp. 54–56. She has some interesting observations on why we should not try to make all African art seem "abstract."

[25] Segy, op. cit., pp. 33–34.

[26] Ademakinwa, op. cit., p. 40. Leo Frobenius is said to have popularized the idea that the Ife bronzes were so natural that Africans couldn't have made them.

[27] They were cast prior to the arrival of Europeans in Yorubaland. We no longer need to feel, as Frobenius did, that Europeans *must* have made them. Elsy Leuzinger, op. cit., p. 117.

classical styles does not rule out the fact that their ancestors did such work. The art of Ife has thus been "returned" to Africa.[28]

Due to the lack of written accounts in West Africa, it is historically impossible to date when certain deities (Orisas) came into being. One Orisa, described in the Yoruba oral tradition is possibly based on the activities of a past leader. The Orisa I refer to is Sango. Sango is the name given to one of the rulers of the Yoruba town of Oyo.[29] He was said to have been so fierce that fire and smoke came out of his mouth. Among the Oyo, Sango is credited with having started the custom of scarring the face, called Eyo. When Oyo was taken from Sango by the Oloyokoro, Sango persuaded his enemies to scar their faces to enhance their looks. While the men were sore from their wounds, Sango organized his troops and retook Oyo.[30] Sango fought many other battles successfully, but his downfall came when he attempted to attract lightning.[31] "While he was doing his magic on a hill, a storm came up and his own house was struck by lightning and was destroyed with his wife, his children, and his property. Alarmed and distracted by this, he abdicated in spite of the efforts of the townspeople to persuade him not to do so. In the end he left for the Nupe country. He was gradually deserted by his followers and he hanged himself on a shea butter tree. After that his followers killed themselves in remorse."[32] This story has evolved to support Sango's deification as the god of thunder and lightning. Art wise, Sango is represented in many ways, particularly by the dance staff carried by worshipers of Sango.

It usually has a double-headed ax with oval indentations, symbolizing the thunderbolts which Sango priests are said to have found after the sky was filled with thunder and lightning.[33] Yorubaland receives a great deal of rain and electrical storms, hence it would seem to be most practical to try and appease the power of Sango, and to adopt his cult for one's protection.[34] It is also important to keep in mind that Sango

[28] Ademakinwa, op. cit., pp. 38–40. Athough some of the "best" Nigerian traditional art remains in European museums and in private collections, outside of Africa.

[29] Thompson, op. cit., Chapter 12/1. Segy, op. cit., p. 193. Idowu, op. cit., pp. 89–92.

[30] Niven, op. cit., p. 40.

[31] Ibid., p. 14.

[32] Ibid., p. 14. Idown, op. cit., p. 90. Thompson, op. cit., Chapter 12/1–2.

[33] Thompson, op. cit., Chapter 12/4, also suggests other explanations for the shape and markings of the Sango staff. See Thompson, "Sons of Thunder," *African Arts* (African Studies Center, UCLA), Spring 1971, p. 13.

[34] Ojo, op. cit., p. 170.

worship stimulated and maintained a patronage that could perpetuate the work of the traditional artists.

A second Orisa, for whom we also have no precise historical date, is Ibeji. Ibeji, Orisa of twins, is another example of how life among the Yoruba is reflected in the traditional religion and related to the powers of the ruler. In Yorubaland there is a high incidence of twinning. "The astonishing high rate of fraternal twins among the Yoruba—42 in a total 177 twin births in a reliable sample—and the relatively higher degree of infant mortality prevalent in twinning combine to suggest one reason for a prodigious quantity of sculptures for departed twins. . . ."[35] In many parts of precolonial Africa, the birth of twins was regarded as unusual and the infants were often put to death. Centuries ago, the Yoruba believed that only monkeys or wretched humans could have twins, and twin births were looked down upon. According to Thompson, a crisis in Old Oyo resulted in which many people died of mysterious causes. In an attempt to stop this crisis, the citizens consulted an oracle. "The word of the oracle was clear: cease killing twins at once and honor them to persuade them from further killing children. . . ."[36] The advice must have been sound because twins are revered in Yorubaland and it is the only part of Africa today with a widespread use of carvings devoted to twinning. The power of twins may derive from their special relationship to Orisa Sango. Sango is variously cited, in praise songs, as the master of twins, the grandfather of twins, and the uncle of twins.[37] "In the Yoruba-influenced provinces of western Cuba the relationship between twins and the Thunder God is faithfully rendered. . . . It is said by some Afro-Cuban informants of Yoruba descent that the Thunder God sired the first pair of twins on earth by a riverain wife."[38] When Twins are about to be born, Idowu tells us, the senior twin says to the junior twin, "You first go out into the world, taste it. If it is sweet, give me a shout, and I will come down."[39] After the birth of twins, they are believed to share the same soul. When one twin dies, the mother may have a small standing statue carved to its memory. The statuette is then washed, clothed, and given food as if it were alive.[40] In this way, the mother has some time to get over the loss of the child; the deceased twin will not feel neglected; and no one has to fear

[35] Thompson, op. cit., p. 8.
[36] Ibid., p. 809. Also Segy, op. cit., pp. 6–7.
[37] Thompson, op. cit., pp. 11–12.
[38] Ibid., p. 11.
[39] Idowu, op. cit., p. 33.
[40] Segy, op. cit., p. 7. Timothy Mobolade, "Ibeji Custom in Yorubaland." *African Arts* (African Studies Center, UCLA) Spring 1971, pp. 14–15.

that the deceased will call the surviving twin to join it in death. Should both twins die, a second statue is carved to let Ibeji know that the family felt honored to have had twins. Another reason for honoring Ibeji is that twins are regarded as having the power to bring prosperity or poverty to the family, depending on how the twins are treated.[41] Suffice to say that the carvings represent the interrelationship between a significant fact of life (abundance of twins), the growth in the Yoruba religious pantheon (from Sango to Ibeji), and provided the artist with one more vehicle by which he could create meaningful form and substance which we can admire.

A different aspect of history and its influence on religion in Yorubaland is seen through the Oshogbu Ogboni Society. Ogboni is a cult related to the powers of the earth and designed to counterbalance the power of the king in Yoruba society. It is possible that Oduduwa may have been an early conqueror of the Yoruba-speaking peoples. If so, his power was such that community leaders established an organization of prominent men to see that Oduduwa's (and his successors) influence did not become oppressive. The name "'Ogbon' can be translated either as 'wisdom' or the number 'thirty.' The word 'Eni' means person. Therefore, the name 'Ogboni' may be deduced to mean either 'the wise ones' or the 'thirty ones.'"[42] The cult limits its active members to thirty persons, and the qualifications for membership are based on one's respect within the community. Roache has outlined several points as being essential to understanding the power of Ogboni. First, Ogboni used to have the power of kingmaking. Second, Ogboni used to conduct judicial proceedings for accused persons. Third, Ogboni meetings contained community forums for the non-royal leaders to debate local issues. Fourth, Ogboni provides for the proper burial of its members. Fifth, Ogboni membership in one town serves to introduce the traveling member to the Ogboni group when he goes to another town.[43]

Artistically, the Ogboni cult is represented most noticeably by brass staffs called Edans. These staffs are usually made of brass over a clay form, depicted as two heads, one male and one female. The heads are attached to each other by a chain at the top. They are often attached to iron rods and often "hold" symbols of the cult (such as a spoon, a rattle, a sword, or another staff) in the Edans "hands." The Edans themselves

[41] Mobolade, op. cit., p. 15. Thompson, op. cit., p. 11.
[42] L. E. Roache, "Psychophysical Attributes of the Ogboni Edan," *African Arts* (African Studies Center, UCLA), Winter 1971, p. 49. See Idowu, op. cit., p. 24, on purpose of Ogboni.
[43] Ibid., p. 49 (Roache).

are so highly regarded that only the members can own them. In life, an Ogboni member may drape the Edans around his neck (by the chain), allowing the staffs to hang down over his collarbone. On the death of a member, the staffs may be stuck in the ground near the gravesite and the chain will be broken, suggesting the severing of the member's life from the earth cult and freeing the member's spirit to join his ancestors.[44]

The Edan not only represent the religious and political power base of Ogboni, but they are religious and powerful objects in and of themselves. Some writers claim an Ogboni member worships his Edan.[45] Edan are suspected of having individual spirits which can leave the brass "body" and do spy and reconnaisance work on behalf of the cult member who owns them. Before the Nigerian Federal government began to reduce Ogboni's power to investigate crimes and to try the accused, Edan were often said to have demonstrated the power to rule on a person's guilt, or innocence, by changing their position[46] (e.g., by falling over after having been stuck in the ground). Related to this, when the Ogboni held a trial, but could not agree on a verdict, retribution would be undertaken by the Edan staffs. Roache has cited three cases in which it was said "that individuals guilty of serious offenses had been found in a desolate area of the bush, their stomachs split open vertically and a small Edan was in the cavity."[47] The Edan would thus become more than a style of art, supporting religion. It could enforce the power of the Ogboni group.

It has been mentioned above that Ife art influenced the art of Benin. Although Benin is not technically in Yorubaland, the religious, political, and artistic ties to the Yoruba warrant including Benin in this paper.

Brass casting flourished in Benin between the 1500s and 1900. Although brass casting has not ceased, the heads commemorating the Obas (kings) are not being made as frequently today as they were in the past. Of the famous Benin brass heads, Talbot wrote, "In the fifteenth century there was no art in Portugal—or indeed throughout the whole of Europe—anything like that practiced in Benin."[48] Benin art is popularly regarded as having been influenced by the art of Ife. Around 900 a migration resulted in people from the Nupe country taking over the

---

[44] Denis Williams, "The Iconology of the Yoruba Edan Ogboni," *Africa*, 1964, p. 146.

[45] Roache, op. cit., p. 50.

[46] Ibid., p. 51.

[47] Ibid., p. 51.

[48] P. Talbot, *The Peoples of Southern Nigeria*, Vol. I. (London, 1926), p. 281.

inhabitants of what was to become Benin City.[49] The rulers in these early dynasties were called Ogisos. When there was no royal heir for the throne, a power vacuum was created. The crisis was settled by sending to Ife for a legitimate ruler.[50] Ife, the story goes, was then being ruled by its first Oni, Oduduwa. Oduduwa had one of his sons, Oranmiyan, designated as the one who would rule the Binis. Oranmiyan stayed at Benin long enough to have a son who became Eweka I, the first Oba of Benin. Oranmiyan then took a long journey back to Ife where he became the Oni there. During his return journey, he left a second son to be the first Alafin (ruler) of Oyo.[51] A successor Oba of Benin, named Cewedo, "was a great idolator, and introduced various gods into Benin, especially the famous Okapannihinrin. Cewedo appointed his adviser, Ogeifa, to be the worshiper of the gods of the earth and royal good luck, that is of the Oba's head."[52] Perhaps this is related to the origin of casting brass heads in the memory of the Obas of Benin. Or would the casting of heads at Ife be the most direct inspiration? Much has been said of the emphasis, in African art, on the head. Some writers claim that the head has always been regarded as the source of the "soul," or spirit, and hence deserves emphasis (or exaggeration) in African art. Others feel that the cast image can assure the departed spirit of a "home," or feeling that his spirit still has an influence on the living. In any case, brass casting in Benin represents a fantastic and dynamic artistic development.[53]

Conclusion

Ife, Orisa Sango, Orisa Ibeji, the Ogboni society, and Benin are all sources of study for future artists and historians. The threads that link the various parts of Yoruba religious history to Yoruba political and physical growth are difficult to measure but are there. Religion has been the inspiration for Yoruba traditional art. The styles and techniques of artists have been influenced by the geography, politics, economics, and shifting populations that have ranged over Yorubaland. The art of Ife and Benin, though not slavishly copied—

[49] Egharevba, op. cit., p. 1.
[50] Ibid., p. 6, W. Fagg, op. cit., p. 31. It also seems probable that the Binis did not actually send for a ruler so much as the powers that were in Ife conquered the Binis and installed one of their own men on the throne.
[51] Egharevba, op. cit., p. 7. Willet, op. cit., p. 151. Niven, op. cit., p. 10.
[52] Egharevba, op. cit., p. 10.
[53] Many writers, following William Fagg, feel that the latest Benin castings demonstrate a decline in brass-casting technique. I feel that these value judgments are useless. After all, the real significance of African art is usually to be found in its use—not in Western concepts of style or beauty.

one from the other—are related to each other as the cities were related within the Yoruba "extended family" of city-states. The Onis of Ife were probably more dependent upon their community leaders, for support, than were the Benin rulers. As the city-states grew, the Orisas increased in number. As the devotees multiplied, the artists produced those objects that would meaningfully serve the needs of religion and life. The success of the artist plying his trade improved as the city-states grew wealthy. But there are still nagging questions about Yoruba art.

Did brass casting end in Ife because an angry Oni had all of the artists put to death? Did brass casting in Benin survive mainly because the Portuguese supplied the Oba with metals (thus making the latest heads of pure bronze)?

Why does there seem to be a decline in the making of religious art objects? The answer lies in the changing needs of devotees. If you teach a devotee of Sango the "scientific" explanation of lightning, he may spend less time worshiping the god of thunder and more time installing lightning rods. If you build bridges across rivers and use better boats on lakes, you may reduce the following of Olokun, goddess of the sea. If you improve the prenatal care for mothers and reduce the number of deaths in twin births, women will no longer need the services of the Ibeji statue carvers. If you institute a system of courts and governmental redress that does not operate through the Ogboni society, you may reduce that group's roll of active members (and therefore fewer members will need to have Edans). If through slavery, imperialism, colonialism, and neocolonialism you wipe out the power of a divine king, how many kings will need to have brass castings made to their memory?

And finally, if the very source of artistic inspiration, traditional religion, is swamped by the incursions of Islam and Christianity (which destroyed the traditional symbols and substituted their own), you have removed—but not completely—the most essential part of the artist-patron cycle that had served the Yoruba world so well in pre-nineteenth century days.

LEONARD BARRETT

Some of the Africans, who were brought to the New World as slaves by the Europeans, came from countries which had developed important cultures, but it was mainly their dynamic and pragmatic religion which helped the slaves survive in their new environment.

The introduction of African slaves in the Caribbean brought with it the establishment of an inhumane system which denied the slaves every right. The slaves responded by resistance through passive opposition or through violence. They united around their religious specialists, the "witch doctors" or *obeah men*. Later the traditional religion of Africa centered around the *myal men and myal women*. The religious Africanization of the Caribbean was fostered by the total separation between slaves and masters and by the lassitude of the Christian Church regarding the spiritual welfare of the Blacks.

In Jamaica, the main African cult is the Cumina-Pukkumina. Cumina was at first a secret society which then merged with the Myal society. When it encountered Christianity, it became known as Pukkumina. Pukkumina appeared in 1860 and centered around native leaders who had been in contact with Christianity. A feature of this cult is the dance accompanied by drums. In Haiti, the African cult is the "Voodoo," or Vodun, which is lightly infused with Catholicism, and which 97 per cent of the people claim to believe in. The author gives an eye-witness account of a Vodun ceremony. In Trinidad, the African cult is the Shango. Each of these cults has its pantheons and rituals which the author traces back to Africa.

In the Caribbean as a whole, the masses have identified with Africa and African religion. African retentions are to be found in the language, the folklore, the market system, the practice of medicine, and the music and the dancing. It is from the Caribbean that African Renaissance and the concept of Negritude emerged.

Leonard Barrett, a native of Jamaica, has traveled and studied extensively in Africa. He is Professor of Religion at Temple University, and the author of *Afro-Caribbean Sects and Cults.**

AFRICAN RELIGIONS IN THE AMERICAS

Source: African Religions: A Sympoisum, Newell S. Booth, ed. New York: Nok, 1974.

At the center of the historical drama of the Caribbean Islands is the African, who at the hands of Portugal, Spain, England, France,

---

* A title in the C. Eric Lincoln Series on Black Religion published by Anchor Press/Doubleday.

Holland, and Denmark, was carried across the Atlantic as human cargo destined to work and die, in the most inhuman conditions of slavery imaginable, for well over three hundred years. No precise figures are available on the number of Africans who came to the various islands, but a conservative estimate would put the over-all figure at over three million.

The early slave trade dealt mainly in Africans from the highly developed kingdoms of the Congo, the Gold Coast, Dahomey, and Nigeria. It was much later that slaves from the interior and from farther south on the continent began to appear. The early slaves were a cross section of the African population; consequently, they brought with them a variety of culture forms which was soon to enrich the Caribbean. Contrary, to the often repeated myth, that the Africans arrived in the New World devoid of culture, it is now generally accepted that the African slaves were the true culture bearers, freedom fighters, and artists of the Caribbean.[1]

The history of West Africa before the entrance of the Europeans provides ample proof that, in the fifteenth century, West Africa had already passed through several centuries of cultural development and had reached a stage comparable to the most developed countries of Europe of that period. Indeed, she had progressed far beyond most of her future oppressors. Richard Wright in his book *Uncle Tom's Children*,[2] describes Africa's complex culture which consisted of iron smelting, the use of brass, ivory, quartz, and granite. Her sculpture in clay, bronze, and wood is still a marvel to Western civilization. Her music, dance, and folklore have captivated the West and in many places displaced all other cultural forms of this *genre*. She mined silver and gold and utilized them with such artistry that, in places like Brazil, the Africans were sought after to work these metals. Africa's legal system was so highly developed before the white man came that, in places like Ghana, the indigenous legal system was never superceded by British laws. The medical knowledge of the traditional doctors of Africa has to be fully explored. But most important is the religious system of Africa. There is

[1] For an interesting discussion of these three contributions, see Frank Bayard's chapter, "The Black Latin American Impact on Western Culture," in the book *The Negro Impact on Western Civilization*, edited by Joseph S. Roucek and Thomas Kiernan; New York, Philosophical Library, Inc., 1970, pp. 287–336.
[2] Richard Wright, *Uncle Tom's Children*, Harper, New York; Musson, Toronto, 1938, p. 13.

no other land in which religion has so permeated the life of its people. St. Paul's statement to the Corinthians, quoting one of the poets of Greece, suitably applies to the Africans, for in their religion they live and move and have their being (Acts 17:28). For all these reasons the slaves who came to the New World should not be thought of as culturally deficient but rather as people from a highly developed culture carrying with them a multitude of skills that enabled them to leave an indelible mark on the New World.

It was African traditional religion, the motivating force of all African peoples, that was first to find expression in their land of bondage. The slave master was able to claim the body of the slave, but the world-view of the African was nurtured in his soul, and this soul was impregnable. This very impregnability was to find expression later in the spiritual, "Jordan river, chilly and cold, chills the body, *not the soul.*" The Africans resistance to spiritual indoctrination is so important a factor that it demands further attention.

The African world-view is dynamic. The universe is a vast system consisting of God, the supreme power who created it, spirits and powers who rule over every aspect of this creation and, at the center, man. All things below man, all lower biological life was created for man, and the inanimate things serve him also. The whole system is alive because it is energized by a spiritual force emanating from the Supreme Being. This force is allotted hierarchically. Flowing from the Supreme Being, it descends to man and through man to all things lower on the scale of life. Man's very being depends upon maintaining a harmonious relationship between himself, his God, and the nature that surrounds him. As long as the vital force which emanates from God is operative throughout the system, and in proper proportion, the universe is considered to be in ritual equilibrium.

But the African is not a mystic. He does not conceive of the world as a place in which to *contemplate* life. He sees his world as an arena for activity. Life for him is a *pragmatic reality*. Gods and Spirits are the sources of his being and all things below him are the agencies of his life. To live strongly, then, is his most engaging concern. His prayers, petition for long life, health, and prosperity; the strengthening of his family, his clan, and his tribe is his great concern because through them he too lives.

This same preoccupation with life force is also manifested in rituals. The Gods are the guardians of life, and if they fail they are reprimanded. The Ancestors, whom we will discuss later, are the guardians of posterity, and men are heavily dependent on them in all aspects of life. They are appealed to for success in birth, marriage, business, and so forth.

The pragmatism in the African world-view finds its greatest expression in African folklore and proverbs. The main theme of the folk tales is the will to survive in adverse conditions. Here we find the ever-recurring theme of the weak against the strong, and here the stress is on cunning, craftiness, and speed. These folk tales gained new significance in the slavery of the New World. And that same pragmatic quality permeates the African proverbs which contain all the reflective wisdom of the African peoples. In them we find instructions for the preservation of life, leading a moral life, living cautiously, loving God, and holding respect for the aged, as well as the wisdom of gratitude and the beauty of temperance. We may conclude, then, that the world-view of Africa is above all life affirming.

It is with this world-view that our forefathers came to the New World. By them the foundation of African culture was laid for all their black descendants. This world-view found expression in the spirituals, music, dance, and the general life-style of later generations who came to be known as Afro-Americans. We will now turn to the Africans in the Caribbean; their period of slavery and the way they adapted to these inhuman conditions; how they Africanized the New World through their traditional religion; and how through this world-view, they survived their oppression. It is the thesis of this paper that the survival of the Africans in the New World was only possible because of this zest for life, which expressed itself mainly in religious terms, and that the Old World environment still remains the unconscious force behind all the combinations and permutations of Afro-Caribbean life to the present day.

Caribbean Slavery: Domination and Resistance

The presence of Africans in the New World became necessary because of the failure of European planters to make a profit using the labor of Indians and white indentured servants. By their very nature the Indians of the Caribbean were unsuitable for sedentary work such as was demanded on European-run plantations. Forced to do such work, they either moved away from the field into the rugged mountain interiors of the islands, or died of the diseases introduced among them by the Europeans. By the middle of the seventeenth century, most of the Indians of the Caribbean had been annihilated either by massacre or by disease. The system of indentured servants was then introduced, but this type of labor was too expensive and temporary to realize the kind of profit demanded by the planters. A new source of labor had to be sought and the lot fell on the Africans.

The leader in bringing slaves to the Caribbean was Spain. By the time the English and the French gained a foothold in the area, slavery was over one hundred years old. By the beginning of the seventeenth century almost all the important islands of the Caribbean held vast plantations. Of course, the price for all this was paid in the suffering of the many Africans who were brought to these regions as slaves.

The introduction of the Africans in the Caribbean was the beginning of a new day for plantation history. Not only were the Africans better workers on the plantations, but their physical condition was uniquely adapted to the brutal climate of the region. The Spaniards soon began to call them "the genius of the tropics" because of their ability to withstand the onslaught of malarial disease. This was incidentally due to the presence of the *sickle cell* developed in Africa over many generations.

This sudden change of fortune for the planters transformed their outlook. The dream of sudden riches, with the chance of returning to Europe to live in splendor, made planters into demons. The profit motive demanded that they drive the slaves to the last inch of their capacity even at the expense of the slaves' lives, as the Minutes of Evidences of 1790-91 indicated. "The object of the overseers was to work the slaves out and trust for supplies from Africa."[3] Slavery had lost every vestige of humanity and the reign of terror had begun. The power of the master over the life of the slave was absolute. The slaves were chattels which meant that they were no different from any other piece of real estate. As such they had no legal or moral rights, but were completely subject to the whims of the master who saw them as nothing more than beasts of burden. The vast number of African slaves in the Caribbean (they outnumbered the whites fifteen to one) meant that such complete minority domination had to be initiated by violence perpetuated by the same. It is essential to understand this aspect of Caribbean life in order to appreciate the reaction of the slaves in later days. Every form of violence known in history was used against the slaves, and all passed under the guise of maintaining law and order.

[3] Orlando Patterson, *The Sociology of Slavery, etc.* (quoting from Minutes of Evidences of 1790-91), London, MacGibbon & Kee, 1967, p. 44.

The myth that the slaves were satisfied and obedient children to white domination is a European fabrication, far from the facts of slave life. It did not take long for the slaves to assert themselves against European domination and inhumanity. In fact, all the evidence clearly shows that the Africans resisted oppression every inch of the way from Africa to the Caribbean and continued to do so right up to the abolition of slavery.

In the Caribbean, slave resistance took two main forms. *First,* there was passive resistance, and *second,* violence. Resistance in the first sense took various forms, running all the way from a simple refusal to work, to complaints of suffering from an undiagnosable disease, to procrastination on the job, to doing the job so badly that it became unprofitable for the master. Another form of passive resistance was simply withdrawing from the plantation into the forest. Such "runaways" started the first communities of Maroons. Examples of Maroon communities can still be found in Jamaica to the present day. Of course, the extreme form of passive resistance was suicide, and even though extreme, it was a frequent occurrence that many of the slaves poisoned themselves and their children with herbs or arsenic; many such potions were known and were readily available to them.

The second form of resistance was violence and this occurred both on the individual and the collective level. Despite the fact that the laws forbid the slaves to even imagine the death of the master, many slaves did much more than just imagine it. Poison was often used for this too. The flora of the Caribbean provided the Africans with an abundance of herbs which were well known to them from Africa. They knew the properties of each herb firsthand, and with their knowledge the unsuspecting master was easy prey. On this subject we have the testimony of Sir Spencer St. John, the British Ambassador to Haiti in the nineteenth century. Of the Africans' herbal knowledge, he observed,

And if it be doubted, that the individuals, without even common sense, can understand so thoroughly the properties of herbs and their combinations, so as to be able to apply them the injury of their fellow-creatures, I can say that tradition is a great book, and that they receive these instructions as a sacred deposit from one generation to another, with further advantage that in the hills and mountains of this island grow in abundance similar herbs to those which in Africa they employ in their incantations.[4]

[4] Sir Spencer St. John, *Haiti or the Black Republic,* London, Smith, Elder and Co., 1884, p. 216.

Still the most significant form of resistance was collective violence. Three aspects of this type of violence stand out. *First*, rebellion was continuous. We have already observed that the slaves actively fought their situation from Africa to the shores of the Caribbean. After reaching the Caribbean, not one year passed between the sixteenth and the nineteenth centuries without a rebellion or the threat of one. *Second*, these rebellions were not simple riots, but in many cases large-scale uprisings which involved thousands of slaves. The end result was usually the massacre of hundreds of slaves and planters. Examples of such crises are the Maroon war of 1735–40, the 1760 Rebellion, and the Sam Sharpe Rebellion of 1831, all of which took place in Jamaica alone. When we turn to Haiti, the history of rebellion is even more full. The *third* point of special interest about those rebellions lies in the fact that their effect on the plantation system was so destructive that the whole system soon became non-productive. It is now commonly believed by Caribbean scholars that the primary factor in the abolition of slavery was not the "humanitarian movement" but the debilitating effect of slave rebellions. The classical example of violent resistance comes from Haiti, where under the leadership of the slaves Boukman, Toussaint, Dessalines, and Christophe, the Haitian slaves proved decisively that they not only loved freedom but were prepared to die for it. It was here that the Africans proved their mettle against the elite soldiers of Napoleon and finally wrestled the island from its slave masters. Very few Europeans have been bold enough to write on the heroism of Caribbean slaves. That entire story is yet to be unfolded.

Africanizing the Caribbean

Like the Hebrews in exile, the early Africans found the Caribbean a "strange land." Here they were separated from family, clan, and tribe but most of all from Guinea—a word which in Haiti became synonymous with Africa—and so from the protection of the Gods and the ancestors. To the Africans this was a psychic shock that could only be handled when explained as the result of witchcraft. Their collective *force vitale* had been totally overcome by the sorcery of the white man. Sorcery or not, the entire world-view of the Africans was shattered and there was, at first, no *hope*, no means in sight through which they could reassemble the pieces of their lives. Anthony F. C. Wallace's concept of the "cultural mazeway" provides a helpful way of viewing the African situation in the Caribbean. According to Wallace,[5] every person in

[5] Anthony F. C. Wallace, "Revitalization Movements" *The American Anthropologist*, Vol. 58, American Anthropological Association, April 1956, p. 266.

a society maintains a mental image of that society and its culture. His conception of the total social complex, involving his own person and the objects of his environment both human and nonhuman, provides a mazeway of experience through which he moves, and this movement must be free and unimpeded in order for him to function in that society. Once this mazeway is mastered by the individual, he functions unconsciously as a member of that society. However, should his mazeway become blocked, he must seek alternative paths through life, paths which are enough for him to continue to function in his culture, otherwise extreme stress will develop. If the mazeway becomes blocked, for a number of persons sooner or later the entire society will suffer from the stress. Cultural distortion will result and, if satisfying alternatives cannot be found, the death of the culture may be the end result. Africans in bondage to the slaver suffered what we will call mazeway disintegration. Slavery threatened the total African personality. The slave was forbidden his language, his religion, his traditional family life, and, in the end, his humanity.

The survival of Africa in the Caribbean must be attributed to the miraculous appearance of those African religious specialists whom the European writers and the slave masters called "witch doctor." Writing of the slaves in Jamaica, Herbert DeLisser observed:

> Both witches and wizards, priests and priestesses were brought to Jamaica in the days of the slave trade, and the slaves recognized the distinction between the former and the latter. Even the masters saw that the two classes were not identical and so they called the latter myalmen and myalwomen; i.e., the people who cured those whom the obeah men had injured.[6]

The function of the legitimate specialists was that of curing those whom the *obeah men* (sorcerers) had injured. Here we have "tangled" evidence that the Africanization of the New World had begun. But even more enlightening is the appearance of the word *Obeah men*, which demands some further discussion in relation to the slave society as a whole.

It now appears quite clear from the records of Caribbean slavery that rather early in the period of slavery there occurred a fusion of the various African tribes, and the new groups centered around the religious specialists. It also appears that much of the religious practice during slavery was directed against the supposed sorcery of the white man. It

[6] H. G. DeLisser, *Twentieth Century Jamaica*, Kingston, Jamaica, 1913, p. 108.

was expedient and prudent for the slave to seek out that tribe whose witchcraft powers were considered most potent. To this base, particularly successful and potent rites from other tribes were added. Thus, in Jamaica and in fact in all the British colonies, the word *obeah* (a select form of African witchcraft) became associated with the whole community. It is also clear that the tribe with the most potent witchcraft became the dominant leaders in the slave community.

The word *obeah* is a shortened form of the Ashanti word *OBAYÉ*, and he who practiced *obayé* is called an *obayifo*.[7] The word can be broken down as follows *oba*, meaning "a child," *yi*, meaning "to take," and the suffix, *fo*, meaning "he who." The full meaning of the word *obayifo* is then read as "he who takes a child away." This suggests the rite that an initiated sorcerer must perform to become a full-fledged practitioner. The appearance of the word also authenticates the dominance of the Ashanti people in Jamaica, and in many other Caribbean islands, and further supports the thesis that the greatest freedom fighters in the British Colonies were none other than the Ashanties.

A similar sort of situation is also found in Haiti. Here again we see the survival technique of many tribes fusing around shared ground of traditional religion. It has been recently suggested that at least one hundred fifteen tribal groups were represented on the island of Haiti,[8] but the name of the religion is *vodun*, a word derived from Dahomey. The leader is a *houngan*, a word from the Congo; the leader of the Haitian rebellion was none other than the Houngan Boukman. And the witchcraft is called *ouanga*, also a Congo word; to this day, the strongest witchcraft in Haiti is still considered that of the Congo variety.

One of the foremost authorities on Haiti, when writing about the Haitian revolution, said of their leaders:

> The belief in their invulnerability was not at all the result of calculation, but was a true state of mind, a sort of autosuggestion which explains very well the chronic heroism of certain leaders of the revolution in Saint Dominque and the war of Independence of 1802–3.[9]

This "invulnerability" was the work of the houngan who empowered the warriors with magical medicine, medicine to make them invulner-

[7] Rev. J. G. Christaller, *Dictionary of the Asante and Fante Language (called Twi)* Second Edition, Basel, The Evangelical Missionary Society, 1933.
[8] Robert Rotberg, *Haiti: The Politics of Squalor*, Boston, Houghton Mifflin Co., 1971.
[9] Dr. J. C. Dorsainvil, *Vodun et Nevrose*, Port-au-Prince, 1931, pp. 33–34.

able to bullets. Madiou, the first Haitian historian, spoke of vodun as "a savage survival" and called it sorcery.[10] We must conclude, then, that the legitimate priests and the illegitimate sorcerers, who came to the Caribbean later, joined forces and pooled their psychic and spiritual powers to free their people from the inhumanity of slavery. It was they who comforted the sorrowing ones; it was they who buried their dead and "sent them off to Guinea"; it was they who led the dance. The dance was the only "recreation" on the plantations, but these African religious men knew the difference between the sacred dance and recreation. It was they who mixed the bullet liquefying potion for the heroes in the slave rebellions and sealed the mouths of the slaves with oaths. They also prescribed the poison against their oppressors and set the *obeah* for both their oppressors and those of their own race who betrayed their secret plottings. This was indeed ritual regression, but the legitimate priests saw this as a necessary evil under a situation of total mazeway distortion. What the African priests and sorcerers were doing here was adapting their own inherited pragmatism to a New World situation.

Witchcraft, however, is inimical to African society. It is an anti-equilibrium device and, if continued, it could have destroyed society. It has been observed that in Africa, whenever the power of witchcraft becomes pervasive, a witchcraft-cleansing cult emerges to rid society of its menace. Members of such a cult must have been what DeLisser referred to as *myalmen* and *myalwomen*. This cult seems to have emerged soon after the 1760 rebellion in which witchcraft was let loose in an unprecedented way. Edward Long, a historian and a member of the planter class, whose book was published in 1774 wrote,

> Not long since [the war of 1760], some of these execrable wretches in Jamaica introduced what they called the Myal-dance, and established a kind of society, into which they invited all they could. The lure hung out was, that every Negro initiated into the Myal society, would be invulnerable by [sic] the white man.[11]

Here, Long missed the true meaning of the Myal society. In truth and in fact, what was happening here was nothing less than the emergence of the traditional religion of Africa. For the first time they began to practice their rites in public. The legitimate priests were now beginning

[10] Thomas Madiou, *Histoire d'Haiti*, Port-au-Prince, 1848, Vol. III, 33.
[11] Edward Long, *History of Jamaica*, Vol. 11, London, 1774, page 416.

to assert themselves and to organize what was later to become the Cumina cult.

The word "Cumina" is a combination of two Ashanti words: *Akom,* "to be possessed," and *ana,* "an ancestor."* Cumina, then, was an ancestral-remembrance cult and myalism came to be identified with the possession-inducing dance that formed part of it. J. H. Buchner, a Moravian missionary writing in 1854, left us a description of the Myal society which seems quite accurate:

> As soon as darkness of evening set in, they assembled in crowds in open pastures, most frequently under large cotton trees, which they worshipped, and counted holy; after sacrificing some fowls, the leader began an extempore song, in a wild strain, which was answered in chorus; the dance followed, grew wilder and wilder, until they were in a state of excitement bordering on madness. Some would perform incredible revolutions while in this state, until, nearly exhausted, they fell senseless to the ground, when every word they uttered was received as a divine revelation. At other times, Obeah was discovered, or a "shadow" was caught; a little coffin being prepared in which it was to be enclosed and buried.[12]

It is necessary to highlight a few of the points quoted above: The pastoral setting under a cotton tree is just the kind of setting popular among the slaves at this period, and the cotton tree is holy to the Africans. This holds to some extent today although the tree has lost its "sacred" quality for modern Jamaicans and this has been replaced by the common fear of ghosts harbored in the trees. Animals are still sacrificed in the Cumina cult in Jamaica and in Vodun in Haiti. The extemporaneous song, with choral response that is found in the Caribbean, is a reflection of the typical statement-response singing of Africa which has come down to us in the Negro spirituals. Also the dance which was known as myal, or spirit possession, is beautifully described by Buchner. The revelatory quality words of those under possession is still felt in Jamaican folk religion. Myalism, the frenzied dance of Cumina, broke out periodically. It appeared at Emancipation in 1834 and again in 1860 during what is known as the Great Revival, when it disrupted the missionary efforts and established what is now known as Pukkumina, a syncretic form of Cumina and Christianity.

The Africanization of the Caribbean was accomplished as the result of many factors. *First,* the numerical strength of the slaves over the masters made communication between the slaves easier. A strong slave

---

* "Cumina" would be more accurately spelled "kumina."

12 J. H. Buchner, *The Moravians in Jamaica,* London, 1885, pp. 139–40.

community was developed around their religious leaders and their religious festivals. The vast numbers of the slaves gave them a feeling of majority, over against the white minority who secluded themselves from the slaves. This lack of interaction between slaves and masters inhibited the acculturation process in the Caribbean. A *second* factor crucial to Africanization was the attitude of the Christian Church to the slaves. The Church in the British slave colonies denied the Africans religious instructions for well over two hundred years. Not only did they deny them Christian teachings, they also sought, through every legal means, to rid the Africans of their traditional religion. Their laws against dancing, drumming, and slave gatherings are enshrined in the slave records. In the Latin slave system, some attempts were made to Christianize the Africans; at least they received technical baptism and were to be present for the sacraments but this was done without enthusiasm and, at the expense of the planters, because the priests demanded payment for their services. An example of the kind of Christianity for form's sake that the slaves received in the Latin system is recorded for us in Ralph Korngold's book *Citizen Toussaint*:

> A hundred or so Negroes freshly arrived from Africa would be herded into a church. Whips cracked and they were ordered to kneel. A priest and his acolytes appeared before the altar and Mass was said. Then the Priest, followed by the acolytes and carrying a basin of holy water walked slowly down the aisle and with vigorous swings of the Aspergillam scattered the water over the heads of the crowd, chanting in Latin. The whips cracked again, the slaves rose from their knees and emerged into the sunlight, converts to Christianity.[13]

This was the extent of the Africans' introduction to the religion of "civilization." In this way Vodun and Christianity were united, with Christianity remaining no more than a gloss over the essentially African slave culture. It has often been said that Vodun is an African religion with a veneer of Catholicism and there can be no denial of this because even those elements of Catholicism which the slaves did absorb were completely Africanized.

African Religion in the Caribbean.

   A. Cumina-Pukkumina in Jamaica. No record of this word Cumina was discovered in Jamaican literature until 1938, when Zora Hurston's book, *Voodoo Gods*, appeared. Hurston was told by informants that the

[13] Ralph Korngold, *Citizen Toussaint*, New York, Little, Brown, 1943, p. 33.

word Cumina meant "the power" and that it was associated with the dead.[14] In the 1950s, Donald Hogg and Joseph G. Moore discovered that the cult was still alive in the eastern part of Jamaica. We may safely assume that Cumina as a family ritual was the first African religious expression among the large body of Akan peoples in Jamaica. As such the meetings were most likely held among the Maroons who inhabited the hills of Jamaica. Later they were taken up by the plantation slaves in the vicinity of Maroon settlements. Soon after the 1760 Rebellion, what we know today as Cumina emerged as a Myal society taking its name from the possession dance which accompanied it. According to Moore, membership in Cumina was inherited, but in some circumstances the rule was altered and people of other tribes could become members, provided they were acceptable to the ancestral community. Membership was determined matrilineally; the spirits who possess the members are the spirits of their mothers' clan. The matrilineal association is further proof of the Akan origin of the cult. Cumina ceremonies generally take place at night and are performed for various purposes: memoralizing the dead, placating the ancestors in the name of someone seriously ill, and celebrating the birth of a child. A Cumina festival may take place during the Christian holidays, especially at Christmas, and it is the opinion of this writer that the popular festival called *Jonkunu* (and various other spellings) originated from a Cumina adaptation of the Yam Festival common to most West African peoples.[15]

The drum is very important in Cumina. Two drums are necessary but as many as six drums can be used along with the African trumpet, the triangle and other instruments for beating out rhythm. Cumina festivals are accompanied by the sacrifice of fowls or goats. The blood is mixed with rum which is a necessity in Cumina, and the meat is cooked and eaten during the festival. The dance leading to possession is the peak of the festival. The woman, "queen," leads the dance and is generally someone who is known to be experienced in spirit possession. Anyone is likely to be possessed, but possession is more frequent in the family who summoned the festival.

We may conclude then that Cumina is the matrix in which many Africanisms were nurtured in Jamaica. In the beginning it was a secret

[14] Zora Hurston, *Voodoo Gods*, Philadelphia, Lippincott, 1938, pp. 56–60.
[15] For a good study of Jonkunu see Sylvia Winters' "Johnson in Jamaica," *Jamaica Journal: Quarterly of the Institute of Jamaica*, Vol. 4, No. 2, June 1970. See also Orlando Patterson, op. cit., pp. 245–46. Evidences of this festival seem to have been widespread in the English colonies of the United States on the eastern coast of the Carolinas.

society that supplied the impetus and framework for the psychic struggle against slavery. About the middle of the eighteenth century it emerged as the Myal society; it grew until the middle of the nineteenth century, when it merged with Afro-Christian cultism and became known as Pukkumina.

B. *Pukkumina.* Pukkumina, the present form of African traditional religion in Jamaica, emerged in 1860 during the Great Revival.[16] In that year a great wave of evangelical emotion swept the island of Jamaica. To the missionaries, this was the work of God made manifest, the result of their efforts, and for a while the churches began to prosper under a great influx of new converts. But the Christians soon realized that the new converts did not follow their "rules" of spiritual behavior. The result was that, what was once construed as Christian movement soon showed its true nature; within a short time the Christian churches were left empty and the Pukkumina cult was born.

This Africanizing process is not surprising when one considers the nature of missionary religion at this period. First of all the churches were under the leadership of European missionaries who had no real sensitivity to the experience of the slaves. One of the ministers who was a contemporary of the famous Revival called the religious enthusiasm of the new converts "wild extravagance and almost blasphemous fanaticism"[17]; and another (obviously considering an isolated incident) was quite pleased that after the first wave of "intense excitement" the evening service was conducted "with perfect quietness and decorum."[18] What the missionaries wanted was nothing short of de-Africanizing the Blacks, making them into carbon copies of themselves. All of the emotional expressions that are part and parcel of the African soul were to be held down. At first, the Africans saw the church as their only hope and, true, some of the churchmen did fight for Emancipation. But their introduction to missionary Christianity appeared to them to be another form of slavery: slavery of the mind and the soul.

Pukkumina centered around native charismatic leaders and most of

[16] For a discussion of Pukkumina in Jamaica, see George Eaton Simpson, "Jamaica Revivalist Cults," Jamaica, *Social and Economic Studies,* Vol. 85, No. 4, 1956, pp. 321–442. Also Donald Hogg, "Jamaican Religion: A Study in Variation," *Unpublished Ph.D. dissertation,* Yale University, 1954. The most authentic analysis of the Cult is done by the former Minister of Finance for Jamaica, Edward Seaga, entitled "Cults in Jamaica," *Jamaica Journal: Quarterly of the Institute of Jamaica,* Vol. 3, No. 2, June 1969.

[17] William James Gardner, *History of Jamaica from its Discovery by Christopher Columbus to the Present Time,* London, 1873, p. 464.

[18] Gardner, *loc cit.*

them had some knowledge of the Christian Bible although they were more influenced by myalism. With their knowledge of the Bible, their charismatic fervor, and their African heritage, they attracted members recently converted and organized their own religious cult. In a short while numerous groups known as "bands," or "societies," were formed all over the island. The head of a band was called "papa," or "mother" or "mami" if a woman. They were also called shepherds and shepherdesses. The band was organized hierarchically; at the head was the charismatic leader, who was all powerful. Below him were subshepherds and subshepherdessess with varying functions. It is not uncommon today to find such names as "wheeling shepherd," who leads the dance, "warrior shepherd," whose work it is to see that order is kept in the meetings, "spying shepherd," whose work is to see the different kinds of spirits functioning in the meeting and to dispatch unwelcome spirits, and so on.

Central to a Pukkumina cult is the drum accompanied dance. Unlike Cumina drums, which are played by drummers sitting astride them on the ground, the Pukkumina drums are played slung on the arm of a standing drummer. The dance generally takes place in the clearing of the cult compound called a "yard." Members form a circle around a flagpole which designates the center of power called the Holy Seal. The movement around the pole is counterclockwise and performed with the aid of the drums; the movement gradually gains momentum until possession takes place. Those possessed may prophesy, or speak in a spiritual language or form of glossolallia.

One of the major functions of Pukkumina is curing and to this end there is generally a balmyard attached to the compound. Here herbal remedies are dispensed for various kinds of *psychosomatic* illnesses. The major function of balming consists in bathing the patient in a herbal concoction, the recipe for which is claimed to have been revealed to the healer by the Spirits. Some medicine is given to the patient in liquid form or raw herbs to be boiled and taken internally. The usefulness of these healers in the health service of Jamaica can be assessed only when it is realized that a trained physician is inaccessible in many parts of the island.

The Pukkumina cult claims almost 15 per cent of the Jamaican population and is comparable only to Vodun in Haiti where 97 per cent of the people claim to be believers.

C. *Haitian Vodun.* A serious study of Vodun will prove that it is the religion of the greatest relevance to the mass of Haitian people. Alfred Metraux calls Vodun a conglomeration of beliefs and rites of

African origin, which having been mixed with Catholic practices, functions for the Haitian peasants as a remedy for ills, satisfaction for needs, and hope for survival. Vodun has had a noble history in Haiti. It is now commonly believed that it was a Vodun priest who started the war of liberation which finally wrestled freedom from France. The three leaders of Haiti in the early days of the Black republic, Toussaint, Dessalines, and Christophe were well acquainted with the powers of Vodun and the recently deceased president, François Duvalier, was a student of Vodun history.

James G. Leyburn suggested four stages of development in the history of Vodun.[19] *First,* the period of gestation in the new environment which covers the years between 1730 and 1790. This was a period of a steady increase in the importation of slaves, and the largest number of these came from Dahomey. *Second,* Leyburn notes the period, between 1790 and 1800, when the numerous African tribes fused under the banner of Vodun and invoked the Gods of Africa in their quest for freedom. The *third* period, between 1800 and 1815, saw the suppression of Vodun by the Black rulers who greatly feared its power. Christophe, though, is said to have had some faith in it. The *last* period falls between 1815 and 1850 when, despite its suppression, Vodun quietly diffused itself among the people and settled into its present form.

The word Vodun is a word derived from Dahomey and refers to the lesser deities of the Dahomean pantheon. The word however is misleading because the Haitian religion is not ruled over by Dahomean spirits alone. Vodun in Haiti stands for the Gods and spirits of all the major peoples of Africa who make up the Haitian nation. At a Vodun service one will hear the voice of the priest calling to Atibon Legba, Damballa, and Agwe, who are gods of Dahomey, and in the same breath he will call for Shango or Ogun, gods of Nigeria, followed by the gods of the Congo. Vodun then is a divine confederacy honed on African pragmatism. It is another example of the flexibility that enabled the Africans to survive.

There are two main Vodun pantheons: *Rada* and *Petro*. The Rada divinities consist of Legba, Damballa, Aizan, Agwe, and Erzulie and include the Nigerian Shango and Ogun, to name only a few. The Petro divinities are Bosu Trois Cornes, Simbi d'leau, Guede, Mait Gran Bois, and Mait Calfour and a host of others. The folklore of the Haitians says that the Rada gods are benevolent, while the Petro ones are malevolent. It was the Petro variety of Vodun that inspired the revolution, and this

[19] James G. Leyburn, *The Haitian People,* New Haven and London, Yale University Press, 1966, pp. 131–65.

is how they acquired their malevolent nature. It is clear, therefore, that this type of malevolence must not be interpreted as evil, but rather as warlike.

The most important Gods of Vodun are Legba, Guede, and Damballa. Legba is the first to be invoked in a ceremony. Like his counterpart in the Dahomean pantheon he is the go-between carrying man's messages to the gods and vice versa. He is the guardian of gates and barriers, the protector of doors and crossroads. No gods will enter nor possess a devotee unless Legba is invoked. Damballa Weda is the God or supreme *mystère* whose symbol is the serpent. Thus, the sign of the serpent is the coat of arms for the Vodun. So strong is his influence in Haiti that the sign of the serpent can even be seen in the architecture of the land. The graceful Yanvalo dance, which depicts the flowing movement of the serpent Damballa, is performed in the Vodun service. In fact, Haiti could easily be called the land of Damballa. The word is the combination of the names of two African provinces, *Adangwe* and *Allada*.

In Haitian Vodun all the gods are called *Loas*, or "powers." It is said that there are over three hundred of them, most of whom have abstract stylistic representations called *vevers*. The vevers are intricate drawings executed on the floor of the Vodun Temple just before the entrance into the service of the specific loa in whose honor the service is being held.

At the center of Vodun is a priest called the *houngan*, who is both feared and respected. His female counterpart is called a *mambo* and has the same authority as the houngan. These leaders are people of knowledge. They are the carriers of the tradition of the people. They know the names, attributes, and special tastes of the gods and must be able to conduct the rites appropriate for the various ceremonies each desires. Only after long and tedious training are they given the *asson*, or rattle, which is the symbol of priesthood. A good Vodun leader is priest, healer, adviser, and teacher. He is respected not only by his followers but by the community at large.

Below the houngan is the *hunsi*, an assistant in the service. Below the hunsi is the *hungenikon*, or the leader of songs, who plays a very exacting role in the service. Next come the drummers, three of whom must be present for a Vodun ceremony. Last, but not least, the *vodunsis*, or the members, who may have formal or loose connections with the cult. The highest group of vodunsis are the canzos, those who have undergone initiation. All the different groups together form a "*société*" which conducts ceremonies in a *houmfort* or temple.

Having given only a bare outline of the Vodun religion, it might be helpful to conclude this section with an eyewitness report of the author's visit to a ceremony. In this way the reader may be able to better appreciate the complexity of the Haitian religion.

In the fall of 1971, while doing research in Haiti, the writer tried in vain to see an authentic Vodun ceremony. But each of the visits planned was of the tourist variety. Then unexpectedly, on the evening of November 21, he was invited by a leading Haitian scholar to see a ceremony which turned out to be the real thing. We arrived at the southern outskirts of the city of Port-au-Prince at 7 P.M. and were led to a houmfort behind a large middle-class dwelling. The houmfort was a substantial extension of the house itself, with a floor space estimated to be about forty feet wide and sixty feet long. At the end of the hall, facing north, was a gallery with rows of seats made of concrete slabs; access to this gallery was through a door close by. We entered the houmfort by the door facing East, which led to several rows of chairs provided for important guests. At the entrance of the eastern door was a small refreshment bar where one could buy beer and soda. Immediately behind the bar was a staircase leading up one flight to a room in which food (roasted mutton and rice) was served to visitors at a small price. In front of the room was a balcony on which stood a large woman about fifty-six years old—graceful and commanding. She was the mambo. From this balcony she directed the early part of the ceremony until her entrance was necessary. At the center of the houmfort was a large concrete column known as the *poteau-mitan* around which the figure of two life-size snakes were entertwined heads down and meeting at the middle of the column. The three drummers were already seated to the right side of the houmfort as we entered and, for a while, they adjusted their drums in the same way the players of an orchestra would tune their instruments before a concert. About thirty minutes after our entrance a large audience was gathered and an air of expectancy was all around us. At 7:30 P.M., a shrill whistle sounded and a man appeared at the northern entrance with a white cock in his hand. He moved in a crouching dance across the floor and disappeared with the rooster into one of the two rooms behind the audience. Immediately following his departure the singers marched in step to the drumbeats and took their places to the south of the houmfort. The hungenikon, or song leader, chanted a tune answered by the chorus and the ceremony was under way. As the singing took on volume and the chorus began to move to the rhythm of the drums, the rooster-man and the woman appeared with their ritual items and placed them at poteau-mitan. First the asson, the symbol of the mambo's power, was brought in, then a bottle of liquor, some candles of various colors, an enamel basin of water, a whip, and finally two candles which were placed in an open space under the poteau-mitan. The ritual items now in place, the assistant priest (the hunsi) took the whip in his right hand and the bottle of liquor in his left, faced the north entrance, and cracked the whip nine times. This was also done at the east entrance and then in front of the poteau-mitan. He next poured libations at the base of the three drums. Filling his mouth with the liquor, he sprayed it at the two entrances, then to the four cardinal points after which he was joined by the woman and they performed a ritual salutation crossing both hands in front of their faces in the form of a cross. First they saluted the drums and the poteau-mitan. During this time the singers chanted the well-known song:

Papa Legba ouvri barrie pour moin ago-e
Papa Legba ouvri chemin pour li ago-e, etc.

Translated:
Papa Legba, open the barrier for
me, pay heed,
Papa Lebga, open the road for him,
pay heed.

The preliminaries now ended, the chorus phased in the dancing. This chorus was largely composed of women, most of them below thirty-five years of age. However, some were as old as sixty-five or more, and their movements were as nimble as those of a teen-ager.

After a brief lull in the singing, during which the chorus continually greeted each other without breaking the momentum of the ceremony, the leader "pitched" into a new song with a faster tempo. All of us in the audience felt that a new dimension of the service had now begun. The woman who performed in the first part of the ceremony reappeared with farina flour in her left hand, saluted the poteau-mitan, as a Catholic priest would do before the altar, proceeded to within three feet of the drums and began to draw one of the intricate vevers on the floor. This ceremony was held in honor of *Guede*, the god of death and sexual potency, this being the season of All Souls, according to the Catholic calendar. A drawing of the vever in my notebook was later checked out against the Guede vever in Maya Deren's book and parts of it were identical; there were, however, several other sections to this elaborate drawing which would need further explanation. The drawing of the vever marked the halfway point of the ceremony. The vever suggested that Guede had now approved the service and his entrance was assured. From here on the spirit would take over under the leadership of the mambo.

Soon after the execution of the vever, the mambo appeared, escorted by the two assistants who led the earlier parts of the ceremony. The atmosphere of the ceremony again changed dramatically; there was a heightened tension all over the houmfort because it is only under the leadership of the mambo that the loa appeared. She took hold of the asson, saluted the drums, the poteau-mitan and then greeted other vodun priests and priestesses who were present. (It was later explained to the author this particular ceremony was a united one.) Each visiting leader was given the asson and each in turn performed a short ritual of salutation similar to that of the presiding mambo. At the end of each salutation by the visiting leaders, a peculiar handshake took place between the visitor and the mambo. The handshake started with the left hand, then the right—each with a sudden release and flipping of the fingers, as if each had experienced an electric shock from the other.

The drum tempo and the singing were now at fever pitch. The audience was sitting on the edge of their seats and those standing were on tiptoes. Something was about to happen. The first appearance of possession was in the mambo herself. Technically, this is not supposed to happen because it is she who controls the service. Possession came while she was performing a ritual around the poteau-mitan. Unexpectedly, she received a sudden bolt which left her limp and falling backward; but just when she was about to lose footing, her assistant sprang into action, caught her in his stride, swung her around while her legs were dragging on the ground almost lifeless. She was a corpulent woman, and a fall could have been serious. The drums changed rhythm and worked her back into consciousness. This experience lasted for about two minutes—but, she was no sooner back at her role when another shock spun her around, again the agile assistant saved her from the hard concrete floor. This time the shock lasted for a longer period and she only recovered after an extended dance to a special rhythm of the drums, all the time propped up in the arms of her assistant. After this dramatic episode, the mambo left, accompanied by her assistants and two of the vodunsis, all of whom were under possession.

After a short while, which appeared to have been an intermission, the audience was directed to rise. The four participants reappeared; the assistant came first, wheeling a machete above his head (the symbol of Ogun); the two vodunsis were each draped with a flag. On one of the flags was the word Guede. (The author was unable to identify the second.) The prevailing colors of the leading participants were red and black—the colors of Guede.

During this part of the ceremony, the gods came down. The drums played evocative polyrhythmic tunes in a dialogue with the spirits. Suddenly the mambo began looking around as if she expected heavenly visitors, and almost at once the participants began to wheel and fall in all directions, completely oblivious of the audience or the concrete below them. Some plunged forward headlong and were only saved from injury by the agility and strength of those who were not possessed. But despite this apparent commotion, there was not any sense of the chaotic: this was a serious matter. Guede, the god of death was present. The possessed regained consciousness after a few minutes and continued dancing or just moved around in a daze shaking hands. They seemed full of indescribable happiness.

Then drumbeats slackened the pace, and the two flags were given to the mambo who gave them to her assistant who draped them in the shape of a V, the two emblems at the ends of the flags meeting at a central point. He extended the points of the flags to the audience; many moved forward, knelt, and kissed the emblems. This was done not only by the visiting cult leaders but by the rank and file of the audience as well. Evidently this ritual was perceived to have healing qualities since many of the people kissing the emblems appeared to have attended the ceremony for reasons of health. The author could get no real explanation of this ritual from those who invited him. They either did not know or did not want to tell what they knew. After this ritual, a libation was poured on the ground, and those who had kissed the emblems of the flags bent over the spot, touching the libation with their left hand and with the same hand touched each other on the forehead. After this, the mambo and her assistants processed to the ritual dressing room. This part of the ceremony seemed to be the high point of the evening. It was accompanied with much pathos, tension, and drama. Afterward, the audience seemed more relaxed and more free.

After a ten-minute lull in the ceremony filled only by drumming, the assistant appeared once more at the door of the ritual room and announced, Guede! The crowd rose and the mambo appeared, this time dressed in black slacks, red blouse, a black hat and with a pistol in her pocket; her face was heavily smeared with white powder signifying death. The assistants all carried mock weapons of war and were dressed in eighteenth-century French military uniforms. One leader, a woman, conducted a drilling ceremony and led a charge against the mambo, who drew her pistol and fired at them; all fell to the ground. This, I was informed was a re-enactment of the Haitian revolution in which the vodun God of death, Guede, played an important part.

The mock battle completed, the meeting switched to a rather comical vein, which pleased the younger element of the audience. In this last part of the ceremony the other function of Guede took over. Guede is not only the god of death, but the god of the erotic; he is also the phallic deity. Such a sudden turn in the ceremony, from a highly mystical experience to one of exaggerated pelvic movements and sexual suggestiveness, could give the casual visitor a distorted picture of Vodun. Maya Deren referred to Guede as "Corpse and Phallus, King and Clown" and said of him: "As Lord of Eroticism, he embarrasses men with his lascivious sensual gestures; but as god of the grave, he terrifies them with the evidence of the absolutely insensate. . . ."[20] A great deal of this part of the ceremony was lost to the author. There was much dialogue between the mambo and the participants, with bursts of hilarious laughter from the audience, but all in Creole. The final portion of the ceremony ended with a short dance of rapid gyration. Afterward there was a feast. In all, the ceremony took seven hours.

A truly meaningful analysis of Vodun in Haiti would demand much more study. It would be necessary to see many different kinds of ceremonies under the leadership of many houngans who are devotees to many different loa. The ceremony discussed above was in honor of Guede and the theme was death and resurrection and in that we observed again the pragmaticism of the African mind. Guede is the god of death and must be feared, but he is also the god of sexuality and life and must be enjoyed. To the Haitians he serves as a terrifying reminder of the tomb which is the inevitable resting place of all men yet he is also the generator of life itself. In this service joy and sorrow mingled; the secular and sacred were united. The experience of possession by Guede acted as a taste of death, but immediately after life sprang forth. As in Africa, death is not to be primarily a time of sorrow, it is also a time to rejoice—dancing, singing, and feasting

[20] Maya Deren, *Divine Horsemen: The Voodoo Gods of Haiti,* New York, Chelsea House, 1970, p. 104.

were all parts of this one experience called Guede or death. When someone dies it is a time to recall the exploits of the ancestors and this was done in the service by re-enacting the Haitian revolution.

One would like to delve more deeply into the Vodun gods: Damballa seemed to have a central place even in this service where Guede was the god being specially honored. Ogun's influence also was evidenced by the machete and the pistol; he is the god of iron and firearms. Legba was the first to be invoked (as he always is), for without him, the other loa would not appear. We need to know more of the significance of alcoholic spirits in Vodun; they also have an important role in African religion. We need to analyze more carefully the symbolic meaning of colors, for example, of the red and black which dominated the ceremony discussed above. And most of all we need to better understand the importance of the drums and the various rhythms used for each section of Vodun ceremonies. A Vodun ceremony is so complex that the visitor on first seeing a service is unable to take in all the simultaneous operations. A Vodun ceremony is an experience of total involvement for audience and actors; all are engaged in a religious experience. In truth, there can be no spectators.

C. Shango in Trinidad. The present author has never been to Trinidad, consequently this section of the paper will be based on the research done by other scholars, especially the work of J. D. Elder,[21] a native of Trinidad, Melville J. Herskovits,[22] and George Eaton Simpson.[23] With the exception of the work of J. D. Elder, much of what has been done on Shango in Trinidad is vague and contradictory. Here, only the bare outline of the religion will be evoked to further our thesis about Caribbean religion in general.

Slavery in Trinidad appears to have been much less severe than slavery in other parts of the Caribbean. The number of slaves from the Spanish period to 1797, when Trinidad was acquired by the British, never exceeded twenty thousand. However, there seems to have been a sufficient number of Yoruba slaves to dominate the population enough to stamp their cultural mold on the other peoples. L. A. A. de Verteuil, writing of Trinidad in 1858, laid great stress on the important place of the "Yarrabas" in the slave society:

[21] J. D. Elder, "The Yoruba Ancestor Cult in Gasparillo," *Caribbean Quarterly*, Vol. 10, No. 3, Jamaica, September 1970, pp. 5–20.
[22] Melville J. and Francis Herskovits, *Trinidad Village*, New York, Alfred Knopf, 1947.
[23] George Eaton Simpson, *The Shango Cult in Trinidad*, Puerto Rico, The Institute of Caribbean Studies, 1965.

Newly imported Africans are, generally speaking, industrious, but avaricious, passionate, prejudiced, suspicious, and many of them still adhering to heathenish practices. The Yarribas or Yarrabas deserve particular notice. . . . They are laborious, usually working for day wages on estates, but preferring job labour. . . . In fact the whole Yarraba race of the colony may be said to form a sort of social league for mutual support and protection.[24]

So, in all of Trinidad, one tribe seems to have dominated the slave community with its cultural patterns and its religion; this pattern repeats itself throughout the Caribbean. We may note the specific emphasis on the *social league,* in the above quotation, which we believe to be none other than the *Egungun,* a secret society of the Yoruba.

Shango, in Yoruba conception the manifestation of the "Wrath of Olodumare," is the god most feared among the common people of Trinidad. Shango manifests himself in lightning and thunder and is still worshiped widely in Yorubaland, where he has an organized priesthood and a cult. Originally, he was king; more specifically, the fourth king of Oyo. Legends about him relate that he was either killed in battle or ascended to heaven. Whichever way, he has long become a god to the Yorubas.

Shango in Trinidad, like Santeria in Cuba and Vodun in Haiti, is the generic name for a confederation of African divinities worshiped collectively by the common people. Like Vodun, it is lightly infused with Catholicism: the gods of Africa have their counterpart in the Catholic Saints. In Cuba, this same combination of traditional African religion and Catholicism is called "Santeria" or the saints. Under the name Shango are found these gods: Shango and his wife, Oya; the trickster deity Esu, another name for the Dahomean Legba; Oshun and Erinle who are river deities; Shakpana, related to Yoruba Sopona, god of epidemics; and Obatala, one of the powerful god-kings of Nigeria. All these gods are called *orishas* by the Shango cultists, a word which simply means *powers.* Along with these unmistakenly Yoruba divinities are names of divinities of the Dahomean pantheon, Legba being the most obvious. Other divinities carry either the names of recent family ancestors or corrupted names of divinities from other areas of Africa.[25]

[24] L. A. A. de Verteuil, *Trinidad: Its Geography, Natural Resources, Present Condition and Prospects,* London, Ward, Lock & Co., 1958, p. 175.
[25] For an authentic study of Yoruba Religion, see E. Bolaji Idowu, *Olodumare: God in Yoruba Belief,* London, Longmans, Green & Co., 1966.

An especially interesting aspect of Shango is the form of witch-craft which the adherents practice. This is none other then the obeah of which we have already spoken. Again our observation is borne out that the African cults were very flexible and pragmatic. Thus we have Yoruba deities at the center of Shango, but the witchcraft of the Akan peoples who appear to have been in the minority yet whose witchcraft was perceived as strongest.

J. D. Elder observed that the major elements which welded to-gether the Africans in Trinidad were:

1. Identical ethnic origin and identity with Africa.
2. A common slave background in their history.
3. Common recognition of African *orishas,* deities, and "powers" of a pantheon interested in the welfare of the living.
4. An ethos in which "Africa" and its culture-heroes serve to inspire morality, a sense of identity in the world, and cultural pride.
5. Intermarriage among the *nations,* with powerful taboos about non-African exogamy.[26]

In Trinidad the word Nations is used to refer to all the collective fes-tivities of the African population. Thus we have the festival of the *Nations,* the drum of the *Nations,* all of which suggests that the people were conscious of the integration that took place in their development. The Shango cult, then, is a conscious, organized attempt of African peoples in exile to reformulate, in one whole, certain aspects remem-bered from their culture. In Trinidad as elsewhere in the Caribbean, the mazeway was reorganized in religious terms.

African Religious Retention in the Caribbean: A Comparative Sum-mary

Anyone who visits the Caribbean will not fail to observe what ap-pears to be two distinct societies existing side by side. At the top of the social scale are the European-oriented elites. This group mainly consists of the mulattoes, the descendants of masters and slaves, who have now come to occupy the positions of slave masters and have imitated their behavior in many ways. Along with the elite are the educated Blacks whose training and upbringing have elevated them in society; they have come to be known as the "Afro-Saxons." Many of these sons of Africa have traditionally rejected any connection with an African heritage.

[26] See Elder, op. cit., p. 15.

Below this small, but dominant, elite is the mass of peasant folk who have traditionally identified themselves with Africa and who are the backbone of the society. It is they who give flavor to every aspect of Caribbean life. They are the people whose pride in their African origin is accompanied with no apologies. Speaking of this largest group of people, Herskovits said:

> African elements are observable in language, folklore, family life and kinship, property, marketing, medicine, magic and religion, exchange-labour, economic organizations. . . . In music, dress, dancing, and domestic life, the African contribution is unmistakable.[27]

Let us analyze a few of these contributions.

A. Language. Throughout Caribbean languages spoken today there are literally thousands of African words that have been retained. The unofficial language of the Caribbean is Creole which is simply an African language structure in which a variety of European words have been introduced. Creole is an important linguistic emergence in the Caribbean, a product of the meeting of Europe and Africa. This new language creation, with its engaging rhythm and great capacity for creative expressions, is just now catching the interest of students of language. It is, however, in the area of religion that we find the most African language retentions. Many of the names of the African gods were transported to the Caribbean in their original form. The names for African religious specialists and for their professions have also survived the transplantation. Under possession, the Caribbean cultists speak an unknown tongue which they claim to be the language of Guinea. And finally, names are generally the day names of Africa, this custom is gradually dying out, but in the island of Jamaica it is still quite common to find people whose names are Cudjoe, Cuffie, Kwaku, Quasie, or Kwamie, all day names of the Akan peoples. The same holds true for the people of Haiti, where we meet personal day names in French.

B. Folklore. In the area of folk tradition, we are on solid ground in claiming that African folklore has dominated all the New World regions from North to South America. In support of this claim, we need only to refer to the animal stories of Br'er Rabbit, Anansi the Spider, the Tortoise, and the famous Uncle Remus stories. In the area of proverbs, Africa reigns supreme again. Examples from

[27] Melville J. Herskovits, *The New World Negro: Selected Papers in Afro-American Studies,* Indiana University Press, 1966.

Jamaica will be sufficient for our limited space. Thus from the Ashanti we have the following:

1. "It is the Supreme Being who pounds fufu for the one without arms" appeared in Jamaica as "When cow lose him tail, God Almighty brush fly."
   In both of these, the providence of God is evident.
2. "When a fowl drinks water, it first shows it to the Supreme Being" appeared in Jamaica as "When fowl drink water him say 'tank God'; when man drink water him say nutten."
   or
   "Chicken 'member God when him drink water."
3. "The Hen's foot does not kill her chicken" appeared in Jamaica as "Fowl tread upon him chicken, but him no tread too hard."
   or
   "Hen neber mash him checken too hot."
4. "When a great number of mice dig a hole, it does not become deep" appeared in Jamaica as "Too much rat nebber dig good hole."
5. "All animals sweat, but the hair on them causes us not to notice it" appeared in Jamaica as "Darg sweat, but long hair cober i'."
6. "When too many people look after a cow, hunger kills it" appeared in Jamaica as "Too much busha, darg Crawney."
7. "Wood already touched with fire is not hard to set alight" appeared in Jamaica as "Ole fire stick no hard fe light."[28]

This is a small sample and taken only from Jamaica. There are literally thousands of these proverbs yet to be collected. All Jamaicans underlay their conversation with them as their ancestors did in Africa. In Haiti and the other islands we find the same oral tradition. J. J. Audain collected and published 1,011 proverbs for Haiti which, we are told, forms only a sample of the enormous body of proverbs existent in that island. They are used by elders to instruct youth in prudence and morals, or to spice up an address in politics and religion.

C. *Marketing*. The African market system has received very little attention from Western scholars and this is because few Westerners know the African concept of marketing. The African market was not only a place for selling and buying produce, it was also a social organization *par excellence*. It was a microcosm of the entire society. The atmosphere of African markets was what we would describe as festive, part religious festival and part carnival. The African markets served as political forums, as communication centers, trysting places,

[28] John Joseph Williams, *Psychic Phenomena of Jamaica*, New York, Dial Press, 1934, pp. 44–47.

as places for meeting old friend, as arenas for the performance of religious rituals, and as a host of other things. It is interesting to note that this market organization was brought into the Caribbean with all its African flavor, and the markets remain African to this day. Anyone who has visited West African markets cannot fail to see that almost every aspect of this social organization is retained in the contemporary Caribbean market.

D. *Medicine.* The Africans found in their lands of exile an abundance of herbal medicines which were well known to them in Africa. It was therefore easy for the African specialist to continue his practice in the islands. His work has recently come to the attention of modern scientists who are now busy testing some of the age-old herbs for their own use. Not only are they experimenting on these herbs, but they are also studying the techniques of African healing. The technique is the key to their success but will prove the hardest to imitate in that it presupposes a special conception of the world. The magico-religious perception of the world is a prerequisite for the proper use of African medicine. For the African specialist, herbs in themselves do not cure; the incantation of power is needed. This is the key to the success of the medicine man. The power of the medicine must be aroused by incantation, therefore, healing in the African view of things is both herbal and ritual. The African healer is not only a doctor, he is a psychiatrist and a pastor. The Western-trained doctor is still at a disadvantage in the Caribbean because much of the illness he confronts is of the psychosomatic variety due to the extreme stress of marginal living conditions. The average peasant in the Caribbean thinks of the professional doctor as ill-prepared to deal with his condition because the doctor's social position makes him so far removed from the poor. The scarcity of trained doctors in the islands and the peoples' faith in the knowledge of the Afro-Caribbean medicine man make it easy to project a long and prosperous future for the African specialists.

E. *Music and Dancing.* The music of Africa was probably the major source by which the Africanization of the Caribbean was accomplished. The Africans cannot live without music. Music is the soul rhythm of the African people, therefore, it was not long after their arrival that we find the white masters in distress over these most disturbing sounds of Africa. The many laws against drumming, blowing of horns, and beating of boards and dancing suggest to us that the whole Caribbean had broken out into one mass African orchestra.

The drum was, and still is, the king of African musical instruments and every variety of this instrument can be found in the Caribbean. From the majestic *assoctor* drum of Haiti, the *tambour* of Vodun, the *dunno* of Shango, and the *akete* of Cumina, they have been calling the gods of Africa to possess their devotees, sending messages across the hills in times of rebellion, or merely pounding out African rhythms to the New World.

The dance is also an expression of the African force vitale. The Caribbean Black also dances in sorrow and in joy; African religion in the Caribbean began as a dance. So we hear of the Vodun dance or the Cumina dance which the masters saw as a simple amusement, having no idea that the dance was the channel through which the African immersed himself in the very force of being. In the dance he became one with the powers of divinity and the ancestors; in the dance he became immortal. Thus the dance became the instrument of rebellion and revolution.

The African dance forms soon replaced all other forms of the dance in the New World. The beat of Africa became the foundation of the shuffle, the fox trot, the mento, the calypso, the meringue, the rhumba, the blues, jazz, rock and roll, and present day "soul."[29] Thus we can see that out of the African traditional religion has come the rhythm that has influenced not only the New World but the fatherland of the slave masters as well. In this sense, the statement "Europe ruled but Africa reigned" is most fitting for the Caribbean.

Conclusion

We cannot conclude this short paper on African retentions in the Caribbean without noting that it is out of the Caribbean that the spirit of African renaissance emerged during the last decades of the nineteenth century. The present return to "things African" came out of the *Zeitgeist* or the African which was nurtured in the soul of such men as Dr. Jean Price-Mars, the father of *Indigenism* in Haiti.[30] It was Price-Mars who called the Haitian people back to an awareness of their folklore and their African past. He made them realize that their cultural roots were not in the French culture, which once

[29] For an interesting study of the influence of African dance form on the New World, see Janheinz Jahn, *Muntu: The New African Culture*, New York, Grove Press, 1961, pp. 61–95.

[30] The classic study of *Indigenismo* is found in Jean Price-Mars, *Ainsi Parla L'oncle . . . Essais d'ethnographie*, Port-au-Prince, 1928. This book is long out of print and has now become a collectors' item.

threatened their destruction, but in their African past, from which they drew their inspiration to fight against oppression. A similar movement known as "Negrismo"[31] came from Cuba. But the movement which caught the imagination of Africans the world over was *Negritude*.[32] It had its origin in Martinique and was fathered by the immortal poet Aimé Césaire. It was the spirit of Negritude that inspired such men as Léopold Sédar Senghor, the present President of the Republic of Senegal, to strip himself of the veneer of French culture and return to an African sense of himself. Negritude was an attempt to redeem the African past and to revive the dynamic and pragmatic philosophy of Africa which had been destroyed by the deadening influence of Europe. Out of this returning, a new African personality was born. Space will not allow us to write at length on the Jamaican prophet of Africanism, Marcus Garvey, the founder of the Back-to-Africa movement. Let it suffice to mention that, in the first decade of this century he organized the Universal Negro Improvement Association both in the Caribbean and in the United States and gathered a following of over two million people dedicated to the reclamation of Africa from colonialism. His motto, "One God, One Faith, One Destiny—Africa for the Africans at Home and Abroad!" is still the inspiration of black movements in our day. His influence is still being felt in such movements as the Black Muslims of America but even more so in the rapidly growing and influential Cult of *Ras Tafari* in Jamaica at the present time.

In no other area of the New World has the African been more dynamic or more influential in keeping the ethos of the motherland alive than in the Caribbean. Out of these small islands have come the culture bearers, freedom fighters, artists, and apostles of Africa in America.

[31] The most important writer on African culture in Cuba was Orlando Ortiz.
[32] The literature is too large to list them here.

SMITH, AUGIER, AND NETTLEFORD

The Rastafarians believe that Ras Tafari is the living God and that salvation can come to black men only through repatriation to Africa. In addition the Rastafarians claim that Ethiopia is the black man's home and that the ways of the white man are evil.

The authors say that the Rastafari brothers are a very heterogeneous group. Centered in Jamaica, they differ widely in their opinions about most things. "Some wear beards, others do not; . . . only a small minority wear the locks . . . some smoke ganja; others abhor it. All brethren agree that Emperor Haile Selassie is the Living God, the Returned Messiah, and the Representative of God the Father." All believe that the black race descended from King Solomon and the Queen of Sheba; hence the black people are the true Israelites.

The authors discuss a variety of differences in doctrinal beliefs within the cult, claiming that one of the most disputed issues is the treatment of the hair (i.e., whether or not to wear beards and locks). They also present diverse Rastafarian views regarding the smoking of the narcotic ganja, the use of violence, and the necessity or the non-necessity of working.

Opportunities in Jamaican society are distributed according to skin color. Whites get the best, coloreds (or browns) are next, and the blacks are most discriminated against in employment, etc. The Rastafarians are, for the most part, black and unemployed. "If the supply of jobs in Kingston were to catch up with the demand for jobs . . . the movement (Rastafarian) would cease to have mass significance." But ". . . a hard core of religious belief . . ." would remain.

This study offers some valuable insights into the continuing problems generated by skin color in the West Indies at a time when in-group color consciousness has lost significant ground to black ethnicity in the United States.

M. G. Smith, Roy Augier, and Rex Nettleford are members of the faculty at the University College of the West Indies in Kingston, Jamaica.

THE RAS TAFARI MOVEMENT

Source: Smith, Augier, and Nettleford, eds., *Report on the Ras Tafari Movement,* Institute of Social and Economic Research, pp. 17–29.

Rastafarians hold in common only two beliefs: that Ras Tafari is the living God, and that salvation can come to black men only through repatriation to Africa. On all other matters the opinions of the brethren vary as widely as the opinions of the rest of the population. Some wear beards, others do not; and only a small minority wear the locks. Some are men of the highest moral fiber, while at the other extreme are men of crime and violence. Some smoke ganja; others abhor it. Some are excellent workmen, while others avoid work. In all matters except two, the divinity of Ras Tafari and the necessity of repatriation, Ras Tafarians are a random group.

They are also very disorganized, and lacking in leadership. Probably the great majority are not attached to any of the many organizations which give themselves names and lists of officers. There is no leader or group of leaders who can speak for the movement as a whole or define its doctrines.

The following description of attitudes to various matters must therefore essentially take the form of "some say this, others say that." This in itself may help to clarify public misconceptions.

The Divinity of Ras Tafari

All brethren agree that the Emperor Haile Selassie is the Living God, the Returned Messiah and the Representative of God the Father. The name "Selassie" means "Power of the Trinity"; Ras was the Emperor's title before his coronation in 1930; Tafari is a personal name of the Emperor Haile Selassie before his coronation. Many brethren nowadays refer to the Emperor only as Haile Selassie, arguing that after his elevation to the throne, the use of his former title would be incorrect. Proverbs 22, Isaiah 43 and John 16 ("For I am in the Father and the Father is in Me") shows that Ras Tafari is the Living God, Old Alpha, the Lion of Judah—invincible and visible, the Redeemer of Israel, who are the black race. A full-length photograph in the *Illustrated London News* of Saturday January 11, 1936 shows the Emperor standing with his right foot on an unexploded Italian bomb. This illustrated his invincibility. Photographs of the Emperor defending Ethiopia against the Italians, and such publications as *"The March of Black Men—Ethiopia Leads,"* support his role as the champion of the black race.

Beyond this point, the religious beliefs of Ras Tafarian brethren diverge widely. Here is an account of one extreme.

(The account which follows is that which is taught by some deeply religious men, who derive from the Bible well-defined views on the role of the Black Man in the divine purpose.)

The Creed of a Ras Tafari Man

The black race are the true Israelites, the House of David, and the Emperor, the Lion of Judah, descended from King Solomon and the Queen of Sheba, is their true head. Those Jews whom Hitler and the Nazis exterminated were merely false Jews of whom the Scripture has said, "Woe unto them that call themselves Israel and they are not." God is black (Jeremiah 8), Haile Selassie is black, Solomon and Sheba were black, and so are the true Israelites. The white men have worshiped a dead God and have taught black men to do likewise. The white man's God is really Pope John XXIII, Pope Pius's successor, the head of the Ku Klux Klan. The Emperor, who as God controls the world and its future, is head of the Nya-Binghi who are champions of the good in the fight against Babylon (Rev. 19) and its defenders, the Ku Klux Klan, who are evil.

The Bible contains the Word of God, but Scripture shows that half of this has not been written save in your hearts. King James I of Britain, a white man, translated the Bible, distorting and confusing its message; but to those who, by virtue of Ras Tafari's divine power, have been given inspiration and prophetic insight, the false passages put in by the white man for his own purposes are easily detected, and accordingly Ras Tafari brethren treat the Bible carefully, using only that part which they regard as the true Word of God. (Psalms 18, 21, 29, 48, 87, 137; Genesis 18; Numbers 6; Leviticus 11, 21; Deuteronomy 16; Isaiah 11, 43; Jeremiah 23, 8; Malachi 1; Hebrews 11; I Corinthians 4; I Timothy 6; I John 4; 2 Thessalonians 3; Ezekiel 5, 13, 23; Revelations 13, 15, 17, 18, 19, 22.) These passages, together with the Ten Commandments, define the principal, behavior, prohibitions and observances of the brethren. But before itemizing these we should define the racial polarities intrinsic to this doctrine.

The black race, having sinned, was punished by God their Father. Punishment was meted out in the form of slavery, conquest, and control by the white man. The four pirates, John Hawkins, Cecil Rhodes, Livingstone and Grant, brought the Africans to the Western world as slaves under Elizabeth I, who has been reincarnated as Elizabeth II. Her former beloved, Philip of Spain, has also been reincarnated as her present husband, Philip, Duke of Edinburgh. The golden scepter which belonged to the House of Judah in Ethiopia and which carried with it the dominion of the world was stolen from Ethiopia by Rome—which then had world empire—and from Rome by Britain which inherited the Roman power. On the coronation of Haile Selassie I in November 1930, King George V of Britain sent his son, the Duke of Gloucester, with this scepter as a gift to the Emperor. The Duke of Gloucester, who is said to have succeeded George V as Edward VIII, while in Ethiopia wandered off into the bush, eating grass, thereby revealing himself as the reincarnated Nebuchadnezzar, King of Babylon. The Emperor Haile Selassie, receiving the scepter, simultaneously recovered the symbol of Ethiopian world power. In return, he is said to have given the Duke of Gloucester a small emblem for King George V. When the Duke returned to Britain and handed this to his father, the latter is said to have been stricken with paralysis and to have died shortly after, although it was some months before this fact was announced to the British public. The Duke of Gloucester then became King and, to fulfill prophecies, abdicated, knowing that he shall resume the throne after the reincarnated Elizabeth I, to rule as the last King of Babylon and to witness its utter defeat. This is clearly apocalyptic, the Messiah being the Emperor and the instrument chosen for the destruction of Babylon being the Bear with three ribs (Rev. 13), that is Russia, which "will come to stamp up the residue thereof so that Babylon shall be a desolation among the nations."

Babylon really covers the Western world. Extreme racialists include Russia but many do not. In its local form, Babylon is explicitly represented by the Government, the Police and the Church. Ministers are Antichrists and preach Antichrist. They are the agents for the mental enslavement of the black man. Their most vicious representatives are black priests, the oppressive allies of the white man. Both the white and black oppressors shall suffer the same fate. The original God of the white man was Adam-Abraham, the leper, Anglo-Saxon bloodsucker and slave master. Pope John has inherited his role. All white men are evil, all colored men are evil, some extreme racialists say all yellow men are evil; some black men are positively evil—these are the allies of the white oppressors. Others live in sin, not knowing that Ras Tafari is the Living God. These mental slaves nonetheless are Ethiopians who will be redeemed by the work of the Church Triumphant, which is the Ras Tafari brethren, and will be brought back to their own vine and fig tree in Ethiopia. Recent events in the Belgian Congo prove the truth of Garvey's prophecy that 1960 is the year of redemption, and herald the future of the white man. The massacre of black men by the white South Africans at Sharpeville in April this year is merely the latest well-known example of how the white treat the black. This shall be repaid in kind. The worst people in Jamaica are the priests, the police and the false prophets who form the Government. Sir Alexander Bustamante and Mr. Norman Manley have shown themselves to be agents of the imperialists, merely concerned to facilitate foreign capital.

Zion is "on the side of the North, the City of the Great King" (Psalm 48). It is known to the uninstructed as Addis Ababa. Ethiopia is the prepared place for Israel, the heaven of the black man, just as Europe is the heaven of the white man and China is heaven for the yellow man. Long ago the entire continent of Africa was known as Ethiopia; the white man called it Africa and carved his empires within it. Now these empires have crumbled. Africa is almost free. South, East and Central Africa are the last white strongholds but these shall surely fall quite soon. The complete collapse of white dominion in Africa is the direct effect of Haile Selassie's will and word. This proves he is the Messiah, presently redeeming his people. "Africa for the Africans at home and abroad"—"One God, one Aim, one Destiny"; this proves that Marcus Garvey was a major prophet whose words are presently being fulfilled. It also assures the brethren that most black Jamaicans will soon accept their doctrine.

Jamaica was a nice island, but the land has been polluted by centuries of crime. For 304 years, beginning in 1655, the white man and his brown ally have held the black man in slavery. During this period, countless horrible crimes have been committed daily. Jamaica is literally Hell for the black man, just as Ethiopia is literally Heaven. Long ago pirates spoke of it as Mount Africa, the slave mart. This it still is. Although physical slavery was abolished in 1838 and Queen Victoria gave £20,000,000 to the island of which £14.25 million were earmarked for the repatriation of the black slaves to Africa, none of them, or their descendants, have ever been sent back. Instead, the Jamaican Government is forcing people to go to Britain, where their slavery will continue.

Black men are Ethiopians. Many do not know this. The brethren do and claim an Ethiopian nationality, as the United Nations charter in its very first paragraph and in Clause 15 entitles them to do. "Everyone is entitled to all the rights and freedoms set forth in this Declaration, without distinction of any kind. . . . No distinction shall be made for the political, jurisdictional or international status of the country to which the individual belongs, whether it be independent, trustee, non self-governing or under any other limitations of sovereignty." (United Nations Charter.) Brethren interpret this to mean that they individually can claim and are fully entitled to Ethiopian nationality. It is obvious that such claims require ratification by the Ethiopian Government on an individual basis, but there are many statements, such as that in the preamble to the Ethiopian World Federation Inc., which states that "Ethiopia is the divine heritage of the black people of the world," that can be cited as evidence of the Emperor's grant of national status. The important point is that this claim for Ethiopian nationality expresses a positive rejection of Jamaican citizenship and national status. Insistence on this Ethiopian claim is the measure of alienation from Jamaica. Only when the issue is pressed can we fully appreciate the intensity and depth of this alienation; and only when we examine the historical and contemporary context of this movement and its devotees can we understand the causes and conditions of this alienation.

It follows that the Ras Tafari brethren do not regard the Jamaican Government as their government. The true believers, or extremists, refuse to vote. To them, the two-party system of which Jamaica is so proud is utterly discredited, and there is some fervent admiration for a one-party state such as Egypt, Czechoslovakia, Russia or China. The Jamaican Government is regarded as the lackey of the British Government, since Jamaica, despite all its recent constitutional changes, remains a colony, is defended by British soldiers, and inspected by the Colonial Secretary, Mr. Ian Macleod. The only true Government is the theocratic government of Emperor Haile Selassie I, the King of Kings and Lord of Lords. The Communist system is far preferable to the present capitalist system of the white and brown Babylonians. Dr. Fidel Castro is showing what can be done in Cuba, but for sixteen years Jamaicans have used their control of government merely to perpetuate and intensify slavery.

The only thing which will satisfy the true brethren is repatriation to Ethiopia. The Emperor has provided land for the black peoples of the West, especially for his worshipers. The Jamaican Government has refused to let the people go, since it wants to keep them in slavery. But as Marcus Garvey said, 1960 (or the '6os) is the time for redemption. If nothing is done, "Watutsi war dance going play here," even though the true believers will never use violence, since their doctrines and laws emphasize redemption by Peace and Love and their ruler is the Prince of Peace.

From these basic doctrines and orientations all the specific symbols and practices follow. The Ethiopian flag of green, yellow, red is the flag of the Ras Tafari movement. Green represents the pastures of Africa, yellow represents the wealth of that land, red the Church Triumphant. Some flags, such as the Ghana flag, may also have a black star; this is not usual, but where found, the black stands for black supremacy as well as for Marcus Garvey's Back-to-Africa movement. The Emperor's photograph is always present; brethren often carry it around with them, together with pompoms or scarves of green, yellow and red which identify them. Beards and long hair are enjoined on men (Numbers 6, Leviticus 21); it is sin to shave or cut the hair. It is sin to touch the dead since Jesus said "Let the dead bury their dead." It is sin for black women to straighten their hair or for women to use cosmetics. Corinthians 1: IV says that women must always have their heads covered. Marriage in a church is regarded as sinful, not merely because the Church is a Babylonian device, but because it is written, "Whom God hath joined together let no man put asunder" and it seems well understood that couples often separate. Concubinage is prescribed in the monogamous form, the "wife" being called a Queen and being treated with great respect. Alcohol is forbidden, together with gambling. Wine may be drunk in small quantities. It is forbidden to co-operate with any Government except that of Ethiopia. Current Jamaican beliefs in obeah, magic or witchcraft are nonsense—these have no empirical validity. Revivalism, whether pocomania or Zion, is a deliberate propagation of Babylonian error through which the mental slavery of the black man is maintained. Pork is forbidden (Leviticus II). The "herb" (ganja) is a gift of God, who enjoined us to smoke it in Genesis 8, Psalm 18 and Rev. 22. God Himself smokes it and we should do likewise to keep His Laws. In the same way, God does not shave his locks or beard and we must do likewise, since He made us in His image and it is sin to deface this by shaving, as do the Babylonians. Education for children is dangerous, since the Babylonian schools enchain them mentally with false doctrines. Some extremists accordingly send their children to private schools run by teachers who are either adherents of this doctrine or sympathetic to it. For this they pay, knowing that their child will not be mocked or shamed because of long locks, beliefs or appearance. Sodomy is advocated by the priests of Babylon, notably the Archbishop of Canterbury, Dr. Fisher (cf. Anglican comments on Wolfenden Report). These are the ways of the white man and his God. The black man knows better.

Worldly possessions are not wanted in Jamaica. The only thing the extremist wants is immediate repatriation. Work is good, but not in the form of slavery, which in Jamaica is now represented by wage employment for unjust masters. What is the use of working when within two or three months we shall again be unemployed for another indefinite period? Property, such as land, if acquired here tends to tie the believer to the Babylonian slavery. To prepare for repatriation, reject wealth, property and everything Jamaica can offer. In fact it does not offer very much to black people. The true brethren share what they have with others in their group. They do not beg, they do not steal, they depend on God's grace for livelihood, knowing that He will look after His own, and that the ganja which they smoke guards them against physical illnesses, curing all complaints and giving them wisdom, love and understanding. It is because the white and brown men know that ganja has these properties that they have forbidden its use by the Blacks and persecute the latter on this account through the police. Since the Jamaican police are mainly black Ethiopians working for Babylon, their persecution of the brethren constitutes a 'tribal war' instigated by the white and brown oppressors. Police are said to use and sell ganja for their own profit. So do the white and brown elite. The herb has been sanctified by Scripture and is freely used in Ethiopia, as magazine photographs and articles show.

Doctrinal Differences

Many people who regard themselves and are regarded as Ras Tafari devotees do not share all of the views summarized above, and may oppose some of them very strongly. We have seen that even the Emperor's title is disputed. Some brethren regard him as God's Representative; the great majority regard him as God. Some brethren distinguish sharply between Ethiopia and Africa; some define black supremacy as a withdrawal of the black men from the countries ruled by white men. Many brethren hold that ganja is evil and befuddles the brain; one or two are puzzled by the failure of Government to enforce its own anti-ganja legislation. Many brethren value education for themselves and their children; some have demanded adult-education facilities, including technical training; others, whose children have recently won scholarships to secondary schools, make genuine sacrifices to try to keep them there. Love and Unity, Peace, Equality and Justice, no exploitation—these are the essential common laws. The beard which is the precept or the wedding garment is the fulfilment of the vows made to God. The Sabbath, commencing on Friday at 7 P.M. and ending on Saturday at the same time, is common to all; so is the taboo on pork. (Deuteronomy 16.) The basic doctrines common to all brethren, whatsoever the degree to which they have been individually alienated from Jamaican society, can now be set out.

1. Ras Tafari is the Living God.
2. Ethiopia is the black man's home.
3. Repatriation is the way of redemption for black men. It has been foretold, and will occur shortly.
4. The ways of the white man are evil, especially for the black.

The brethren do not speak of people joining their cult. In their view, the doctrine is in them at birth but unfolds and comes into consciousness when they recognize the Emperor as God and themselves become fully conscious. When this happens, the convert makes a private vow or pledge to his God, usually to a photograph of the Emperor, that he will abide by the laws of God and the rules of the doctrine. Many are called but few are chosen, and for this reason many brethren do not fulfill all the laws, such as those regarding their hair. On this basis some differentiation is made between the "true," "partial" and "false" brethren, and this is sometimes expressed as the elect and the non-elect, or the priests and the members; but whenever these distinctions are declared, groups reject their applicability to themselves. All are one and one are all.

An important and extremely complex set of ideas cluster around re-incarnation. Some brethren affirm that they personally and physically experienced the whips of the slave drivers. These hold the doctrine of reincarnation illustrated already by reference to Elizabeth I and II of England and the two Philips, of Spain and Greece. Despite these illustrations, there is no general rule that an individual should have the same name on reincarnation. One Brother held that men are reincarnated through the male line, females through the female line; for this reason, it is not possible for the brethren in Jamaica to be repatriated by reincarnation. Another man held that this doctrine of reincarnation was false on mathematical grounds, since there are not enough dead souls to meet the requirements of an expanding population. A third view is rather more sophisticated: reincarnation is the reaffirmation of one's lost culture and traditions. In this view, the Africans brought to Jamaica had "our culture beaten out of us, our language, and all that our forefathers did. We reincarnate in this culture through Almighty God Ras Tafari."

All brethren who regard Ras Tafari as God regard Man as God. Man are those who know the Living God, the brethren. Men are the sinners who do not, and some of these sinners are the oppressors. "Thirty Locks men" is wrong speech; correctly stated it is "Thirty Locks man," for man is one, in God and with God. For this reason there are no leaders, only brethren and members. For this reason there is no belief, only knowledge, prophecy and inspiration.

Men die, being sinners. Man (the believers) do not die. For this reason the dead should be left to bury their own dead, since death only applies to sinners. God being Man and eternal, Man lives eternally, in the flesh as well as the spirit. Heaven, which is in Ethiopia, is waiting to receive the brethren. Duppies, ghosts and the like are nonsense. Prophecy has various forms, and sometimes dreams are messages.

Black Nationalism

All Ras Tafari brethren agree that the black man is exploited in the Western world and must get back to Africa. For some this is a secular doctrine, derived from the history of the Negro during slavery and since. For others it is a religious doctrine, enshrining the proposition that the black man is the chosen race of God.

The secular view is rooted both in history and in the contemporary social structure of Jamaica. Everybody recognizes that Negroes were exploited during slavery. Ras Tafarian brethren assert that Negroes are still exploited.

When challenged, they point to the contemporary situation, where economic and racial lines run close together. Eighty per cent of Jamaica's population is black, about 2 per cent is white, and most of the rest is colored. By and large, the economic system is a pyramid with whites at the top, coloreds in the middle, and Blacks at the bottom. Nobody can pretend that in Jamaica today the average black child, brown child, and white child have equal chances at birth.

The slums of Kingston are an excellent breeding ground for black nationalism. Unemployment is endemic and widespread in Kingston, and many persons who actively seek employment have for years had only occasional casual labor. The areas where many Ras Tafari brethren live have no water, light, sewage disposal or collection of rubbish. It is not strange that those who live in these conditions would like to emigrate.

Marcus Garvey taught that the black man would find his soul only by turning his back on white civilization and returning to Africa, to live under black government. All Ras Tafari brethren believe this to be true.

Beards and Locks

The most obvious source of division and dispute among the brethren is the treatment of the hair. The brethren fall into three categories: the Locksmen, whose hair is matted and plaited and never cut, neither their beards; the Beardmen, who wear their hair and beards but may trim them occasionally and do not plait the hair, but keep it clean. Both these groups wear mustaches. Thirdly there is the Baldhead, or "clean-faced" man, who is not obviously distinguishable from the ordinary Jamaican except by some article such as the yellow, green and red pompom or scarf. Clean-faced men are mostly employed. Many employed men who have not overtly declared themselves to be brethren are deeply sympathetic to or interested in their doctrines and movement, and some of these wear beards. Not all Beardmen in Kingston are Ras Tafari brethren; many criminals have adopted the beard as a form of disguise and because it enables them to penetrate Ras Tafari groups in the slums and facilitates access to ganja and information; many who profess the doctrine in any of its forms may do so for ulterior motives. The Ras Tafari brethren are themselves very conscious of this.

The dispute about beards and hair centers on the interpretation of Scripture and of the brethren's role in contemporary Jamaica. Clean-faced men argue that beards, in view of current Jamaican attitudes which are hostile to the Ras Tafari, deprive people of employment. We have met many cases in which persons were refused work because of their beards; and others in which employed persons, who had adopted the doctrine and begun to grow the beard as a symbol of their creed, soon lost employment. Beardmen are divided among themselves, some, who have fairly regular jobs and carry themselves with dignity, hold that the beard and long hair are enjoined on brethren but should be kept neat and clean as the Emperor keeps his beard and hair. Others who lack employment blame their condition on the Babylonian conspiracy, holding Government as well as the public responsible, and take pride in the beard as the precept or cross which they bear for their religion among the heathen. It is a short step from this position to that adopted by the Locksmen, whose vows are Nazarite. Locksmen point with pride to photographs of East African tribesmen whose coiffure is almost identical with their own. They regard themselves as the most elect and purest adherents to the doctrine, the persons who have suffered most for their religion and race and the vanguard, the Ethiopian warriors. Many Beardmen and almost all clean-faced, or Baldhead, men take a sharply different view. To these people, the Locksmen have discredited the Ras Tafari movement and are bringing it into further disrepute through their associations with ganja, crime and verbal violence. The division here is basically between persons with some commitment to the standards by which self-respect and self-improvement are measured in Jamaican society, and those whose commitment is to standards which are totally alien. For the Locksmen do have their own standards, and these are as genuine as any others. To them, racial pride and religious observance together require a physical appearance almost identical with that of some East African tribes. Similarly, ganja is an article of use in East Africa and is regarded as sanctified by God. The criminality of which they are accused seems to Locksmen to be simply a Babylonian lie. The violence which some of them emphasize pales by comparison with passages from Ezekiel, Isaiah, Revelations and the like, the Bible of Babylon.

Ganja

Some brethren will have nothing to do with ganja, while others accord it religious significance. It is identified by its users with the herb of Genesis 8, Psalm 18, and Revelation 22.

Those who smoke ganja say that it has therapeutic effects and keeps away illness. They deny that it is harmful. To those who assert that ganja smoking makes some men violent, they reply that so also does drinking rum, and if it is not illegal to drink rum, why is it illegal to smoke ganja?

One difference between rum and ganja, which the brethren do not recognize, is that while an overdose of rum incapacitates, an overdose of ganja does not. Thus, when a man predisposed to violence drinks too much rum, he ceases to be dangerous. But such a man, on smoking ganja, becomes more dangerous the more he smokes.

Those of the brethren who object to ganja complain that it is used by influential people merely for exploitation. They assert that many policemen sell ganja, and that the police could stop the sale of ganja if they wanted to do so. In every country of the world there are some corrupt policemen who protect the trade in narcotics; but there is no evidence that Jamaica's policemen are more deeply involved than policemen in other countries.

Violence

The team had no contact with the followers of the Reverend Claudius Henry, who are, in any case, a small minority of the Kingston Brethren.

The great majority of Ras Tafari brethren are peaceful citizens who do not believe in violence. Nevertheless, since the movement is heterogeneous and includes all types, its members range from complete pacifists at one end to criminals, the mentally deranged and revolutionaries at the other end.

The language of the movement is violent. This is because it is the language of the Bible, and especially of the Old Testament. It is apocalyptic language, in which sinners are consumed with fire, sheep are separated from goats, oppressors are smitten, and kings and empires are overthrown. All Christians use this violent language, in their religious services and elsewhere. The use of such language does not mean that they are ready to fight in the streets. It does, on the other hand, mean that the concepts of revolution are neither frightening nor unfamiliar.

Recent events have increased the acceptability of revolutionary ideas. We have already shown that relations between Ras Tafari brethren and the police have deteriorated sharply over the last few years. They have deteriorated even more sharply in the last four months, in the course of which the police have carried out extensive raids, made numerous arrests, and, in the heat of the moment, have indulged in many arbitrary acts against Ras Tafarians. The brethren have a strong sense of persecution, which draws them together. In this mood an explosion of violence is quite feasible.

We have no evidence that Ras Tafarians, as a group, are being manipulated by non-Ras Tafarians with violent beliefs, such as Communists. Ras Tafarian doctrine is radical in the broad sense that it is against the oppression of black men, much of which derives from the existing economic structure. But it has no links with Marxism, either of analysis or of prognosis. The movement has been infiltrated by a number of criminals, but these people are essentially individualists and have little ideological influence.

For Jamaican leftists the violent part of the Ras Tafari spectrum is a gift; capitalist, bourgeoisie and proletariat can be directly translated into white, brown and black. Revolution becomes Redemption, with Repatriation as the issue provoking bloodshed. The Marxist vanguard wears a Niyabingi cloak. Ras Tafari brethren themselves often speak of the wolf in sheep's clothing among them. The Leftist doctrine attracts the young unemployed and those with schooling, as well as the disinherited. In our survey we encountered certain groups among which the Marxist interpretation and terminology predominated over the racial-religious. Events in Cuba, China, Egypt and elsewhere endow the Marxist analysis with a pragmatic validity and power. In so far as this political philosophy employs the ideology of Ras Tafari racism, its spread throughout the bulk of the population is assured unless Government takes positive steps to meet the legitimate needs of the lower classes, including the Ras Tafari group. The choice before Jamaica is that between social reform which is planned, peaceful and rapid on the one hand, or changes of a different sort. It is certain that Jamaican society cannot continue in its present form. Since economic development presumes social stability, this means that any successful development depends on an intelligent programme of social reform. The recent spread of Ras Tafari doctrines among educated middle-class youth is largely due to the appeals of ganja and Marxism, but this spread will surely continue so long as Jamaican society fails to provide the young with significant ideals of social justice for which to strive and opportunities for their achievement.

Work

The attitudes of Ras Tafari brethren to work do not differ from those of the rest of the population. At one extreme, the movement includes some excellent workmen, highly skilled and industrious. At the other extreme are not a few who avoid work. In the middle are the great majority of average disposition.

Though the attitudes of Ras Tafarians are similar, the brethren differ from the rest of the population in that a much larger proportion are unemployed; not because Ras Tafarians are difficult to employ, but because it is the unemployed who are most easily attracted to the movement.

Much of the psychology of the brethren is the psychology of the unemployed in any part of the world and is similar in its essentials to that of the unemployed working class in Europe or in the United States during the nineteen thirties. There is the same sense of shiftlessness and of despair. In the absence of organized relief, many brethren live on the charity of their fellows. And many have become so used to not finding work that they have ceased to look for it.

The movement is rooted in unemployment. If the supply of jobs in Kingston were to catch up with the demand for jobs, a hard core of religious belief would remain, but the movement would cease to have mass significance. This is well recognized by those Ras Tafari extremists who say that they do not want the Government to take any special measures to improve the economic lot of Ras Tafari brethren.

INDEX

Abel, Sherry, 271n
Abraham, 296; Adam-, 344
Acts, Book of, 313
Adam-Abraham, 344
Addis Ababa, 344
Address to the Slaves . . . , 19n
Ademakinwa, J. A., 300n, 302–3,
304n, 305n
Africa(ns), 15, 16n, 69ff., 97, 206ff.,
268ff., 273–310 (*see also* Slaves and
slavery; South Africa; specific
countries, peoples); camp meetings
influenced by, 52, 57, 61;
Rastafarians and, 344ff., 349, 351
African, 308n
African Art and Culture, 303n, 304n
African Arts, 305n; Mobolade in,
306n, 307n; Roache in, 307n, 308n
African Methodist Episcopal (A.M.E.)
Church, 12, 21ff., 29, 58–60, 114.
See also specific churches, clergymen
African Methodist Episcopal (A.M.E.)
Zion Church, 12, 22ff., 114, 158ff.
See also specific churches, clergymen
African Religions and Philosophy, 274,
287n, 297n
African Sculpture Speaks. See Segy,
Ladislas
African Union Society, 21
African Worlds, 293n
Afro-American, 223n, 232n, 234, 235
Afro-Saxon Mind, 156, 161–63
After Auschwitz, 139n
Ahmad, Mirzā Ghulām, 247
Ahmadiyah movement, 247
Ainsi Parla L'oncle . . . , 339n

Ajayi, Jacob, 300n, 301n
Akamba, the, 277, 278, 282ff.
Akan, the, 276ff., 280, 283, 285–99,
323, 335, 336
Akɔm Ho Hkɔmmɔbɔ, 297n
Akuffo, B. S., 296n
Alcohol (liquor), 176, 329, 333, 347;
rum, 352
Alinsky, Saul, 204
Allah, 105, 236, 238, 244ff.
Allen, Richard, 10ff., 15, 24, 25, 73,
122, 158–59; song collection, 56–57
All Nations Pentecostal Church, 200
A.M.E. *See* African Methodist
Episcopal
Amen Corner, 83
American Anthropologist, The, 317n
American Bible Society, 17
American Board of Foreign Commis-
sioners for Foreign Missions, 17
American Dilemma, An, 22n
American and Foreign Anti-Slavery
Society, 16
American Jewish Yearbook, 271n
American Society for Colonizing Free
People of Color . . . , 13ff.
American Sunday School Union, 17
American Tract Society, 17
Amos, 92, 104
Ampom-Darkwah, K., 297n
Ancestors, 287, 293–94, 314
Anglican Church, 11
Anglo-American Magazine, 19n
Antubam, Kofi, 292n
Apostolic Church of God, 204
Apostolic Church of Jesus Christ, 201

355

Index